Tantra Across the Buddhist Cosmopolis

Tantra Across the Buddhist Cosmopolis

Richard K. Payne

OXFORD
UNIVERSITY PRESS

OXFORD
UNIVERSITY PRESS

Oxford University Press is a department of the University of Oxford.
It furthers the University's objective of excellence in research, scholarship,
and education by publishing worldwide. Oxford is a registered trademark of
Oxford University Press in the UK and in certain other countries.

Published in the United States of America by Oxford University Press
198 Madison Avenue, New York, NY 10016, United States of America.

CIP data is on file at the Library of Congress

ISBN 9780195368475 (pbk.)
ISBN 9780195368482 (hbk.)

DOI: 10.1093/9780197825105.001.0001

The manufacturer's authorized representative in the EU for product safety is
Oxford University Press España S.A. of Parque Empresarial San Fernando de Henares,
Avenida de Castilla, 2 – 28830 Madrid (www.oup.es/en or product.safety@oup.com).
OUP España S.A. also acts as importer into Spain of products made by the manufacturer.

To Bonnie, without whose assistance, support, and encouragement this work would not have been possible. You patiently read every chapter in repeated drafts, including several that do not appear in this volume. Your questions, suggestions, and comments clarified both my thinking and my writing.

Contents

Acknowledgments ix
Préludes xi

I. Recognizing Tantra When You See It 1
II. South Asia: From Vedic Ritual to the Mahāsiddhas 34
III. East Asia: Instituting Tantra: Recitation and Pilgrimage 74
IV. Southeast Asia: State Formation and Monuments 106
V. Inner Asia: Decaying Corpses and Hungry Ghouls 135
VI. Networks: Travelers and Praxes 161
VII. Closing Reflections: Tantric Buddhism and Religious Studies 188

Glossary 219
Bibliography 233
Index 279

Acknowledgments

Many people have responded to inquiries, made suggestions, and given encouragement. This project has stretched out over more than two decades and, consequently, some of the assistance kindly provided to me has been lost in the mists of my imperfect memory. I hope that anyone not mentioned will forgive my oversight.

Andrea Acri
Naomi Appleton
Lara Braitstein
Courtney Bruntz
Megan Bryson
Ronald Davidson
J. F. Marc des Jardins
Timothy Fitzgerald
David Gray
Georgios Halkias
Glen Hayes
Roger Jackson
Casey Kemp
Kristin Largen
Jared Lindahl
John R. McRae†
Franz Metcalf
Scott Mitchell
Jan Nattier
Charles Orzech
Klaus Pinte
C. Pierce Salguero
Tansen Sen
Peter Sharrock
Jonathan Silk
Henrik H. Sørensen
Tony Stewart†

Jacqueline Stone
Bruce Sullivan
Mark Unno
Michael Witzel

I thank all the members, present and past, living and dead, of the Society for Tantric Studies and of the American Academy of Religions Tantric Studies Unit.

Special thanks go to my OUP acquisitions editor, Theodore Calderara, whose patience and support were no doubt pressed at times by my repeated failures to make promised deadlines—but who continued to believe that this was a worthwhile undertaking. And thanks to my OUP project editor, who helped shepherd this work through the stages of production.

And thanks also to the faculty, staff, students, and Board of Trustees of the Institute of Buddhist Studies, who, over decades, provided the supportive context within which I was able to pursue this research and writing.

Part of Chapter III on the Shikoku pilgrimage draws on research published in the *Bulletin of the Research Institute of Esoteric Buddhist Culture* (*Mikkyō Bunka Kenkyūsho Kiyō* 密教文化研究所紀要), Koyasan University, 12 (February 1999): 114–94 (reverse numbering).

Préludes

My own academic training has been such that the authorial voice you will encounter in the rest of this work is almost always a neutral, third-person one—even when some of the experiences described are my own. This set of *préludes*, however, allows me to speak directly to you in the first person.

During years of teaching, I discovered that several of my colleagues located religious studies in the humanities, along with philosophy, literature, cultural studies, performing and visual arts, and so on. Framed in this way, religious studies is understood to be a creative or constructive undertaking, and religious studies education as something akin to music appreciation. Although primarily trained in philosophy, much of my education also emphasized the social sciences—anthropology, sociology, psychology, history, and economics. And, for many years, I taught logic, symbolic logic, and critical thinking. Consequently, for me, religious studies is located in the social sciences—as a discipline formed by accurate description, hypothesis formation, generalization (as opposed to generalities), and reason. And for many of those years the main subject of my work has been Buddhism.

This work, therefore, operates at the intersection of religious studies and Buddhist studies. Further within that intersection, the leitmotif of this work is methodological—that is, the discussion (*logos*) regarding matching theories (ideas about how things work) and methods (for evaluating those ideas).

Over decades of teaching, I came to understand that the history of religious studies reveals that it not only originated out of the concepts, categories, and concerns[1] of late nineteenth-century liberal Protestant Christian theology, but that those continue to form the field of religious studies from the inside. More than half a century ago, this was for me more of an intuition, but in the intervening decades I have benefited from the critical reflections on theory and method of many, many scholars.[2] And the opportunity to teach graduate

[1] "Concepts, categories and concerns," that is, the ideas considered natural, the organization of information, and the motivating issues for the discourse of religious studies.

[2] These methodological influences include, but are not limited to, Talal Asad, Timothy Fitzgerald, Tomoko Masuzawa, David Chidester, Roy Rappaport, Urs App, Geoffrey Samuel, Bruno Latour, Robert Wardy, and several others.

students and doctoral candidates sharpened my sensibility that methodology (asking good questions and figuring out how to answer them) is essential.

Historically, beginning in the mid-nineteenth century, religious studies developed out of liberal Protestant Christian theology. And, in the last half century, religious studies became in large part the academic setting for Buddhist studies in the United States.[3] It is, therefore, important for scholars of Buddhist studies to critically reflect on the cultural preconceptions informing the field of religious studies.

Prior to the second half of the nineteenth century, Buddhism did not participate in that sociohistorical context and did not share the concepts, categories, and concerns of European and American religious discourse. Today those are in common (that is, unreflective, uncritical) use in both popular and academic discourse about religion, making it all too easy to employ them as unproblematic universals.[4]

Several years ago, when I presented this material to a seminar, one student thought that I was saying that there was something wrong with Protestant Christianity and took serious offense. That, however, is not the case—the issue here is not Protestant Christianity *per se*. Instead, the problem is that the concepts, categories, and concerns of Protestant Christianity have been generalized out of their sociohistorical context and treated as if universally true of all religions. And, in that process, the category of religion has been abstracted and universalized to include Buddhism—or rather, a representation of Buddhism has been created that fits into that category.

What is problematic, therefore, is the presumption that the categories, concepts, and concerns native to Protestant Christianity can be "sublated" (in the Hegelian sense of being "lifted up") out of that context and applied to Buddhism. Despite many, and seemingly unending, efforts to universalize "religion" itself as an object of study, these concepts, categories, and concerns still trail behind it, shrouds of unexamined intellectual commitments.

Over the course of the following chapters, a variety of topics and issues will be introduced. The topics include forms of tantric Buddhism found

[3] For example, the Buddhism program unit in the American Academy of Religion began in 1984, and quickly grew into one of the largest at the annual meeting. Since that time several spin-off and related program units focused on more specialized areas within Buddhist studies have been added to the academy's annual meeting.

[4] For this reason, one of the keystone essays I regularly assigned to graduate students was Gregory Schopen's classic "Archaeology and Protestant Presuppositions in the Study of Indian Buddhism" (*History of Religions* 31.1 [Aug. 1991]: 1–23), which has the added benefit of emphasizing the value of nontextual sources for the study of Buddhism.

on the global stage today and their recognizable continuity with tantric Buddhism's past, adaptation of Vedic ritual and its interiorization, dhāraṇī as praxis and pilgrimage as institution, state formation (creation, maintenance, and protection), meditation on corpses and skeletons as a pan-Buddhist practice, and the movement of praxes through the networks of the Buddhist cosmopolis.

The issues addressed include the problems of definition, praxis as the dialectic between doctrine and practice, how tantric Buddhism has been institutionalized, how sectarian conflicts have at times resulted in attempts to erase tantric Buddhism, how various components and practices become tantric through context, use, and designation, and networks as an alternative to nation-states and regions that can reveal different aspects of Buddhist history. Taken cumulatively, these topics and issues provide an overview of the tantric Buddhist tradition and some of the ways that it challenges received ideas about the nature of religion and its study.

Since its inception in the early medieval period in India, tantric Buddhism spread throughout the community of Buddhist practitioners, adherents, and institutions, that is, throughout the Buddhist cosmopolis. Looking for the coherence and continuity of tantric Buddhism across a variety of settings requires a more fine-grained analysis of the movement as a set of interrelated praxes. The components that constitute these praxes include practices and beliefs, rituals and texts, buddhas and bodhisattvas, guardian deities and masters, art and architecture, and so on. However, there is no definitive or comprehensive list of what a praxis comprises—it can be constructed from different components constellated into different patterns. Those components are not inherently tantric, but rather are tantric in a tantric context, when put to a tantric use, and when designated as tantric. The same (or, rather, what we abstract from different contexts and can consider to be the same) component can be used in different ways, located in different contexts, and called by different names. Some of these contexts, uses, and designations may be tantric, and others not.[5]

More explicitly, this work makes two methodological contributions to the fields of religious studies and Buddhist studies. The first is that context, use, and designation are the means by which we can delineate tantra, rather than any attempt to define tantra. The second is that praxes are the appropriate

[5] For example, the Heart Sutra recited as part of a morning service in a Zen temple is not tantric. As part of a morning service in a Shingon temple, it is.

objects for the study of tantric Buddhism as an historical movement, rather than abstract entities such as "religion" or "Buddhism," or entities more limited in scope such as a text, a ritual, or a teacher.

Those are the *préludes* to what follows. Or, to employ another metaphor, having imagined the journey ahead, let us go out the door and set our feet upon the path unfolding before us.

I

Recognizing Tantra When You See It

The tantric Buddhist movement is a network of interrelated systems of thought and practice, each integrally organized by a central deity.[1] That movement extends both over the course of Buddhist history since the early medieval period and across the variety of cultures into which Buddhism has been introduced. Four contemporary instances provide an initial glimpse of this movement in our present time.

Glimpsing Tantra in the Present

Shoreline

Over four days in May 2001, the Dalai Lama gave a series of teachings at the Shoreline Amphitheater, south of San Francisco, in Mountain View, California, a venue that holds twenty-two thousand audience members—and which was filled by devotees, adherents, and the merely curious. The first three days concentrated on the Heart of Wisdom teachings, while on Sunday, the final day, he gave teachings focused on the Medicine Buddha (Skt. Bhaiṣajyaguru).[2] The days were clear, sunny, and hot in the open-air theater, despite which each day thousands of participants came to listen to perhaps the most widely recognized Buddhist teacher of our day.[3]

These teachings culminated with the Dalai Lama giving initiations to participants enabling them to engage in ritualized meditation (Skt. *sādhana*, "method" or "technique") on the figure of the Medicine Buddha. Such

[1] Although the terms have broader application, here in the context of the study of the tantric Buddhist movement, dialectically integral systems of thought and practice, organized around the figure of a central deity, will be referred to throughout as "praxis" in the singular and "praxes" in the plural.

[2] The event was sponsored by the Land of Medicine Buddha, a Tibetan center located in California's Santa Cruz Mountains, further south from Mountain View, and closer to Santa Cruz.

[3] Transcripts of the lectures provided the primary source for Geshe Thupten Jinpa, trans. and ed., *Essence of the Heart Sutra: The Dalai Lama's Heart of Wisdom Teachings* (Boston: Wisdom Publications, 2005).

Tantra Across the Buddhist Cosmopolis. Richard K. Payne, Oxford University Press. © Oxford University Press 2025.
DOI: 10.1093/9780197825105.003.0001

teachings, practices, and initiations are instances of the tantric Buddhist movement as it exists today. That movement also includes annual New Year's fire rituals performed in many temples of the Shingon tradition of Japan.

Sacramento

Each year beginning before the break of dawn on New Year's Day, at the Northern California Koyasan Temple—a Shingon temple in Sacramento—the head priest performs a homa (Jpn. *goma*), a ritual in which offerings are made into a fire. When I first attended this ceremony in 1980, a congregation of two hundred or more people had gathered in the predawn darkness of the temple. As the ritual started, a *taiko* drum began to keep a steady beat. In time with the drum, members of the sangha[4] started chanting the Heart Sutra in unison, the same text as had formed the basis for the Dalai Lama's teachings at Shoreline. On the altar in the front of the temple the head priest built a fire in a hearth. Each time the priest added oil to the fire, flames lit up the darkness. Smoke and incense filled the hall, until despite the cold outside, windows were opened. About an hour later, the ritual ended, and the sun was up. As is typical of many Japanese temples at New Year's, beans were handed out to all the members of the sangha, and led by the head priest, the beans were thrown in all directions, accompanied by shouts of "Oni wa soto, fuku wa uchi"—"Demons outside, good fortune inside."

Differences

Initially, these two events may appear quite different from one another. From one perspective, that of the functions served, one was a ritual for initiation, and the other a ritual for protection. On the closing day, the Dalai

[4] The simplest meaning of the term "sangha" (Skt. *saṃgha*) is "community." It is used in Buddhist discourse to identify specific groups, and it can have a variety of more nuanced meanings. In some cases, the usage is limited to ordained monks and nuns, or to the fourfold community of monks, nuns, laymen, and laywomen. But used as a loanword in contemporary English, it refers to any identifiable community of Buddhist adherents, regardless of their monastic or institutional status. To evoke the complex meanings of the term in Buddhist history, the term "sangha" (treated as a loanword, that is, without diacritics and not italicized) is used here in preference to glosses such as "congregation." See Thomas Borchert, "The Sangha as an Institution," in *The Oxford Encyclopedia of Buddhism*, ed. Richard K. Payne and Georgios T. Halkias, 2061–2075 (New York: Oxford University Press, 2024; https://doi.org/10.1093/acrefore/9780199340378.013.194).

Lama distinguished two kinds of initiations he would give. The majority of those in attendance at Shoreline were authorized to engage in a devotional practice in which the deity evoked is worshipped for the sake of receiving blessings.[5] This exoteric version of the initiation was contrasted with the tantric initiation. A tantric initiation, or empowerment, authorizes the practitioner to engage in a particular *sādhana*, that is, practices that usually involve visualization and evocation of a buddha, bodhisattva, or protector deity.[6] This *sādhana* centered on ritual identification between the practitioner and Medicine Buddha. Experiencing oneself as Medicine Buddha in body, speech, and mind, that is, in all dimensions of human existence, the practitioner thereby realizes their already and always awakened nature. In the context of Buddhist tantra, practices of this kind lead to "realization" or "attainment" (Skt. *siddhi*). In this case, the *sādhana* enables the practitioner to manifest the healing power of the Medicine Buddha.[7]

The New Year's homa ritual performed at the Sacramento Shingon temple is performed for the protection of sangha members throughout the coming year. Offerings representing our own mistaken conceptions and misplaced affections[8] are made into a purifying fire. During the ritual, the fire is first identified as Agni, the Vedic deity who conveys the offerings in purified form as scent to the deities. Following Agni, the central deity (Jpn. *honzon*) in the Sacramento temple's New Year's ritual is the Immovable Wisdom King (Skt. Acalanātha Vidyārāja, Jpn. Fudō Myōō), who is portrayed as a strong youth holding a dragon-enwrapped sword in his right hand and a lasso in his left—the lasso to entangle those who would escape from him, and the sword to cut away their delusions.

A Thought Experiment

Were it possible for tantric practitioners from eighth-century India, eighteenth-century Tibet, and eleventh-century Java to come to

[5] "Evoked" is used throughout this work to identify the ritual actions, including speech, that bring the deity into the ritual enclosure or practice space, as distinct from "invoke," which is used to identify the use of speech to communicate with a deity by calling their name.

[6] Luis O. Gómez, "Meditation," in *Encyclopedia of Buddhism*, ed. Robert Buswell (New York: Macmillan, 2004), 525.

[7] Ngawang Losang Tempa Gyältsän, *Medicine Buddha Sadhana*, trans. Lama Thubten Zopa Rinpoche (Taos, NM: FPMT, 2004), 11–12.

[8] These are my own renderings for the two *vāsanās*—latent tendencies, habits, predispositions. These two are *jñeyavāsanā*, those consistently mistaken ways in which we think about the world, and *kleśavāsanā*, those emotional attachments (both clinging and rejecting) we have to things that will not satisfy us.

twenty-first-century Sacramento to see a Shingon homa performed in English, we can easily imagine that they would all recognize it as familiar, even substantially the same as practices that they themselves have performed.[9] They would recognize not just simply the broad, general outlines of what is going on, but many of the specifics as well. Such details as the hand gestures (mudras), verbal formulae (mantras), the shape of the hearth in which the fire is built on the altar, and the symbolic colors, ritual implements, and offerings show a high degree of consistency over the centuries of tantric Buddhist history, and across linguistic and cultural boundaries.[10] In the same fashion, one can well imagine that the figure of the Medicine Buddha and the *sādhana* practice into which adherents were initiated would have also felt familiar to these visitors from other times and places in the history of the tantric Buddhist movement. Although speculative, this thought experiment indicates the overall coherence of tantric Buddhism as a movement.

The differences between the two events described above are multiple and important to the goals of this work. In one instance, an internationally renowned religious teacher brings together a group of thousands into a temporary association to listen to him expound the teachings of a particular strain of Buddhist religio-philosophic thought and receive initiation into a practice centered on a particular buddha. In the other, a long-standing local group, including both natal and convert Buddhists, comes together on a regular basis at the beginning of the New Year to participate in a ritual performance, receive the benefits of protection, and drive away demonic influences.

These events take place within what is here being called the Buddhist cosmopolis—the system of concepts, practices, teachings, narratives, communities, texts, and institutions that make up the lived world through which lay adherents and monks can move and be recognized as members of that community. The Buddhist cosmopolis is diffuse, not limited by the geographic boundaries of modern nation-states. Some of its social institutions have had political and juridical authority over members. From its beginning

[9] Epistemologically, thought experiments can only definitively establish what is logically not impossible and do not demonstrate the truth of one's claim. Our claim here regards the possibility of shared recognition, and therefore, shared participation in an historically and culturally broader movement.

[10] Richard K. Payne and Michael Witzel, eds., *Homa Variations: Ritual Change Across the* Longue Durée (Oxford: Oxford University Press, 2016).

with the direct disciples of Śākyamuni, and the communities that supported the early sangha, it has extended across wide geographic stretches and constitutes an ordered lived-world, a "transregional culture–power sphere,"[11] a "cosmos."[12]

Similarities

Both events are end products of a shared history stretching back at least four thousand years to the Vedic ritual culture of India, a culture that developed long before the life of Śākyamuni Buddha. That shared history is evident in tantric praxes, that is, the multifaceted practices and ideologies that interact with one another. This dialectic is one in which, as Richard Nance succinctly puts it, "Doctrine . . . both shapes, and is shaped by, practice."[13] For much of the history of tantric Buddhism, a foundational idea supporting practice explains it as the means for realizing one's own always and already awakened mind, and to do so in this lifetime.[14]

A practice or a doctrine, indeed, any component of the tantric movement, is only meaningful as part of a pattern of relations with other components.[15] As a pattern of relations, praxis is the context that makes any component meaningfully tantric. Despite their differences, both the New Year's fire ritual and the Medicine Buddha initiation are instances of praxes that are markedly tantric in character. The following two examples are also tantric, but more ambiguously so.

[11] Sheldon Pollock, *Language of the Gods in the World of Men: Sanskrit, Power, and Culture in Premodern India* (Berkeley: University of California Press, 2006), 12.

[12] See Stephen Toulmin, *Cosmopolis: The Hidden Agenda of Modernity* (Chicago: University of Chicago Press, 1992).

[13] Richard Nance, "Indian Buddhist Preachers Inside and Outside the Sūtras," *Religion Compass* 2.2 (2008): 134–159, 135, DOI: 10.1111/j.1749-8171.2007.00057.x.

[14] This complex of ideas, that is, making manifest the always and already awakened mind in this lifetime through ritual identification, is central to many tantric traditions. This is further linked with ideas of secrecy and requirements for initiation. But for reasons explained more fully in the final chapter, it should not be taken as a single defining characteristic, but rather as a suggestive rule of thumb.

[15] This understanding of "meaning" as context dependent is intentionally consistent with structuralist linguistics. See Luca Gasparri and Diego Marconi, "Word Meaning," in *The Stanford Encyclopedia of Philosophy* (Fall 2019 edition), ed. Edward N. Zalta, https://plato.stanford.edu/archives/fall2019/entries/word-meaning/, 32.

Ohara

In 1982, the trip to the town of Ohara, north of Kyoto and in the foothills of Mt. Hiei, took about forty-five minutes or more by bus. Ohara is near the well-known temple Sanzen-in, a Tendai temple founded by Saichō (767–822) in 788. During Japan's Warring States period (*Sengoku jidai*, 1467–1615), the Tendai sect was a major military power, equal to many of the major clans. In 1571, as part of his attempt to unify Japan under his rule, Oda Nobunaga (1534–1582) ordered that the temple-shrine complex on Mt. Hiei be destroyed and its temples burned. Escaping the destruction, many Tendai monks fled down the mountain, taking refuge at Sanzen-in.

Ohara is in the Takanogawa River Valley, a major tributary of the Kamogawa River that runs down the east side of Kyoto. Like many river valley towns, Ohara's origins as a farming village are evident in its rambling, scattered spread across the narrow valley floor. I had met a fellow American in the Kyoto expatriate community who was a Zen priest. Having been trained by a famous American Zen teacher, he had come to Japan to practice Zen under the guidance of a Japanese Zen master. That teacher concluded that he was ready to sustain his practice independently, and he had been assigned to care for a small hermitage in Ohara, intended as the retirement home of the teacher.

My wife and I made the bus trip up the river valley to Ohara and found the proper stop at which to get off. Not sure what to expect, we came to a modest, newly built house, nicely designed and landscaped in a contemporary Japanese style and very up-to-date. Our friend greeted us and ushered us into the entryway. I was immediately struck by the presence in the entry of a statue of a guardian deity (Skt. *lokapāla*), one of the four great kings (Skt. *caturmahārāja*) of heaven, protector deities associated with the four directions. Recognizing the figure from Shingon mandalas, I asked my friend about it, and he told me that burning incense for the figure was part of his daily round of duties.

Later, after the usual guest/host ritual of tea and cookies, in the restroom I encountered a small scroll with a verbal formula (Skt. *dhāraṇī*) hanging on the wall. This dhāraṇī is recited specifically for protection in toilet areas, and it is found in all the Shingon temples with which I was familiar—both in Japan and the United States. Again inquiring of my friend, I realized that for him, these two items—a *lokapāla*, a deity whose origins are in Indian Buddhist cosmology, and a protective *dhāraṇī* recited in Japanese pronunciation of the Chinese pronunciation of Sanskrit—were simply part of Zen.[16] What to me were clearly tantric components had become so deeply integrated into Zen praxis that he saw them simply as part of the tradition.[17] In other words, these two were so naturalized as part of Zen that the tantric associations I saw were rendered invisible.[18] In this context, then, these components are not "tantric." Instead, they are traces of the tantric tradition at the historical roots of Sōtō Zen—the Tendai tradition in which Dōgen Zenji, founder of Sōtō in Japan, had originally trained, a tradition that has its own strong tantric dimension.[19]

Fushimi Inari

Later that same year, I saw an announcement of a large outdoor fire ritual (Jpn. *saitō goma*) to be held at Fushimi Inari, a famous Shintō shrine in southeast Kyoto—this was an outdoor version of the New Year's homa ritual at the Sacramento Shingon temple. Taking the train down from our home, we arrived amid several hundred other visitors to the shrine. In a field behind the shrine, three massive bonfires had been constructed for the performance of the *saitō goma*, which was being conducted by Shugendō practitioners (Jpn. Shugensha, also, *yamabushi*). Shugendō is organized according to the mountains that form the center of their activities and is the

[16] This is not to say that scholarly monks or historians of Japanese religions would be unaware of the historical relations between Zen and tantra, grounded, for example, in Dōgen's training in the Tendai tradition of Hieizan, which had an esoteric dimension. However, rhetorics of legitimacy propagated, for example, by Sōtō Zen apologists and the scholarship that depends on sectarian historiography have emphasized Dōgen's connection to China, thereby minimizing the role of his Tendai training. Claims to legitimacy are based, for example, on direct, or "face-to-face" transmission from Chinese masters. Steven Heine, "Did Dōgen go to China? Problematizing Dōgen's Relation to Ju-Ching and Chinese Ch'an," *Japanese Journal of Religious Studies* 30.1–2 (2003): 27–59, 35. Similarly face to face, the importance given to oral transmission texts (Jpn. *kuden*) is that they also function as a legitimating device. Jacqueline Stone, *Original Enlightenment and the Transformation of Medieval Japanese Buddhism* (Honolulu: University of Hawai'i Press, 1999), 97–152.

[17] This is not an argument regarding authenticity, which is always an assertion of power, but rather a description of the historical processes by which tantric elements pervade the Buddhist tradition.

[18] This invisibility seems at least in part a consequence of the purposeful rhetorical distancing of Japanese Mahāyāna from tantra by early modern Japanese Buddhist scholars. This was in parallel to the rhetoric of purity being promoted in regard to Pāli Buddhism by European and American scholars in the nineteenth century, and which contrasted that putatively original and therefore authentic tradition with the supposed decadence of Tibetan "lamaism." See Griffith Foulk, "Ritual in Japanese Zen Buddhism," in *Zen Ritual: Studies of Zen Buddhist Theory in Practice*, ed. Steven Heine and Dale S. Wright, 21–82 (Oxford: Oxford University Press, 2008), 30.

[19] William M. Bodiford, "Zen and Esoteric Buddhism," in *Esoteric Buddhism and the Tantras in East Asia*, ed. Charles D. Orzech, Henrik H. Sørensen, and Richard K. Payne, 924–935 (Leiden: Brill, 2011).

modern manifestation of mountain worship that dates to very early in Japan's history.[20] In 1613, during the Edo period (1603–1868), the Tokugawa government mandated that Shugendō groups affiliate with either Tendai or Shingon. Consequently, the tantric influences already part of Shugendō became more central, and teachings and practices were systematized to better accord with tantric Buddhist praxis.[21]

However, in 1947 a new constitution was established for Japan. This made a policy of religious freedom official, and the required association of Shugendō organizations with Tendai and Shingon was eliminated. And present-day Shugendō groups do not have any specific institutional connection with Shintō—yet here Shugendō practitioners were officiating a *saitō goma* performance on the grounds of a famous Shintō shrine.[22] The boundaries were further blurred when I observed some members of the audience reciting the mantra and forming the mudra of Fudō Myōō, the tantric Buddhist deity found at Shingon temples across Japan, and who was the focus of the protective homa at the Sacramento Kōyasan New Year's ceremony.

Thought Experiment, Revisited

If our imagined tantric practitioners from India, Tibet, and Java were also to join in examining the Zen hermitage in Ohara, and the Shugendō fire ceremony at Fushimi Inari, they would again no doubt recognize familiar tantric components—though again also inflected differently from their own forms. To trace the pervasive spread of tantric praxes through the Buddhist cosmopolis, these juxtapositions of similarities and differences necessitate formulating a way of thinking about tantra that is expansive—inclusive rather than exclusive.[23] Methodologically, an expansive approach can illuminate components of the tantric movement that have (inadvertently) been cast into the shadows by constricted academic approaches. Necessarily, then,

[20] See Gaynor Sekimori, "Shugendō and Its Relationship with the Japanese Esoteric Sects: A Study of the Ritual Calendar of an Edo-Period Shugendō Shrine-Temple Complex," in *Esoteric Buddhism and the Tantras in East Asia*, ed. Charles D. Orzech, Henrik Sørensen, and Richard K. Payne, 997–1008 (Leiden: Brill, 2010).

[21] Barbara Ambros, "Tōzanha Shugendō in the Early Modern Period," in *Esoteric Buddhism and the Tantras in East Asia*, ed. Charles D. Orzech, Henrik Sørensen, and Richard K. Payne, 1018–1023 (Leiden: Brill, 2010).

[22] In another instance, Shugendō practitioners performed *saitō goma* at the grand opening of a new Shingon temple built on the road between Hashimoto and Kōyasan.

[23] While we are intentionally taking this approach for the purposes of this work, other works motivated by different questions may well reasonably take more exclusive approaches.

our approach here lacks sharp-edged definitional distinctions that are usually expected as conceptual strategies in the academic world.

Orientations to This Work

This work has two goals. The first goal is to support three interconnected claims regarding tantric Buddhism. The second goal is to raise methodological issues regarding the study of religion. Briefly, the three claims are that tantra is pervasive, invisible, and coherent. After these three claims are explained more fully, two fundamental issues are discussed. These are the problematics of definition and the regional organization of this work. In closing this chapter, the overall structure of the work is outlined with an overview of the chapters that follow.

Three Claims

This work asserts three claims regarding the tantric Buddhist tradition—that since its origins in early medieval India, tantra has become pervasive throughout the Buddhist cosmopolis, that it has often been rendered invisible, and that when understood as a set of interrelated praxes, it constitutes a movement. Within that broader, largely coherent, and continuous movement, particular instances of tantra have existed as independent institutions, as unrecognized forms within a larger institution, or as established alternatives within a larger tradition, which itself may or may not be explicitly designated as tantric.[24]

Tantra as Pervasive

From the early medieval period into the present, tantric praxes—that is, dialectically interrelated doctrines and practices—built on existing aspects of the broader Buddhist tradition and have been integral to it. These praxes have not always been explicit or central, but they have been influential.

[24] This summary is based on ideas shared by the late Tony Stewart, via email, April 22, 2023, and this gives me another opportunity to thank him for generously sharing his insights. For fuller presentation of Stewart's ideas, see Richard K. Payne and Glen A. Hayes, "Tantric Studies: Issues, Methods, and Scholarly Collaborations," in *The Oxford Handbook of Tantric Studies*, ed. Richard K. Payne and Glen A. Hayes, 1–26 (New York: Oxford University Press, 2024), 5–6.

An obstacle to recognizing the pervasive role of tantra is that its presence may not be evident to scholars who are not already familiar with it, an instance of the iterative process of understanding known as the hermeneutic circle.[25] As the academic study of tantra has become increasingly legitimate, greater understanding of it has become increasingly possible.[26] And with greater understanding has come increased visibility.

The Invisibility of Tantra

The second claim is that the role of tantra in Buddhist history has often been obscured—accidentally, or intentionally, or by lack of familiarity, or because components have been naturalized into a different context. Historical accidents have probably been responsible for many instances in which tantra has been obscured—the death of a teacher, destruction of a temple, loss of a text. Events such as these may have obscured a connection to the tantric movement, leaving only traces in a local religious culture. In some cases, tantric connections were purposely obscured, perhaps for the sake of sectarian identity, or because of the ill repute that tantra has in some quarters. Many tantric texts enjoin secrecy, which would also purposely contribute to the invisibility of the tradition.[27] Some teachings are said to be "self-secret"; that is, even if someone hears or reads about the teachings, they will not be able to understand them, and so they ignore or forget them. This is analogous to the history of scholarly neglect, whether motivated by disdain or by lack of interest. And in some instances, such as the dhāraṇī and protector deity at the Zen hermitage in Ohara, tantric components were so deeply rooted in a religious culture that they are just taken as naturally part of that culture.[28] And in some instances tantric connections seem to have simply been forgotten, due to the passage of time, loss of records, shifts in the religious culture, or other unintentional factors. Whatever the process by which tantra has become invisible, increasing familiarity, knowledge, understanding, and appreciation will make it easier to recognize it when one sees it.

[25] Jeff Malpas, "Hans-Georg Gadamer," in *The Stanford Encyclopedia of Philosophy* (Fall 2022 edition), ed. Edward N. Zalta, https://plato.stanford.edu/archives/fall2022/entries/gadamer/, 14.

[26] See, for example, Richard K. Payne and Glen A. Hayes, eds., *The Oxford Handbook of Tantric Studies* (New York: Oxford University Press, 2024).

[27] My thanks to my friend and colleague Georgios T. Halkias for emphasizing that the contents of many texts are sealed by dharma protectors and other guardians. The contents are not to be shared publicly, and to do so would be a breach of *samaya* vows.

[28] This claim should not be misunderstood as a claim that such elements, in Zen or elsewhere, are not authentic. Both claims of authenticity and accusations of inauthenticity are as noted above best understood as strategic moves toward gaining rhetorical power.

Tantra as a Coherent and Continuous Movement

The coherence and continuity of tantric Buddhism are evident when it is understood not as a monolithic entity but as a series of interrelated and overlapping praxes.[29] While centering on different deities, these praxes also share a range of practices and doctrines.[30] In this sense, a praxis constitutes a natural and coherent unit of study. Reflecting how practitioners themselves often conceptualize their own activities, it is a more natural unit than such artificial modern categories as "world religions."[31] The coherence of praxes over time and across cultural boundaries is evidenced repeatedly in Buddhist history. Indeed, from the perspective of Buddhism as a living tradition, it makes sense to think of it as the praxis focused on the figure of Śākyamuni, of which there are a wide variety of culturally located instances, but which cumulatively constitute a movement.

Methodological Issues

The study of tantric Buddhism is an opportunity for critical reflection on methodological issues in the study of religion. This is not, however, intended to facilitate a refinement of academic conceptions—claims regarding, or understandings of—of "religion." That is, the goal is not a more accurate conception of religion. Instead, it seeks to problematize the conception as a scholarly category, one still apparently considered by some scholars in religious studies to be unproblematically universalizable. By bringing attention to the preconceptions that are projected onto cultural phenomena when they

[29] My friend and colleague Glen A. Hayes suggests that this pattern may be understood in terms of "blending theory," in which reblending creates "emergent structures" that integrate thought and practice, which then themselves in turn serve as inputs for subsequent blending (personal communication, via email, November 5, 2023). Hayes has developed both metaphor theory and blending theory as tools for understanding tantra. See his "Exploring Metaphors and Conceptual Blending in Vaiṣṇava Sahajiyā Texts," in *The Oxford Handbook of Tantric Studies*, ed. Richard K. Payne and Glen A. Hayes, 755–786 (Oxford: Oxford University Press, 2024; online 2023: https://doi.org/10.1093/oxfordhb/9780197549889.013.28), which includes several of his other publications in the References list.

[30] The term "praxis" is used here instead of "cult." Despite the classic meaning of cult as "the set of practices directed toward a particular figure, such as the cult of Mithras or the cult of Heracles" (Georgios T. Halkias and Richard K. Payne, "Editors' Introduction," in *Pure Lands in Asian Texts and Contexts: An Anthology*, ed. Georgios T. Halkias and Richard K. Payne, 1–25 [Honolulu: University of Hawai'i Press, 2019], 11), it has been so deeply stained by negative interpretations as to be a distraction in the context of this work.

[31] Tomoko Masuzawa, *The Invention of World Religion: Or, How European Universalism Was Preserved in the Language of Pluralism* (Chicago: University of Chicago Press, 2005).

are categorized as religion, the constructed and conventional character of the category is highlighted.

Before turning in more detail to the topics of definition and regional organization, other methodological issues are raised in the following chapters. Four of these will be directly and more fully discussed in the closing chapter. In summary, these include the academic history of elevating the concerns, concepts, and categories of Protestant Christianity out of their native context and employing them in this abstracted form as universal to all religions—that is, "sublation."[32] Integral to this sublation is the overdetermined way by which some selected concerns, concepts, and categories are highlighted, while others are derogated. Second is the rhetoric of decadence, which identifies the narrative arc that structures how the history of religions is written. A corollary to this is the "disappearing tradition" narrative found in discussions of both South and East Asian Buddhist history. This work also develops a critique of the presumption that doctrine is fundamental and practice derivative, the third issue. Throughout this work, doctrine and practice are understood to exist in a dialectic relation, forming a more complex whole referred to as "praxis." The fourth issue is the appropriate object of study for religious studies. Rather than abstract generalities such as religion or Buddhism, which may be useful for delineating a field of inquiry, the sets of activities centered on some deity, that is, a praxis, is a more concrete object of study.

Strategies for Delineating, Not Defining, Tantra

As a category, "tantra" is neither purely subjective, nor is it entirely objective.[33] Instead, it is intersubjective; that is, its significance is constituted by

[32] As used here, the concept "sublation" (Ger. *Aufhebung*) derives from Hegel, for whom it "means to cancel, preserve, and raise up" (Robert C. McDonald, "Slavoj Žižek and Communication Studies," in *The Oxford Research Encyclopedia of Communication*, n.p. [New York: Oxford University Press, 2018]; https://doi.org/10.1093/acrefore/9780190228613.013.593). The use here does not intend to apply the idea in a formally dialectical manner, but rather to highlight that when abstracted from one intellectual context into another, a concept retains ("preserves") the meanings and values it had—the concepts, categories, and concerns that constituted its previous context remain spectrally present.

[33] Stipulative definitions—pointing to a particular instance by way of definition—may make it seem as if tantra is something existing in the communal world and which, therefore, exists objectively. Stipulative definitions are, however, at best a starting point. Generalization on the basis of stipulative instances becomes an unending task of identifying similarities and differences—one that is strained when one is trying to take into account such divergent instances as a South Indian blood offering to Kali and a Tendai homa ritual to the mountain deity.

use in discourse, both popular and scholarly. The boundaries of the category are fluid, moving as the concept is employed to identify instances as belonging in the category—a dialectic interplay between our ideas (subjective) and things in the world (objects).[34] To the extent that such a dialectic interplay proceeds in a disciplined fashion, the concept can become more refined, more heuristically useful. Such fluidity means that the boundaries of the category "tantra" are fuzzy; that is, it is not a sharply bounded category.[35] This way of understanding the category differs from most standard scholarly approaches, which generally privilege sharp delineations between categories.

Previous attempts to define tantra are problematic in one way or another. Rather than "defining," what is proposed here is "delineating," that is, suggesting ways in which tantra can be identified. After evaluating previous attempts at defining tantra, two steps toward delineating it are introduced. The first is bibliographic, that is, tantra as a label attached to texts, and as employed in canon formation. The second expands on this by looking at context, use, and designation as the factors that make some component of a culture tantric.

Previous Definitional Strategies

Etymology

Many scholars follow a customary practice of beginning a discussion of tantra with the term's etymology. In his study of tantric yoga, James Hartzell explains that the Sanskrit root √*tan* means "to stretch, extend or spread, weave, etc."[36] As the weft, sutra is also part of the weaving metaphor, while tantra is taken as referring to the warp; that is, sutra and tantra are the two directions of thread in woven cloth. André Padoux explains that from the "the verbal root *TAN*, which means 'to extend,' 'to spread,' hence 'to spin

[34] Throughout this work, we use the term "dialectic" simply to describe an ongoing interaction between two concepts, such that changes to one effect changes to the other. Philosophically sophisticated readers may think first of the Hegelian usage, which is that there is a constantly improving interaction. That, however, is not intended, but instead something closer to the negative dialectic of Adorno. Lambert Zuidervaart, "Theodor W. Adorno," in *The Stanford Encyclopedia of Philosophy* (Winter 2015 edition), ed. Edward N. Zalta, https://plato.stanford.edu/archives/win2015/entries/adorno/, 15.

[35] While this concept is borrowed from its use in set theory and logic, it is used here without the additional implication that the degrees of applicability can be specified.

[36] James F. Hartzell, "Tantric Yoga: A Study of the Vedic Precursors, Historical Evolution, Literatures, Cultures, Doctrines, and Practices of the 11th Century Kaśmīri Śaivite and Buddhist Unexcelled Tantric Yogas," PhD diss. (Columbia University Press, 1997), 5.

out,' 'weave,' 'display,' 'put forth,' and 'compose' [the term comes by extension to mean] 'system,' 'doctrine,' or 'work.' A Tantra is thus a work, a text—any text."[37] However, after noting that "tantra" is simply another word for a book or a work similar to a sutra, Kees Bolle emphasizes the ritual dimensions of tantric texts, explaining that the root "tan" has a meaning more general than that associated with weaving. That meaning is "to do" or "make," and that with "the common meaning of doing things in the right way in rituals, 'tantra' is distinct (which in no way means separated) from *mantra*, the prescribed, sacred formula."[38] To apprehend the tantric Buddhist movement, however, etymological explanations are only a preliminary, scholarly glimpse of the term's meaning.

A Monothetic Approach: Ritual Identification

Some scholars have attempted to identify a single defining characteristic that clearly indicates whether some instance is or isn't tantra—a monothetic definitional strategy.[39] The key example of a minimal defining characteristic for Buddhist tantra is ritual identification.[40] In tantric practice, ritual identification involves visualizing the body, speech, and mind of the deity evoked in the ritual as identical with the body, speech, and mind of the practitioner.[41] This actively engages the practitioner with the teaching that they are already and always awakened. Considering the wide range of ritual practices that could be considered tantric, Michel Strickmann suggested that "Such rites are 'Tantric' if we accept as a minimal definition of this imprecise but useful term that they center upon the visualization by the officiant of the

[37] André Padoux, *The Hindu Tantric World* (Chicago: University of Chicago Press, 2017), 7. Playing on this imagery, Rae Erin Dachille employs the term "suture" not simply in the sense of sewing something together, but in relation to the way exegetes create interpretations that appear "seamless" (*Searching for the Body: A Contemporary Perspective on Tibetan Buddhist Tantra* [New York: Columbia University Press, 2022]), 12.

[38] Kees W. Bolle, *The Persistence of Religion* (Leiden: E.J. Brill, 1971), 43.

[39] Padmanabh Jaini employed a monothetic definition of tantra as "fusion of the mundane and the supermundane" to claim, incorrectly, that the Jain tradition did not have a tantric dimension. Padmanabh Jaini, *The Jaina Path of Purification* (Berkeley: University of California Press, 1979), 245n20, cited in Ellen Gough, *Making a Mantra: Tantric Ritual and Renunciation on the Jain Path to Liberation* (Chicago: University of Chicago Press, 2021), 114.

[40] See, for example, Ferdinand Lessing, "The Thirteen Visions of a Yogācārya: A Preliminary Study," in *Ritual and Symbol: Collected Essays on Lamaism and Chinese Symbolism*, ed. Ferdinand Lessing (Taipei: The Chinese Association for Folklore, 1976), 83.

[41] Just one of many descriptions of this practice in tantric literature is found in Ferdinand Lessing and Alex Wayman, trans., *Mkhas Grub rJe's Fundamentals of the Buddhist Tantras* (The Hague: Mouton, 1968), 163. For a discussion of this idea in the work of Tsongkhapa, and its critique by Ngorchen Kunga Sangpo, see Ronald M. Davidson, *Indian Esoteric Buddhism: A Social History of the Tantric Movement* (New York: Columbia University Press, 2002), 119.

deity to whom the rite is addressed, with whom the officiant then proceeds to identify himself or otherwise unite."[42] In his view, the tantric metamorphosis of Vedic ritual is effected by the addition of this component—in other words, that ritual identification is the minimal defining characteristic that distinguishes tantra from earlier Indic ritual traditions.[43]

However, while ritual identification is found in many tantric traditions, such as Buddhist, Jain, and Hindu, there are some important and, therefore, interesting exceptions.[44] There are, for example, traditions that self-identify as tantric and employ ritual techniques identifiably similar to other tantric traditions, but which are metaphysically dualistic. In the rituals of such traditions, there is a very limited role for any kind of identification between the practitioner and the deity. In Śaiva Siddhānta, for instance, Śīva is the ultimate and supreme reality, distinct from any human person (Skt. *jiva*), and it is Śīva alone who liberates. Being fundamentally distinct, a person never becomes identical with Śiva in the way that the practitioner and deity become identified in many tantric Buddhist praxes. Yet practitioner and deity are of the same essence, and through proper initiation (Skt. *dīkṣā*), a practitioner can embody the agency of Śiva. Thus, for example, the Śaiva Siddhanta fire ritual, as described in the *Somaśambhupaddhati*, does not include an act of ritual identification. However, while the context of initiations required for performing the fire ritual maintains a dualist separation between Śiva and the practitioner, at the same time, they allow the latter to be the vehicle by which the liberative agency of Śiva can be made manifest.[45]

Also problematic is that the significance of ritual identification has not always been the same. Regarding the place of ritual identification in tantric Buddhist praxis, Ronald M. Davidson has argued that mandala symbolism, essential to the development of tantric praxis, originates in the political realities of an imperial court organized according to the system of early medieval Indian feudalism.[46] In this context, "imperial maṇḍala" rites focused

[42] Michel Strickmann, "Homa in East Asia," in Frits Staal, ed., *Agni: The Vedic Ritual of the Fire Altar*, 2 vols. (Berkeley, CA: Asian Humanities Press, 1983), 418. He later developed this comment more fully; see Michel Strickmann, *Mantras et mandarins: Le bouddhisme tantrique en Chine* (Paris: Gallimard, 1996), 25. Strickmann provides no sources for his claim in either publication.

[43] For an early discussion, see Ferdinand Lessing, "The Thirteen Visions of a Yogācārya: A Preliminary Study," in *Ritual and Symbol: Collected Essays on Lamaism and Chinese Symbolism*, ed. Ferdinand Lessing (Taipei: The Chinese Association for Folklore, 1976), 83.

[44] Gough, *Making a Mantra*, 114.

[45] Richard K. Payne, "Ritual Studies in the *Longue Durée*: Comparing Shingon and Śaiva Siddhanta *Homas*," *Pacific World: Journal of the Institute of Buddhist Studies*, third series, no. 13 (Fall 2011): 223–262, 236–238.

[46] Davidson, *Indian Esoteric Buddhism*, 139.

instead on the acquisition of power. The practitioner is identified with the central deity and surrounded by that deity's retinue. Each member of the retinue is, in turn, surrounded by his own retinue, just as a "king of kings" (Skt. *rājādhirāja*) is surrounded by vassals, each of whom is head of his own dominion.[47] While there is a continuity of symbolism, this is not the same as the idea that ritual identification is instrumental for awakening.

In contrast to medieval India, contemporary religious culture conceives the defining goal of religious practice as transforming the self, or one's consciousness. This psychologized, interiorized, and individualized (or privatized) understanding of religion is widely presumed in much of Westernized popular religious culture. This understanding, however, has its roots in Enlightenment and Romantic conceptions of the self. In that framework it would be easy to interpret ritual identification as a kind of psychospiritual transformation and with that interpretation see it as definitive of the tradition of tantric Buddhism. Some modern interpreters may find it appealing to define tantra in terms of ritual identification simply because it fits so well with their own cultural preconceptions about individual transformation. Despite this easy congruence, the Buddhist tradition does not share that intellectual history.

Ritual identification is not universal among tantric traditions, its meaning within Buddhist tantra has changed over time, and its appeal as the defining characteristic is fostered by an anachronistic affinity with contemporary preconceptions. Consequently, as important as the concept of ritual identification is for understanding tantric praxis, it cannot be used monothetically as the unique defining characteristic of tantra.[48] Even if not explicitly proposing a single characteristic as definitive, some authors highlight sex and death,[49] others focus on transgressive acts more broadly,[50] while still others emphasize the importance of mantra. Strictly monothetic approaches, then, identify a single necessary and sufficient characteristic as definitive. Alternatively, "multifactorial monothetic" approaches identify all of some set of several characteristics as both necessary and sufficient.

[47] Davidson, *Indian Esoteric Buddhism*, 139.

[48] It seems plausible that the role that ritual identification has had as the defining characteristic of tantra in Western scholarship follows from the early work of Ferdinand D. Lessing and Alex Wayman, *Mkhas Grub Rje's Fundamentals of the Buddhist Tantras* (The Hague: Mouton, 1968); see, for example, the "Discussion of Self Generation," 163–171.

[49] Hartzell, "Tantric Yoga," 15–16.

[50] Thomas B. Ellis, "Disgusting Bodies, Disgusting Religion: The Biology of Tantra," *Journal of the American Academy of Religion* 79.4 (Dec. 2011): 879–927.

Multifactorial Monothetic Approaches: Lists Without Number

Several scholars have proposed definitions based on lists of characteristics, all of which are required: a multifactorial definition.[51] Axel Michaels, for example, describes the commonalities of both Hindu and Buddhist tantric texts: "What is common to these texts is that they object to the Veda as (the sole) authority, stress the importance of ordination (*dīkṣā*), acknowledge the significance of spiritual practices (*sādhana*), and suggest that the sought-after deity can be realized by various means—e.g., through worship (*pūjā*), sacred diagrams (*maṇḍala, yantra*), or visualization."[52] This description is useful as a preliminary orientation. However, any approach based on listing elements is made problematic by the fact that each component on the list either has a prior history or is found in explicitly nontantric settings.[53] Mantras date back to Vedic ritual, mandalas are found in a variety of nontantric traditions, and bodily postures (Skt. *asanas*) and mudras are employed in art and dance, and so on.

Following his summary of the *Sarvatathāgatādhṣṭhānahṛdaya-guhyadhātukaraṇḍamudra-nāma-dhāraṇī-sūtra* (commonly referred to as the Karaṇḍamudrā Dhāraṇī),[54] Gregory Schopen's comments provide another instance of the list approach to defining tantra. He says that there is

> nothing at all "Tantric" about our text if by "Tantric" we mean that phase of Buddhist doctrinal development which is characterized by an emphasis on the central function of the *guru* as religious preceptor; by sets—usually graded—of specific initiations; by esotericism of doctrine, language and

[51] Some theorists consider such a definition is "monothetic, if the multiple factors are all required" (Kevin Schilbrack, "The Concept of Religion," in *The Stanford Encyclopedia of Philosophy* [Summer 2022 edition], ed. Edward N. Zalta, https://plato.stanford.edu/archives/sum2022/entries/concept-religion/, 45n4).

[52] Axel Michaels, *Hinduism: Past and Present*, trans. Barbara Harshov (Princeton, NJ: Princeton University Press, 2004), 61.

[53] Yukei Matsunaga, "A History of Tantric Buddhism in India, with Reference to Chinese Translations," in *Buddhist Thought and Asian Civilization: Essays in Honor of Herbert V. Guenther on His Sixtieth Birthday*, ed. Leslie S. Kawamura and Keith Scott (Emeryville, CA: Dharma Publishing, 1977), 167–181.

[54] Peking vol. 11, no. 508, 112–2–2 to 114–4–7. (Schopen's citation of page, folio, and line numbers apparently follows the Suzuki edition of the Peking canon; corresponding Chinese versions in the Taisho: T. 1022a/K. 1287, T. 1022b, and T. 1023/K. 1113.) Schopen's claim that the text is not tantric is part of his argument against the idea that the association of a dhāraṇī recorded in that text with the Abhayagiri indicates a tantric dimension of that sangha. If to determine the affiliation of the text we consider the bibliographic categorization (see discussion below), instead of Schopen's list of characteristics, the situation is ambiguous. Although not included in the tantric section of the Tibetan canon (it is in the *mdo sde* rather than *rgyud 'bum*), it is included in the tantric section of the Taisho edition of the Chinese canon, in vol. 19, of the 密教部 Esoteric section.

> organization; and by a strong emphasis on the realization of the goal through highly structured ritual and meditative techniques. If "Tantric" is to be used to refer to something other than this, then the term must be clearly defined and its boundaries must be clearly drawn. Otherwise the term is meaningless and quite certainly misleading.[55]

Schopen asserts that the goal of definition is sharply distinguished categories, while also arguing that all of the characteristics he lists are necessary to identify a tantric text.

Like strictly monothetic approaches, multifactorial monothetic approaches are also dysfunctional. Probably as a consequence of differing areas of expertise, different scholars suggest different lists. Essentially, this means that the selection of items on a list is idiosyncratic, rather than a universalizable set of (necessary and sufficient) characteristics.[56] Likewise, a multifactorial list that might work in one cultural context, such as Tibet, may well not work in a different cultural context, such as Japan. Another alternative to monothetic approaches is the polythetic approach, which, having become popular in religious studies, deserves closer scrutiny.

Polythetic Approaches: Lists Without End

Yet other scholars have claimed that something can be tantra if it has some but not all of the characteristics on the list they propose—an approach to definition known as polythetic, or metaphorically "family resemblances." This is the intuitively accessible idea that one can identify members of a family by noting the various ways in which they are alike, even though no two of them have all the same characteristics, and no single characteristic is shared by all of them. One family member may have Uncle Josh's eyes, but Grandmother Betty's hair color, and so on. A second metaphor for this is the separate strands that make up a rope.[57] No single strand runs the entire length of the rope, yet the rope forms a coherent whole.

In her discussion of different approaches to defining "religion," Caroline Schaffalitzky de Muckadell explains that theorists employing polythetic

[55] Gregory Schopen, "The Text on the 'Dhāraṇī Stones from Abhayagiriya': A Minor Contribution to the Study of Mahāyāna Literature in Ceylon," *Journal of the International Association of Buddhist Studies* 5.1 (1982): 100–108, 105.

[56] See, for another example, Stephen Hodge, *The Mahā-Vairocana-Abhisaṃbodhi Tantra with Buddhaguhya's Commentary* (London: RoutledgeCurzon, 2003), 4–5.

[57] This metaphor is Wittgenstein's. Rodney Needham, "Polythetic Classification: Convergence and Consequences," *Man* 10.3 (1975): 349–369, 350.

approaches consider religion to be "a familiar term of ordinary language, but—perhaps because of its very complex history—it is a vague concept which refers to something with indistinct boundaries and gray areas."[58] Accordingly,

> polythetic approaches account for vagueness roughly by arguing that there are various elements that religions often have in common, but that there is no set of necessary and sufficient conditions that must be met. Rather, these elements are more or less overlapping traits, and this means that something can be more or less religion-like depending on how many of the relevant elements it has.[59]

Perhaps the earliest application of a polythetic approach to defining tantra was made in discussions at the first meeting of the Society for Tantric Studies in 1987. Several of the participants had been students of Jonathan Z. Smith, and following his explanation of polythetic definition,[60] it became part of an attempt by participants to clarify the concept.[61] Douglas Renfrew Brooks systematized the discussion and argued for this approach in his groundbreaking study of Hindu Śakta tantra.[62]

Such an approach may also allow for the creation of a scale of "tantricness"; that is, the more items from the list, the more tantric the text. Henrik Sørensen has gone further to suggest that the degree of tantric-ness correlates to a developmental chronology, with earlier works having fewer of the characteristics and later works having more.[63]

Upon examination, however, sometimes the claim that a polythetic definition is being employed is simply a list of characteristics accompanied by the disclaimer that any instance may have only some of the characteristics

[58] Caroline Schaffalitzky de Muckadell, "On Essentialism and Real Definitions of Religion," *Journal of the American Academy of Religion* 82.2 (June 2014): 495–520, DOI: 10.1093/jaarel/lfu015: 500.

[59] Schaffalitzky de Muckadell, "On Essentialism and Real Definitions of Religion," 500.

[60] Jonathan Z. Smith, *Imagining Religion: From Babylon to Jonestown* (Chicago: University of Chicago Press, 1982), 1–8.

[61] Payne and Hayes, "Tantric Studies," 5.

[62] Douglas Renfrew Brooks, *The Secret of the Three Cities: An Introduction to Hindu Śākta Tantrism* (Chicago: University of Chicago Press, 1990), 52–72.

[63] Henrik H. Sørensen, "Spells and Magical Practices as Reflected in the Early Chinese Buddhist Sources (c. 300–600 CE) and Their Implications for the Rise and Development of Esoteric Buddhism," in *Chinese and Tibetan Esoteric Buddhism*, ed. Yael Bentor and Meir Shahar, 41–71 (Leiden: Brill, 2017).

listed.[64] Bradley L. Herling explains the polythetic definition of "religion" in just this fashion, saying that a polythetic definition

> constructs a list of characteristics that, taken together, describe what religion is generally about. Not all individual instances have all the characteristics, nor is there any one single characteristic that they all must have to be considered "religions." But there is overlap and resemblance among these characteristics—enough to suggest that there is a consistent, continuous reality behind the term, even [if] it cannot be pinned down to one absolute, essential quality.[65]

Important questions, such as where specific characteristics begin and end, how they are related to one another, and how they hold together, are left unanswered—or even unasked. Developing an actual polythetic definition *per se* should mean more than a list of shared characteristics and the caveat that they are not all shared universally by the members of the set being defined. It should derive from an analysis that identifies at least the longer "strands" in the rope, where they begin and end, and how they are interwoven with other strands. The strands of a rope hold together physically. However, the strands of a religious tradition are held together by factors other than the physical. In other words, a polythetic definition should discuss what the strands are, whether some are more significant than others, and how many characteristics something needs to have in order to be included in the category, as well as how the various strands are interwoven in such a fashion as to hold together as an identifiable whole over time.[66] While such criteria for clarity may, of course, be pushing the rope and strand metaphor too far, in some cases, "polythetic" appears to function more as a rhetorical flourish than as an actual strategy for definition.

Whether monothetic, multifactorial, or polythetic, scholarly attempts to define tantra have often taken an outside, that is, an etic perspective. An etic stance is, of course, itself a matter of choice, an artifice, a handy fiction, a claim to authority. Highlighting this is not intended to engage the politicized rhetoric that attempts to privilege either an insider or an outsider view.

[64] On the application of polythetics, see Needham, "Polythetic Classification," 351.

[65] Bradley L. Herling, *A Beginner's Guide to the Study of Religion*, 2nd ed. (London: Bloomsbury, 2016), 37.

[66] These questions generally go unasked, and consequently, claiming to employ a polythetic definition is little different from claims that a category is a term of art or claiming common usage.

Rather, it is simply to emphasize that an etic perspective is an intellectual stance taken in a modern academic context—a choice made, not imposed, and despite being "outside" is still a particular perspective on the object of study. In that context, "tantra" is then a "term of art," that is, a concept or category used by members of the scholarly community who, as participants in that academic discourse, have a shared understanding. In this context, "tantra" is constrained by its history of use within the discourse community.

An alternative, one that looks at tantra from the perspective of participants in a living tradition, would be an emic approach; that is, how do insiders to the tradition understand it? Etic and emic approaches are not necessarily mutually exclusive, as some etic scholarly studies have drawn on emic definitions. Noteworthy figures within the history of Buddhist tantra have offered their own definitions. Consistent with Strickmann's monothetic definition given above, Tsongkhapa (1357–1419) offers a definition of tantra using the term "deity yoga" for ritual identification. Tsongkhapa distinguishes two divisions of the Mahāyāna, referred to as the sutra and mantra vehicles. While the former emphasize the Perfection of Wisdom, the latter are distinguished not by motivation or the perfections to be accomplished, but rather by the practice of ritual identification. As Jeffrey Hopkins explains, Tsongkhapa's distinction focuses on

> the additional technique of deity yoga. A deity is a supramundane being who himself or herself is a manifestation of compassion and wisdom. Thus, in the special practice of deity yoga one joins one's own body, speech, mind, and activities with the exalted body, speech, mind, and activities of a supramundane being, manifesting on the path a similitude of the state of effect.[67]

Emic definitions of tantra, such as Tsongkhapa's, may be integrated into academic discourse. Its emic status, however, is only an indication of how concepts were understood by someone standing within the tradition, at a particular time and place. As such, they are not automatically privileged as authentic, accurate, or definitively final, any more than etic definitions are. Like etic definitions, emic ones are constrained by the historical, cultural,

[67] Jeffrey Hopkins, "Preface," in Tsongkhapa, *The Great Exposition of Secret Mantra, Volume One: Tantra in Tibet*, trans. and ed. Jeffrey Hopkins, vii–xii (1977. Rev. ed. Boulder, CO: Snow Lion, 2016), ix.

linguistic, and sectarian locations of the figures proposing them.[68] Despite such constraints, they can be taken as data for identifying factors shared across the boundaries between different tantric Buddhist traditions.

These problems with various approaches to defining tantra result in large part from it being an intersubjective category—its meaning is in part conceptual (subjective), but it also allows us to identify specific instances existing in the communal world (objective). That is, intersubjective categories point both at some set of objects and at a concept. What constitutes the object, however, is itself socially determined, and at the same time the concept is determined by context, use, and designation. Consequently, the boundaries around "tantra"—what things in the world are tantric and what the concept means—change over time and lack sharp edges; that is, the category is both fluid and fuzzy.

Context, Use, and Designation—How to Not Define Tantra

The protector deity and the dhāraṇī found in the Zen hermitage in Ohara have recognizably tantric associations for someone trained in Buddhist tantra. However, in that context, neither was used nor designated by the hermitage's occupants as tantric—they were understood as unproblematically part of the Zen tradition. In the context of the Shingon temple where I had done my own training, both were used and designated as tantric. Similarly, in the context of canon formation, some dhāraṇī sutras are classed as tantric and others not—we may speculatively suggest that these decisions were due to use and sectarian designation.

Context, use, and designation are ways of delineating tantra—not defining it. Metaphorically, to define is like drawing a line around the instances to be included, creating a boundary, claiming a territory, enforcing inclusion by exclusion. In contrast, to delineate is to make connections, to draw lines between instances, creating an interconnected pattern. Again, unlike the ideal of definition, delineation does not create sharp divisions, but instead indicates relations across boundaries. It does, however, reflect the actual complexity of lived religion and of actual people engaged in living religion, rather than abstracted categories.

[68] Similarly, as valuable as definitions based on usages as found in particular bodies of literature are for understanding the categories as native to those literatures, they do not provide a means of understanding tantra across as wide a range as we are considering here. See, for example, Henrik H. Sørensen, "On Esoteric Buddhism in China: A Working Definition," in *Esoteric Buddhism and the Tantras in East Asia*, ed. Charles D. Orzech, Henrik H. Sørensen, and Richard K. Payne, 155–175 (Leiden: Brill, 2011).

A particularly clear and salient instance of designation is the bibliographic category of tantra as it is employed in categorizing the variety of Buddhist texts found in canonic collections. A (strictly) canonic bibliographic category can also then be extended meaningfully into extracanonic and nonbibliographic settings. Context, use, and designation provide means by which it is possible to delineate what is tantric. This is, in other words, a way of recognizing tantra when one sees it, rather than trying to create a definition that draws a boundary from a position above the ongoing history of the movement.

"Tantra" as a Bibliographic Category

This work selectively examines important dimensions of the tantric movement in the history and culture of the Buddhist cosmopolis, ranging chronologically from the early medieval period to the present, and culturally from the Indian subcontinent to the rest of Asia, and globally. This scope requires an understanding of tantra that is constrained neither by sectarian or institutional conceptions, nor by academic preconceptions. Delineating the category by bibliographic designation employs the work of the Buddhist tradition's own practitioners, compilers, editors, and bibliographers. This takes advantage of the collective history of judgments about what is and isn't tantra—judgments made by Buddhist practitioners and scholars over centuries, that is, emic judgments employed toward an etic delineation.

Grounded in this fashion, an initial delineation of "tantra" would be as a bibliographic category.[69] Pointing out that the term identifies a set of texts is simple, but not simplistic; obvious, but not inconsequential. It is distinct and clear, providing an objective referent for inquiry.[70] Even as a bibliographic category, however, "tantra" has fuzzy edges and, therefore, cannot be applied unreflectively in a mechanical manner of inclusion and exclusion.

Three aspects of the bibliographic category make this delineation fuzzy.[71] First, different canonic collections themselves employ different category

[69] Such an approach has been dismissively rejected by many scholars. A recent instance is Julian Strube, who asserts that "While there are scriptures called the *tantras*, their content is highly diverse and can hardly help to delineate a monolithic tradition or doctrine." The argument being made in this volume is that there is no reason to attempt to "delineate a monolithic tradition or doctrine," and that in fact such attempts prove to be dysfunctional by imposing constraints onto the movement. Julian Strube, *Global Tantra: Religion, Science and Nationalism in Global Modernity* (New York: Oxford University Press, 2022), 1.

[70] The first use of the term "tantra" in English dates from 1799 when it was used to identify a type of text. Herbert Guenther, *The Tantric View of Life* (Berkeley, CA: Shambhala, 1972), 1.

[71] The concept of "fuzzy" is being used in a technical sense. See Petr Cintula, Christian G. Fermüller, and Carles Noguera, "Fuzzy Logic," in *The Stanford Encyclopedia of Philosophy*

systems and include different texts in the category of tantras. For example, as a consequence of differing historical conditions, the structures of the Chinese and Tibetan canons are not the same, and they do not include the same set of texts. Even where the "same" text is included, they are (obviously) different translations.[72] Second, the term "tantra" is found in the titles of several works that are outside our field of interest here. Donald Lopez calls attention to the *Uttaratantra*, the title of one of the five works of Maitreya that are associated with the Yogācāra tradition, as an instance.[73] Third, not all texts that are of interest have the specific term "tantra" in their title. The *Root Manual of the Rites of Mañjuśrī* (*Mañjuśrīmūlakalpa*) is important to the tantric praxis of Mañjuśrī, though it is identified as a "kalpa" (manual of rites) rather than a tantra.

As a literary category, the term "tantra" has a wide semantic range across the history of Indian religious literature. Gerald Larson has called it a portmanteau (that is, an expression "that combines two separate meanings") or perhaps a homograph (two words written the same, but having different origins and meanings).[74] In contrast, however, Friedhelm Hardy has noted that the term "in its concrete sense . . . denotes quite innocuously a particular genre of religious texts (parallel, say, to the Upaniṣads or Purāṇas)."[75]

In the context of Indian Buddhism, tantra has a more specific significance of just this sort. Davidson notes that "The word 'tantra' is a polysemic term in India, but as employed in Buddhism came to denote the esoteric scriptures, even though these often were identified with other terms in their titles, such as kalpa, sutra, and so on."[76] Despite this fuzziness, as a bibliographic category, "tantra" comprises a set of texts produced during the medieval period

(Summer 2023 edition), ed. Edward N. Zalta and Uri Nodelman, https://plato.stanford.edu/archives/sum2023/entries/logic-fuzzy/.

[72] For example, although there is a great deal of similarity between the Chinese and Tibetan translations of the *Vairocanābhisaṃbodhi tantra*, there are also significant differences. See Hodge, *The Mahāvairocana-Abhisaṃbodhi Tantra*, 16. It seems worth emphasizing at this point that the concept of "text" is itself an abstract social convention. For example, the "text" of the Lotus Sutra can refer to many different specific translations in many languages.

[73] Donald S. Lopez, Jr., *Elaborations on Emptiness: Uses of the Heart Sutra* (Princeton, NJ: Princeton University Press, 1996), 84.

[74] Gerald James Larson, "The Terms 'Tantra' and 'Yoga' as Portmanteau or Homographic Expressions," AAR paper 2008: 1.

[75] Friedhelm Harvey, *The Religious Culture of India: Power, Love and Wisdom* (Cambridge: Cambridge University Press, 1994), 153.

[76] Ronald M. Davidson, "The Problem of Secrecy in Indian Tantric Buddhism," in *The Culture of Secrecy in Japanese Religion*, ed. Bernhard Scheid and Mark Teeuwen, 60–77 (London: Routledge, 2006), 74n1.

of Indian Buddhism, together with the extensive literature that developed on the basis of those texts throughout the spread of Buddhism.[77] Several of these texts are taught by buddhas other than Śākyamuni, and they often focus more on practice than on doctrine. The practices include a wide variety of rituals and visualizations, as well as initiations, recitations, and yogic practices, many of which were adapted into Buddhist use from the wider cultural context, including Vedic, Brahmanic, and Śaivite traditions. Indicative of the permeability of these categories, deities were also adopted by one tradition from the other, both from Buddhist to Hindu traditions and vice versa.[78] The relation between Buddhist and Hindu (that is, Śaiva, Śakti, and Vaiṣnava) and Jain forms of tantra is an important area of contemporary scholarship.[79]

The bibliographic significance of the term "tantra," and its corollaries, as found in the titles of specific texts, can be given greater nuance by considering the categories employed in Buddhist canons. Canon construction is not, of course, itself an objective project,[80] and the range of tantric literature goes beyond the contents of any specific canon. One of the more significant examples of this is the Nyingma, "old school," texts (the Nyingma *rgyud bum*) that were expunged from the Tibetan canon on the grounds that there was no clear Sanskrit original, though in some cases this criterion appears to have been applied selectively in light of political considerations.[81] Additionally, "explanatory tantras" are associated with some tantras, as well

[77] A more extensive understanding then also includes textual resources from traditions influenced by tantric Buddhism, such as Bon, Daoism, and Shinto.

[78] Gudrun Bühnemann, "Buddhist Deities and Mantras in the Hindu Tantras: I The *Tantrasārasaṃgraha* and the *Īśānaśivagurudevapaddhati*," *Indo-Iranian Journal* 42.4 (1999): 303–334; and "Buddhist Deities and Mantras in the Hindu Tantras: II The *Śrīvidyārṇavatantra* and the *Tantrasāra*." *Indo-Iranian Journal* 43.1 (2000): 27–48.

[79] See the chapters on Jain tantra in Richard K. Payne and Glen A. Hayes, eds., *The Oxford Handbook of Tantric Studies* (New York: Oxford University Press, 2024). See also Gough, *Making a Mantra*.

[80] See Steven Collins, "On the Very Idea of the Pāli Canon," *Journal of the Pali Text Society* 15 (1990): 89–126; and David Gray, "On the Very Idea of a Tantric Canon: Myth, Politics, and the Formation of the Bka' 'gyur," *Journal of the International Association of Tibetan Studies* 5 (Dec. 2009): 1–37; and Richard Salomon, "An Unwieldy Canon: Observations on Some Distinctive Features of Canon Formation in Buddhism," in *Kanonisierung und Kanonbildung in der asiatischen Religionsgeschichte*, ed. Max Deeg, Oliver Freiberger, and Christoph Kleine, 161–207 (Vienna: Verlag der Österreichischen Akademie der Wissenschaften, 2011).

[81] Robert Mayer, "Rnyingma Tantras," in *Brill Encyclopedia of Buddhism: Literature and Languages*, ed. Jonathan Silk, Oskar von Hinuber, and Vincent Eltschinger, 390–397 (Leiden: Brill, 2015). Also, Tsering Namgyal, "Buton Rinchen Drub" (Treasury of Lives, 2012; https://treasuryoflives.org/biographies/view/Buton-Rinchen-Drub/2845). See also Lisa Stein and Ngwang Zangpo, trans., *Butön's History of Buddhism in India and Its Spread to Tibet* (Boulder, CO: Snow Lion, 2013), 372–373.

as commentaries, compendia of ritual instructions, and cycles of texts.[82] Also to be considered are ancillary works that may not be canonic in the sense of being members of the edited collections ("formal canon"), but which are regularly used by practitioners ("practical canon"). Anne Blackburn explains that this phrase "refers to *the units of text actually employed in the practices of collecting manuscripts, copying them, reading them, commenting on them, listening to them, and preaching sermons based upon them that are understood by their users as part of a tipiṭaka-based tradition*."[83] For Buddhist tantra, a "practical canon" would include ritual manuals, yogic instructions, and other resources prescribing tantric praxes.

Texts have been important as the tantric movement extended across continents and endured for a millennium and a half. It has not, however, been defined by any particular text in the way that, for example, Christianity is today largely self-defined by the Bible. The prototypical role of Christianity for the field of religious studies creates an implicit assumption that there is, or ought to be, some book that is central to the movement as a whole. While, for example, the *Guhyasamāja tantra* has been called "the most renowned and influential of the Buddhist Mahāyoga Tantras,"[84] it is not definitive of the movement as a whole, nor are the mahāyoga tantras as a group definitive.[85] For example, Dorji Wangchuk has called attention to another tantra, the *Guhyagarbha tantra*, as being essential for the Nyingma tradition.[86] Also in relation to the Nyingma tradition, Jacob Dalton has pointed to the *Gathering of Intentions* (*Dgong pa 'dus pa'i mdo*) as "the canonical backbone of the Nyingma school."[87] Steven Weinberger identifies yet another text, the *Sarva-tathāgata-tattva-saṃgraha* (STS, *Compendium of Principles*) "and the tantric traditions associated with it in India [as having] formed the substance of mainstream tantric traditions in Tibet."[88] In

[82] An instance is the cycle of texts that are the source for the "Tibetan Book of the Dead"; see Donald S. Lopez, Jr., *The Tibetan Book of the Dead: A Biography* (Princeton, NJ: Princeton University Press, 2011), 124.

[83] Anne Blackburn, "Looking for the *Vinaya*: Monastic Discipline in the Practical Canons of the Theravāda," *Journal of the International Association of Buddhist Studies* 22.2 (1999): 281–309, 284.

[84] Christian Wedemeyer, *Making Sense of Tantric Buddhism: History, Semiology, and Transgression in the Indian Traditions* (New York: Columbia University Press, 2013), 106.

[85] The problematic character of textual fundamentalism will also be discussed below in relation to interpreting the nature of Borobudur.

[86] Dorji Wangchuk, "An Eleventh-Century Defence of the Authenticity of the *Guhyagarbha Tantra*," in *The Many Canons of Tibetan Buddhism*, ed. Helmut Eimer and David Germano, 265–291 (Leiden: Brill, 2002), 268.

[87] Jacob P. Dalton, *The Gathering of Intentions: A History of a Tibetan Tantra* (New York: Columbia University Press, 2016), xviii.

[88] Steven Weinberger, "The Yoga Tantras and the Social Context of Their Transmission to Tibet," *Chung-Hwa Buddhist Journal* 23 (2010): 131–166, 133.

addition to the *Sarvatathāgatatattva saṃgraha*, the *Vairocanābhisaṃbodhi* and **Susiddhikara tantras* have been central to the development of tantric Buddhism in East Asia.[89] Each of these is, in fact, important for some specific group of practitioners, but fundamentally sectarian designations of centrality do not serve for the entirety of the tantric movement.

The collective nature of the Buddhist bibliographic project stretches across several different canons in different languages, meaning that taken together, the work of the compilers serves to blunt, though not eliminate, sectarian commitments from the textual whole of tantra. Again, understanding "tantra" by referring to its use as a bibliographic category may not be perfect, but for understanding tantra across Buddhist history, it is more adequately grounded than the definitional strategies discussed above. Compared to the concrete nature of the textual collections, those definitional approaches are abstract, idiosyncratic, and dysfunctional. There is no particular text that is foundational or definitive for the tantric Buddhist movement as a whole. Instead of being a singular entity, the movement comprises many praxes, and the variety of texts encompassed in the movement's formal and practical canons reflects the variety of different praxes, each one of which may hold different texts in special regard.[90]

For these reasons, the bibliographic delineation is not intended to be definitive, but instead, a starting point. It provides a clear foundation for knowing what components—deities, practices, concepts, graphic representations, and so on—have been considered tantric by members of the Buddhist tradition itself. It also limits the scope of inquiry, that is, justifies decisions regarding what not to include.

Other Category Terms Pointing to the Movement

Practitioners, lineages, institutions, and scholars have adopted a variety of terms to identify tantric praxes. These include not only tantra but also mantranaya, mantrayāna, and vajrayāna, together with equivalents for these terms in other languages. These terms differ not so much in substance as in emphasis, highlighting different aspects of the movement.

[89] Cf. Richard K. Payne, "Buddhism," in *The Cambridge Companion to Literature and Religion*, ed. Susan M. Felch, 169–185 (New York: Cambridge University Press, 2016). An asterisk in front of the Susiddhikara indicates that the title is reconstructed in Sanskrit from the Chinese, in this case from Śubhakarasiṃha's translation of 726 (T. 893, K. 432).

[90] This does not mean that they are "sacred texts," which is a category created as part of Western religious studies from the nineteenth century onward.

Some scholars have articulated careful historical distinctions based on the differences between some of these terms. Explaining their decision to avoid the term "tantric," Thomas Cruijsen, Arlo Griffiths, and Marijke J. Klokke offer a helpful explanation that identifies three categories and their historical relations:

> The term Mantranaya is used within Mahāyāna Buddhist tradition during this period [second half of the first millennium CE]—including in ancient Java—to distinguish the path of mantras from the longer path called Pāramitānaya, that requires continual cultivation of virtues over countless lives before reaching Buddhahood. The term Vajrayāna is first attested toward the end of the 7th century, and refers to the strand of Mantranayic Buddhism in which the symbol of the *vajra* holds a prominent place, both in its literature as also in the ritual context. The term Mantrayāna does not appear to have come into use before the 11th century.[91]

Davidson has noted a related problem in the study of specific lineages of practice, saying that modern scholarship has suffered from "a totalizing response . . . to issues of Buddhist ritual and its hermeneutics, so that the differentiation into specific traditions has been under emphasized."[92] Determined by social convention, "movements" comprise a variety of different particular entities that overlap in different ways, such as belief systems, practices, organizing commitments, and so on.

For clarity in the study of the movement in China, Andrew Goble makes another terminological distinction. One term of the distinction is "esoteric Buddhism" as the "body of early Mahāyāna ritual and spell texts in Chinese translation,"[93] that is, primarily an object constructed by historical reflection. The other term is "Esoteric Buddhism," as the "Tang dynasty Buddhist school" identified with Śubhākarasiṃha, Vajrabodhi, and Amoghavajra, that is, what we can call a lineage of practice.[94] According to Goble, later historical understandings rarely made this distinction, and this failure to distinguish

[91] Thomas Cruijsen, Arlo Griffiths, and Marijke J. Klokke, "The Cult of the Buddhist *Dhāraṇī* Deity Mahāpratisarā Along the Maritime Silk Route: New Epigraphical and Iconographic Evidence from the Indonesian Archipelago," *Journal of the International Association of Buddhist Studies* 35.1–2 (2012 [2013]): 74n7. (Internal references elided.)

[92] Ronald M. Davidson, "Reframing *Sahaja*: Genre, Representation, Ritual, and Lineage," *Journal of Indian Philosophy* 30 (2002): 45–83, 45.

[93] Geoffrey C. Goble, *Chinese Esoteric Buddhism, Chinese Esoteric Buddhism: Amoghavajra, the Ruling Elite, and the Emergence of a Tradition* (New York: Columbia University Press, 2019), 1.

[94] See also Sørensen, "On Esoteric Buddhism in China."

between the lineage of practice (Esoteric Buddhism) and the corpus of esoteric Buddhist texts contributed to the idea that tantric Buddhism had disappeared after the Tang dynasty (an historiographic trope known as the "disappearing tradition narrative" discussed in the final chapter). However, as Goble notes, "Of course, Esoteric Buddhism did not cease to exist in China. The Esoteric *ācāryas* did not disappear from the world in the eighth century, only their self-representations in elite textual sources did."[95] Goble's latter point highlights the value of context, use, and designation as alternative ways of delineating tantra. Often the scholarly literature employs categories that refer to doctrines or to doctrinal schools. However, the study of ritual praxes deserves the same kind of fine-grained study that doctrines and doctrinal texts receive, and it offers at least as much insight into the history of Buddhism.

Narrow terminological distinctions can be of value at the level of granular detail, which is often key to understanding larger issues. But, because it has a different set of goals, the scope of this work necessarily steps back from these precise historical distinctions for the sake of being able to see not only the tantric movement more widely but also to make its influences and spread more visible, along with reflecting on its corrective value for religious studies. This is the normal dialectic of scholarship in which specific studies inform general ones, and general studies provide structure and direction to specific ones.

The Sanskrit terms listed above—mantranaya, mantrayāna, vajrayāna—provide an overview of key concepts in the formation of the tantric movement. *Mantranaya* is the "mode of mantra," a usage that highlights the central role of mantras, verbal formulae that originate in Vedic ritual practice. In the context of meditation practice, "mantra" is sometimes explained in a quasi-etymology as "mind protector," referring to the way in which concentrating on a mantra, reciting it either mentally or verbally, serves to focus the mind and protect the practitioner from being distracted by other thoughts and appearances.[96]

The "mantra vehicle" (Skt. *mantrayāna*) emphasizes the important role of mantra in the tradition, now employing the terminology of "vehicles"

[95] Goble, *Chinese Esoteric Buddhism*, 244.

[96] See Sthaneshwar Timalsina, "Attention, Memory, and the Imagination: A Cognitive Analysis of Tantric Visualization," in *The Oxford Handbook of Tantric Studies*, ed. Richard K. Payne and Glen A. Hayes, 731–751 (Oxford: Oxford University Press, online 2023: https://doi.org/10.1093/oxfordhb/9780197549889.013.53).

(Skt. *yāna*) widely used by systematizers of Buddhist praxis. Equivalents in East Asia also emphasize the central place of mantra, being translations of mantra as "true word" (Ch. *zhenyan*, Jpn. *shingon*). Other terms used in East Asia emphasize the secrecy of the teachings and the initiatory character of the tradition: "secret" or "esoteric" tradition (Ch. *mizong*), and "secret" or "esoteric" teachings (Ch. *mijiao*, Jpn. *mikkyō*). The phrase "secret mantra vehicle" (Skt. *guhymantrayāna*) is also employed in Tibetan treatments of the topic.

One way of emphasizing the tantric idea of sudden awakening, or awakening in this very lifetime, is to juxtapose tantra and sutra. The "vehicle of sutra teachings" (Skt. *sūtrayāna*) is also known as the "mode of perfection" (Skt. *pāramītānaya*), both of which refer to conceptions of the path as gradual.[97] Symbolically, sudden awakening is represented by the vajra, itself a semantically complex symbol. "Vajra" is rendered sometimes as "thunderbolt" or as "diamond," and it gives us the category term "vajrayāna." The bivalence of the term "vajra" as lightning and as indestructible can be interpreted as first the conception of awakening as sudden illumination, like the sudden vision of one's surroundings revealed by a thunderbolt on a dark night. The second suggests that it is stronger than anything else, as in the rendering of *vajrayāna* as the "adamantine" or "diamond vehicle."

The variety of terms discussed above reflects the history and complexity of the tantric movement, and each emphasizes some particular aspects of the movement. As perhaps the most general term, and because it is grounded in the concrete referent of the texts designated by the bibliographic category, the term "tantra" will (continue) to be employed in this work to identify the movement.

Regional Organization

The next four chapters of this work are organized regionally. Beginning first with South Asia, the following chapters then move to East Asia, Southeast Asia, and Inner Asia. The purpose for using regions as the overall organizing principle is to overcome the limitations and blind spots that follow from the more common default that takes modern nation-states as an organizing

[97] See Jeffrey Hopkins, "Supplement," in *The Great Exposition of Secret Mantra, Vol. 1: Tantra in Tibet*, trans. and ed. Jeffrey Hopkins, 163–231 (1977. Reprint. Boulder, CO: Snow Lion, 2016), 163–171.

principle.[98] Modern nation-states are frequently taken as the "natural" organizing schema for Buddhist studies—producing such phrases as "Chinese Buddhism," "Korean Buddhism," "Cambodian Buddhism," and so on.[99] While those phrases are appropriate for studies delimited by modern nation-states, when employed without qualification, they distort the study of Buddhist history. Jinhua Chen makes this point strongly, saying that

> Applying these divisions in their own work, researchers often overlook substantial shifts and currents (byways or roads) that have long connected places and people across these regions. Modern nation states have blocked the scholarly view from the dynamic interconnections between these different regions on the one hand and on the other, the significant impact from the marginal regions to the "centers."[100]

For example, the implied unity of something as complex as the history of the variety of Buddhisms that were practiced in continental East Asia by the phrase "Chinese Buddhism" both obscures and marginalizes much of the actual history. Structuring that history in terms of modern nation-states also often means a focus on national capitals, privileging the elite traditions of the "center," to the detriment of our understanding of the "periphery." And sectarian understandings of Buddhist history propagated by the elites of the center become hegemonic in our perception of that history.[101] In some cases at least, use of nation-state categories has been in the service of nationalistic

[98] For a more comprehensive treatment of these issues, see Richard K. Payne, "Buddhist Studies Beyond the Nation-State," in *Oxford Handbooks* (Oxford: Oxford University Press, 2016; DOI: 10.1093/oxfordhb/9780199935420.013.13).

[99] The dysfunctions of naturalizing nation-state categorization can be exacerbated by rhetorical claims valorizing one form over another. For example, referencing the Muslim invasion of India and the collapse of the Tang dynasty, Robert Thurman has asserted, "Fortunately, during the last flowering at the end of the first millenium, Chinese Buddhist traditions were transmitted to Japan, and the Indian Buddhist traditions were transmitted to Tibet" ("Buddhist Hermeneutics," *Journal of the American Academy of Religion* 46.1[March 1978]: 19–39, 21). The reader of such a claim might reasonably assume that the two strains (Chinese and Indian) are disjunct from one another, creating the sense of rupture rather than continuity. This, then, plays upon a general rhetoric of origins and authenticity, reinforced by the notion that since India is the source of Buddhism, and Tibet received it from there, Tibetan Buddhism is more authentically Buddhist than the marginal or derivative Japanese Buddhism.

[100] Jinhua Chen, "A Chemical 'Explosion' Triggered by an Encounter Between Indian and Chinese Medical Sciences: Another Look at the Significances of the Sinhalese Monk Śākyamitra's (567?–668+) Visit at Mount Wutai in 667," in *What Happened After Mañjuśrī Migrated to China? The Sinification of the Mañjuśrī Faith and the Globalization of the Wutai Cult*, ed. Jinhua Chen, Guang Kuan, and Hu Fo, 3–18 (London: Routledge, 2022), 3.

[101] Megan Bryson, "Buddhist Geography and Regionalism," in *Oxford Research Encyclopedia of Religion* (New York: Oxford University Press, 2018; DOI: 10.1093/acrefore/9780199340378.013.626).

assertions of some unique and privileged sectarian form of Buddhism identified with that nation-state. For these reasons, regional categories, rather than modern nation-states, structure the body of this work. At the same time, it is important to emphasize that these categories are simply descriptive. They do not imply any underlying essential unity to the Buddhisms of the region, nor any causal relation from region to forms of Buddhist praxis. In other words, regions are not explanatory. The sixth chapter specifically seeks to subvert the separations implied by regional categories by focusing instead on networks of relations, patterns that have consistently run across regional divisions.

The study of tantric Buddhism provides a fulcrum point for critiquing the academic field of religious studies. The concluding chapter highlights methodological reflections on the way that tantra does not fit easily into the concepts, categories, and concerns standard to religious studies as it is practiced today.

Facets of Tantra

Tantra is a multifaceted movement, and this work is structured to reflect that multifaceted character. It is an intentional methodological decision that rather than employing a single interpretive or analytic framework, the work examines a variety of topics and issues relevant to the study of tantra. While organized regionally, the following chapters examine several different facets. South Asia is the first region, as it is where tantra originated. The chapter examines the ritual foundations of tantric practice, how those were transformed into interior practices, and a group of practitioners who engaged in such interiorized practices. East Asia is the next region, and the chapter examines two ways in which tantra has been institutionalized—the recitation of verbal formulae, specifically the practices and conventions of *dhāraṇī*, and pilgrimages, specifically the one that encircles the island of Shikoku in Japan. Turning to Southeast Asia, the fourth chapter looks at the role of tantra in state formation, and monuments as expressions of state tantra. Inner Asia is the focus of the fifth chapter, which examines the variety of death, decay, and corruption imagery that range widely across the entire Buddhist tradition, and which take a specifically tantric form in the practice of severance (Tib. *chöd*). The sixth chapter then works to subvert the regional structuring as such, employing the metaphor of networks to examine the strands and nodes that make up networks, the travelers who went from node to node, and the way that it was not "tantric Buddhism" that moved over the networks but rather praxes focused on particular buddhas, bodhisattvas, or protectors. The final chapter turns again to methodological discussions, here focused specifically on critiquing the presumptions and practices of academic religious studies.

II

South Asia

From Vedic Ritual to the Mahāsiddhas

Introduction

Indic religious culture comprises a wide range of ritual practices, many of which, originating in Vedic ritual culture, predate the time of Śākyamuni Buddha.[1] In Kerala state, on the southwest coast of the Indian subcontinent, an ancient Vedic ritual tradition has been maintained by Nambudiri brahmins.[2] Arguably the most elaborate Vedic ritual to actually be performed is the *agnicayana*, "piling up" of an altar for Agni, the Vedic fire deity.[3] After a twenty-year hiatus since its last performance in 1955, it was again performed in 1975 by Nambudiri brahmins in the hamlet of Panjal, when it was extensively studied by a team of researchers and scholars.[4] The performance took place over twelve days, including constructing the large bird-shaped altar. Preparations for the ritual, however, took much longer, some having been initiated a year previously. The altar requires over one thousand fired

[1] On the lengthy history of Vedic culture, see David W. Anthony, *The Horse, the Wheel and Language: How Bronze-Age Riders from the Eurasian Steppes Shaped the Modern World* (Princeton, NJ: Princeton University Press, 2007).

[2] It seems improbable that practice of the Vedic tradition as found among the Nambudiri in Kerala is unbroken, and unchanged from the Vedic era into the present—a "strong claim" of continuity. The claim that Staal makes, however, is that the Vedic tradition as practiced by the Nambudiri is " 'living,' and not 'revivalistic' " (Staal, *Agnicayana* I.174). This more nuanced claim is that while the tradition has changed over time, it has not been "corrected" to accord with normative conceptions from outside that tradition. Kim Plofker makes a qualified challenge to Staal on this point, saying that modern practices of the geometry of the brick altar "may have originated in a form of 'Vedic revivalism' in some post-Vedic period rather than in a continuous ritual praxis going back to the composition of the *Śulba-sūtras*" (*Mathematics in India: 500 BCE to 1800 CE* [Princeton: Princeton University Press, 2009], 18, n. 10). Plofker's critique is, however, directed at a strong version of the claim of continuity, rather than at Staal's nuanced claim.

[3] The qualification "to actually be performed" is necessary because Vedic ritualism proposes the possibility of massively expanded rituals, far beyond what could actually be performed. The mechanism for such expansion is a key point in Frits Staal's development of a syntactic analysis of ritual.

[4] Frits Staal, *Agni: The Vedic Fire Ritual*, 2 vols. (Berkeley, CA: Asian Humanities Press, 1983), I.188. The agnicayana was again performed in 2011. See Michael Witzel, "Reminiscences of Frits Staal and the *Agnicayana*," in *On Meaning and Mantra: Essays in Honor of Frits Staal*, ed. George Thompson and Richard K. Payne, 601–622 (Berkeley, CA: Institute of Buddhist Studies, 2016).

Tantra Across the Buddhist Cosmopolis. Richard K. Payne, Oxford University Press. © Oxford University Press 2025.
DOI: 10.1093/9780197825105.003.0002

clay bricks in a variety of specific shapes and sizes, which are stacked in five layers, forming the altar. The ritual also requires the preparation of offerings, of ritual implements, and of the enclosure within which the ritual will be performed. Key among the offerings is *soma*, the famed "drink of the gods."

During the twelve days, seventeen priests and officiants participated first in stacking the bricks (five days) and then making offerings accompanied by recitations of Vedic texts and mantras. At the end of the performance, the altar was abandoned and the enclosure burned. Although vastly more complex, the *agnicayana* is part of the ritual tradition that provided models for tantric homa rituals, including the homas at the Sacramento Shingon Temple and the Fushimi Inari Shrine described in the preceding chapter.

Vedic Ritual

Vedic India's ritual practices and teachings date from about 1500 to 500 BCE, during the millennium preceding the time of the historical Buddha, Śākyamuni.[5]

Much of Vedic ritual involves making votive offerings into fire. These include large or communal rituals (Skt. *śrauta*, solemn rites) and household rituals (Skt. *gṛhya*, domestic rites).[6] Personified as Agni, fire was conceived as the agent by which offerings were purified and transmitted to the deities. Being fire as such, Agni is both domesticated and wild fire; it is both productive and destructive.[7] Agni as a deity and as fire is an identity—not a symbolic relation between a deity as a transcendent reality and a mundane entity that is taken as merely a symbol referencing the deity.[8]

[5] Stephanie Jamison and Michael Witzel, "Vedic Hinduism," in *The Study of Hinduism*, ed. Arvind Sharma, 65–113 (Columbia: University of South Carolina Press, 2003); references here are to the "long version" dated 1992, available online at http://www.people.fas.harvard.edu/~witzel/vedica.pdf.

[6] This distinction was perhaps not as straightforwardly dichotomous as it often seems. See Frederick M. Smith, "The Āvasathya Fire in the Vedic Ritual," *Adyar Library Bulletin* 46 (1982): 73–92.

[7] This ambivalent character is not uncommon among powerful deities. Plague demons, for example, can both inflict plague and prevent it. For more on this complexity, see Christopher Bell, "Tibetan Demonology," in *Oxford Research Encyclopedias* (New York: Oxford University Press, online 2020; https://doi.org/10.1093/acrefore/9780199340378.013.700).

[8] Some theories employed in religious studies construct a progressive hierarchy of an increasingly sophisticated form of religiosity, such as that proposed by Lucien Levy-Bruhl. See Souleymane Bachir Diagne, "Négritude," in *The Stanford Encyclopedia of Philosophy* (Summer 2018 edition), ed. Edward N. Zalta, 19, https://plato.stanford.edu/archives/sum2018/entries/negritude/. Whether explicitly referencing Levy-Bruhl or not, theories of religion that embrace notions of progress implicitly reflect the values of the theory's social location. See Mark C. Taylor, "The Politics of Theo-ry," *Journal of the American Academy of Religion* 59.1 (Spring 1991): 1–37. Denying that the relation

Relatively little is known about the earliest phase of Vedic ritual, the period of the Ṛg Veda. The later development of the public rituals (Skt. *śrauta*) is better known, and it is possible to delineate developmental phases—increasing elaboration, systematization, and codification—of ritual within the Vedas.[9] The goal here, however, is to establish the Vedic background to the development of tantra. For our purposes, "Vedic ritual" refers to general patterns, particularly as found in *śrauta* ritual. Stephanie Jamison and Michael Witzel highlight the importance of ritual for the Vedic tradition, stating that "the central role of elaborate ritual activity throughout the Vedic period cannot be overemphasized."[10] The critical function of fire is one of the key elements in establishing lateral relations between Vedic religious practice and both the Avestan tradition in Iran, and classic Greek and Roman sacrificial practices, and vertically with tantric traditions that developed later.[11]

Making offerings to selected deities is central to Vedic rituals. Offerings include praises voiced and songs performed, as well as incense, food, and drink, the latter being ritually consumed by the fire. "The model of Vedic ritual is then that of a formal meal, ceremonial hospitality, offered to particularly worthy dignitaries."[12] Feasting an honored guest structures ritual offerings to the gods, part of a system of reciprocal exchange between humans and gods.[13] This metaphor is not only fundamental for Vedic ritual but also for Hindu rituals of worship (Skt. *pūjās*) of the medieval and modern periods, as well as structuring tantric ritual performances—such as the homa ritual.

Making offerings, whether oblations of vegetable and dairy products, animal sacrifices, or, the most highly prized oblation, *soma*,[14] is both centrally

between Agni and fire is symbolic is intended to avoid the imposition of an exogenous value system onto Vedic and tantric praxes.

[9] See Michael Witzel, "Vedas and Upaniṣads," in *The Blackwell Companion to Hinduism*, ed. Gavin Flood, 68–98 (Oxford: Blackwell, 2003), 75.

[10] Jamison and Witzel, "Vedic Hinduism," 29.

[11] Jamison and Witzel, "Vedic Hinduism," 30; see also Richard K. Payne, "Tongues of Flame: Homologies in the Tantric Homa," in *The Roots of Tantra*, ed. Katherine Anne Harper and Robert L. Brown, 193–210 (Albany: State University of New York Press, 2002).

[12] Jamison and Witzel, "Vedic Hinduism," 35. See also Carlos Lopez, "Food and Immortality in the Veda: A Gastronomic Theology?" *Electronic Journal of Vedic Studies* 3.3 (1997): 11–19, 15.

[13] See Witzel, "Vedas and Upaniṣads," 78. Ritualization is frequently a matter of taking an ordinary activity and giving it greater form and structure. In such cases the ordinary activity, such as a feast, functions as the "ritual metaphor," and consequently there are metaphoric entailments that follow and which serve to further structure and give meaning to the ritual activities.

[14] *Soma* is the "drink of the gods" and the "nectar of immortality." What the libation was originally made from and how it was made is much debated in the literature. Vedic ritualists have employed several substitutes. Staal, *Agni*, I:105.

important and structurally central in Vedic ritual.[15] "The offering of this chief oblation will generally occur at the exact center of the ritual, for Vedic rituals are bilaterally symmetrical, leading up to and away from the climactic moment."[16] In addition to sharing the ritual metaphor of feasting an honored guest, Vedic and tantric rituals also share this ritually symmetrical structure.[17]

Although the era in which Śākyamuni and other renunciate teachers (Skt. *śramaṇa*) were active saw significant new developments, practices based in the Vedas continued, in some places into the present.[18] Both Vedic practices and the new developments of the *śramaṇa* period contributed to the conceptual milieu—rituals, yogas, doctrines, deities—from which tantric traditions later developed. Indo-Iranian influences on the development of tantra in the early medieval period have also been suggested.[19] Tantric Buddhist praxis developed within this milieu, actively adapting and reinterpreting it in Buddhist ways. For instance, Vajrapāṇi ("vajra-in-hand") developed from a local deity, a *yakṣa*, who became a guardian to Śākyamuni in the first centuries CE, to a Mahayana bodhisattva, and then into tantric form as Vajradhara, the primordial buddha (Skt. *ādhibuddha*).[20] Similarly, Vairocana, the buddha who preaches the *Vairocanābhisaṃbodhi tantra* (discussed in the following section), evidences the role of classical and medieval solar cults, which Ronald M. Davidson considers to be "influential, yet under-acknowledged."[21]

During the same historical period that Buddhist and various Hindu tantric forms were being systematized, the Jain tradition also developed forms of tantric practice, known as *mantraśāstra*. These practices employ both

[15] Stephanie W. Jamison, *The Ravenous Hyenas and the Wounded Sun: Myth and Ritual in Ancient India* (Ithaca, NY: Cornell University Press, 1991), 22–23.

[16] Jamison and Witzel, "Vedic Hinduism," 35. Internal annotations deleted.

[17] The symmetrical structuring of these rituals is noteworthy because it is not in fact universal.

[18] In addition to Kerala, see David M. Knipe, *Vedic Voices: Intimate Narratives of Living Andhra Traditions* (New York: Oxford University Press, 2015).

[19] Holly Grether, "The Ritual Interplay of Fire and Water in Hindu and Buddhist Tantras," in *Homa Variations: The Study of Ritual Change Across the* Longue Durée, ed. Richard K. Payne and Michael Witzel, 47–66 (Oxford: Oxford University Press, 2016).

[20] Ronald M. Davidson, "Esoteric Buddhism in the Matrix of Early Medieval India: An Overview," in *On the Regional Development of Early Medieval Buddhist Monasteries in South Asia*, ed. Abhishek Singh Amar, Nicolas Morrisey, and Akira Shimada, 1–40 (RINDAS Series of Working Papers, #34. Kyoto: Ryukoku University, 2021. RINDAS Series of Working Papers, #34), 15. An alternative explanation is that *vajrapāṇi* originates from an epithet of Indra. "When adopted by Buddhism, Indra was regarded either as king of the gods, or (later in Mahāyāna Buddhism) as Vajrapāṇi among the Eight Great Bodhisattvas; or as the minor deity Vajrapāṇi, ruler of the 'secret one' (*guhyaka*)." Alex Wayman, *The Enlightenment of Vairocana* (Delhi: Motilal Banarsidass, 1992), 83. The adoption of Vedic deities into Buddhist praxis is not unique to tantra. See John Clifford Holt, *The Buddhist Visnu: Religious Transformation, Politics, and Culture* (New York: Columbia University Press, 2004).

[21] Davidson, "Esoteric Buddhism in the Matrix of Early Medieval India," 16.

mantra and geometric diagrams (Skt. *yantra*) comparable to mandala.[22] Ellen Gough describes the similarities and differences between Hindu and Jain practices:

> If the "essentials" of *mantraśāstra* are the use of *mantras*, the structure of the *maṇḍala*, and the significance of certain syllables, colours, etc., then yes, Hindu and Jain *mantraśāstra* are very similar. If, however, the "essentials" of *mantraśāstra* are the particular *mantras* used, the specific symbols of a *maṇḍala*, and how these images are worshiped, then Jain and Hindu *mantraśāstra* at times differ considerably.[23]

Gough highlights the interplay of two different perspectives—specific components and more general categories. Seeing similarities at a more general level is important—it allows understanding tantra in terms of systematic patterns in which components are configured into praxes. The components may change, but the configurations endure.[24] This is analogous to ripples on the surface of a stream as it goes around a rock—the ripples seem stationary, but they are composed of the constantly flowing waters of the stream.

During the early medieval period, revisions of Vedic ritualism, which was not itself a uniform pan-Indian system, were being made across the wide range of Indic religious culture, such as early mandala forms being developed from the domestic earthen fire altar (Skt. *sthaṇdila*) and initiation rites based on royal consecrations. Buddhist practitioners (Skt. *dharmabhāṇakas*) integrated some of these into their own praxis, that is, modifying practices and generating new interpretations.[25] Of course, this was not a simple straight line of development from Vedic to tantric ritual practices. Nor was this simply a matter of Buddhist interpretations being applied to Vedic or Brahmanic ritual.

A complex variety of sources influenced the development of tantra from its prelude in the third to sixth centuries, to the closure of the Buddhist tantric era in India, and its enduring role in sub-Himalayan cultures. The complexity

[22] Ellen Gough, "Jain Tantric Diagrams of the Goddess Padmāvatī," in *The Oxford Handbook of Tantric Studies*, ed. Richard K. Payne and Glen A. Hayes, 679–702 (Oxford: Oxford University Press, 2024).

[23] Ellen Gough, "Jain *Mantraśāstra* and the *Ṛṣimaṇḍala Yantra*," Centre of Jain Studies Newsletter, March 2009, 4: 36–38. See also Ellen Gough, *Making a Mantra: Tantric Ritual and Renunciation on the Jain Path to Liberation* (Chicago: University of Chicago Press, 2021).

[24] Perhaps an extreme example is the homa for Jesus and the Saints created by Yogi Chen, who is discussed in the last chapter of this volume.

[25] Davidson, "Esoteric Buddhism in the Matrix of Early Medieval India," 13.

of this process is such that Davidson has referred to some components of the religious culture as "pre-existing." By this he means that though those components "themselves are not representative of the eventual emergent system" of tantric praxes, they instead provide "raw material—ritual, ideological, terminological, functional, or other—for its development."[26] Davidson points out that "magicians, sorcerers, witches or seers" were part of Indic religious culture for more than a millennium before the formation of identifiably Buddhist or Hindu forms of lineage-based tantra, and these kinds of praxes "made an observable contribution . . . to the eventual emergence of tantrism in the sixth or seventh century."[27]

Davidson's suggestion of "pre-existing" contributes to resolving a variety of tendentious theoretical issues. First, it serves as a complement to "proto-tantric." Proto-tantric implies a teleological development with greater coherence than does "pre-existing."[28] Second, Davidson discusses the distortions created by presuming a simple diffusionist model, in which tantra begins at some particular place and time and then spreads out from there. He notes that an historiography based on the diffusion of elite sources may "implicitly or explicitly encode a political position and covert hegemony."[29]

Scholarly preference for elite textual and intellectual traditions is the obverse to which neglect and marginalization of nonliterate and living traditions is the reverse. Given that textual studies and philology hold methodological privilege in both religious studies and Buddhist studies, scholars in those fields can at times be incognizant of this preferential focus and its distorting consequences.

The Tantric Era on the Indian Subcontinent

Tantra has no single, easily identifiable "origin." That is, there is no one particular event that initiated it, no specific founder who established it, no unique authoritative text the writing of which is the doctrinal basis for it. Rather than having one specific setting of origin, forest, village, city, and monastery all contributed to its formation. There is, in other words, no

[26] Ronald M. Davidson, "Magicians, Sorcerers and Witches: Considering Pretantric, Nonsectarian Sources of Tantric Practices," *Religions* 8.188 (2017): 1, DOI:10.3390/rel8090188.

[27] Davidson, "Magicians, Sorcerers and Witches," 1.

[28] "Proto-tantric" is relevant to particular instances, but it cannot be applied without discriminating between how different components endured or did not.

[29] Davidson, "Magicians, Sorcerers and Witches," 3.

moment that marks a rupture in historical continuity when tantra emerged into the temporal order—putatively intruding into the ongoing flow of history from some eternal, timeless realm, and thus forever dividing time into a "before" and an "after." While much of the history of religion is structured by this rhetoric of rupture, the historiographic narrative of rupture is itself fundamentally religious—a myth, not history.[30]

History can be written in different ways, and the brief history of tantric Buddhism in South Asia here first considers the social and political context, and second the literary history of the Buddhist tantras. This summary attempts to avoid periodizing or categorizing in a way that either implies a teleological development from inferior to superior, or imposes an organic metaphor—such as that of birth, growth, maturity, senescence, and death.

Changing Social and Political Context

Collapse of the Gupta and Vākaṭaka

The region in which there was the most tantric Buddhist activity was the central plain (the area known as the Deccan) and north India.[31] Two dynasties were dominant in this region, the Gupta and Vākāṭaka, and the classical period for both lasted from approximately 320 to 550 CE. This was a period of at least relative stability across middle and northern India, which allowed for Mahāyāna forms of Buddhism to flourish and to develop institutionally.[32] At the end of the sixth century, however, both kingdoms collapsed.

Period of Strife

The collapse of the two empires marks the beginning of a period complicated by almost incessant conflict, what Davidson has termed "the culture of military opportunism."[33] During this period of turmoil, the status and security

[30] For religious studies, the model for historiography is grounded in the Christian narrative of a new dispensation—the rupture created between the old Hebraic religion of a god limited to a particular tribal group and a god whose dominion is universal. One of the most influential figures promoting rupture as effectively inherent to religion was Mircea Eliade. See, for example, his *The Sacred and The Profane: The Nature of Religion*, trans. Willard R. Trask (San Diego, CA: Harcourt, Brace, Jovanovich, 1987), and *The Myth of the Eternal Return: Cosmos and History* (1954. Reprint. Princeton, NJ: Princeton University Press, 2018).

[31] Ronald M. Davidson, *Indian Esoteric Buddhism: A Social History of the Tantric Movement* (New York: Columbia University Press, 2002), 30.

[32] Davidson, "Esoteric Buddhism in the Matrix of Early Medieval India," 1.

[33] Davidson, *Indian Esoteric Buddhism*, 62. Davidson has provided a detailed summary of the complex political and dynastic history of this time; see Davidson, *Indian Esoteric Buddhism*, 30–62.

of Buddhist institutions and practitioners were under threat, and Davidson notes that the "Chinese historical records indicate that the late 7th through the 8th century was a particularly unruly time."[34] Buddhist institutions lost patronage and protection, and amid the ongoing conflict, monks moved out of the regions that had been controlled by the dynasties, and toward the north and south of the subcontinent. Lacking patronage, many monasteries became landed estates. This institutional transformation led to the rise of "great monasteries" (Skt. *mahāvihara*), which provided the institutional support for the creation of new, more intellectual monastic curricula.[35] This is, in other words, the period when critical reflection began to move Buddhist thought in directions away from the early abhidharma, which focused on systematizing the teachings, to the later abhidharma, which shifted toward a more interpretive orientation, as well as the Mahāyāna systems of Yogācāra and Madhyamaka.

Rise and Stability of the Pāla

In Bengal, in northeast India, Gopāla (c. 750–775) initiated the Pāla dynasty, which lasted into the early thirteenth century. Although conflict and warfare continued, the Pāla provided relative stability in which Buddhist institutions such as Nalānda were able to thrive. Buddhists also adapted to these changing social conditions by adopting models of social hierarchy and central authority into their symbolic system. The feudal system of vassal relations (Skt. *samanta*)[36] provided a conceptual framework for structuring the tantric pantheon, and royal consecration became the model for ritual initiation, specifically into the mandalic structure portraying a central authority surrounded by peripheral vassals.

Muslim Conquest

Beginning in the seventh century, Muslim merchants and traders arrived on the southwest coast of India and settled into communities and intermarried with local populations. Then, beginning in the eighth century, Muslim armies began to move into the areas now known as Afghanistan and Pakistan, seeking to control a central node in the trade routes connecting the Indian

[34] Davidson, "Esoteric Buddhism in the Matrix of Early Medieval India," 23.
[35] Davidson, *Indian Esoteric Buddhism*, 77.
[36] For an explanation of the *samanta* system, see Roger Jackson, *Saraha: Poet of Blissful Awareness* (Boulder, CO: Shambhala Publications, 2024), 8.

Ocean and the Silk Route. Buddhist institutions continued to operate under Muslim rule in this area into the eleventh century.

This situation changed when Muhammad Ghuri (1162–1206) overthrew the Turkish Muslim Ghaznavid dynasty in Afghanistan and began to invade India. By 1206 his invasion stretched across the whole of northern India. Although exaggerated in Buddhist literature, this invasion did lead to the destruction and sacking of major Buddhist monasteries, including Nalanda, Odantapuri, and Vikramasila. The loss of these centers led to the flight of Buddhist monastics, including tantric masters, to Tibet. Johan Elverskog notes the irony that "it was the particular form of Tantric Buddhism that subsequently developed in Tibet—especially its rituals concentrating on power and its projection—that would result in it being adopted by imperial courts across Asia, most notably among the Mongols."[37]

Ongoing Tradition in the Himalaya

It is often claimed that Buddhism "disappeared from the land of its origin" as a result of the Muslim invasions. Despite nostalgia for the lost tradition, as well as the clean slate it provides for scholars, Buddhism continued as a living tradition in Nepal and the wider Himalaya. Will Tuladhar-Douglas tells us that Nepal "probably has the oldest continuous tradition of Buddhism in the world."[38] This form was largely continuous with the tantric forms of Buddhism, such as that carried by the refugees from the Muslim conquest. It employed Sanskrit as its canonic language, and it claims authority on the basis of its Indic sources. Thus, although sometimes confused with Tibetan Buddhism—easy to do in the present with many Tibetan teachers and institutions relocated to the Kathmandu Valley—it has its own independent status.

Literary History

Tantric literature provides another way of thinking about the trajectory of the movement's changes. Tantric texts underwent revision and expansion

[37] Johan Elverskog, "Buddhist and Muslim Interactions in Asian History," in *The Oxford Research Encyclopedias: Asian History* (New York: Oxford University Press, 2019; doi.org/10.1093/acrefore/9780190277727.013.418), 8.

[38] Will Tuladhar-Douglas, *Remaking Buddhism for Medieval Nepal: The Fifteenth-Century Reformation of Newar Buddhism* (London: Routledge, 2006), 9.

over time, sometimes by incorporating previously existing material.[39] As Tsunehiko Sugiki notes,

> Many Buddhist tantras are evolving texts; they were gradually compiled, enlarged, and organized by different compilers over decades or in some cases even centuries. In this process of compilation, compilers also took ideas and texts from other scriptures of the same or foreign traditions and integrated them into the scriptures they were working on. Therefore, the final version of a tantra often contains both ancient and new elements. It is also common that different versions of a tantra were developed separately by different groups of compilers.[40]

Texts have histories of change and development, and the histories of different texts often overlap with one another. As a guide for the historical development of Buddhist tantra, therefore, textual history does not provide clearly marked dividing lines, but instead broad and fuzzy periods. Rather than looking at individual texts, some authors have suggested developmental trajectories of one kind or another. For example, Alexis Sanderson has argued that over time the compilers of Buddhist tantras, in a fashion he disparagingly describes as both uncritical and incompetent, increasingly appropriated deities, practices, and texts from Śaiva tantra, a process he calls "śāktization."[41] Other scholars have suggested an approximate correlation between historical development and the different categories of tantras.[42] However, the existence of differing category systems makes this also an only approximate indicator.[43]

[39] See, for example, Ronald M. Davidson, "Studies in *Dhāraṇī* Literature III: Seeking the Parameters of a *Dhāraṇī-piṭaka*, the Formation of the *Dhāraṇīsaṃgraha*s, and the Place of the Seven Buddhas," in *Scripture:Canon::Text:Context: Essays Honoring Lewis Lancaster*, ed. Richard K. Payne, 119–180 (Berkeley, CA: Institute of Buddhist Studies and BDK/America, 2014), 127.

[40] Tsunehiko Sugiki, "On the Chronology of Buddhist Tantras," in *The Oxford Handbook of Tantric Studies*, ed. Richard K. Payne and Glen T. Hayes, 1057–1082 (New York: Oxford University Press, 2024; doi.org/10.1093/oxfordhb/9780197549889.013.32), 1075.

[41] Alexis Sanderson, "The Śaiva Age," in *Genesis and Development of Tantrism*, ed. Shingo Einoo, 41–349 (Tokyo: Institute of Oriental Culture, University of Tokyo, 2009), 145. In Sanderson's portrayal, tantric Buddhism appears both derivative and inferior. More recently, Ronald M. Davidson has challenged much of Sanderson's portrayal, for example in his "Magicians, Sorcerers and Witches," 2.

[42] For example, Stephen Hodge, "Considerations on the Dating and Geographical Origins of the *Mahāvairocanābhisaṃbodhi-sūtra*," in *The Buddhist Forum* 3 (1991–1993; https://www.shin-ibs.edu/research/archived-publications-and-research-projects/the-buddhist-forum/the-buddhist-forum-volume-iii/), 57–83, 58.

[43] While the fourfold system prevalent in Tibetan scholasticism is often deployed as if simply given, there are other category system as well. One system is structured into nine categories; see,

Collecting Dhāraṇīs and Putting Them to Work

From about the third century on, the practice of reciting the verbal formulae known as dhāraṇī became increasingly popular.[44] Dhāraṇī are similar to mantra, being verbal expressions employed in ritual and yogic practice.[45] Like mantra, they are instances of extraordinary language, that is, language that does not serve the ordinary communicative function of language.[46]

Probably around the fifth century, dhāraṇīs and ritual instructions for their application began being systematically gathered together into collections (Skt. *dhāraṇīsaṃgraha*).[47] Attributed to Atikūṭa, one such "Collection of Dhāraṇī" (*Dhāraṇīsaṃgraha*, T. 901) was compiled and translated into Chinese in 654, making it in Davidson's estimation "[a]rguably the earliest surviving tantric work."[48] Like the other components of tantric praxis, dhāraṇī are not inherently tantric but are so by context, use, and designation. Jacob P. Dalton, for example, has argued that rather than looking at dhāraṇī in the abstract, it is essential to understand how they were actually used and what it meant to put them to use.[49] The dhāraṇī collections from Dunhuang that Dalton examines are practical manuals, compiled for use, and meeting the needs of the individual compiler.[50] Dhāraṇī collections "functioned as liturgies, created for recitation in a prescribed ritual order."[51] Some were formalized in such a fashion as to be called dhāraṇī sutras, and some of these

for example, Martin Boord, "The Vajrakīla Tantras," in *The Oxford Encyclopedia of Buddhism*, ed. Richard K. Payne and Georgios T. Halkias, 2635–2656 (New York: Oxford University Press, 2024), 2640.

44 Paul Williams, with Anthony Tribe, *Buddhist Thought: A Complete Introduction to the Indian Tradition* (London: Routledge, 2000), 194.

45 Although functionally similar in many settings, mantra and dhāraṇī are not synonymous. See Ronald M. Davidson, "Studies in Dhāraṇī Literature I: Revisiting the Meaning of the Term *Dhāraṇī*," *Journal of Indian Philosophy* 37.2 (Apr. 2009): 97–147, DOI: 10.1007/s10781-008-9054-8.

46 See Richard K. Payne, *Language in the Buddhist Tantra of Japan: Indic Roots of Mantra* (London: Bloomsbury, 2018).

47 Michel Strickmann first identified these works as "proto-tantric," and despite criticism of the category, its use has recently been supported by Jacob P. Dalton, who refined the meaning of the term by examining the ritual context within which dhāraṇī were used. Jacob P. Dalton, "How *Dhāraṇīs* WERE Proto-Tantric: Liturgies, Ritual Manuals, and the Origins of the Tantras," in *Tantric Traditions in Transmission and Translation*, ed. David B. Gray and Ryan Richard Overbey, 199–229 (New York: Oxford University Press, 2016).

48 Ronald M. Davidson, "Initiation (*Abhiṣeka*) in Indian Buddhism," in *The Oxford Handbook of Tantric Studies*, ed. Richard K. Payne and Glen A. Hayes, 29–51 (New York: Oxford University Press, 2024), 36.

49 Dalton, "How *Dhāraṇīs* WERE Proto-Tantric," 200.

50 These are then instances of the category of texts described by Anne Blackburn as the "practical canon," as distinct from the "formal canon" ("Looking for the *Vinaya*: Monastic Discipline in the Practical Canons of the Theravāda," *Journal of the International Association of Buddhist Studies* 22.2 [1999]: 281–309).

51 Dalton, "How *Dhāraṇīs* WERE Proto-Tantric," 205.

in turn came to have ritual manuals (Skt. *dhāraṇī vidhi*) appended. Dhāraṇī ritual manuals began being compiled and systematized "in the second half of the fifth and especially the sixth centuries."[52] The liturgical and ritual functions of these manuals and collections focus on image worship, and this was an important part of the historical trajectory from proto-tantric texts to the systematic tantras that began appearing more than a century later.

Koichi Shinohara has segmented this transition from "proto-tantric" texts to tantric ones into three steps, each marked by increasingly complex ritual scenarios. The first was simply the repeated recitation of dhāraṇī, sometimes empowering a cord (Skt. *pratisara*) which would then be tied to the body. Image worship marked the second step, developing into more elaborated ritual scenarios involving not only recitation but also offerings. As image worship developed, stages of the ritual came to be accompanied by specific dhāraṇī, and more elaborate images and altars were employed. In turn, this led to mandalas devoted to a central deity surrounded by ritual implements and images of other deities—and this then allowed for initiatory rites to be developed wherein the aspirant was authorized by the master to engage in ritual practices focused on the central deity.

In Shinohara's analysis then, the third ritual scenario involved the entire pantheon being brought into the mandala, a ritual known as the "All-Gathering Maṇḍala Ceremony,"[53] and this ceremony marks the start of the systematization of tantric praxes.

Early Systems

Sometime after the mid-sixth century such systematic texts began to be produced, some of which will be mentioned as exemplifying the historical development of tantra.[54] These systematic texts were not simply collections of dhāraṇī and ritual instructions, but were organized into more coherent, extended ritual programs, like the All-Gathering Maṇḍala Ceremony described by Shinohara. As David Gray says, "These texts gradually became more complex, reaching a critical mass in the seventh century, becoming the

[52] Dalton, "How *Dhāraṇīs* WERE Proto-Tantric," 208, 219.

[53] Koichi Shinohara, *Spells, Images, and Mandalas: Tracing the Evolution of Esoteric Buddhist Rituals* (New York: Columbia University Press, 2014), xvi.

[54] The next three periods might roughly be correlated with the "mantranaya" (way of mantra), the "vajrayāna" (vajra vehicle), and the "mantayāna" (mantra vehicle) terminology proposed by Thomas Cruijsen et al., in "The Cult of the Buddhist *dhāraṇī* Deity Mahāpratisaā Along the Maritime Silk Route: New Epigraphical and Iconographic Evidence from the Indonesian Archipelago," *Journal of the International Association of Buddhist Studies* 35.1–2 (2012 [2013]): 71–157, 74n7. The three terms have connotations and valorizations that make them inapt for our purposes here.

textual basis for a new Buddhist tradition that was deemed by its advocates to be distinct from the larger Mahāyāna tradition from which it emerged."[55]

Scholars have often highlighted that some tantras are taught by a buddha other than Śākyamuni.[56] This is the case with three of the earliest tantras, the *Vajrapāṇyabhiṣeka*, the *Vairocanābhisaṃbodhi tantra*, and the *Sarvatathāgatatattvasaṃgraha tantra*. All three of these tantras are taught by Vairocana, whose name means "the resplendent,"[57] perhaps indicating originating as a solar deity. Davidson suggests that Vairocana is indicative of the influence of solar cults in classical and medieval Indian Buddhism and that, although little acknowledged, solar cults are significant early sources of Buddhist tantra.[58]

Stephen Hodge indicates that the *Vairocanābhisaṃbodhi tantra*[59] was probably composed around 640 in northeastern India, at or near the famous Buddhist monastery Nālandā.[60] It was one of the texts collected in India by the Chinese pilgrim Wuxing around 680, giving further support to the dating of the text to the mid-seventh century.[61]

Middle Era Developments: Mid-Eighth to Mid-Ninth Century

Noteworthy texts compiled during this period include the *Vajraśekhara*, which was important for its role in the development of tantric Buddhism in East Asia, and the *Nāmasaṃgīti*, which comprises multiple epithets of Mañjuśri, "each of which is understood to be a syllabic manifestation of Mañjuśrī as the perfectly enlightened buddha."[62] The *Nāmasaṃgīti* is described as the most important Mañjuśri text for both monastics and lay-people in northeast India, and this importance is reflected by it having 22 commentaries and 130 ancillary texts. In this way it is like many tantras that

[55] David Gray, *The Buddhist Tantras* (New York: Oxford University Press, 2023), 13.

[56] This is not entirely unique to the tantras. For example, the famous Vimalakirti Nirdeṣa Sutra, although framed as being introduced by Śākyamuni, is taught by the layman Vimalakirti.

[57] In East Asia, Vairocana is frequently equated with Mahāvairocana, the latter being rendered as "great sun" (Jpn. Dainich, 大日).

[58] Davidson, "Esoteric Buddhism in the Matrix of Early Medieval India," 16.

[59] Also know as the *Mahāvairocanābhisaṃbodhi tantra*.

[60] Hodge, "Considerations on the Dating and Geographical Origins of the *Mahāvairocanābhisaṃbodhi-sūtra*," 70, 74.

[61] According to David Gray, his record makes this tantra "the earliest known dateable tantric text," also making it contemporaneous with the *Dhāraṇīsaṃgraha* of Atikūta discussed above. As to precedence of one text over the other, part of the issue may be slightly variant understandings of what constitutes a "tantric text." David Gray, *The Buddhist Tantras*, 10.

[62] Laura Harrington, "Mañjuśrī," in *The Oxford Encyclopedia of Buddhism*, ed. Richard K. Payne and Georgios T. Halkias, 1497–1512 (New York: Oxford University Press, 2024), 1500.

are themselves at the center of a cluster of related texts which expand the tantric literature.

Also dating from this period is the *Cakrasaṃvara tantra*, which is a key text within what are known as the "Yoginī tantras." David Gray tells us that the term "yoginī" for this category of tantras indicates that they "seem to have developed among and/or been influenced by liminal groups of renunciant yogins and yoginīs, who collectively constituted what might be called the 'siddha movement'."[63] The mahāsiddhas constitute an important subgroup within this broader movement. Conventionally numbering eighty-four, the mahāsiddhas are discussed in more detail later in this chapter.

Davidson argues that "the central and defining metaphor for mature esoteric Buddhism is that of an individual assuming kingship and exercising dominion. . . . [The practitioner] metaphorically becoming the overlord (*rājādhirājā*) or the universal ruler (*cakravartin*)."[64] This imperial symbolism motivates the development of the mandala as a structure portraying a buddha's retinue and as a location of initiation—initiation rituals themselves being modeled on royal consecrations.

While the systems employed to categorize the tantras have been revised over time, an important one for this period is the sequence of yoga tantras, "great yoga" tantras (Skt. *mahāyoga tantras*), and "unexcelled yoga" tantras (Skt. *anuttarayoga tantras*). The Dunhuang tantric texts provide an historical archive of different strata reflecting this ongoing development of tantric praxis. Jacob Dalton has outlined three stages of development, identified as these three categories of tantras. The yoga tantras, originating in the early eighth century, taught the practitioner to visualize oneself as identical with the buddha and to direct ritual activities to oneself as the buddha. Developing in the century from c. 750 to c. 850, the "great yoga" tantras taught yogic sexual practices. And, beginning to be compiled in the first half of the ninth century and then formalized in the tenth, the "unexcelled yoga" tantras taught the manipulation of interior bodily energies.[65] Mahāyoga tantras, such as the Guhyasamaja, are from this period.

[63] David B. Gray, *The* Cakrasamvara Tantra *(The Discourse of Śrī Heruka)* (New York: The American Institute of Buddhist Studies at Columbia University, and Columbia University's Center for Buddhist Studies and Tibet House US, 2007), 7.

[64] Davidson, *Indian Esoteric Buddhism*, 121.

[65] Jacob Dalton, "The Development of Perfection: The Interiorization of Buddhist Ritual in the Eighth and Ninth Centuries," *Journal of Indian Philosophy* 32 (2004): 1–30, 3.

Final Stage

The *Kalacakra tantra* was compiled in the eleventh century,[66] and it is one of the most important texts in the final stage of tantra in India. It is classed as a member of the unexcelled yoga tantras, and it is thought to be the last tantra in that class to be produced.[67] As with several Buddhist texts, the text we have is said to be an abridged version (Skt. *laghu-tantra*) of a much larger original text, in this case called the *Paramādibuddha*.

Key to the teachings of the *Kālacakra* is the intepretation of yoga as the nondual union "of bliss and emptiness, or of method and wisdom."[68] The text presents the "nonduality of wisdom and method as an expression of nondual gnosis, without which Buddhahood could never occur."[69]

Here we have presented a few exemplary tantras in brief summary as instances of the textual history of Buddhist tantra in India. There are many additional texts that are also important and which could provide different perspectives on the development of the tradition. As noted above, the *Vairocanābhisaṃbodhi tantra* is an early text and therefore provides an important window into the development of tantric ritual practice at a key period.

The *Vairocanābhisaṃbodhi Tantra*

The previous chapter argued for delineating tantra by context, use, and designation. As an explicit instance of designation, bibliographic categorization allows us to focus on the contents of those texts identified as tantras, constituting an initial pool of praxes identifiable as "tantric." Like the category tantra itself, bibliographic categorization is fuzzy. For example, though located in the tantric sections of both the Tibetan and Chinese canons, the *Vairocanābhisaṃbodhi tantra* is also known as a sutra.[70] Compiled around the mid-seventh century, it has been called "the earliest known dateable tantric Buddhist text."[71] As an early Buddhist tantra, examining its contents gives

[66] Dalton, "The Development of Perfection," 2n3.

[67] Vesna Wallace, *The Inner Kālacakratantra: A Buddhist Tantric View of the Individual* (Oxford: Oxford University Press, 2001), 3.

[68] Wallace, *The Inner Kālacakratantra*, 7.

[69] Wallace, *The Inner Kālacakratantra*, 7.

[70] Similarly, the *Gathering of Intentions* is identified not only as a tantra but also as a sutra. Jacob P. Dalton, *The Gathering of Intentions: A History of a Tibetan Tantra* (New York: Columbia University Press, 2016), 1.

[71] Gray, *Buddhist Tantras*, 16.

us access to an early systematization of tantric Buddhist praxis.[72] It is also one of the most influential tantric texts in China and Japan, and therefore, provides insight into the tantric movement across its East Asian expansion.

The *Vairocanābhisaṃbodhi tantra* begins by orienting the reader into the conceptual world of Mahāyāna Buddhist thought.[73] Because many of these ideas are familiar, it is important to understand that their meanings are contextualized by tantric praxis. In other words, rather than simply being concepts located in a decontextualized, abstract realm of Mahāyāna doctrine or of "philosophy," the teachings are contextualized by their dialectic relation with the practices, just as the practices are contextualized by the teachings.[74] While the tantra's first chapter provides the conceptual rationale for the practices described in the balance of the text, it is important, therefore, that we understand the text as a whole.[75] Focusing solely on the doctrinal content of the first chapter of the *Vairocanābhisaṃbodhi tantra* in isolation from the rest of the text severs thought from action, artificially severing praxis into two parts.

Organizing tantric praxis in this text is a system of cause, root, and culmination, which parallels the more familiar schema of ground, path, and goal. The opening chapter of the tantra provides a framework of ideas regarding the basis of awakening (cause), of compassion (root), and of the ability to engage in compassionate action upon awakening (culmination).

This chapter opens by setting the kind of dramatic scene found throughout Buddhist literature.[76] The Buddha Vairocana is introduced as "dwelling in

[72] Hodge locates the text in the early seventh century. See Stephen Hodge, *The Mahā-Vairocana-Abhisaṃbodhi Tantra, with Buddhaguhya's Commentary* (London: RoutledgeCurzon, 2003), 14. Nakamura gives a slightly later estimate of the second half of the seventh century. See Hajime Nakamura, *Indian Buddhism: A Survey with Bibliographical Notes* (1980. Reprint. Delhi: Motilal Banarsidass, 1987), 321. More recently, Kazuo Kano says that its composition is prior to 674. "Vairocanābhisaṃbodhi," in *Brill's Encyclopedia of Buddhism*, vol. I: Literature and Languages, ed. Jonathan A. Silk, 382–389 (Leiden: Brill, 2015), 382.

[73] There are two complete English translations of this text, one from Chinese by Rolf Giebel and one from Tibetan by Stephen Hodge. Giebel's, being available online, is more easily accessible and will be the version most frequently referenced here. Hodge's includes a translation of an important commentary on the text by Buddhaguhya. Both Giebel and Hodge will be referenced to explicate important points. See also Wilhelm K. Muller, "Shingon-Mysticism: Śubhākarasiṁha and I-hsing's Commentary to the Mahāvairocana-sūtra, Chapter One, an Annotated Translation," PhD diss. (University of California, Los Angeles, 1976).

[74] For a more extended discussion of this dialectic relation between thought and practice, see Richard K. Payne, "Doctrine and Practice: Dialectic and Nondual," *Berkeley Journal of Religion and Theology* 9.1 (2024): 122–152.

[75] See, for example, Ryūjun Tajima, *Étude sur le Mahāvairocana sūtra* (Paris, 1936; English translation by Alex Wayman, trans. and ed., *The Enlightenment of Vairocana* [Delhi: Motilal Banarsidass, 1992]).

[76] Regarding differing styles of such opening scene setting in Pāli and Mahāyāna texts (but not tantras), see David McMahan, "Orality, Writing, and Authority in South Asian Buddhism: Visionary

the abode" of the awakened ones (Skt. *tathāgatas*). He is approached by an assembly of bodhisattvas led by Samantabhadra and an assembly of "vajra holders" (Skt. *vajradharas*) led by Vajrapāṇi. According to Buddhaguhya (fl. c. 700 CE, and therefore close in time to the compilation of the tantra), "vajra" here means "the insight that destroys incorrect views."[77]

The first question that Vajrapāṇi asks Vairocana is how he became awakened; that is, how did he "obtain the knowledge of an omniscient one"?[78] Describing this knowledge as "free from all differentiation, without differentiation and without nondifferentiation," Vajrapāṇi goes on to ask "what is the cause, what is the root, and what is the culmination of this knowledge?"[79] Vairocana replies that "The *bodhi*-mind is its cause, compassion is its root, and expedient means [awakened compassionate action] is its culmination."[80] *Bodhi*-mind (Skt. *bodhicitta*) is the intention to awaken and the text says that *bodhi* "means to know one's mind as it really is."[81] Much depends on properly understanding that *citta*, the term rendered as "mind" in these translations, refers to conscious activity broadly. In classic Indian Buddhist thought it is contrasted with the material aspects (Skt. *rūpa*) of existents, including one's own body. *Citta* includes sensation (Skt. *vedanā*), perception (Skt. *samjñā*), conditioning habits (Skt. *saṃskāra*), and discriminative consciousness (Skt. *vijñāna*).[82] Buddhaguhya expands on the meaning of *bodhi*-mind by explaining the two aspects of bodhicitta, "the mind (*citta*) directed towards Enlightenment (*bodhi*) and the mind whose intrinsic nature is Enlightenment."[83]

Literature and the Struggle for Legitimacy in the Mahāyāna," *History of Religions* 37.3 (Feb. 1998): 249–274, 249–251.

[77] Hodge, *The Mahā-Vairocana-Abhisaṃbodhi Tantra*, 48. For further on Buddhaguhya, including his dates, see Jake Nagasawa, "Buddhaguhya," *Treasury of Lives*, 2017. https://treasuryoflives.org/biographies/view/Buddhaguhya/10546.

[78] Giebel, *The Vairocanābhisaṃbodhi Sutra*, 4.

[79] Giebel, *The Vairocanābhisaṃbodhi Sutra*, 5.

[80] Giebel, *The Vairocanābhisaṃbodhi Sutra*, 6. Buddhaguhya explains that these are the perfections, such as the perfection of generosity, etc. (Hodge, *The Mahā-Vairocana-Abhisaṃbodhi Tantra*, 55). On the perfections, see James B. Apple, "Perfections (Six and Ten) of Bodhisattvas in Buddhist Literature," in *Oxford Research Encyclopedia of Religion*, ed. John Barton (Oxford: Oxford University Press, 2016; DOI: 10.1093/acrefore/9780199340378.013.193).

[81] Giebel, *The Vairocanābhisaṃbodhi Sutra*, 6.

[82] What *citta* does not mean is the contemporary English usage of mind, standing for reason, as opposed to heart, standing for emotion. Nor is this structured as the opposition between mind and body (or mental and material, or spiritual and physical) as in post-Cartesian Western thought, which privileges the mind as the active agent.

[83] Hodge, *The Mahā-Vairocana-Abhisaṃbodhi Tantra*, 54. Like so many key terms in Buddhist thought, "mind" in this context requres nuancing as its use is more specific than in conversational English. For a brief discussion, see Hodge, *The Mahā-Vairocana-Abhisaṃbodhi Tantra*, sv. "Mind (*citta*)," 567.

As the root, compassion also has two aspects. First, the intention to attain awakening should be firmly rooted in the intention "to remove the afflictions of suffering from beings."[84] Compassion also serves as the root for firmly remaining in the world as an awakened being (Skt. *apratiṣṭhā-nirvāṇa*), rather than entering nirvana without remainder (Skt. *nirupadhiśeṣa-nirvāṇa*). Expedient means (Skt. *upaya*) is the perfecting of such characteristics as generosity (Skt. *dana-parāmitā*) and the other "perfections" (Skt. *parāmitā*). Expedient means is the culmination because it is the compassionate action of an awakened one who remains in this world.

The text goes on to describe the character of an awakened one's awareness, which is free from the delusion of a permanent, eternal, absolute, unchanging self-essence of persons or any other entity. Moving through a variety of stages in the development of insight and wisdom, the bodhisattva practitioner attains fearlessness. When the knowledge of emptiness is born, awareness of emptiness can be cultivated by means of mantras, which are themselves empty. Understanding the emptiness of mantras is facilitated by reflection on ten similes, which are familiar as literary tropes in Mahāyāna, and perhaps especially Madhyamaka, thought. These are that dependent arising is "like an illusion, a mirage, a dream, a reflection, a *gandharva* [celestial musicians] city, an echo, the moon [reflected] in water, bubbles, a flower in empty space, and a whirling wheel of fire."[85] Just as each of these—illusions, mirages, and so on—lacks any permanent, eternal, absolute, or unchanging essence, so also are mantras empty, and mantra practice thus leads to the realization of emptiness. Understanding this, one will then "completely possess the riches of the Dharma, bring forth great knowledge with various skills, and fully know all notions about the mind as it really is."[86]

Entry into the Mandala: Initiation (Abhiṣeka)

Except perhaps for the unfamiliar names of the interlocutors, Vajrapāṇi and Vairocana, up to this point, a modern reader already familiar with Mahāyāna thought would find the presentation largely unsurprising.[87] The tantra points us in the direction of values and concepts of the bodhisattva quest and

[84] Hodge, *The Mahā-Vairocana-Abhisaṃbodhi Tantra*, 55.
[85] Giebel, *The Vairocanābhisaṃbodhi Sutra*, 17.
[86] Giebel, *The Vairocanābhisaṃbodhi Sutra*, 18.
[87] On Vajrapāṇi, see Wayman, *The Enlightenment of Vairocana*, 83–85.

its accomplishment, exemplified by the compassionate action of a person awakened to the impermanence and inconstancy of all existing things, and who voluntarily chooses to remain in the world out of compassion, intent on assisting others to attain awakening. However, beyond the tantra's first chapter is less familiar territory, that of tantric ritual practice.

The theme of the next chapter of the *Vairocanābhisaṃbodhi tantra* is initiation (*abhiṣeka*), which is important throughout the tantric tradition.[88] The system of mandala construction found in the *Vairocanābhisaṃbodhi* chapter on initiation develops from a systematization of earlier, disparate rites. In Davidson's account it is in what he calls the *Vajroṣṇīṣa* texts, known from eighth-century Chinese translations, that earlier disparate rites are formalized into the system of mandala construction "recognizable across texts."[89] The initiation ceremony for Bhaiṣajyaguru given by the Dalai Lama at Shoreline Amphitheatre described in Chapter I had two dimensions. The exoteric initiation authorized devotional contemplation of Bhaiṣajyaguru, while the esoteric one authorized practice of the tantric sādhana involving ritual identification between the practitioner and the chief deity.[90]

Here in the *Vairocanābhisaṃbodhi tantra*, initiation is referred to as "entering into the mandala," that is, becoming a member of the retinue of Mahāvairocana Buddha. Entry into Mahāvairocana's mandala establishes a connection between the practitioner and Vairocana Buddha and his retinue. This connection is requisite for the practitioner to engage in ritual identification.[91]

The *Vairocanābhisambodhi tantra* prescribes the construction of a mandala, that is, the ritual enclosure within which the initiation will take place. The initiate enters into the assembly of buddhas, bodhisattvas, and guardians who constitute the mandala as an imperial entourage. While present-day temples, such as those in Japan, may have permanent mandala altars available for ritual performances, this chapter begins with instructions for constructing the initiatory mandala.[92] The teacher (Skt. *ācārya*,

[88] See Ronald M. Davidson, "Abhiṣeka," in *Esoteric Buddhism and the Tantras in East Asia*, ed. Charles D. Orzech, Henrik H. Sørensen, and Richard K. Payne, 71–75 (Leiden: Brill, 2011), and Davidson, "Initiation (*Abhiṣeka*) in Indian Buddhism."

[89] Davidson, "Esoteric Buddhism in the Matrix of Early Medieval India,"23.

[90] See, for example, Shakya Gelong Kelsan Thubten Wangchug, *A Manual for the Self-Generation of the Mandala of the Seven Gone to Thus*, trans. Fabrizio Palloti (Portland, OR: FPMT, 2011), 9.

[91] Initiation, or "empowerment," is also in some cases interpreted as making that existing karmic connection manifest, that is, "discovering" the karmic connections a practitioner already has with the buddha.

[92] Later, when permanent mandala came to be employed for initiations as in Japan, only vestigial versions of both the construction and the destruction of the mandala remain in symbolic form.

"accomplished one"; also *mantrin*, one who has mantra) is instructed to clear the site of "pebbles, broken earthenware, potsherds, skulls, hair, chaff, ashes, cinders, thorns, bones, rotten wood, and so on, as well as insects, ants, dung beetles, and poisonous or stinging" creatures.[93] Similar instructions are found in other tantric texts as well.[94]

Once cleaned, the site can be empowered and offerings made.[95] After preparing the surface, the teacher visualizes Vairocana and the other deities of the mandala and paints circles with white sandalwood indicating the locations of the deities. That night the teacher will have auspicious dreams, and in the morning, he will receive the initiands at the site. While they may have other shortcomings, the initiands are expected to have confidence; be born of a pure lineage; revere the Three Jewels (Skt. *ratnatraya*: buddha, dharma, sangha); be wise, perseverant, and energetic; adhere to the standards of moral behavior; be patient, generous, and firm; and be intrepid in fulfilling their vows of practice.[96] The teacher then has the initiands take the triple refuge (Skt. *triśaraṇa*: seeking safe haven in the buddha, dharma, and sangha) and confess their faults, and then the teacher gives them offerings that they present to the deities. Determining that they are worthy, he encourages them in their practice, and that night they also have auspicious dreams.

The following day, as the initiands enter the mandala space, the teacher purifies them with perfumed water (Skt. *argha*), and then together they move through the various quarters occupied by different deities of Vairocana's retinue. The descriptions of the members of the retinue become increasingly detailed, starting with the four buddhas located in the four directions around Vairocana, each of whom, in turn, has their own retinue. There follow additional details about the construction of the mandala, and the text again

Richard K. Payne, "From Vedic India to Buddhist Japan: Continuities and Discontinuities in Esoteric Ritual," in *Esoteric Buddhism and the Tantras in East Asia*, ed. Charles Orzech, Henrik Sørensen, and Richard K. Payne, 1040–1054 (Leiden: Brill, 2011), 1048–1051.

[93] Giebel, *The Vairocanābhisaṃbodhi Sutra*, 22.

[94] See, for example, Dharmachakra Translation Committee, trans., *Root Manual of the Rites of Manjusri*, Toh. 543. (84:000: Translating the Words of the Buddha, 2020, https://84000.co/translation/toh543), §2.122, and Gyurme Dorje, "The Guhyagarbhatantra and Its XIVth Century Commentary *phyogs-bcu mun-sel*," PhD diss. (School of Oriental and African Studies, University of London, 1987), 756–782.

[95] See also Tenzin Gyatso, *Kalachakra Tantra: Rite of Initiation*, trans. and ed. Jeffrey Hopkins (1985. Rev. ed. Boston: Wisdom Publications, 1989), 167.

[96] § 5b: Giebel, *The Vairocanābhisaṃbodhi Sutra*, 26 (dBET 23).

asserts the centrality of emptiness and the importance of meditative concentration (Skt. *samādhi*) as a direct awareness of the emptiness of mind.[97]

After explaining various concentrative meditations, *samādhis*, the chapter continues with a detailed discussion of the characteristics of mantra. The meanings of key "dharma phrases" are explained by their association with different agents. For example, if mantra have the

> ... word *namaḥ* ("homage"), *svāhā*, and so on,
> These are the marks of [mantras of] practitioners of quiescence cultivating *samādhi*.
> If they have the word *śānta* ("pacified"), the word *viśuddha* ("purified"), and so on,
> You should know that they are able to fulfill all wishes:
> These are the mantras of Perfectly Awakened Ones, sons of the Buddha, and world-saviors.[98]

The characteristics of mantras are explained as simply existing—they are not caused or created by Vairocana. "That is to say, mantras are naturally mantras."[99] The text then refers to the "mantra teachings," which associate individual syllables with a characteristic, the name of which begins with that syllable. For example, the first syllable of the Sanskrit syllabary, A, is explained as a gateway to samādhi "because all *dharmas* are originally unborn (*ādyanutpāda*: "original non-arising").[100] The text then continues with the syllables KA, KHA, GA, and so on through the full sequence of thirty-four syllables of the Sanskrit syllabary. In each case, the text says that the characteristic cannot be apprehended in any existing entity (dharma); that is, those entities are empty of that characteristic, indicating that contemplating that emptiness is the gateway to samādhi.

Next, the text discusses further preliminaries for the initiation: both offerings to be gathered and prepared, and preparations of the initiands. Once they are made ready, each initiand throws a flower onto the mandala, and whichever deity the flower falls upon is the deity that the initiand reveres.[101] The teacher then performs a homa ritual of pacification

97 § 9a: Giebel, *The Vairocanābhisaṃbodhi Sutra*, 43 (dBET 38).
98 § 10a: Giebel, *The Vairocanābhisaṃbodhi Sutra*, 48 (dBET 41–42).
99 § 10a: Giebel, *The Vairocanābhisaṃbodhi Sutra*, 48 (dBET 42).
100 § 10a: Giebel, *The Vairocanābhisaṃbodhi Sutra*, 49 (dBET 42–43).
101 This same action is reported by Kūkai (774–835) when he was initiated in Chang'an during his visit to China, and it is performed as part of Shingon initiations today on Mt. Kōya in Japan.

(Skt. *śāntika*) and instructs the initiands regarding gifts to be given to the teacher.[102] A second mandala altar is then constructed, protective deities and bodhisattvas installed, and offerings made. Once inside, the teacher instructs each initiand and leads them into the mandala. There the teacher reveals the verses of the vows (Skt. *samaya*,[103] "sacramental commitments") the initiands make to complete the initiation:

> "Son of the Buddha, henceforth, not begrudging of life or limb,
> You should never abandon the Dharma, forsake the *bodhi*-mind,
> Be miserly with any *dharmas*, or do anything that does not benefit beings.
> The Buddha has taught the *samaya* for you who abide well in the precepts,
> And just as you guard your life, so too should you guard the precepts."[104]

Regarding the samaya vows, Charles Orzech and Henrik Sørensen explain that

> These vows—to uphold the true teaching, to uphold the seed of enlightenment, to share the Buddhist teachings, and to avoid harming sentient beings--are unremarkable in the context of Mahāyāna Buddhism. But in the context of *abhiṣeka* they signify a dramatic transformation. . . . The *abhiṣeka* ritual itself reenacts the enlightenment of Siddhartha in the Akaniṣṭha palace at the summit of the universe as set out in the *Mahāvairocanābhisaṃbodhi sūtra* [*Vairocanābhisaṃbodhi tantra*] and the *Sarvatathāgata-tattva-saṃgraha*, with master and disciple taking the roles of Mahāvairocana and Vajrasattva (in the *MVS*) or Mahāvairocana and Vajradhātu (in the *STTS*). The *samaya* vows are thus realized through ritual practice as the disciple replicates Siddhartha's enlightenment.[105]

[102] § 11b: Giebel, *The Vairocanābhisaṃbodhi Sutra*, 54–56 (dBET 47–48).

[103] *Samaya* is another polysemous term in Buddhist usages. See Yoshito S. Hakeda, *Kūkai: Major Works* (New York: Columbia University Press, 1972), 89n26. Also, James Duncan Gentry, "Tibetan Buddhist Power Objects," in *The Oxford Encyclopedia of Buddhism*, ed. Richard K. Payne and Georgios T. Halkias (New York: Oxford University Press, online 2019: https://doi.org/10.1093/acrefore/9780199340378.013.657); and Jessica Locke, "Ethics and Buddhism," in *The Oxford Encyclopedia of Buddhism*, ed. Richard K. Payne and Georgios T. Halkias (New York: Oxford University Press, online 2023: https://doi.org/10.1093/acrefore/9780199340378.013.714).

[104] § 12b: Giebel, *The Vairocanābhisaṃbodhi Sutra*, 59 (dBET 51). These four are employed by Kūkai in the establishment of Shingon practice (Hakeda, *Kūkai*, 95–96).

[105] Charles D. Orzech and Henrik H. Sørensen, "*Mudrā*, Mantra, Mandala," in *Esoteric Buddhism and the Tantras in East Asia*, ed. Charles D. Orzech, Henrik H. Sørensen, and Richard K. Payne, 76–89 (Leiden: Brill, 2011), 85–86.

This explanation highlights that the vows are not simply a set of ethical injunctions existing in isolation. Reenacting Śākyamuni's awakening, they are an integral part of the initiation and are congruent with ritual identification at the center of many tantric rituals.

Vajrapaṇi then asks how much merit is gained by taking the *samaya* of entering the mandala. Vairocana replies that entry into the mandala is equivalent to the merit that may be accumulated from the first arising of the aspiration for awakening (Skt. *bodhicitta*) through to becoming a completely awakened tathāgata.[106] The chapter closes with Vairocana entering different samādhis, manifesting miracles, and teaching several additional mantras and *vidya* to his audience.[107]

The *Vairocanābhisaṃbodhi tantra*'s chapter on initiation demonstrates the integral character of tantric praxis. The mandala is not an abstract diagram, or a symbol referencing a "higher reality," but rather the ritual space within which the protector deities, bodhisattvas, and buddhas are manifest.[108] The mandala is constructed both by means of circles, colors, and figures, and simultaneously by means of mudrās, mantras, and the visualizations performed by the tantric master. These are all ritual actions, and as such it is an interpretive artifice to divide them into physical and mental. Likewise, the mantra are not only verbal formulae, but they are the deities, who are also made present in particular sections of the mandala by colors, figures, and mudrā.

If we avoid the presumption that action derives from thought, or in this case, ritual from doctrine, it is then this chapter on initiation that stands out—if only because it is by far the longest chapter in the text and seems to have been the core around which other materials were gathered. Later chapters provide further ritual details that complement and expand on those of the initiation ritual, or prescribe ancillary rituals. A plausible textual history would begin from the initiation ritual itself, to which literary framing, such as the dialogue between Vairocana and Vajrapaṇi, was added. That

[106] § 12b: Giebel, *The Vairocanābhisaṃbodhi Sutra*, 59 (dBET 51).

[107] § 12c–13b: Giebel, *The Vairocanābhisaṃbodhi Sutra*, 61 (dBET 52–54). *Vidya* literally means "wisdom," but the term is used for mantras with a feminine grammatical form. See Richard K. Payne, *Language in the Buddhist Tantra of Japan: Indic Roots of Mantra* (London: Bloomsbury, 2018), 78–79.

[108] It seems entirely plausible, therefore, that architectural sites structured as mandala served as more permanent sites of initiation than the temporary sites described in the text here. For an extensive examination of such sites, see Swati Chemburkar, "Mandalas and Monarchs: Tantra and Temple Architecture in Buddhist Southeast Asia," in *The Oxford Handbook of Tantric Studies*, ed. Richard K. Payne and Glen A. Hayes, 581–678 (New York: Oxford University Press, 2024).

expanded text then had several chapters providing ritual details added—like appendices. From this perspective, the first chapter now seems more of a preface, framing the ritual in Buddhist doctrinal terms as an editorial afterthought. Further textual study is needed to determine more firmly the textual stratigraphy of the *Vairocanābhisaṃbodhi tantra*, including, for example, the relation between the verses (Skt. *gatha*) and narrative components of the second chapter. Further study, however, must avoid the distorting presumption that the first chapter is primary or foundational simply because of its focus on familiar Mahāyāna doctrines, and that all the ritual chapters are to be explained as deriving from or as expressions of those doctrines.

Complex rituals integrating mudrā, mantra, and mandala, like those described above and in Chapter I, are characteristic of much of tantric Buddhism. Also prevalent are interiorized yogic practices, which may be considered a second and contrasting form of tantric praxis.

Interiorizing Ritual

The Cartesian dualism of mind and body is pervasive not only in popular religious culture in the West but also in the field of religious studies. The opposition of mind and body correlates to additional oppositions, such as those between mental and physical activity, spirit and matter, and doctrine and practice. This same opposition also structures the distinction commonly made in contemporary Western thought between ritual and meditation—ritual being bodily, physical, and material, and meditation being mental and spiritual. In large part, religious studies discourse naturalizes mind–body dualism, as if it were just the way things are—a universally true and unchanging reality. Tantric yogas, however, confound the belief that mind–body dualism is somehow natural, and that it can be applied uncritically to all religious traditions. Instead of mind–body dualism, the conceptual framework appropriate for tantric yoga is interiority, which does not necessarily mean "mental."[109] Interiorized interpretations of practice develop progressively from Vedic and Brahmanic ritual practices to tantric yogas.[110]

[109] Michael Witzel, personal communication, April 19, 2007.

[110] Shaman Hatley provides a perspective that emphasizes the integration of internal and external. "Aguably, such integration of inner and outer processes is characteristic of tantric ritual, broadly conceived, as reflected in the ubiquitous dichotomy of *antarayāga* ("inner worship") and *bahiryāga* ("external worship")." Shaman Hatley, "The Lotus Garland (*padmamālā*) and Cord of Power (*śaktitantu*): The *Brahmayāmala*'s Integration of Inner and Outer Ritual," in *Śaivism and the*

Interiorization (also "internalization") is a multivalent term, referring to a variety of ritualized visualization practices performed "inside" the body. Yael Bentor explains the range of meanings, saying that interiorization "may pertain to a mental performance of the ritual, to the replacement of the ritual with a continuous process of life such as breathing or eating, to a particular way of life such as renunciation, to an actual performance with an inner interpretation, to the replacement of the external ritual with an internal one, and so forth."[111]

In a somatic understanding of tantric practice, external practices may be homologized with internal bodily functions.[112] For example, the fire of the homa ritual may be equated with digestive or sexual "fires." The symbolism is further amplified by equating the fire with wisdom, and the burning of offerings in the fire to the transformation of the obscurations (Skt. *āvaraṇa*) that keep one karmically entangled in samsara. Another instance of somatic interiorization is an interpretation of breathing as mantra recitation, found for example in Japan. Inhalation and exhalation of the breath are equated with the two syllables "a" and "hum." Thus, breathing itself is conceptually transformed into the recitation of mantra.[113]

The historical record of tantric praxis in the eighth and ninth centuries studied by Dalton reveals the progressive development of interiorization. "Buddhist authors at the time described what was unfolding as an internalization of ritual performance; in contrast to the earlier 'external' methods of worship, they termed the new techniques the 'internal yogas.'"[114]

Tantric Traditions: Essays in Honour of Alexis G. J. S. Sanderson, ed. Dominic Goodall et al., 387–408 (Leiden: Brill, 2020), 392.

[111] Yael Bentor, "Interiorized Fire Rituals in India and in Tibet," *Journal of the American Oriental Society* 120.4 (Oct./Dec. 2000): 594–613, 596.

[112] Bengali texts from the sixteenth century show esoteric physiology being adopted into Sufi traditions of practice. Shaman Hatley, "Mapping the Esoteric Body in the Islamic Yoga of Bengal," *History of Religions* 46.4 (2007): 352–368.

[113] For example, "esoteric nembutsu," see James H. Sanford, "Breath of Life: The Esoteric Nembutsu," in Esoteric Buddhism in Japan, ed. Ian Astley (Copenhagen: Seminar for Buddhist Studies, 1994), reprinted in Richard K. Payne, ed., *Esoteric Buddhism in East Asia* (Boston: Wisdom Publications, 2006), 161–189. See also Jacqueline Stone, "Just Open Your Mouth and Say 'A': A-Syllable Practice for the Time of Death in Early Medieval Japan," *Pacific World: Journal of the Institute of Buddhist Studies*, third series, no. 8 (Fall 2006); and Yael Bentor, "Interiorized Fire Offerings of Breathing, Inner Heat, and the Subtle Body," in *Tibetan Studies: Proceedings of the Seventh Seminar of the International Association for Tibetan Studies, Graz 1995*, ed. Helmut Krasser, Michael Torsten Much, and Ernst Steinkellner, 51–58 (Vienna: Verlag der Österreichischen Akademi der Wissenschaften, 1997); see also Yael Bentor, "Interiorized Fire Rituals in India and in Tibet," *Journal of the American Oriental Society* 120.4 (Oct.–Dec. 2000): 594–613.

[114] Dalton, "The Development of Perfection," 2.

These internal yogas were not a rejection of ritual, nor did they constitute a spiritualized or psychologized reinterpretation of earlier tantric ritual. Instead, this involved a literal embodying of tantric praxis—"The tantric subject had become the site for the entire ritual performance; the body's interior provided the devotee, the altar, the oblations, and the buddha to be worshipped."[115] Dalton has further traced interiorization across the eighth to eleventh centuries, arguing that this is a key change in tantric Buddhist praxes in India.

Focusing his examination on yoga tantra materials from Dunhuang, Dalton argues that there was an historical progression of interiorization, already mentioned briefly above. That progression moved through three stages corresponding to three categories of tantras: from the *yoga tantras*, which focus on yogic rather than ritual practices, through "great yoga" tantras (Skt. *mahāyoga tantras*), to "supreme yoga" tantras (Skt. *anuttarayoga tantras*).[116]

[115] Dalton, "The Development of Perfection," 2.

[116] Much contemporary Western academic scholarship continues to employ a Tibetan scholastic system for categorizing the tantras. That system obscures the history of tantric Buddhism because it has been decontextualized and dehistoricized—sublated from an emic set of bibliographic categories into one employed in both academic and popular discussions of the tantras.

This scholastic system is a fourfold classification that divides the tantras into action tantras (*kriyā tantras*), performance tantras (*carya tantras*), yoga tantras, and supreme yoga tantras (*anuttarayoga tantras*). (For a focused presentation of teachings related to the supreme yoga tantras, see Daniel Cozort, *Highest Yoga Tantra: An Introduction to the Esoteric Buddhism of Tibet* [Ithaca, NY: Snow Lion Publications, 1986].) Although it is only one of several, this fourfold system is today frequently treated as the single authoritative way to classify the tantras. (For an extensive emic discussion of various category systems, see Jamgön Kongtrul Lodrö Tayé, *The Treasury of Knowledge: Book Six, Part Four; Systems of Buddhist Tantra*, trans. Elio Guarisco and Ingrid McLeod [Ithaca, NY: Snow Lion Publications, 2005].) This system was probably established as late as the twelfth century in Tibet, and it is only one of several doxographies—that is, organizing systems structured as a sequence of increasingly higher teachings (Jacob Dalton, "A Crisis of Doxography: How Tibetans Organized Tantra During the 8th–12th Centuries," *Journal of the International Association of Buddhist Studies* 28.1 [2005]: 115–181, 158–161).

Dalton emphasizes that in India the principle by which teachings were organized was not doctrinal, but rather that "the tantric classification systems of India . . . are largely concerned with differences in *ritual practice*" (Dalton, "A Crisis of Doxography," 119; emphasis in original). After two centuries of "contention and confusion," Tibetan systems employed doctrine as the primary organizing principle, that is, "doxography" in the Western sense became the norm (Dalton, "Crisis of Doxography," 121).

Despite the tendency to dehistoricize the fourfold categorization, commentators such as Buddhaguhya, who was active in the eighth century around Vārāṇasī (modern Benares), reflect the problematic nature of the categories. He says in his commentary to the *Vairocanābhisaṃbodhi*:

> In this way, although the *Tattvasaṃgraha* and so on are mainly about inner yoga, outer practice is also not lacking. Likewise, although the Kriyā Tantras are mainly concerned with outer practice, they also do not lack inner practice. In the *Vidyādhara Collection*, immersion in the Three Gates of Liberation and so forth is spoken of, and you should understand this in a similar manner for those who engage in practice by way of the Perfections, according to the circumstances.
>
> Thus, although the *Mahā-vairocana-abhisaṃbodhi-vikurvati-adhiṣṭhāna-tantra* is a Yoga Tantra which deals mainly with expedient means (*upāya*) and insight (*prajñā*), it

The three categories of tantras correspond then to three periods "in the development of tantric ritual, each of which focused the Buddhist subject's attention further inwards, first from the external altar to himself, then to his physical anatomy and embodied experience, and finally to the subtleties of his internal physiological processes."[117] The early editions of the *mahāyoga* tantras began to appear over the course of approximately a century (c. 750 CE to c. 850 CE), a middle stratum layered between the earlier *yoga tantras* and the subsequent *anuttarayoga tantras.* Dalton suggests that the contents of the *mahāyoga tantras* were in large part extensively revised and emended in light of changing expectations and understandings in Tibet after this time. Despite this, he proposes that the earlier contents of the mahāyoga tantras can be discerned.[118] He suggests that the *mahāyoga tantras* "presented for the first time the ritualized sexual practices . . . [and] focused on the body's interior, on the anatomical details of the male and female sexual organs and the pleasure generated through sexual union."[119] The interiorization of ritual thus runs across a much wider range of conceptions than is possible in the framework of an exclusively mind–body or physical–spiritual dualism.

The interiorization of ritual corresponds to conceptions of a "subtle body" (Skt. *sūkṣmakāya, sūkṣmadeha*).[120] The subtle body is esoteric in the sense of something that is hidden or concealed, not part of ordinary, physical presence of the body—what C. Pierce Salguero describes as "supra-anatomical."[121]

> also teaches practices which accord with the *Kriyā* Tantras so that those trainees who are oriented towards rituals may also be attracted. Hence it can be considered as a *Kriyā* Tantra or as a Dual (*ubhaya*) Tantra (Hodge, 43).

Despite this fourfold system often being presented as a progression, this is a scholastic artifice of doctrinal progression, and not an historical sequence. Like other doxographic systems and formations of canon, the fourfold categorization was created to serve sectarian or political ends. Not only is it assertions about what is included or excluded, and which parts are more important than others, but it is also a claim to the authority to make those judgments—judgments which in this case continue to affect the understanding of tantra a millennium later.

117 Dalton, "The Development of Perfection," 3.

118 Note that this obsuring of the middle period was not a matter of bowdlerizing, but rather the result of constant reworking of texts to "bring them up-to-date with the latest ritual technologies" (Dalton, "The Development of Perfection," 4), a consequence of both a highly creative and highly competitive religious milieu.

119 Dalton, "The Development of Perfection," 3.

120 See Gavin Flood, *The Tantric Body: The Secret Tradition of Hindu Religion* (London: I.B. Taurus, 2006); Geoffrey Samuel, "The Subtle Body in India and Beyond," in *Religion and the Subtle Body in Asia and the West: Between Mind and Body*, ed. Geoffrey Samuel and Jay Johnston, 33–47 (London: Routledge, 2013).

121 C. Pierce Salguero, "Buddhist Medicine and Its Circulation," in *Oxford Research Encyclopedias: Asian History* (Oxford: Oxford University Press, 2022; doi.org/10.1093/acrefore/9780190277727.013.215), n.p.: 3 of 26. See also Tsutomu Yamashita, "Sanskrit Medical Literature," in *The Oxford Handbook of Science and Medicine in the Classical World*, ed. Paul T. Keyser and

Dominik Wujastyk distinguishes tantric subtle body physiology from earlier sources, such as *Āyurvedic* medicine, noting that "āyurveda knows no *cakras*, nor the spinal conduits of breath (*prāṇa*) known from tantric literature."[122] Tantric conceptions of physiology developed into more complex systems in which the breath (Skt. *prāṇa* or "winds" Tib. *lung*) "provided connectivity between the mind, the body, the senses, and the cosmos at large."[123] Breath moved along channels (Skt. *nāḍī*) within the body, linked to the cakras, where it could be collected. These and other related concepts contributed to the formation of practices found in various of the Buddhist tantras.[124]

What are known as the "Six Dharmas of Naropa"[125] (Tib. *Naropa chos drug*) bring together in systematic fashion subtle body teachings as a yogic technology.[126] Who codified this specific set of six interiorized yogic practices and when that was done are both uncertain.[127] However, Tilopa (b. 988) is credited with having drawn together practices from several tantras and taught them to Naropa (1016–1100). Naropa's Tibetan disciple Marpa (1012–1097) received these practices and, in turn, conveyed them to his disciple, the well-known Tibetan yogi, Milarepa (1040–1123).

The six practices include consciousness transfer, inner heat, illusory body, lucid awareness, clear light, and the control of rebirth destiny. The "transfer of consciousness" (Tib. *phowa*) involves separating the subtle body from the coarse body, enabling the practitioner to eject their consciousness out through the top of the head and travel to a buddha land. "Inner heat" (Tib. *gtum mo*) integrates "visualizations, breath-control, and physical yoga

John Scarborough, 95–104 (Oxford: Oxford University Press, 2018; doi.org/10.1093/oxfordhb/9780199734146.013.66), 96.

122 Dominik Wujastyk, "The Science of Medicine," in *The Blackwell Companion to Hinduism*, ed. Gavin Flood, 393–409 (Oxford: Blackwell, 2003), 397.

123 Salguero, "Buddhist Medicine and Its Circulation," 3 of 26.

124 On the variety tantras, see Ching Hsuan Mei, "The Early Transmission of 'Pho ba Teachings," *The Tibet Journal* 29.4 (Winter 2004): 27–42.

125 The name is also commonly rendered in English as "the six yogas of Naropa." While in English "dharma" is usually used to refer specifically to the teachings of the Buddha Śākyamuni, or to the teachings of Buddhism more generally, the Sanskrit, Tibetan, and Chinese terms refer not simply to conceptual or doctrinal matters but also to yogic and ritual practices. It is only from the perspective of the categories embedded in English that one could describe the term as polysemous—in context, its meaning is broader than any of the more specific English terms used.

126 Casey Kemp, "The Tibetan Book of the Dead (*Bardo Thödol*)," in *The Oxford Encyclopedia of Buddhism*, ed. Richard K. Payne and Georgios T. Halkias, 2467–2487 (New York: Oxford University Press, 2024), 2471.

127 Glenn H. Mullin, *The Six Yogas of Naropa* (1996. Reprint. Ithaca, NY: Snow Lion Publications, 2005), 29.

exercises . . . for gaining mastery over subtle mind-body processes."[128] Other practices in this set of six are attaining an "illusory body," which is pure; lucid awareness, which enables the practitioner to manipulate dream states[129]; "clear light" practices in which the natural luminosity of consciousness is experienced; and the well-known *bardo* teachings in which the state between death and rebirth is entered into consciously so that the practitioner can attain full awakening—or at least a more beneficial rebirth.[130]

In addition to their role in the formation and transmission of the six yogas, Tilopa and Naropa are members of a group of yogis said to be "great realized adepts" (Skt. *mahāsiddas*).[131] "Siddhas" (adepts[132]) identifies a major category of yogic practitioners in medieval India, formative for the tantric movement generally. "Mahāsiddhas" identifies a specific group of figures who are important in the history of tantric Buddhism, usually numbering eighty-four. Mahāsiddhas are characterized by Sonya Lee, who says that

> Coming from both princely and lowly backgrounds in Indian society, mahasiddhas are celebrated for their magical feats and audacious violations of traditional Buddhist values. Their transgressions signal not only their profound understanding of the laws of nature and the ability to manipulate them but also their transcendence of them altogether.[133]

Many figures in this group focused on interiorized yogic practices, but also some at times criticized such practices as impeding awareness of the naturally enlightened mind.

[128] Georgios T. Halkias, "Buddhist Meditation in Tibet: Exosteric and Esoteric Orientations," in *The Oxford Handbook of Meditation*, ed. Miguel Farias, David Brazier, and Mansur Lalljee, 263–287 (Oxford: Oxford University Press, 2021; DOI: 10.1093/oxfordhb/9780198808640.013.52), 280.

[129] For a modern discussion of Bon dream yoga, see Tenzin Wangyal, *The Tibetan Yogas of Dream and Sleep* (Ithaca, NY: Snow Lion Publications, 1998).

[130] For a guide through the vast English language literature on "The Tibetan Book of the Dead," see Donald S. Lopez, Jr., *The Tibetan Book of the Dead: A Biography* (Princeton, NJ: Princeton University Press, 2011).

[131] David Gray, "Tantra and Tantric Traditions of Hinduism and Buddhism," in *The Oxford Encyclopedia of Buddhism*, ed. Richard K. Payne and Georgios T. Halkias, 2301–2324 (New York: Oxford University Press, 2024; DOI: 10.1093/acrefore/9780199340378.013.59), 2305.

[132] David Gordon White gives an etymologically informed explanation: "As a common noun, *siddha* means 'realized, perfected one,' a term generally applied to a practitioner (*sādhaka*, *sādhu*) who has through his practice (*sādhana*) realized his dual goal of superhuman powers (*siddhis*, 'realizations, 'perfections') and bodily immortality (*jīvanmukti*)." *The Alchemical Body: Siddha Traditions in Medieval India* (Chicago: University of Chicago Press, 1996), 2.

[133] Sonya Lee, "Buddhist Art and Architecture," in *Oxford Research Encyclopedias: Asian History* (Oxford: Oxford University Press, 2022; DOI: 10.1093/acrefore/9780190277727.013.398), n.p.: 29 of 42.

Mahāsiddhas

As noted above, the mahāsiddhas are a group of eighty-four "greatly accomplished" figures considered particularly important for the development of Buddhist tantra. They are part of the broader siddha movement in Indic religious history, which continues into the present. In this section, we will be looking more closely at one particular mahāsiddha: Saraha.

The tantric movement is not a singular, authoritatively defined institution—instead, some parts of it contradict others. The mahāsiddhas are noteworthy not only for their yogic practices but also for the use of poetry in popular folk form to convey their teachings and to describe their transformative experiences. Although the form is different, this links both back to the *Theragātha* and *Therīgātha* collections, and into the present as well.[134] Being composed in regional languages, rather than Sanskrit, the songs helped to preserve vernacular literary forms.[135] Such "songs of awakening" (or "songs of realization," Tib. *mgur*) constitute a genre that originated in India and continued in Tibet.[136] The songs stand out from other literary genre because of their "sincere and detailed descriptions of personal thoughts and experiences as related to one's own spiritual path."[137] In Davidson's view, the personal quality of the siddha's songs is a revival, in that "not since the poems of the early *arhats* did Buddhists express themselves in such a rich autobiographical first-person form, often playful and not infrequently with pathos."[138] In addition to the collections of songs attributed to the mahāsiddhas, such "adamantine songs" (Skt. *vajragīti*) are also found in tantras.[139] While the

[134] For the Therigatha, see Charles Hallisey, *Therigatha: Poems of the First Buddhist Women* (Cambridge, MA: Harvard University Press, 2015), and C. A. F. Rhys Davids and K. R. Norman, *Poems of Early Buddhist Nuns* (Oxford: Pali Text Society, 1989). For the Theragatha, see K. R. Norman, *Poems of Early Buddhist Monks* (1997. Rev. ed. Oxford: Pali Text Society, 2022). A modern example is by Jivan Tova Green found in "Jivan Tova Green's Reflection," in *The Hidden Lamp: Stories from Twenty-Five Centuries of Awakened Women*, ed. Florence Caplow and Susan Moon, 339–341 (Somerville, MA: Wisdom Publications, 2013), 339.

[135] Davidson, "Esoteric Buddhism in the Matrix of Early Medieval India," 25.

[136] John A. Ardussi, "Brewing and Drinking the Beer of Enlightenment in Tibetan Buddhism: The *Dohā* Tradition in Tibet," *Journal of the American Oriental Society* 97.2 (1977): 115–124. Davidson compares these with the songs attributed to later figures in India, such as Kabir, Sūrdas, and Mira, as well as others (Davidson, "Esoteric Buddhism in the Matrix of Early Medieval India," 27). Linda Hess has addressed the continuity betweeen the mahāsiddhas and Kabir, and how Kabir might be characterized as tantric in her general introduction to the forthcoming Kabir volume in the Murty Classical Library of India, Harvard University Press.

[137] Jennifer Divall, "Empty Stone Caves and Celestial Palaces: Embedding the Transcendent in the Tibetan Landscape in Godrakpa's 'Songs of Realization,'" *Tibet Journal* 39.2 (Autumn/Winter 2014): 37–56, 37.

[138] Davidson, "Esoteric Buddhism in the Matrix of Early Medieval India," 26.

[139] Gray, *The Buddhist Tantras*, 68.

surrounding text is Sanskrit, the songs are given in a different, earlier literary language, Apabraṃśa. This is a late Middle Indo-Aryan literary language in which the songs of the mahāsiddhas, such as Saraha, were recorded.

Saraha

Saraha is prominent among the mahāsiddhas in part because the Tibetan traditions that embraced the idea of the "great seal" (Skt. *mahāmudrā*) consider him to be the founder from whom many of the lineages of Mahāmudrā teachings descend.[140] Found initially in the Mahāyoga and Yoginī tantras, mahāmudrā is a polysemous term indicating, among other things, the accomplishment of "a full understanding of the nature of reality."[141] Proponents of the Mahāyoga and Yoginī tantras, the mahāsiddhas made mahāmudrā and the idea of the spontaneously awakened nature of the natural mind key to their practices and teachings. This tradition is an important thread linking Indic and Tibetan forms of tantric Buddhism. Given our strategy for delineating tantra, context and designation make Saraha and the other mahāsiddhas, along with the Mahāmudrā teachings and lineages, tantric.

Of the mahāsiddhas, some practitioners and teachers consider Saraha to be singularly important, with incidents from his life often recounted along with the songs attributed to him. Yet some of the songs attributed to Saraha—and other siddhas—appear to be openly critical of particular practices associated with yoga, rejecting systematic practices in favor of direct awareness of the pure nature of mind.[142] For example, in one of his collections of songs, the *vajragīti*, Saraha ridicules the practices of the subtle body:

> Drawing energies up and down in the turning centres [*cakra*]:
> Guided by these methods, the truth cannot be found;
> Although you may grasp and eject and unite and ignite,

[140] Roger Jackson, "Mahāmudrā: Natural Mind in Indian and Tibetan Buddhism," *Religion Compass* 5.7 (2011): 286–299, 289, DOI: 10.1111/j.1749-8171.2011.00283.x.

[141] Jackson, "Mahāmudrā," 288.

[142] Klaus-Dieter Mathes, "Mind and Its Co-emergent (*sahaja*) Nature in Advayavajra's Commentary on Saraha's *Dohākoṣa*," *Zentralasiatische Studien* 44 (2015): 17–34; and Casey Alexandra Kemp, "Merging Ignorance and Luminosity in Early Bka' brgyud *Bsre ba* Literature," *Zentralasiatische Studien* 44 (2015): 35–50.

> There is no difference between these breath-control practices and a fool suffering from asthma.[143]

Lara Braitstein summarizes Saraha's views of systems of Buddhist thought, saying

> Saraha's references to these schemes—*pāramitā* and *upāya*,[144] the Four Seals, etc.—are for the most part deeply critical. He dismisses and mocks whatever has made its way into mainstream thought and practice, with his own typical flair.[145]

At this distance in time and cultures, interpreting Saraha's rejection of practice inevitably requires some speculation. It should not necessarily be taken only literally but may better be understood as also focusing attention on the goal of "a non-conceptual, blissful gnosis of reality—the natural mind."[146] The value of this latter emphasis is that it helps the practitioner avoid mistakenly believing that mastering the practice in which one has been instructed is itself the goal.[147]

How best to conceive of Saraha is a matter of debate. Is he to be thought of as a specific, historically real living person or as a literary figure, one who takes on different meanings in different contexts. Kurtis R. Schaeffer, commenting on Herbert Guenther's study of Saraha, says "Herbert Guenther has provocatively remarked, 'as is so often the case with major figures in the intellectual history of India, almost nothing factual is known about Saraha.'

143 Lara Braitstein, "Saraha's Adamantine Songs: Texts, Contexts, Translations and Traditions of the Great Seal" (PhD diss., McGill University, 2004), 78.

144 RKP: "Pāramitā" is perfection and refers to the gradual path of the Perfection of Wisdom, leading to insight into emptiness. "Upāya" is skillful means and commonly refers to compassionate action on the part of the bodhisattva. According to Mahāyāna conceptions of the bodhisattva, insight into emptiness and arising of compassion are often presented as balancing one another.

145 Lara Braitstein, "The Direct Path: Saraha's Adamantine Songs and the Bka' brgyud Great Seal," in *Mahāmudrā and the Bka'-brgyud Tradition*, ed. Roger R. Jackson and Matthew T. Kapstein, 55–88 (Andiast, Switzerland: International Institute for Tibetan and Buddhist Studies GmbH, 2011), 84.

146 Roger Jackson, "Mahāmudrā in India and Tibet," in *The Oxford Encyclopedia of Buddhism* (New York: Oxford University Press, 2024; online: 2016; DOI: 10.1093/acrefore/9780199340378.013.184), 1477. See also Roger Jackson, *Mind Seeing Mind: Mahāmudrā and the Geluk Tradition of Tibetan Buddhism* (Boston: Wisdom Publishing, 2019).

147 My thanks to Roger Jackson for helping to clarify this for me. Roger Jackson, personal communication via email, March 7, 2018. Regarding these ideas in mahāyoga texts, see Sam van Schaik, "The Sweet Sage and *The Four Yogas*: A Lost Mahāyoga Treatise from Dunhuang." *Journal of the International Association of Tibetan Studies* 4 (Dec. 2008): 1–67, 5, and in the Mahāmudrā of Gampopa (1079–1153), see Ulrich Timme Kragh, *Tibetan Yoga and Mysticism: A Textual Study of the Yogas of Nāropa and Mahāmudrā Meditation in the Medieval Tradition of Dags po* (Tokyo: The International Institute for Buddhist Studies, 2015), 21.

But even this admittal presumes that there are 'facts' to be known about the person of Saraha, if only we could read the sources correctly, or had access to more sources."[148] Schaeffer indicates, in other words, that there may be no "facts" available from which to construct a biography of the sort that Western historical conventions might lead us to desire.[149] Braitstein specifies that there is no firm consensus as to Saraha's dates, the language in which he wrote, or where he lived and worked.[150] One way of understanding "Saraha," therefore, is as the collection of ideas and teachings found in the collections of songs attributed to him, and the figure as described in the various life stories, all held together by the name. In the most comprehensive study of Saraha, Jackson agrees that there is nothing that can be said with certainty about Saraha. Avoiding the extreme view of Saraha as an empty signifier, however, Jackson reasonably suggests that we can know something about "the general milieu in which Saraha seems to have flourished [which] was that of the Buddhist culture of India sometime between the eighth and eleventh centuries."[151]

Prominent in the stories of Saraha and other mahāsiddhas are consorts, who in one of the consistent tropes of the literature play a key role in the mahāsiddha's yogic practices—imagery that is also suggestive of the inspirational function of ḍākinī. Two sets of stories associated with Saraha are identified by different consorts, the "radish girl" and the "fletcheress."[152] As in the following story regarding the radish girl, tantric consorts are often portrayed as teaching the practitioner.

> One time he asked for a dish of radishes, but by the time his woman returned with them, he had entered into meditation. Having been instructed not to

[148] Kurtis R. Schaeffer, *Dreaming the Great Brahmin: Tibetan Traditions of the Buddhist Poet-Saint Saraha* (Oxford: Oxford University Press, 2005), 14. Internal quote is from Herbert Guenther, *Ecstatic Spontaneity: Saraha's Three Cycles of Dohā* (Berkeley, CA: Asian Humanities Press, 1993), 3.

[149] Such historical difficulties are not unique to Saraha. Nāropa (Skt. Nādapradā, 1016–1100) is one of the key members of the Gelug lineage, having been the student of Tilopa and the teacher of Marpa. As such, he is at the transition between India and Tibet. He is usually identified as having been from a Brahmin family and to have held high office (Gatekeeper of the North) at Nalanda monastery. However, the brief biography in the *Caturaśīti-siddhi-pravṛtti* by Abhayadatta, the collection of brief biographies of the eighty-four mahāsiddhas referred to above, claims that he was from a family of wine sellers and makes no mention of Nalanda (Abhayadatta, *Buddha's Lions: The Lives of the Eighty-Four Siddhas*, trans. James B. Robinson [Berkeley, CA: Dharma Publishing, 1979], 93–95).

[150] Lara Braitstein, "Exploring Saraha's Treasury of Adamantine Songs," *The Tibet Journal* 33.1 (Spring 2008): 40–65, 40–41.

[151] Jackson, *Saraha*, 5.

[152] On the fletcheress, see Schaeffer, *Dreaming the Great Brahmin*, 19–25.

disturb him during his meditations, she did not and the meditation period extended to twelve years. Upon arising from meditation he asked for the radishes. Learning what had happened, and being chided by his woman for continuing to be attached to the idea of radishes, Saraha abandons "names and conceptions. By experiencing the essential meaning, he obtained the highest siddhi of Mahāmudrā [the 'great seal' system of yogic realization], and furthered the aims of living beings. He, together with his woman, entered the realm of the Ḍākas."[153]

Saraha is also mentioned in the lineage of teachers listed by Tsongkhapa in his commentary to the Guhyasamāja tantra, the *Brilliant Illumination of the Lamp of the Five Stages*. Introducing his translation of this work, Robert Thurman expands on the mention of the "Glorious Saraha," recounting additional pieces of the stories about Saraha. In contrast to Visukalpa, the figure preceding Saraha in the lineage, Thurman claims that

> There is a bit more information about Saraha, who was a Brahmin, but who was attracted by a female arrow-maker when strolling through a bazaar, humbled, and then taught how to make a straight arrow. To take up such a profession was to abandon his status as a high caste Brahmin and to live among the lowliest castes, typical behavior of the great adepts. He became enlightened as a great adept and eventually taught the great Nagarjuna.[154]

Again, the "information" here should be understood as referring to Saraha the literary figure.

Like many other tantric consorts, both the radish girl and the fletcheress are central actors in the story of Saraha, as well as an essential part of our understanding of the nature of the practices engaged in by the siddhas. As Serinity Young notes, "*Mahāsiddha* biographies reveal that several male *siddhas* practiced sexual union with actual women, though their practice is not usually elaborated upon."[155] One mahāsiddha life story, that of Babhala, does give a brief description:

[153] Robinson, *Buddha's Lions*, 43. Ḍākas are the male counterparts of ḍākinī.

[154] Tsong Khapa Losang Drakpa, *Brilliant Illumination of the Lamp of the Five Stages (Rin lnga rab tu gsal ba'i sgron me): Practical Instruction in the King of Tantras, The Glorious Esoteric Community*, ed. Robert A. F. Thurman (New York: Columbia University, 2010), 19.

[155] Serinity Young, *Courtesans and Tantric Consorts: Sexualities in Buddhist Narrative, Iconography, and Ritual* (London: Routledge, 2004), 140.

In the lotus maṇḍala of your partner,
A superior, skillful consort,
Mingle your white seed
With her ocean of red seed.
Then absorb, raise and diffuse the elixir
And your ecstasy will never end.
Then to raise the pleasure beyond pleasure
Visualize it inseparable from emptiness.[156]

Focusing on the end of the stanza, Young comments that "Through meditative skill the sensation of sexual pleasure is experienced as emptiness, the profound realization that all beings and all things are essentially empty, without individuality and nonenduring."[157] This doctrinally refined interpretation of the stanza emphasizes the experiential realization of emptiness (Skt. *śunyatā*).[158] The stanza, however, does not indicate a purely mental transformation resulting from meditative visualization. The stanza's context is the physiology of the subtle body, of embryology, and of the practices that followed from those conceptions.[159]

Rather than being an instance of a purposely obscure tantric code,[160] the imagery at the center of the stanza is fairly straightforward: The lotus mandala is the consort's vagina, the white seed is semen, and the red seed is menstrual blood.[161] Each of these—lotus mandala, white seed, red seed, and vagina, semen, menstrual blood—can of course be interpreted as referring to doctrinal themes such as the unification of wisdom and compassion in the mind of the practitioner. It might be suggested that there are (at least) three different modes of interpretation: symbolic, literal, and doctrinal.

[156] Keith Dowman, *Masters of Mahamudra: Songs and Histories of the Eighty-Four Buddhist Siddhas* (Albany: State University of New York Press, 1985), 216.

[157] Young, *Courtesans and Tantric Consorts*, 140.

[158] Cf. White, *The Alchemical Body*, 138–39.

[159] The association between embryological conceptions and tantra is also found in Tibet and East Asia. See Francis Garrett, *Religion, Medicine and the Human Embryo in Tibet* (Oxon, UK: Routledge, 2015), and Anna Andreeva and Dominic Steavu, eds., *Transforming the Void: Embryological Discourse and Reproductive Imagery in East Asian Religions* (Leiden: Brill, 2016).

[160] This is one interpretation of the Skt. term *sandhyābhāṣā*. The term is also rendered "intentional language" or "twilight language." Carol Lorea, "Singing Tantra: Aural Media and Sonic Soteriology in Bengali Esoteric Lineages," in *The Oxford Handbook of Tantric Studies*, ed. Richard K. Payne and Glen T. Hayes, 991–1021 (New York: Oxford University Press, 2024), 1005.

[161] This symbolism of white/semen and red/menstrual blood, and the commingling of the two, is also found in Daoist imagery.

However, none of these three is the "true" understanding, but rather alternative frameworks of interpretation.

What is less obvious is the reference to absorbing, raising, and diffusing the elixir. Embryos were thought to result from the union of female blood and male semen in the vagina. The goal of practice referred to here is the resorption of commingled male and female sexual fluids back into the body of the male practitioner and its introjection up into the spinal column, rising through the spinal cakras to the cakra at the crown of the head.[162]

Per Kvaerne has explained that the tantric Buddhist tradition identifies semen with bodhicitta, noting that awakening "results from the upward march of the *bodhicitta*—not as in classical Mahāyāna, through the Ten Stages, but through the various *cakras* (psychic centers) of the body."[163] The particular yogic practice that Kvaerne examines is a solo one and differs from sexual yoga with a partner, such as described in Babhala's song quoted earlier. Kvaerne explains that in this solitary practice "Caṇḍālī is the female force, represented as the scorching heat of the Sun and symbolised by the letter *A*; she is situated in the *nirmāṇacakra*,"[164] which is the first of four cakras in this system of esoteric physiology, located at the practitioner's navel.[165] This solo version focuses exclusively on semen (bodhicitta), rather than on both semen and menstrual blood, as is the case with the sexual yoga with a partner described in Babhala's song. Despite this difference, both practices point to a shared grounding in esoteric physiology of the subtle body.[166] At the same time, these introjected, interiorized forms differ from the consumption of commingled sexual fluids,[167] and it

[162] A similar idea is found in the *Secret of the Golden Flower*, a Chinese text evidencing both Taoist and Buddhist concepts, including the notion that the "tathāgata" is an embryo within the body of the male practitioner. This embryo, once fully gestated, becomes the source of the infinite manifestation of bodies that the practitioner can emanate. See Richard K. Payne, "Sex and Gestation: The Union of Opposites in European and Chinese Alchemy," *Ambix* 36.2 (1989): 66–81 (http://dx.doi.org/10.1179/000269889790418612).

[163] Per Kvaerne, *An Anthology of Buddhist Tantric Songs: A Study of the* Caryāgīti (Oslo: Universitetsforlaget, 1977), 30–31.

[164] Kvaerne, *An Anthology*, 31.

[165] For a discussion of the different systems of cakras, and relation to kundalini, see Flood, *The Tantric Body*, 157–162. Note that Flood reminds us that the *cakra* system is not the only one found in tantric praxis: "it is important to remember that there are other systems of mapping the cosmos on to the body" (Flood, *The Tantric Body*, 157).

[166] Loosely, this may also be called "kundalini yoga." See Lilian Silburn, *Kundalini: Energy of the Depths, A Comprehensive Study Based on Scriptures of Nondualistic Kaśmir Śaivism*, trans. Jacques Gontier (Albany: State University of New York Press, 1988). On contemporary expressions of these ideas, see Sudhir Kakar, *Shamans, Mystics and Doctors: A Psychological Inquiry into India and Its Healing Traditions* (Chicago: University of Chicago Press, 1982).

[167] White, *The Alchemical Body*, 137.

may constitute either parallel or later forms from within the same range of practices.[168]

Tantric consorts, such as the radish girl, are usually described as being young—reportedly in this case fifteen years old, but in the case of two other siddhas, as young as twelve. This reflects Indian conceptions of female sexual potency. Serinity Young explains that

> It is believed that younger women have more female seed than older women. In a tantric context this means the male adept will receive greater benefits from a young woman. Women are also believed to be more sexual than men; indeed they are thought to be insatiable and sexually aggressive, thus mature women pose a real threat to men by taking their semen.[169]

Projections regarding the sexuality of women are a complex matter. Amy Langenberg calls attention to the methodological importance of taking into account the perspective of a text's author. When texts are authored by men, representations of female sexuality easily "fall into the category of male fantasy and projection."[170]

Like that of the fletcheress, the social status of the radish girl is also noteworthy, as it contributes to both the rhetoric of transgression and the maintenance of control by the male adept over his consort who is not only female and younger but also of a lower caste. Other consorts are identified as prostitutes, barmaids, and outcastes—*ḍombī* and *caṇḍālī* are terms for female outcastes and are commonly used in reference to tantric consorts.

Along with the radish girl, the fletcheress is also described as a tantric teacher and consort to Saraha. Upon taking the fletcheress as his tantric consort, he is said to have exclaimed:

> Until yesterday I was not a monk,
> From today onward I am a monk.[171]

[168] David Gray notes that in the Cakrasamvara tantra, the euphemism "nondual hero worship" is used for "the gathering and consumption of the mixed sexual fluids, semen and uterine blood" (*Cakrasaṃvara Tantra*, 107). See also White, *The Alchemical Body.*

[169] Young, *Courtesans and Tantric Consorts*, 140–141. This fear of female sexuality, expressed in the idea of women taking men's potency by taking semen, appears also in Chinese "Daoist" contexts.

[170] Amy Langenberg, "Reading Against the Grain: Female Sexuality in Classical South Asian Buddhism," *Religion* 49.4 (2019): 728–734, 729. See also Amy Langenberg, "Buddhism and Sexuality," in *The Oxford Handbook of Buddhist Ethics*, ed. Daniel Cozort and James Mark Shields, 567–591 (Oxford: Oxford University Press, 2018; DOI: 10.1093/oxfordhb/9780198746140.013.22).

[171] Quoted from Drakpa Dorje's biography. Schaeffer, *Dreaming the Great Brahmin*, 54.

Just as with his breach of Brahmanical caste rules, here Saraha is portrayed as breaching the Buddhist monastic rule of celibacy. It is typical of the teachings attributed to the mahāsiddhas that he inverts this relation between rule and identity, claiming that by having breached the rule for a monk, he is now a monk. Such seemingly paradoxical claims are also reminiscent of the Perfection of Wisdom literature and are found in many of the related song traditions from India.[172]

The Tantric Character of the Mahāsiddhas

Aside from the songs and hagiography, all we have of Saraha are retrospective constructions. These have been built up largely either in the frame of sectarian claims of lineal authority,[173] or as part of a historical strategy seeking origins. Saraha and the other mahāsiddhas can also, however, be framed in several different discourses, such as figures in the Indian tradition of folk poetry, or as mythic trickster figures.[174] A different orientation emphasizes their role as lineal progentors of Tibetan Mahāmudrā, so that from that perspective they are designated as tantric.

Saraha is a centripetal figure, who brings together literary elements—poems, hagiographic tales, and so on. In this, he functions in the same way that the central deity of a praxis brings together rituals, texts, artwork, and so on. The attempt to construct a unitary conception of Saraha is a speculative project in hagiography, and not an historical project. There is, consequently, no need to reconcile the apparent contradiction between representations of Saraha as a great tantric practitioner and founder of the Kagyü tantric lineage, and those in which he is portrayed as apparently being critical of yogic practices commonly considered tantric.

In the figure of a tantric master, Saraha warns "against reifying the distinction between path and fruition."[175] Although referencing the scheme of path and fruit (that is, goal: awakening), the tantric perspective expressed

[172] Carola Erika Lorea, "'I Am Afraid of Telling You This, Lest You'd Be Scared Shitless!': The Myth of Secrecy and the Study of Esoteric Traditions of Bengal," *Religions* 9.6 (2018).

[173] See Jackson, *Mind Seeing Mind*, 100, 120, etc.

[174] See, for instance, the figure of "Bengal Blackie," Kāṇha (Kṛṣṇācārya), one of the eighty-four mahāsiddhas as described by Lee Siegel, "Bengal Blackie and the Sacred Slut: A Sahajayāna Buddhist Song," *Buddhist-Christian Studies* 1 (1981): 51–58. Cf. Reginal Ray, "Reading the Vajrayāna in Context: A Reassessment of Bengal Blackie," *Buddhist-Christian Studies* 5 (1985): 173–189, and Lee Siegel, "Bengal Blackie Rides Again," *Buddhist-Christian Studies* 5 (1985): 191–192.

[175] Braitstein, "Saraha's Adamantine Songs," 79.

asserts that path and fruit are radically nondual. This is in contrast to seeing the two as distinctly separate, the path leading to the fruit of awakening—as cause leads to effect.[176] The nondual identity of path and fruit is another way of asserting that tantra is the sudden vehicle, that is, the thunderbolt vehicle (Skt. *vajrayāna*)—being always and already awakened, the practitioner attains full awakening speedily in this very lifetime.[177] Here it is Saraha in use, that is, as a master teaching radical nonduality, that makes Saraha a tantric figure.

Radical nonduality also suggests a conceptual congruence between the intellectual system of Madhyamaka and tantra. Asserting the nonduality of path and fruit recalls the relation between seed and sprout, as explained by Nagārjuna, who says that "the sprout does not exist in the seed which is its cause."[178] In Saraha's view, when path and fruit are understood as a whole, then they are *mahāmudrā*, the "great seal." Braitstein tells us that Saraha describes Mahāmudrā as "unborn, free of conventions, free of distinctions, the highest union of thought and non-thought, the innate nature of all, instantaneous full awakening, blissful, and uncontrived—to cite but a few of his descriptions."[179] Because of Saraha's teachings, Tibetan formulators of the Mahāmudrā designate him as a founder of a tantric lineage, exemplifying the institutional facet of tantra, by which it is delineated by designation.

Summary

This chapter first introduced the basis of tantric ritual practice in Vedic ritual culture, the historical development of Buddhist tantra, and then focused on the mandala initiation of the *Vairocanābhisaṃbodhi tantra*. The *Vairocanābhisaṃbodhi* serves first as an instance of the bibliographic delineation of tantra, as a window onto the key ritual of early tantra, and as a text central to East Asian tantric Buddhism. The medieval period, from the Gupta (early fourth to sixth century) through the Pāla (ca. 750–1161), is also

[176] This formulation also connects with the phrase *phalayāna*, the "vehicle of the fruit," and with the Sakya school's *lamdre* (*lam 'bras*) or "path and fruit" stream. See Cyrus Stearns, ed. and trans., *Taking the Result as the Path: Core Teachings of the Sakya Lamdré Tradition* (Boston: Wisdom Publications, 2006).

[177] Two of the several terms used to identify this complex of ideas include *sahaja* and *phalayāna*.

[178] Jan Westerhoff, *The Dispeller of Disputes: Nāgārjuna's* Vigrahavyāvartanī (Oxford: Oxford University Press, 2010), 19.

[179] Braitstein, "The Direct Path," 84.

the time in which the mahāsiddhas were active, known for yogic practices rather than ritual ones. Yogic practices developed through the interiorization of ritual practices and employ conceptions of the subtle body. The songs of awakening of Saraha and other mahāsiddhas promoted immediate experiences of nondual awareness, and as a genre they continued in Tibetan literature as well.

While this chapter employed the threefold system of context, use, and designation as ways to delineate tantric Buddhism, the next chapter turns to the categories of praxis and pilgrimage as institutional forms. Praxes associated with the verbal formulae known as *dharāṇī* allow us to consider tantra as being framed not only by the yogic practices of the subtle body but also by linguistic practices and conceptions of the power of language. Then, the pilgrimage route encircling the island of Shikoku provides entrée to an institutional form centering on Kūkai, a key figure in East Asian Buddhist tantra.

III

East Asia

Instituting Tantra: Recitation and Pilgrimage

Smooth stone slabs lead the white-clad pilgrim's feet back to where he began. The path stretches a mile or so through giant cypress, reminiscent of the redwoods of his California home; he approaches the temple that is the focus of this vast ancient cemetery. Offering water to the assembled buddhas and bodhisattvas, he crosses the stone bridge for the last approach to the temple where Kūkai, founder of the lineage into which the pilgrim has been initiated, is entombed. He climbs the long stairway to the large temple, bowing, going around to the back where the mausoleum is. There he recites the mantra of Kūkai, *namu daishi henjo kongo*, that he has recited at the Kūkai shrine at each of the eighty-eight temples of the Shikoku pilgrimage, and bows.

Culminating with a return to Kūkai's mausoleum on Kōyasan contextualizes the pilgrim and the route he followed as part of the tantric cosmopolis. The facet of the tantric movement that this chapter examines is institutionalization, as evidenced by two tantric institutions. "Institution" is being used here broadly to refer to structures or forms of social order that govern individual behavior and that reproduce themselves.[1]

Focusing on East Asia, this chapter discusses two kinds of tantric institutions. One is the practice of dhāraṇī recitation, and the other is the pilgrimage route around the island of Shikoku. Both are tantric by context, use, and designation, and both are examples of the social institutions that maintain tantric praxis over time, and across linguistic and cultural boundaries.

[1] Seumas Miller, "Social Institutions," in *The Stanford Encyclopedia of Philosophy* (Fall 2024 edition), ed. Edward N. Zalta and Uri Nodelman, https://plato.stanford.edu/archives/fall2024/entries/social-institutions/.

Tantra Across the Buddhist Cosmopolis. Richard K. Payne, Oxford University Press. © Oxford University Press 2025.
DOI: 10.1093/9780197825105.003.0003

Dhāraṇī as a Tantric Institution

Dhāraṇī are formulaic verbal expressions similar to mantra, such as the Kūkai mantra pilgrims recite at the mausoleum on Kōyasan. The important role of dhāraṇī practices in the development of tantric Buddhism was discussed in the previous chapter in relation to its textual history. An initial, and only very rough rule of thumb to distinguish mantra and dhāraṇī is that (most) mantra are (relatively) short, and (most) dhāraṇī are (relatively) long. Some mantra are so short that they comprise a single "seed" syllable (*bīja mantra*), for example the syllable *A*. This is the first in the sequence of the Sanskrit syllabary, and the sequence of syllables is interpreted in Indic theories of the linguistic sequence through which the cosmos emanates.[2] As the first syllable, *A* is interpreted as the origin of the cosmos.[3] In the Buddhist tradition, there is the famously short Perfection of Wisdom sutra in a single syllable, the syllable *A*.[4] Another Perfection of Wisdom sutra, the Heart Sutra, both ends with a mantra and is often treated as a mantra in its entirety. To further complicate the usage of both terms, they are at times used synonymously, and in tantric practices both mantra and dhāraṇī are sometimes recited, and sometimes written or visualized.

Another text that promoted the practice of a single syllable is "The Procedure for Mañjuśrī's Single-Syllable Mantra."[5] This is a short text of seven lines that first introduces and praises the single syllable. The text prescribes what it calls a dhāraṇī for several healing functions, including toothache, wounds, indigestion, bloating, diarrhea, and "illnesses of the brain."[6] The Tibetan translation lacks either a Sanskrit title or an opening salutation, both of which would be normally expected in a text found in the Tibetan canon. This suggests that, when it was translated, this particular text

[2] See Ben Williams, "Cosmogenesis and Phonematic Emanation," in *The Oxford Handbook of Tantric Studies*, ed. Richard K. Payne and Glen A. Hayes, 795–818 (New York: Oxford University Press, 2024).

[3] Richard K. Payne, *Language in the Buddhist Tantra of Japan: Indic Roots of Mantra* (London: Bloomsbury, 2018), 127.

[4] *Prajñāpāramitā sarvatathāgatamātā Ekākṣarā*, Toh. 23. For a translation, see Stefan Mang, trans., "One-Syllable Prajñāpāramitā," Lotsawa House, 2019, https://www.lotsawahouse.org/words-of-the-buddha/one-syllable-perfection-of-wisdom. Other instances of single-syllable mantra are also known, as for example, Tibetan Classics Translators Guild of New York, trans., *The Noble Procedure for Mañjuśrī's Single-Syllable Mantra* (84000: https://read.84000.co/translation/toh550.html).

[5] Toh. 550, known only in Tibetan translation.

[6] Tibetan Classics Translators Guild of New York, trans, *The Noble Procedure for Mañjuśrī's Single-Syllable Mantra*, 10.

was in circulation as simply an independent piece of healing magic, and that it had not been edited as "scripture."[7]

Taking into account the physical materials that constitute our record of dhāraṇī texts, Davidson comments that "the boundaries between practices, coded phrases [dhāraṇī], texts, and textual bundles are very fluid, a point that is evident the more one looks into *dhāraṇī* materials."[8] Like mantra, dhāraṇī are found throughout the Mahāyāna tradition, and they relate to older practices recorded in the Pāli traditions, which in turn are rooted in Vedic ritual. Dhāraṇī texts began being produced before the compilation of systematic tantras, and they continued to be produced and employed throughout the tantric era in India.

Because of this widespread use and divergence from more ordinary doctrinal texts, dhāraṇī have been the object of a now rather long-standing debate in Western scholarship regarding what they are or how they can be defined, and whether they, and the texts that record and transmit them, are properly considered tantric or not.[9] Like other components of tantric praxis, dhāraṇī are doctrinally flexible and difficult to define succinctly.[10] Not only modern academics but also Buddhist scholastics have attempted to define and categorize dhāraṇī. The Sanskrit root is √dhṛ, meaning to hold, and more broadly to grasp, to retain, and to uphold.[11] This semantic range informs the frequent Buddhist explanations that dhāraṇī are mnemonic devices—an aid "to retain the words of Buddhist scriptures (dharmadhāraṇī), to retain magical incantations (mantradhāraṇī), and to imbue oneself with the bodhisattva virtue of patient acceptance (kṣāntilābābhāya dhāraṇī)."[12] In addition

[7] The Tibetan translation is placed after the start of the ninth century, but before the time of the "History of Buddhism" written by Buston (1290–1364). See Tibetan Classics Translators Guild of New York, trans., *The Noble Procedure for Mañjuśrī's Single-Syllable Mantra*, § i.3.

[8] Ronald M. Davidson "Studies in Dhāraṇī Literature I: Revisiting the Meaning of the Term *Dhāraṇī*." *Journal of Indian Philosophy* 37.2 (April 2009): 97–147, 127. DOI: 10.1007/s10781-008-9054.

[9] See Ryan Richard Overbey, "Vicissitudes of Text and Rite in the *Great Peahen Queen of Spells*," in *Tantric Traditions in Transmission and Translation*, ed. David B. Gray and Ryan Richard Overbey, 257–283 (Oxford: Oxford University Press, 2016), 260. See also Jacob Dalton, "How Dhāraṇīs WERE Proto-Tantric: Liturgies, Ritual Manuals, and the Origins of the Tantras," in *Tantric Traditions on the Move*, ed. David B. Gray and Ryan Overbey, 199–229 (Oxford: Oxford University Press, 2016).

[10] Ryan Richard Overbey, "Memory, Rhetoric, and Education in the Great Lamp of the Dharma Dhāraṇī Scripture," PhD diss. (Harvard University, 2010), 11. Because of this flexibility and definitional difficulty, the various glosses that have been offered would each need to be contextualized. In this work, we instead choose to leave the term untranslated.

[11] Overbey, "Memory, Rhetoric, and Education," 6.

[12] Overbey, "Memory, Rhetoric, and Education," 6–7.

to the mnemonic, many other benefits such as protection are said to follow from reciting dhāraṇī.[13]

It is claimed, for example, that the dhāraṇī of the Noble King of the Sound of the Drum[14] will—if recited properly—assure the practitioner a vision of the Buddha Aparimitāyus[15] in his pure land.[16] Similarly, the dhāraṇī text, "The Dhāraṇī 'Essence of Immeasurable Longevity and Wisdom,'" makes it clear that proper practice involves not only reciting with the proper pronunciation but also prostrating, being dressed in clean clothes, and making offerings of flowers and incense. The practice is to be sustained over ten days, three times during the day, and three times during the night.

Attempting to conclusively define dhāraṇī and their functions, however, would produce an ahistorical and decontextualized understanding. Recognizing the variety and flexibility of functions ascribed to dhāraṇī highlights the importance of context, use, and designation in forming categories. Instead of abstract categories, our interest here is with dhāraṇī praxes. Such praxes have been widespread in the Buddhist cosmopolis, enduring into the present.

While scholars have debated how to think about dhāraṇī as a particular linguistic form, bibliographers have generally classified dhāraṇī texts as tantras. Two examples are "The Discourse of the Dhāraṇī of the Buddha's Essence"[17]and "The Noble Dhāraṇī of the Tathāgata Jñānolka That Purifies All Rebirths,"[18] located in the tantric section of both the Chinese and Tibetan

[13] Overbey notes that this "use of *dhāraṇīs* as apotropaic charms and magical incantations" has been an embarrassing fact for those committed to a modernist vision of Buddhism as a rational system of ethical self-improvement. Overbey, "Memory, Rhetoric, and Education," 7. This also probably contributed to the dismissive attitude toward tantric Buddhism long held by Western scholars. Although these attitudes persist in some of the secularizing discourse, that is outside the concerns of this work. See Richard K. Payne, ed., *Secularizing Buddhism: New Perspectives on a Dynamic Tradition* (Boulder, CO: Shambhala Publications, 2021).

[14] Amṛtadundubhisvararāja. Although this name has a variety of possible meanings, it is generally taken to be another name for Amitābha or Amitāyus. Dharmachakra Translation Committee, "The Dhāraṇī 'Essence of Immeasurable Longevity and Wisdom'" (84000: Translating the Words of the Buddha, https://read.84000.co/translation/toh676.html), § i.8.

[15] Although generally taken to be another name for Amitāyus, there is also reason to consider that, in addition to Amitābha, this a third buddha. This also highlights the malleability of the concept of "buddha," as distinct from the singular identity often assumed by analogy with Christian conceptions.

[16] Dharmachakra Translation Committee, "The Dhāraṇī 'Essence of Immeasurable Longevity and Wisdom,'" §1.13.

[17] Āryabuddhahṛdayanāmadhāraṇīdharmaparyāya: Shobusshindarinikyō T. *Mikkyō* 2, vol. XIX, no. 918; and Toh. 514, Dege Kangyur, vol. 88 (rgyud 'bum, na), folios 27.b–29.b (1737, f. 44.b–46.b in later printings). "The Discourse of the Dhāraṇī of the Buddha's Essence," trans. The Dharmachakra Translation Committee (84000: Translating the Words of the Buddha, 2020, https://read.84000.co/translation/toh514.html).

[18] Āryajñānolkanāmadhāraṇīsarvagatipariśodhanī, T. *Mikkyō* 4, vol. XXI, no. 1398; Toh. 522, Degé Kangyur, vol. 88 (rgyud 'bum, na), fol. 42.a–43.b (in 1737, fol. 59.a–60.b in later). "The Dhāraṇī

canons. However, these categories are porous and not sharply definitive.[19] Bibliographic categories are themselves fuzzy, and therefore need to be complemented by considering context and use, as well as bibliographic designation. As a type of practice, dhāraṇī recitation is supported by a system of thought, and the dialectic between the two has enabled dhāraṇī as a praxis to endure as an institution through the Buddhist cosmopolis.

Dhāraṇī and Agency

That a dhāraṇī is the centripetal figure at the focus of a praxis raises the issue of agency. In the field of religious studies, and in Western thought generally, agency is usually located in an anthropomorphic figure, and it is taken to imply the existence of conscious intent, or will. In tantric praxis (and Indic religious culture more generally), however, the concept of agency is more complex. For example, a dhāraṇī is itself considered to have agency directly, in some cases as an expression of the karmically effective commitments of buddhas and bodhisattvas. Similarly, some dhāraṇī are talked about as powers that bodhisattvas possess. Rather than always serving as prayer, invocation, entreaty, spell, or petition directed toward some anthropomorphic supernatural agent, dhāraṇī and mantra are often understood as having direct agency—though that agency may lie in the power of speech as such or derive from another source.[20] "The Dhāraṇī 'Essence of Immeasurable Longevity and Wisdom'" is part of the praxis of a relatively little known buddha, Aparimitāyus. A buddha and that buddha's name constitute an identity, as indicated when the Buddha who teaches the dhāraṇī goes on to explain:

of the Tathāgata Jñānolka," trans. Dharmachakra Translation Committee (84000 Translating the Words of the Buddha, 2021, https://read.84000.co/translation/toh522.html).

[19] For example, in neither the Tibetan nor the Chinese canon are all dhāraṇī texts classed in the tantric volumes. An instance of this is the "Dhāraṇī of the Jewel Torch," which is found in the "general sūtra section" (*mdo sde*) of the Tibetan canon and in the volume of Kegon (Avataṁsaka sūtra) texts in the Chinese. Ratnokāldhāraṇī, T. *Kegon* 2, vol. X, no. 299; Toh. 145, Degé Kangyur, vol. 57 (*mdo sde, pa*), fol. 34.a–82.a, trans. David Jackson (84000: Translating the Words of the Buddha, 2020, https://read.84000.co/translation/toh145.html).

[20] The distinction between ordinary language and extraordinary language is, like the others discussed throughout this volume, not a sharp delineation.

> "Monks, any monk, nun, male lay practitioner, or female lay practitioner who bears in mind the name of the Thus-Gone Aparimitāyus will never have to face any dangers from fire, dangers from water, dangers from poison, dangers from weapons, dangers from yakṣas, and dangers from rākṣasas, except for those that arise due to the ripening of previous actions."[21]

The protective agency is the *name* of Aparimitāyus. In other cases, such as that of Avalokiteśvara, the bodhisattva is said to manifest to protect the devotee when their name is recited; that is, the dhāraṇī is understood to evoke the bodhisattva's presence.[22]

Many dhāraṇī, such as those found in several chapters of the Lotus Sutra, are treated simply as existing, and they are "held" by bodhisattvas, like powerful objects of some kind. Others are "established" by a buddha or bodhisattva, such as the Great Compassion Dhāraṇī (which is also called a mantra, demonstrating the porosity of these categories). The Great Compassion Dhāraṇī is understood to be an expression of the compassion of Avalokiteśvara Bodhisattva.[23] The historical spread of dhāraṇī praxes demonstrates their importance in the history of tantric Buddhism in East Asia.

What Came Before and Continues After the Tang: Dharāṇī Praxes

Dhāraṇī have been part of East Asian Buddhist practice from relatively early, and they constitute an important part of the background upon which the tantric movement developed in China. And dhāraṇī practices have continued to be an important part of East Asian Buddhism right into the present. Laypeople who use and share these practices seem to have little concern with the kind of questions scholars have asked, such as whether dhāraṇī are meaningful or are tantric, but are instead concerned with the efficacy of dhāraṇī recitation.[24]

[21] Dharmachakra Translation Committee, "The Dhāraṇī 'Essence of Immeasurable Longevity and Wisdom,'" §1.16

[22] The distinction between evoke, to make present by sounding the name, and invoke, to call to a superior power, is important, especially as most tantric ritual evokes the presence of buddhas, bodhisattvas, and guardians into a ritual space.

[23] Maria Dorothea Reis-Habito, *Die Dhāraṇī des Großen Erbarmens des Bodhisattva Avalokiteśvara mit tausend Händen und Augen: Übersetzung und Untersuchung ihrer textlichen Grundlage sowie Erforschung ihres Kultes in China* (Nettetal: Steyler Verlag, 1993).

[24] The debate over whether mantra and dhāraṇī are language often fails to make pragmatic distinctions. Some arguments that mantra and dhāraṇī are language hinge on a lexical understanding

Dhāraṇī in Indic Buddhism

Dhāraṇī are found throughout Buddhist history, and they are one kind of "extraordinary language," that is, linguistic expressions that are not communicative in the way that language is ordinarily understood to function.[25] Like other components of tantric praxis, there is nothing "inherently" tantric about dhāraṇī. They are part of Buddhist practice from its early history, and they are one of the practices that conveyed beliefs and symbolism from that early period into tantra and then on into the present. Given the continuity of these beliefs and practices, they are only identifiably tantric when located in a tantric context, put to a tantric use, or designated as tantric. The issues of continuity in relation to changing context, use, and designation are evidenced by the Great Peahen Queen of Spells (*Mahāmayūrīvidyārajñī*).[26]

Both the symbolism of the peahen and the function of protective recitations (Pāli *paritta*) are found in the Pāli texts.[27] The protective function of the peahen can be traced further back to peahens as slayers of snakes, noted for example in the Atharvaveda.[28] Because it is both early in China and exists in several different recensions, the Great Peahen Queen of Spells (*Mahāmayūrīvidyārajñī*) is an important instance of this literature.[29]

of language, that is, the possibility of rendering terms into meaningful English words. But the ability to do so does not mean that in use the mantra or dhāraṇī is communicative in the way that ordinary language is—hence the need for a new category, that is, "extraordinary language."

[25] Richard K. Payne, "On Not Understanding Extraordinary Language in the Buddhist Tantra of Japan," *Religions* 8.10 (2017): 223; https://doi.org/10.3390/rel8100223; Payne, *Language in the Buddhist Tantra of Japan*.

[26] English translation from the Tibetan version: Dharmachakra Translation Committee, trans., "The Queen of Incantations: The Great Peahen" (84000: Translating the Words of the Buddha, 2023, https://read.84000.co/translation/toh559.html). Ch. trans. T. 982, by Amoghavajra. A very important study of this latter text is J. F. Marc des Jardins, *Le sūtra de la Mahāmāyūrī: rituel et politique dans la Chine des Tang (618–907)* (Québec: Les Presses de L'Université Laval, 2011).

[27] See, for example, V. F. Gunaratna, trans., "The Peacock's Prayer for Protection," #8 in *The Book of Protection:* Paritta (Access to Insight, https://www.accesstoinsight.org/lib/authors/piyadassi/protection.html#s8).

[28] Atharvaveda VII/56. P. Gupta, "Hymns of Garutman in Atharva Veda," *Proceedings of the Indian History Congress* 47.1 (1986): 130–137, 132.

[29] The simplest version of this text (T. 986) was translated into Chinese in the late fourth century (Overbey, "Memory, Rhetoric, and Education," 258, also Overbey, "Vicissitudes of Text and Rite"). Henrik Sørensen has suggested that this early recension of the *Mahāmayūrīvidyārajñī* may include "one of the earliest references in Chinese to the type of yogic mastery of supramundane powers connected with the use of spells . . . that we encounter with greater frequency in the later esoteric Buddhist literature." (Henrik Sørensen, "The Spell of the Great, Golden Peacock Queen: The Origin, Practices, and Lore of an Early Esoteric Buddhist Tradition in China," *Pacific World: Journal of the Institute of Buddhist Studies*, third series, no. 8 [Fall 2006]: 89–123, 95.) Amoghavajra is credited with translating another version of the Great Peahen Queen of Spells (T. 982). These are two of the several Great Peahen texts, which survive "in many versions, including six Chinese translations, a Tibetan translation, in Sanskrit manuscripts, and as part of a later ritual collection called the

And the dhāraṇī itself has several different transcriptions.[30] Lokesh Chandra has rendered the dhāraṇī into English as follows:

> Adoration to the Triple Gem. Adoration to the noble Avalokiteśvara, bodhisattva-mahāsattva, the Great Compassionate One. Om. Having paid adoration to One who protects in all dangers, here is the [recitation] of the names of Nīlakaṇṭha [i.e., a name for Avalokiteśvara], as chanted by noble Avalokiteśvara. I shall enunciate the heart [dhāraṇī] that ensures all purposes, is pure and invincible for all beings, and that purifies the path of existence. Thus: Om. Oh Effulgence, World-Transcendent, come oh Hari, the great bodhisattva, descend, descend. Bear in mind my heart-dhāraṇī. Accomplish, accomplish the work. Hold fast, hold fast, Victor, oh Great Victor. Hold on, hold on, oh Lord of the Earth. Move, move, oh my immaculate image. Come, come, Thou with the black serpent as Thy sacred thread. Destroy every poison. Quick, quick, oh Strong Being. Quick, quick, O Hari. Descend, descend, come down, come down, condescend, condescend. Being enlightened, enlighten me, O merciful Nīlakaṇṭha. Gladden my heart by appearing unto me. To the Siddha, hail. To the Great Siddha, hail. To the Lord of Siddha Yogins, hail. To Nīlakaṇṭha, hail. To the Boar-Faced One, hail. To One with the face of Narasiṁha, hail. To One who has a lotus in His hand, hail. To the Holder of a cakra in His hand, hail. To One who sports a lotus[?] in his Hand, hail. To Nīlakaṇṭha the Tiger, hail. To the mighty Śaṅkara, hail. Adoration to the Triple Gem. Adoration to noble Avalokiteśvara, hail.[31]

Fivefold Protection (Pañcarakṣā)." (Overbey, "Vicissitudes of Text and Rite," 257. An extensive study of the rakṣa literature is found in Peter Skilling, "The Rakṣā Literature of the Śrāvakayāna," *Journal of the Pali Text Society* XVI (1992): 109–182. Two of the five are available in English translation: the "Great Upholder of the Secret Mantra" (*Mahāmantrānudhāriṇī*, Toh. 563, https://read.84000.co/translation/UT22084-090-007.html) and "Destroyer of the Great Trichiliocosm" (*Mahāsāhasrapramardanīnāsūtra*, Toh. 558 https://read.84000.co/translation/UT22084-090-002.html), both Dharmachakra Translation Committee, tr., 84000: Translating the Words of the Buddha (https://84000.co/).

[30] "There are at least eight different Chinese transcriptions of this dhāraṇī and two Tibetan transcriptions, suggesting that different Sanskrit recensions of the spell were in circulation" ("Qianshou jing," in *The Princeton Dictionary of Buddhism*, ed. Robert E. Buswell, Jr., and Donald S. Lopez, Jr. [Princeton, NJ: Princeton University Press, 2014], 689). One example is found in William J. Giddings, "The Sūtra on the Dhāraṇī of the Vast, Complete, and Unobstructed Great Compassion of the Bodhisattva Avalokiteśvara with a Thousand Hands and a Thousand Eyes," in *Buddhism and Medicine: An Anthology of Premodern Sources*, ed. C. Pierce Salguero, 252–285 (New York: Columbia University Press, 2017), 260.

[31] Lokesh Chandra, *The Thousand-Armed Avalokiteśvara* (New Delhi: Indira Gandhi National Centre for the Arts, 1988), 133.

This dhāraṇī makes it clear that it is the *names* of Avalokiteśvara that evoke the bodhisattva and the protection promised in the sūtra. Despite the appearance of semantic content in Chandra's rendering, Giddings explains that the dhāraṇī is "[t]ypically recited in transliteration with little concern for its literal meaning."[32]

The Pure Land sutras tell us that reciting the *name* of Amitābha assures birth in Sukhāvatī, the Western Pure Land. That result, however, is achieved without Amitābha's direct intervention, but rather through the power of Amitābha's vow.[33] In the same way it is "holding" the Great Compassion Dhāraṇī that is effective in gaining aid from "virtuous gods and dragon-kings" when the dhāraṇī holder is in peril.[34] Despite the apparent semantic significance that can be elicited from dhāraṇī, for many practitioners the value is not semantic—they are not "saying" anything in the sense of communicating cognitive content to another person. In his *Bodhisattvabhūmi*, Asaṅga (fl. fourth century CE) makes this point quite clearly. His text identifies four kinds of dhāraṇī, one of which is for the attainment of forbearance. A specific instance of a dhāraṇī for forbearance is the mantra *iṭi miṭi kiṭi bhikṣānti padāni svā hā*—again delineating the absence of any sharp delineation between mantra and dhāraṇī. Asaṅga goes on to explain that

> Having correctly undertaken [the practice of] these mantra spells and without having heard their meaning from anyone else, he or she realizes it in the following manner: "There is no realization of the meaning of these mantra spells. They do not contain any meaning. Their meaning is that they have no meaning." Following that, he or she does not seek any further meaning. In this way, he or she gains a correct realization of the meanings of these mantra spells.[35]

32 Giddings, "The Sūtra on the Dhāraṇī," 253.

33 From the perspective of the sutras, the vow is effective because Amitābha has become a buddha and thus fulfilled the terms of the vow. But that also means that, as a buddha, Amitābha has ceased being reborn and no longer exists. Only the vow continues to exist and be active; that is, it is the vow that has agency.

34 Lee Kane, "Great Compassion Mantra: Purification, Healing and Protection, the Maha Karuna Dharani Sutra—Benefiting All Beings," https://buddhaweekly.com/great-compassion-mantra-purification-healing-protection-maha-karuna-dharani-sutra-benefiting-beings.

35 Ārya Asaṅga, *The Bodhisattva Path to Unsurpassed Enlightenment: A Complete Translation of the* Bodhisattvabhūmi, trans. Artemus B. Engle (Boulder, CO: Snow Lion, 2016), 449.

In other words, mantra and dhāraṇī are not meaningful in the same way that ordinary language is.[36] This problematizing of meaning de-reifies language and undermines the habitual mistaken belief that language works because it refers to substantially existing essences of one kind or another.[37] Dhāraṇī are instances of extraordinary language—that is, they do not communicate information, nor do they have referential meaning.[38]

The understanding of dhāraṇī presented by Asaṅga—that they are meaningless and therefore a means for realizing the emptiness of language—is not shared by all Buddhist teachers, however. Boting Xufa (1641–1728), for example, asserted not only that dhāraṇī are semantically meaningful, but that they should be translated. Xufa is primarily remembered as a Huayan scholar because of his work in reviving the tradition during the Qing dynasty (1636–1912).[39] He also, however, studied tantric teachings, mostly through the translations attributed to Amoghavajra. For Xufa, translating dhāraṇī was an expression of "the compatibility between the exegetical and esoteric traditions."[40] Although recognizing that several earlier scholars had resisted the translation of dhāraṇī, based on other sources, he argues that while perhaps the full meaning cannot be rendered into contemporary vernacular, it is better to render at least some part of the meaning than not. In Xufa's view, translating dhāraṇī generates merit, just as does translating sutras. Such debates over the semantic significance of dhāraṇī, however, seem to have been of intellectual concern, rather than having had any direct effect on the use of dhāraṇī, either in ritual *per se* or as a popular act of devotion or petition.

[36] Speaking of Tang-era China when printed dhāraṇī were buried as part of funerary offerings, T. H. Barrett points out that "The fact that these printed words were never destined for human readers indicates the perils of attempting to understand Buddhist printing solely in light of the European experience" ("Buddhism and Print Culture in China," in *The Oxford Encyclopedia of Buddhism*, ed. Richard K. Payne and Georgios T. Halkias, 319–332 [New York: Oxford University Press, 2024; online 2019: https://doi.org/10.1093/acrefore/9780199340378.013.636], 320).

[37] Buddhist literature does include interpretations of dhāraṇī as semantically significant, or as communicating performatively. The category of extraordinary language, however, applies to these views when their nuances are taken into account. See Ryan Richard Overbey, "'Why Don't We Translate Spells in the Scriptures?': Medieval Exegesis on the Meaning and Function of *Dhāraṇī* Language," *Journal of the International Association of Buddhist Studies* 42 (2019): 493–514.

[38] The informative function of language is taken as fundamental to other functions, such as questions and commands—which are seen as variations of the informative. And, while there is some similarity to exclamatory and performative functions, these grammatical categories are also not fully accurate representations of extraordinary language.

[39] Chi Chen Ho, "The Śūraṃgama Dhāraṇī in Sinitic Buddhist Context: From the Tang Dynasty through the Contemporary Period," PhD diss. (UCLA, 2010), 107.

[40] Ho, "The Śūraṃgama Dhāraṇī in Sinitic Buddhist Context," 111.

Ideas regarding the efficacy of extraordinary language also extended to sutras as a whole. The Heart Sutra not only closes with a mantra but is considered to be a dhāraṇī in its entirety[41]—quite appropriately in the sense of helping one to retain the buddhadharma in memory, since it includes summary lists of many key Buddhist concepts. Other entire texts, such as the Diamond Sutra[42] and the Lotus Sutra,[43] have also been thought to be directly efficacious. Similarly, the title of the Lotus Sutra is also considered by some to be directly effective.[44] This complex of conceptions regarding the agency of dhāraṇī and the potency of spoken sounds provides an important conceptual basis for the development of tantric Buddhism in East Asia.

Dhāraṇī as Ground for the Mantra School (Zhenyan): Third Century to Tang

Dhāraṇī and related ritual practices were part of the cultural foundations for the establishment of Chinese tantric Buddhism (Zhenyanzong, mantra school, or Kaiyuanzong, school of the Kaiyuan era [713–741],[45] or Mizong, esoteric school) in the Tang era (618–907). Prior to the Tang, a variety of Buddhist works, including dhāraṇī texts, were translated into Chinese. Representative of the dhāraṇī texts is the *Mo teng ch'ieh ching (Mātangīsūtra*[46]) translated by Chu Lü-yen (also called Chu Chiang-yen) in 230 CE. This sutra not only includes six dhāraṇīs but also instructions for

[41] Jan Nattier, "The *Heart Sūtra*: A Chinese Apocryphal Text?" *Journal of the International Journal of Buddhist Studies* 15.2 (1992): 153–223, 153. See also Donald S. Lopez, *Elaborations on Emptiness: Uses of the* Heart Sutra (Princeton, NJ: Princeton University Press, 1996).

[42] Shih-shan Susan Huang, "Illustrating the Efficacy of the *Diamond Sutra* in Vernacular Buddhism," *National Palace Museum Quarterly* (2018): 35–120.

[43] Yoshiko K. Dykstra, "Miraculous Tales of the Lotus Sutra: The *Dainihonkoku Hokkegenki*," *Monumenta Nipponica* 32.2 (Summer 1977): 189–210.

[44] Jacqueline Stone, "Nichiren," in *The Oxford Encyclopedia of Buddhism*, ed. Richard K. Payne and Georgios T. Halkias, 1760–1779 (New York: Oxford University Press, online 2020: https://doi.org/10.1093/acrefore/9780199340378.013.575, 2024). Again, these conceptions regarding the power of sound or of the spoken word, not its conceptual content, remain a part of present-day popular Buddhist understandings. For example, a web search for testimonials to the power of the title of the Lotus Sutra (*daimoku*) yielded dozens of pages making just that claim.

[45] This name refers to the arrival of Śubhakarasiṃha in the capital, Chang'an, in the fourth year of the Kaiyuan era, that is, in 716. Wei Wu, *Esoteric Buddhism in China: Engaging Japanese and Tibetan Traditions, 1912–1949* (New York: Columbia University Press, 2024), 32.

[46] T. 1300, K. 766, Toh. 358, the title of which has been rendered from the Tibetan as "The Exemplary Tale of Śārdūlakarṇa," 84000: Translating the Words of the Buddha (https://read.84000.co/section/O1JC114941JC14668.html).

ritual actions that accompany their recitation.[47] Chu Lü-yen's collaborator Chih Ch'ien also translated several texts of dhāraṇīs, though these do not include instructions for ritual, and several other figures produced translations of tantric materials.[48] Various other tantric texts were translated from the third century on, and several individual tantric practitioners were active. These translations and activities served to make tantra accessible in East Asia, providing a cultural reservoir of concepts and practices for the establishment of an institutional form of tantra.[49] Instrumental in institutionalizing tantric praxis in East Asia are three figures: Śubhākarasiṃha (637–735), Vajrabodhi (671–741), and Amoghavajra (705–774).[50] Śubhākarasiṃha arrived in the capital city of Ch'ang-an in 716 CE.[51] Shortly thereafter, in 720 CE, Vajrabodhi came to China, where Amoghavajra became his disciple.[52]

[47] One of these rituals is a simple fire ritual, which seems to be the earliest known ritual use of fire in East Asian Buddhism. The homa ritual *per se* is a particularly important marker of tantric Buddhism, as it is a key element found throughout tantra—Hindu, Buddhist, and Jain, in India, East Asia, and today globally, from its earliest recorded beginnings into the present. Despite the *Mātangīsūtra*'s fire ritual having been taken by some scholars as a predecessor to the homa in East Asia, it seems at most to provide a kind of symbolic antecedent. Michel Strickmann, "Homa in East Asia," in *Agni: The Vedic Ritual of the Fire Altar*, ed. Frits Staal, 2 vols. (Berkeley, CA: Asian Humanities Press, 1983), II: 426.

[48] Other translators and monks who are known to have worked with tantric materials during this time include the following: Master Dharmarakṣa, early fourth century; Fo-t'u-ch'eng, died 348 CE; Śrīmitra, died between 335 and 342 CE; She-kung, died 380 CE; Dharmakṣema/T'an-wu-ch'an, died 433 CE; T'an-yao, mid-fifth century; the translator of the *Mo-li-chih-t'ien ching* (*Mārīcīdhāraṇī*, T. 1256, K. 311), Liang dynasty (618 to 906 CE); Atigupta/A-ti-ch'u-to, mid-seventh century; Punyodaya, mid-seventh century; and I-ching, 635 to 713 CE. Chou Yi-liang, "Tantrism in China," *Harvard Journal of Asiatic Studies* 8.3/4 (March 1945): 241–332, 242–246, reprinted in Richard K. Payne, ed., *Tantric Buddhism in East Asia* (Boston: Wisdom Publications, 2005).

[49] Daoism provided another cultural reservoir; see Christine Mollier, *Buddhism and Taoism Face to Face: Scripture, Ritual, and Iconographic Exchange in Medieval China* (Honolulu: University of Hawai'i Press, 2009).

[50] Conventionally sometimes referred to as the "three founders," this appellation reflects the sectarian historiography of Shingon and has polemical significance—for which reason we will avoid it here. We note that the received tradition regarding the history of tantric Buddhism in China has been molded by the Japanese sectarian scholarship and the implicit utilization of Japan's "three countries" model of the history of Buddhism, a teleology of ongoing progress in the teachings as they were first exported from India, to China, and then on to Japan, though there were also counternarratives of decline as well.

[51] Regarding the Sanskrit back-translation of Shanwuwei's name, see Charles Willemen, "Tripitaka Shan-wu-wei's Name: A Chinese Translation from Prākrit," *T'oung Pao* 67 (1981): 362–365. Here we follow the common practice of rendering it as Śubhākarasiṃha.

[52] Our present understanding of these figures is in large part drawn from the work of the monk Zanning (919–1001 CE), who served the Song emperor Taizong (939–997). During the Song dynasty, Zanning became the head of the sangha, and based on several earlier works, between 982 and 988 CE, he compiled a collection of biographies known as the "Lives of Eminent Monks Composed in the Song" (Chou, "Tantrism in China," 248–250). As important as Zanning is as a source, Geoffrey Goble has noted that "Zanning's explanations are multiple and seemingly contradictory" (Geoffrey C. Goble, *Chinese Esoteric Buddhism: Amoghavajra, the Ruling Elite, and the Emergence of a Tradition* [New York: Columbia University Press, 2019], 212). On Amoghavajra's background, see Mariko Namba Walter, *Sogdians and Buddhism*, Sino-Platonic Papers 174 (Philadelphia: Department of

Tang (618–907): Dhāraṇī and Dhāraṇī Praxes

Dhāraṇī praxes—that is, dhāraṇis themselves, beliefs about their efficacy, the practices employed to put them into effect, material objects on which they were inscribed, and the texts recording them—constitute an important part of the broad flow of tantric praxis beginning in the third century, running through the pivotal period of the Tang dynasty, and continuing into the present. The importance of dhāraṇī for Tang society is evident by the fact that, dating from second half of the eighth century, the first printed text is a dhāraṇī. As condensations of the Buddha's teachings, they functioned like relics—making present the potency of the dharma.[53]

Also evidencing the idea that dhāraṇī are potent are dhāraṇī pillars, which are constructed as "a free-standing stone column, most often octagonal in shape."[54] Erecting such pillars, known in Chinese as "banners" (Ch. *chuang*), is a visible expression of a dhāraṇī praxis. These pillars "are mostly found in the central, eastern and southern parts of China .... [and] are also known in Vietnam, Korea, and Japan, where they are not necessarily octagonal."[55] Many dhāraṇī pillars were engraved with the dhāraṇī known as the "Incantation of the Glorious Buddha's Crown" (*Budhoṣṇīṣa vijayā dhāraṇī*[56] variously rendered, e.g., "Incantation of Glory"[57]). This dhāraṇī was promoted by Amoghavajra, who encouraged memorization and regular recitation by monks for the protection of the Tang state.[58] Praxes centering on the "Incantation of the Glorious Buddha's Crown" include copying out the sutra and placing the copy in a high location so that those seeing it have its shadow cast upon them—such as by a pillar—or are touched by dust that had been in contact with it.[59] Anyone engaging with the dhāraṇī in these ways

East Asian Languages and Civilizations, University of Pennsylvania, 2006): 30 (www.sino-platonic.org).

[53] Barrett, "Buddhism and Print Culture in China," 320.

[54] Liying Kuo, "Dhāraṇī Pillars in China: Functions and Symbols," in *China and Beyond in the Mediaeval Period: Cultural Crossings and Inter-Regional Connections*, ed. Dorothy C. Wang and Gustav Heldt, 351–385 (New Delhi: Manohar, 2014), 351.

[55] Kuo, "Dhāraṇī Pillars in China," 352.

[56] Various translations, T. 967, 968, 969, 970, 971; Kuo, "Dhāraṇī Pillars in China," 380. However, T. 967 was the only translation employed for dhāraṇī pillars; Kuo, "Dhāraṇī Pillars in China," 356.

[57] See Paul Copp, *The Body Incantatory: Spells and the Ritual Imagination in Medieval Chinese Buddhism* (New York: Columbia University Press, 2014), xiv.

[58] Kuo, "Dhāraṇī Pillars in China," 361.

[59] For a detailed study of one such pillar, see Angela F. Howard, "The *Dhāraṇī* Pillar of Kunming, Yunnan: A Legacy of Esoteric Buddhism and Burial Rites of the Bai People in the Kingdom of Dali (937–1253)," *Artibus Asiae* 57.1/2 (1997): 33–72.

"will be purified from all sins and freed from all unfortunate states of rebirth .... [and] will receive the prediction made by all the Tathāgatas that they will obtain complete and perfect awakening."[60] Devotees of the dhāraṇī are advised to offer flowers and incense, banners, and parasols. After constructing stupas engraved with the dhāraṇī at crossroads, devotees circumambulate them. Sprinkling dust consecrated with the dhāraṇī on a corpse will assure the deceased rebirth in heaven.[61] In the present, practices focused on dhāraṇī "has now been rediscovered in Taiwan and Hong Kong, where Buddhist communities are beginning to erect dhāraṇī pillars."[62]

From Tang to Heian: Shingon

At the beginning of the ninth century, Saichō and Kūkai traveled to China as members of an official delegation to the Tang court.[63] These two monks were to become prominent in the history of Buddhism in Japan, playing key roles in the introduction and propagation of tantric Buddhism there.

Saichō (767–822) was older and already well-established, and in China he received training in the Tiantai tradition. Upon his return to Japan, he would establish the Tendai tradition, which, like its Chinese antecedent, focuses on the Lotus Sutra. Saichō, however, had also had some contact with tantric Buddhism during his time in China and was directed by the emperor to develop an esoteric component for his school along with the Lotus Sutra component.

In the eighth century, tantric texts were available in Japan. Kūkai (774–835), a younger contemporary of Saichō, tells us that he read the *Vairocanābhisaṃbodhi*, but he did not understand it and could find no one

[60] Kuo, "Dhāraṇī Pillars in China," 361.

[61] In Japan this same belief is attached to the "Clear Light Mantra" (*kōmyō shingon* 光明真言) popularized by Myōe Kōben (1173–1232). Mark Unno, *Shingon Refractions: Myōe and the Mantra of Light* (Boston: Wisdom Publications, 2004).

[62] Kuo, "Dhāraṇī Pillars in China," 352.

[63] The complexity of institutional forms in both China and Japan means that the "received wisdom" that organizes history according to the system of modern sects is a misleading artifice. Sectarian history of this kind (along with a focus on founders) has, for example, contributed to the contemporary scholarly focus on Kūkai and Saichō, and the consequent marginalization of several other monks who traveled to China and returned with significant collections of tantric texts (George Keyworth, "Did the Silk Road(s) Extend from Dunhuang, Mount Wutai, and Chang'an to Kyoto, Japan? A Reassessment Based on Material Culture from the Temple Gate Tendai Tradition of Miidera," in *Buddhism in Central Asia II—Practices and Rituals, Visual and Material Transfer*, ed. Yukiyo Kasai and Henrik H. Sørensen, 17–67 [Leiden: Brill, 2022], 36–37).

to explain it to him. He managed to be named to the same delegation to Tang; once there, he sought out the Qinglong Monastery (Green Dragon) in Chang'an, capital of the dynasty. There he was initiated into the ritual cycles of the diamond realm (Skt. *vajradhātu*, or "thunderbolt" realm) and womb realm (Skt. *garbhadhātu*, or "matrix" realm), the two assemblies of buddhas, bodhisattvas, and guardian deities that form the retinue of Mahāvairocana Buddha.[64] It was this dual tradition that he brought back to Japan. After some delay, he was authorized to establish a training center on Kōyasan, and he was given responsibility for a temple at the eastern gate to Heian, Tōji.

According to Ryūichi Abé's convincing analysis, Shingon began as an interpretive discourse about Buddhist praxes, based on the tantric teachings newly introduced by Kūkai. According to this discourse, tantric teachings were simultaneously superior to and already inherent in the Buddhist traditions of Heian Japan in the form of mantra and dhāraṇī. As explained by Abé, Kūkai presented tantric Buddhism as extending the existing forms of Buddhism, not as competing with them.[65] Avoiding direct confrontation, Kūkai represented tantra as a higher, more powerful form of Buddhist teaching complementing and augmenting existing forms, rather than contradicting them. In considering the institutionalization of tantra, Abé's understanding is important as it shifts away from projecting modern institutional categories of sectarian identity onto previous periods.

According to Abé, Kūkai did not set out to establish a competing institution, that is, establish yet another Buddhist sect. Instead, Kūkai promoted a discourse within which components of practice already existing in the six sects of Buddhism established during the preceding Nara period (710–794) and which continued into the Heian (794–1185) could be better actualized by the systematic praxes of tantric Buddhism.

Abé explains that "Shingon was presented as of complementary utility, as a new conceptual and linguistic tool for closing the gap in Nara Buddhist discourse between theory and practice—the gap in which esoteric elements

[64] These assemblies are portrayed in two mandalas, representations of which are found throughout the Shingon tradition. See chapters 2 and 3 in Elizabeth ten Grotenhuis, *Japanese Mandalas: Representations of Sacred Geography* (Honolulu: University of Hawai'i Press, 1999). Also, Aaron Proffitt, "Shingon," in *The Oxford Encyclopedia of Buddhism*, ed. Richard K. Payne and Georgios T. Halkias, 2173–2196 (Oxford: Oxford University Press, online 2022: https://doi.org/10.1093/acrefore/9780199340378.013.767).

[65] Ryuichi Abé, *The Weaving of Mantra: Kūkai and the Construction of Esoteric Buddhist Discourse* (New York: Columbia University Press, 1999). See also Ryuichi Abé, "Saichō and Kūkai: A Conflict of Interpretations," *Japanese Journal of Religious Studies* 22.1–2 (1995): 103–137.

of Nara Buddhism were situated."[66] By highlighting existing components of Nara Buddhism that could be interpreted as tantric, Kūkai changed the context of those components. "To fully grasp the hidden logic behind mantras, mudrās, and other esoteric elements already embedded in their religious practices, the Nara clerics needed to study the *Mahāvairocana Sūtra* [*Vairocanābhisaṃbodhi tantra*], the *Vajraśekhara Sūtra*, and their ritual systems of abhiṣeka [initiation], in which the esoteric language theories of the three mysteries [body, speech and mind] were elucidated."[67] Thus, rather than simply asserting the superiority of Shingon as a new and therefore competing sect, Kūkai presented Shingon as superior "not only because it introduced new types of scriptures and ritual systems but because these texts and rituals would provide the Nara clerics with a theoretical foundation to authenticate their belief in the efficacy of existing Buddhist ritual services in early Heian Japan."[68]

Viewing Kūkai's Shingon as an interpretive discourse about existing practices, and as providing additional authority to the Nara priesthood, avoids presuming that sectarian institutions in competition with one another are the natural institutional form for traditions.[69] This also helps to explain how the tantric teachings were adopted so widely and quickly, becoming pervasive throughout Japanese Buddhism—such that the Zen hermitage in Ohara described in the first chapter would have a directional guardian in its entry and a dhāraṇī in its bathroom.[70]

Kūkai's strategy of presenting Shingon as a unifying discourse that placed tantric understandings at the pinnacle of Buddhist thought was, however, gradually displaced by the institutionalized forms of sectarian Japanese

[66] Abé, *The Weaving of Mantra*, 270.

[67] Abé, *The Weaving of Mantra*, 270.

[68] Abé, *The Weaving of Mantra*, 270.

[69] This historical narrative of Shingon as originally an interpretive discourse is a radical challenge to the modern model of church, sect, and cult that has been normative in religious studies, influential in Buddhist studies, and adopted for the representation of a "Japanese Buddhism." The compound of factors standard to religious studies representations of traditions as religions—deity, founder, unique doctrinal teaching, authoritative text, church preserving the founder's teaching, and so on—is an interpretation, convincing because of its easy application and familiarity, but which organizes the historical record in such a fashion as to make complexity and nuance invisible.

[70] The influence of tantric praxis on the later development of Buddhism in Japan was deep and pervasive, involving both state entities and religious institutions. The relation was framed by Kuroda Toshio as the "esoteric–exoteric system" (*kenmitsu taisei*). Kuroda Toshio, "The Development of the *Kenmitsu* System as Japan's Medieval Orthodoxy," trans. James Dobbins, *Japanese Journal of Religious Studies* 23.3–4 (1996): 233–269. These relations have been extensively studied, and ideas about them have been refined since their introduction. For critiques, see Taira Masayuki, "Kuroda Toshio and the *Kenmitsu Taisei* Theory," trans. Thomas Kirchner, *Japanese Journal of Religious Studies* 23.3–4 (1996): 427–448.

Buddhism. This happened first by the power and authority transmitted through a linked set of lineages and the temples in their charge. Then, in the Tokugawa era (1603–1868), the shogunate authorized institutional structures and limited sectarian activities to specific regions. This finalized the convergence toward institutional uniformity evidenced by Japanese Buddhism as we find it in the present.

Alternatively, framing Shingon as the praxis of Kūkai provides a different perspective. He is the main focus for many adherents, much more so than the figure of Dainichi Nyorai (Mahāvairocana Tathāgata).[71] While the Shikoku pilgrimage discussed below is one dimension of the praxis of Kūkai, many more visitors travel to the mausoleum (Okunoin) on Mt. Kōya, where Kūkai is said to be in deep samādhi. The cemetery on Mt. Kōya developed over centuries and is today a national record of historically important individuals and families. That history effectively begins in 921 when the tomb was opened to announce to Kūkai that he had received the posthumous title of Kōbō Daishi from the emperor Daigo (884–930, r. 897–930). At that time, it was discovered that his hair and nails had grown, which was taken to mean that he was not in fact dead, but rather in deep concentrative meditation, awaiting the arrival of the future buddha, Maitreya.[72]

The continuing living presence of Kūkai on Kōyasan is key to the praxis of Kūkai. George Tanabe notes that the "apotheosis of Kūkai began shortly after his death when admiring disciples expressed their adoration by writing legends of the virtues and miraculous feats of their master."[73] Kūkai had from the time of his early writings expressed his expectation that he would meet Maitreya, the next buddha. Kōyasan was identified as the site at which Maitreya will descend to this earth, and a long-held belief is that Kūkai will emerge from his meditation when Maitreya arrives. Traveling widely in fundraising for Kōyasan, the "holy men of Kōyasan" (*Kōya hijiri*) promoted the practice of having one's ashes located close to Kūkai, establishing karmic connections for when that auspicious event takes place centuries in the

[71] In Shingon thought Dainichi is the active dharmakāya and source of tantric teachings and practices. It is this active dharmakāya that is the teacher in the *Vairocanābhisambodhi tantra*.

[72] Karen L. Brock, "Awaiting Maitreya at Kasagi," in *Maitreya, the Future Buddha*, ed. Alan Sponberg and Helen Hardacre, 214–247 (Cambridge: Cambridge University Press, 1988), 238.

[73] George J. Tanabe, Jr., "The Founding of Mount Kōya and Kūkai's Eternal Meditation," in *Religions of Japan in Practice*, ed. George J. Tanabe, Jr., 354–359 (Princeton, NJ: Princeton University Press, 1999), 354.

future.[74] These fundraising activities spread the praxis of Kūkai across much of Japan.[75]

The Shikoku Pilgrimage as Tantric Institution

Examining the Shikoku pilgrimage shows how some tantric institutions are built. There are two different approaches to writing history, that is, two historiographies. One, probably the more common for religious studies, is the perspective that highlights a singular dramatic act of founding—an event that can definitively be located in a specific time and place, attributed to the actions of specific individuals. This is the "rhetoric of rupture," that is, the claim that some critically significant event separates time into two—the time before that event, and the time after. The other perspective is one that emphasizes gradual development, a focus on changes across the *longue durée*. Metaphorically, this may be described as examining the layers of historical sediment underlaying the present.

Choosing one or the other implicitly conditions what questions can be asked and what answers can be judged satisfactory. Although either historiography could be chosen in response to the research questions being asked, in practice the presuppositions of religious studies focus on the acts of a founder that establish something new and different, creating a rupture from what went before. Within that conceptual framework institutional histories are "naturally" written as involving ruptures and heightening the unique historical acts of the founder. The argument here is not that there is one correct way to write history, but rather that the writing of history requires choices about narrative frames—rupture or continuity—within which the history will be written.[76] Such choices may be made unreflectively in accord with the

[74] *Hijiri* is a modern analytic category grouping together a variety of historical religious categories that shared important similarities. The term was established in English language religious studies literature by Ichiro Hori. See his "On the Concept of the Hijiri (Holy-Man)," *Numen* 5.2 (April 1958): 128–160, and "On the Concept of the Hijiri (Holy-Man) (Continued)," *Numen* 5.3 (September 1958): 199–232. The category of *hijiri* is trans-sectarian, and members were reclusive, itinerant, and practiced austerities in remote locations, such as mountains and forests.

[75] Donald Drummond, "Negotiating Influence: The Pilgrimage Diary of Monastic Imperial Prince Kakuhō—*Omurogosho Kōyasan gosanrō nikki*," PhD diss. (Graduate Theological Union, 2007), 121. Many *hijiri* were active in raising funds for different temple building or restoration projects (*kanjin*, hence *kanjin hijiri*). Janet Goodwin, "Alms for Kasagi Temple," *Journal of Asian Studies* 46.4 (Nov. 1987): 827–841, 829; see also Janet Goodwin, *Alms and Vagabonds: Buddhist Temples and Popular Patronage in Medieval Japan* (Honolulu: University of Hawai'i Press, 1994).

[76] Paul Nietupski makes a similar analysis regarding the Labrang Monastery. He points out that from one perspective the monastery is an extension of the Gelug authority located in Lhasa. Another

presuppositions of the field or, more intentionally, in service to an explicit research program or motivating question.

Institutions such as monasteries might seem to be "naturally" ones with a clear moment of founding, particularly when associated with some charismatic figure. Just two examples are Kūkai's founding of Kōyasan in 819 and the establishment of Sera Monastery by Tsongkhapa in 1409.[77] The rhetoric of rupture contributes to the legends that Kūkai also established the Shikoku pilgrimage.

The historical study of the Shikoku pilgrimage, however, is more convincingly written as a process involving change, continuity, and gradual development. As summarized by Ian Reader,

> The pilgrimage appears to have developed over a number of centuries, out of the travels of ascetics from Kōya, who went to Shikoku to seek out sites connected with the holy founder of their religious institution. Gradually, from the twelfth through the seventeenth centuries, Shikoku came to be a major focus of Daishi [i.e., Kūkai] devotion, and by the mid-seventeenth century a pilgrimage route around the island, incorporating various local temples and mountain religious centers, with eighty-eight sites in all (a number for which no reliable reason has been ascertained) had come into existence.[78]

Countless pilgrims following the route for individual reasons, each with their own ideas about its meaning and significance, have collectively enacted, and continue to enact the institution of the Shikoku pilgrimage. Visiting the two shrines at each temple—one for the chief deity of the temple[79] and one for Kūkai—and reciting mantra and the Heart Sutra, their clothing inscribed with syllables in Siddham script, their pilgrimage books recording each stop

perspective is that it is a complex local institution (Paul Kocot Nietupski, *Labrang Monastery: A Tibetan Buddhist Community on the Inner Asian Borderlands, 1709–1958* [Lanham, MD: Lexington Books, 2011], xviii–xix). Both perspectives are important for a more fully adequate understanding.

[77] José Ignacio Cabezón and Penpa Dorjee, *Sera Monastery* (Boston: Wisdom Publications, 2019), 5.

[78] Ian Reader, "Legends, Miracles, and Faith in Kōbō Daishi, and the Shikoku Pilgrimage," in *Religions of Japan in Practice*, ed. George J. Tanabe, Jr., 360–369 (Princeton, NJ: Princeton University Press, 1999), 361.

[79] For a detailed list of the chief deity of each temple, see Michael Pye, *Japanese Buddhist Pilgrimage* (Sheffield, UK: Equinox, 2015), 83–86.

at a temple with a stamp and calligraphic insignia—this entire complex of practices constitutes the pilgrimage as a tantric institution.[80]

The pilgrimage route encircles the island of Shikoku, covering approximately 759 miles, leading the pilgrim along the coast, into river valleys, and up into the mountains of the island. Although the pilgrimage route is associated with Kūkai, not all the temples are Shingon. Of the eighty-eight temples, five are not Shingon, the affliliations of these being Rinzai (nos. 11 and 33) and Sōtō Zen (no. 15), Tendai (no. 43), and one of the few temples extant today of the otherwise almost forgotten "Ji" sect of Pure Land Buddhism (no. 78).[81] Shikoku lore portrays a founding myth in which Kūkai is "constantly wandering the island dispensing benefits and aiding pilgrims and those that help pilgrims."[82] This myth "originated in the latter-Heian-era travels of ascetic devotees from Mt. Kōya to sites associated with the life of Kūkai (Kōkō Daishi) on the island of his birth, but only coalesced into a pilgrimage route in the latter part of the Muromachi and earlier parts of the Tokugawa eras."[83]

Each of Shikoku's four traditional provinces (now prefectures) has a doctrinal significance attributed to it. The four describe the path of awakening starting with the arising of the intent to awaken (Jpn. *hosshin*) in the first province, Awa (Tokushima Prefecture), temples 1 to 23. The second stage, in Tosa (Kōchi Prefecture), temples 24 to 39, is the stage of practice (Jpn. *shugyō*)—often referring to the practice of austerities. Awakening (Jpn. *bodai*, Skt. *bodhi*) is the third stage in Iyo (Ehime Prefecture), temples 40 to 65. And the final stage is cessation (Jpn. *nehan*, Skt. *nirvana*) from temple 66 to 88 in Sanuki (Kagawa Prefecture).[84] While this structure provides one understanding of the Shikoku pilgrimage, the following offers a rough typology of temple origins. Rough because the categories are not mutually exclusive, nor is the typology comprehensive—in other words, some temples belong to more than one category, and additional categories might be suggested.

[80] An overall description and brief history of the Shikoku pilgrimage is found in the first chapter of Ian Reader and John Schultz, *Pilgrims Until We Die: Unending Pilgrimage in Shikoku* (New York: Oxford University Press, 2021; https://doi.org/10.1093/oso/9780197573587.001.0001), 25–48.

[81] Pye, *Japanese Buddhist Pilgrimage*, 82. On the Jishū sect, see Caitilin J. Griffiths, *Tracing the Itinerant Path: Jishū Nuns of Medieval Japan* (Honolulu: University of Hawai'i Press, 2016), 127–128; revision of "Tracing the Itinerant Path: Jishū Nuns of Medieval Japan," PhD diss. (University of Toronto, 2010).

[82] Reader and Swanson, "Pilgrimage in the Japanese Religious Tradition," 244.

[83] Reader and Swanson, "Pilgrimage in the Japanese Religious Tradition," 244.

[84] Pye, *Japanese Buddhist Pilgrimage*, 78–79.

The goal is to elucidate the dynamics of the gradual development of a tantric institution and the importance of not automatically defaulting to an historiography of rupture.

Dynamics of Temple Origins

Examining the geographic relations between historically important sites supplements traditional historical methods.[85] Discussed in the next chapter, for example, the significance of Borobudur is much more evident when considered in its geographic relation to two other monuments, those of Pawon and Chandi Mendut. In the case of the Shikoku pilgrimage, such a perspective contributes to our understanding of the variety of dynamics by which the temples that became the route were established. The following categories are not mutually exclusive, as the development of any particular temple probably involved a complex of dynamics, some reinforcing each other and others conflicting. Consequently, the typology below is broadly descriptive and suggestive of general patterns.

Trade Routes

Beginning about ten kilometers inland from the sea, the first ten temples form a line along the northern edge of the Yoshino River Valley. This sequence of temples runs about another thirty kilometers inland (i.e., from east to west). The first ten temples are located just up on the side of the hills that line the river valley. Such a position is typical of many of the temples along the entire route, as well as elsewhere in Japan. It seems likely that placing temples on the hillside was in order to not take up valuable agricultural land. Similarly, one suspects that the choice of the north side of the valley, so that a temple faces south, was because this orientation provides more sunlight, particularly during the winter months. The way that these first ten temples line up also suggests that this may have been an old trade and travel route. The Yoshino River goes far up into the mountainous center of the northwest end of the island and would have been a fairly natural communications route,

[85] See, for example, Lionel Rothkrug, "Religious Practices and Collective Perceptions: Hidden Homologies in the Renaissance and Reformation," *Historical Reflections/Réflexions Historiques* 7.1 (Spring 1980): 1–251.

especially given the proximity of the mouth of the Yoshino River across the Seto Inland Sea to both Wakayama and, via the intermediary island of Awaji, to Kobe. The suggestion that these may be old transportation routes is supported by similarities to patterns of local systems in China studied by G. William Skinner[86] and P. Steven Sangren.[87]

Practice

From no. 10, the route turns south, crosses the now relatively narrow valley, and leads to no. 11, which is located on the southern edge of the valley. The next temple, Shōsan-ji (no. 12), is an example of a second category of temples on the route. It is located very high up in the mountains (800 m/2,400 ft[88]), far from any city or village (it is, for example, approximately 30 km from no. 11 to no. 12, and another 30 km from no. 12 to no. 13[89]). As in the case of other, more famous temples, for example, Hiei-zan and Kōya-san, such a location might have been chosen because of its remoteness, or because of some preexisting mountain worship. Other temples in this group are Kakurin ji (550 m/1,650 ft; no. 20), Tairyō ji (610 m/1,800 ft; no. 21), Yokomine ji (700 m/2,100 ft; no. 60), and Upen ji (911 m/2,700 ft; no. 66).[90] Being located at high altitudes also means that they are deep in the mountains, distant from other locales.

Although not so notably high, another temple that could be considered part of this group is Iwaya ji (no. 45). This temple is located in an old river gorge where there are very steep bluffs. When running high, the river carved grottoes and caves into the walls of the gorge. The legend of the site is that it was "donated to Kōbō Daishi by a mysterious female recluse named Hokke-sennin."[91] The site is reputed to have been a location "where recluses and mountain wanderers once took ascetic disciplines."[92] Probably chosen for practice because of its remote location, the site is also continuous with the

[86] G. William Skinner, "Cities and the Hierarchy of Local Systems," in *The City in Late Imperial China*, ed. G. William Skinner, 275–351 (Stanford, CA: Stanford University Press, 1977); and "Marketing and Social Structure in Rural China, Part I," *Journal of Asian Studies* 24.1 (1964): 3–43.

[87] P. Steven Sangren, *History and Magical Power in a Chinese Community* (Stanford, CA: Stanford University Press, 1987).

[88] Taisen Miyata, *Henro Pilgrimage* (Sacramento: Northern California Koyasan Temple, 1984), 14.

[89] *Shikoku Hachi-ju Ha ka Sho* (2 vols., 1982), II.268.

[90] Miyata, *Henro Pilgrimage*, 14.

[91] Miyata, *Henro Pilgrimage*, 96.

[92] Miyata, *Henro Pilgrimage*, 96.

practice of Buddhist monks throughout Asia, who chose natural caves and grottoes alongside rivers or excavated caves as sites for practice.[93]

Imperial Temples

A third category of temples are those established as an expression of imperial power. These include the four Kokubun ji (Jpn. "national temples") that are found on the pilgrimage, one in each of provinces that comprise the "four countries" of Shikoku: no. 15 in Tokushima prefecture, no. 29 in Kochi, no. 59 in Ehime, and no. 80 in Kagawa. These were established by Emperor Shōmu's edict of 741 and appear to have been part of an effort to create a clearly hierarchical social organization throughout the nation paralleling the cosmic organization described in the *Avataṃsaka sūtra* (*Kegon gyō*).[94] Also in this category would be such temples as Kongō fuku ji (no. 38), which is located at the very tip of Cape Ashizuri, the most extreme southeast point of the island, facing the emptiness of the Pacific Ocean. It was founded by Kōbō Daishi, but with the support of Emperor Saga.[95] Establishing a temple at such an extreme location would have expressed the reach of the emperor's power. Several other temples were also established at the direction or support of Emperors Shōmu (701–756, r. 724–749) and Saga (784–842, r. 809–823).

Dual Occupancy

Constituting a fourth category, several of the temples are juxtaposed to a Shintō shrine that probably preexisted the establishment of the temple. Such temples thereby appropriated the existing sacrality of a site. Michael Pye refers to these as situations of "dual occupancy," as distinct from instances of "displacement."[96] According to Pye, the term "applies to cases where Buddhist

[93] Similarly: Ajaṇṭā, Ellora, Kizil, and Dunhuang. On the construction of the caves at Dunhuang, see Michelle C. Wang, "Dunhuang Art," in *The Oxford Encyclopedia of Buddhism*, ed. Richard K. Payne and Georgios T. Halkias, 781–806 (New York: Oxford University Press, online 2018: https://doi.org/10.1093/acrefore/9780199340378.013.173); see also Sunkyung Kim, "Seeing Buddhas in Cave Sanctuaries," *Asia Major* 24.1 (2011): 87–126, 88–89.

[94] G. B. Sansom, *Japan: A Short Cultural History* (1931. Rev. ed. Stanford, CA: Stanford University Press, 1978), 126–128. See also Eric Huntington, "Buddhist Cosmology," in *The Oxford Encyclopedia of Buddhism*, ed. Richard K. Payne and Georgios T. Halkias, 478–493 (New York: Oxford University Press, 2024; online: https://doi.org/10.1093/acrefore/9780199340378.013.1050).

[95] Miyata, *Henro Pilgrimage*, 85.

[96] Pye, *Japanese Buddhist Pilgrimage*, 23–24.

pilgrimage temples on the main pilgrimage routes are located at the top of hills or small mountains which had previously been sacred sites in their own right. Thus the effective displacement of local divinities by Kannon-sama or other Buddhist divinities is not at all unknown, even though it may not fit the common stereotype of religious tolerance."[97] "Displacement" encompasses often violent acts of subjugation characteristic of tantric Buddhist history.[98] The kami at the center of Shintō shrines are themselves complex, combining territorial, functional, and ancestral significance.[99] Although all temples have their own unique histories, it seems likely that some dual-occupancy sites served the needs of state formation, including relations between the court in Kyoto and more local and regional state powers.[100]

Dual-occupancy sites are usually called *jingūji*, combining the terms for Shintō shrine (Jpn. *jingū*) and Buddhist temple (Jpn. *ji*). *Jingūji* "are combinatory worship sites where Buddhist temples were built adjacent to shrines. The purpose of a *jingūji* was to provide a site where Buddhist monks could recite sutras. . . and perform rituals for the *kami* of the shrine, who were believed to be suffering and in need of Buddhist salvation."[101] In much the same fashion, rituals are performed for the benefit of the two mountain deities who gave Kūkai permission to establish his training center there.[102]

[97] Pye, *Japanese Buddhist Pilgrimage*, 24.

[98] See Ronald M. Davidson, "Reflections on the Maheśvara Subjugation Myth: Indic Materials, Sa-skya-pa Apologetics, and the Birth of Heruka," *Journal of the International Association of Buddhist Studies* 14.2: 197–235; Jacob P. Dalton, *The Taming of the Demons: Violence and Liberation in Tibetan Buddhism* (New Haven, CT: Yale University Press, 2011); Richard K. Payne, "Lethal Fire: The Shingon Yamāntaka Abhicāra Homa," *Journal of Religion and Violence* 6.1 (2018): 11–31; and Mark W. MacWilliams, "Temple Myths and the Popularization of Kannon Pilgrimage in Japan: A Case Study of Ōya-ji on the Bandō Route," *Japanese Journal of Religious Studies* 24.3–4 (1997): 391.

[99] The complexity is summarized by Fabio Rambelli, who says that "Shinto worships spirit-gods called Kami (also addressed with honorific forms such as *mikoto, shinmei, myōjin, gongen*, etc.), a wide category of sacred entities that includes natural objects (mountains, waterfalls, stones, the sea, stars), anthropomorphic deities whose deeds are described in myths recorded in the earliest books ever written in Japan, such as *Kojiki* (712), *Nihon shoki* (720), and *Fudoki* and *Man'yōshū* (both mid-eighth century) (several of these gods are related to the imperial family, especially the highest deity of the entire pantheon, sun goddess Amaterasu Ōmikami), cultural heroes (warriors, emperors, model citizens, etc.), clan divinities (more or less related to imperial deities through myths and legends), local spirits (often without a name and a clearly defined shape), and even imported deities (from India, Korea, and China)" (Fabio Rambelli, "Buddhism and Shinto," in *The Oxford Encyclopedia of Buddhism*, ed. Richard K. Payne and Georgios T. Halkias, 332–349 (New York: Oxford University Press, 2024; online 2018: https://doi.org/10.1093/acrefore/9780199340378.013.612), 332–333.

[100] For this aspect in Shinto history, see Helen Hardacre, *Shinto: A History* (New York: Oxford University Press, 2017), 71–72.

[101] Lisa Kochinski, "Negotiations Between the *Kami* and Buddha Realms: The Establishment of Shrine–Temples in the Eighth Century," *Journal of Asian Studies at Kyushu University* 1 (Spring 2016): 39.

[102] These include ritualized debates, which are practiced not only on Kōyasan but in other Buddhist sects in Japan and Tibet into the present. See Asuka Sango, "Debate Traditions in Premodern Japan," in *The Oxford Encyclopedia of Buddhism*, ed. Richard K. Payne and Georgios

Tantric rituals of state formation, including creation, maintenance, and protection, provided the larger framework within which the temple-shrine complexes and their practices developed. Pilgrimage to such sites reflects the opening of these temple-shrine complexes to a public wider than the aristocratic clans who established them. In Allan Grapard's explanation, state protection (Jpn. *chingo kokka*) "means 'protection through means of stabilization' (*chingo*) of 'the imperial house and its satellite lineages' (*kokka*)."[103] While the ideological system supported the legitimacy of the imperial lineage and the aristocratic social structure, it was also "made palatable to nonaristocrats by the inclusion of folk beliefs and practices in the elite cults. This accounts for the enormous complexity of any given cultic site in Japan."[104] Found throughout the Shikoku pilgrimage, this complexity is not "syncretism," which usually connotes the rhetoric of purity and impurity. Instead, Grapard identifies the process as "a self-conscious mechanism obeying rules of combination that appear in the various modes of expression of those combinations: poetic, literary, iconographic, and ritual."[105] The complexity of these dual-occupancy temples is an instance of this combinatory logic.

Noteworthy among the dual-occupancy temples is Dainichi ji (no. 13). At present this temple is on one side of the street, while an Ichi no Miya shrine is on the other. According to the temple priest, however, the two had formed a single institution until they were separated during the Meiji era (1868–1912).[106] This was part of the extensive attempts to "modernize" Japan's society and culture known as the "separation of kami and buddhas" (Jpn. *shinbutsu bunri*).

T. Halkias, 747–763 (New York: Oxford University Press, 2024; online 2022: https://doi.org/10.1093/acrefore/9780199340378.013.954), and Jonathan Samuels, "Debate in the Tibetan Tradition," in *The Oxford Encyclopedia of Buddhism*, ed. Richard K. Payne and Georgios T. Halkias, 729–747 (New York: Oxford University Press, 2024; online 2021: https://doi.org/10.1093/acrefore/9780199340378.013.752).

[103] Allan G. Grapard, "Institution, Ritual, and Ideology: The Twenty-Two Shrine-Temple Multiplexes of Heian Japan." *History of Religions* 27.3 (Feb. 1988): 246–269, 258.

[104] Grapard, "Institution, Ritual, and Ideology," 261. The inclusion of "folk beliefs and practices" as part of "elite cults" may not have been as purposely manipulative as Grapard seemingly suggests. Some literary sources from early Japan, such as The Tale of Genji, give extensive evidence of aristocratic elites participating equally in such folk beliefs and practices.

[105] Grapard, "Institution, Ritual, and Ideology," 264. See also Barbara Ambros, *Emplacing a Pilgrimage: The Ōyama Cult and Regional Religion in Early Modern Japan* (Cambridge, MA: Harvard University Press, 2008), 2.

[106] Personal communication (presentation following morning service), July 12, 1993.

Also in this group is Kōnomine ji (no. 27). Adjacent to the entry to this temple is a *torii* through which a track leads to a Shintō shrine further up the mountain, and Eifuku ji (no. 57), which is located on the site of a Hachiman shrine.[107] Maegami ji (no. 64), constructed in the form of a Shinto shrine, is dedicated to Zaō-gongen, an avatar who is understood to be a manifestation of Śākyamuni and Amitābha.[108] The name of the temple may be understood to mean "in front of the kami." Similarly, although formally named Kōshō in (no. 79), it is popularly called Tennō ji because the remains of the exiled Emperor Sōtoku were brought here following his assassination at Tsutsumi-ga hill.[109] Architecturally, this temple's style is exactly that of a Shintō shrine.

A noteworthy reversal of this general pattern is Ichi no miya ji ("temple of the first shrine," no. 83), which was originally founded as a Buddhist temple by the monk Gien in 704 and at that time named Daihō in. However, in 716 the Tamura Shrine was built in its courtyard and the name of the temple changed to its current one. While the more typical chronological order is reversed, this example demonstrates the integral and combinatory character of Japanese religion more generally.[110] After repeated encounters of this connection between Buddhist temples and Shintō shrines (the institutional separation of which derives only from the latter half of the nineteenth century, during the Meiji era), I was not particularly surprised to discover that the entrance to Ryōkō ji (no. 41) is marked by a *torii*, the red-orange gateway standard to Shintō shrines. I noted in my journal that day "that there is simply Japanese religion which is in some places colored more Shinto and in others more Buddhist."[111]

The Life Story of Kūkai

A fifth category comprises those temples associated with more specific events in the life of Kūkai. Given the convention that the entire route and every temple along it is associated with Kūkai, to base a category on his life might seem problematic.[112] However, if we start from the mix of history and myth

[107] Miyata, *Henro Pilgrimage*, 109.
[108] Miyata, *Henro Pilgrimage*, 116.
[109] Miyata, *Henro Pilgrimage*, 135.
[110] Anna Andreeva, *Assembling Shinto: Buddhist Approaches to Kami Worship in Medieval Japan* (Cambridge, MA: Harvard University Asia Center, Harvard University Press, 2017).
[111] Sunday, July 18, 1993.
[112] Pye, *Japanese Buddhist Pilgrimage*, 80.

that makes up the narrative strands of Kūkai's life story rather than from the pilgrimage, there are certain temples that stand out. These include Zentsū ji (no. 75), which is Kōbō Daishi's birthplace; Kōyama ji (no. 74), which is the location of the Mannō dam and irrigation project attributed to Kūkai; and Shusshaka ji (no. 73), where at seven years of age, Kūkai climbed a cliff and asked if his desire to save all beings would be achieved. If not, then he would offer his life to all the buddhas. Jumping off the cliff, he was rescued by Śākyamuni Buddha.

Others with significant associations to the life of Kūkai include Mandara ji (no. 72), where Kūkai resided here after his return from China. The name means "Temple of the Mandala" and derives from Kūkai having dedicated the dual mandalas (Taizōkai, Garbhadhātu, and Kongōkai, Vajradhātu) here. Also there is Tairyō ji (no. 21), where Kūkai is said to have achieved an awakening by practicing the recitation of the mantra of Kokuzo (Ākāśagarbha); and Hotsu-Misaki ji (no. 24), the site where at age nineteen Kūkai determined to become a Buddhist monk. At this site he had been practicing the Gumonji practice,[113] and on the final day the morning star entered into his mouth. And there is Ido ji (no. 17), where Kūkai dug a well in one night with the aid of his staff in order to help farmers who had no other source of water in the area.[114]

The analysis here identifies the dynamics of temple establishment into five broad groups, either historical or geographical: those established along trade and travel routes; those established in remote locations considered appropriate for Buddhist practice, such as atop mountains, and in one case a river gorge; those established as expressions of imperial power; those established in juxtaposition to Shintō shrines; and those established because they were sites important in the life of Kōbō Daishi.

The temples associated with the legends of Kūkai in turn reveal the multiple layers of the religious history of Japan—such sedimentation is an important aspect of the history of other tantric institutions. At least twenty-five of the temples claim to have been founded by Kūkai's famous predecessor, Gyōgi (668–749).[115] Ordained in 682, unlike other monks of his time,

[113] Recitation of the dhāraṇī of Kokuzō, Akaśagarbha, which is believed to improve memory. David Gardiner, *Kūkai: Japan's First Vajrayana Visionary* (Berkeley, CA: Institute of Buddhist Studies, and BDK America, 2024), 124.

[114] Miyata, *Henro Pilgrimage.*

[115] Nos. 1, 2 [legendary, doubtful by modern scholarship], 3, 18, 19, 23, 27, 28, 31, 35, 37, 39, 48, 49, 50, 51, 53, 54, 59, 65, 71, 78, 80, 86, 87, and 88. Miyata, *Henro Pilgrimage.*

Gyōgi was active preaching to general audiences outside the monastery. He is known for several construction projects, such as roads and bridges, monasteries, and irrigation systems. Notably charismatic, he gathered a following large enough to draw suspicion from the authorities. However, when Emperor Shōmu set about construction of Tōdaiji in Nara, he needed to raise funds for the project. Gyōgi was enrolled in this fundraising, and in 741 he and some 550 of his followers received official ordination.[116] Then, in 745, Gyōki was given the status of supreme priest (Jpn. *daisōjō*).

There are also two temples that claim to have been established by En no Ozunu (or, En no Gyoja), the semi-legendary figure considered to be the founder of the Shugendō tradition of practicing austerities in the mountains.[117] En no Ozunu (b. 634) drew from both Daoist and Buddhist sources in his ascetic practices. In addition to engaging in austerities in pursuit of longevity or immortality, he is also said to have deployed the "peacock spell," probably an allusion to the Great Peahen Queen of Spells (*Mahāmayūrīvidyārajñī*) discussed previously in this chapter.[118]

Many of these temples claim to have been in some way re-sacralized by Kūkai.[119] Thus, there is a layering of religious significance resulting from actions attributed to Kūkai in relation to the religious activities of his predecessors.[120] This layering, or sedimentation of religious significance on the pilgrimage route, did not end with Kūkai. Many of the temples are connected with the lives of figures who are important later in Japanese religious history.

Kuya shōnin (903–972, also Kōya) was an itinerant monk who was famous for promoting recitation of the mantra of Amida, and devotion to Kannon,[121] who is said to have lived at Jōdo ji (no. 49) for three years. He took an active concern in the well-being of others, so much so that he has been described as "an early medieval Japanese street activist, ... concerned about care of the sick, accessibility of potable water, disposal of corpses, digging wells, and building

[116] Richard Bowring, *The Religious Traditions of Japan, 500–1600* (Cambridge: Cambridge University Press, 2005), 79.

[117] Nos. 60 and 64. Other historically important founders include Ganjin (Ch. Chi'en chen), no. 84; Dōryū (Wake no Michitaka), no. 77; Wake no Michimaro (Enchin's grandfather), no. 76; Prince Shōtoku, no. 61.

[118] Hardacre, *Shintō*, 105.

[119] Nos. 1, 18, 19, 23, 28, 35, 37, 39, 48, 50, 51, 54, 59, 60, 64, 65, 71, 78, 80, 87, and 88.

[120] This seems to parallel Bashō's relation to Saigyo and Gyōgi. See William R. LaFleur, *The Karma of Words* (Berkeley: University of California Press, 1983), 152–162.

[121] Robert F. Rhodes, *Genshin's* Ōjōyōshū *and the Construction of Pure Land Discourse in Medieval Japan* (Honolulu: University of Hawai'i Press, 2017), 66.

bridges."[122]

Ippen shōnin (1239–1289), who established the Ji-shū (originally known at the Yugyō school), a denomination of Pure Land Buddhism, trained at Hanta ji (no. 50). The sect developed on the basis of groups of itinerant practitioners devoted to chanting the mantra of Amida, and unlike monastic groups, these groups often included both men and women.[123] As noted above, one of the eighty-eight temples, Gōshōji (no. 78), is a Ji sect temple.

Considered to be the premier scholar of his times, Gyōnen (1240–1321) authored *The Essentials of the Eight Traditions* (*Hasshū kōyō*)[124] while residing at Emmei ji (no. 54, or perhaps at Emmyō ji, no. 53). His early work is an important source for our understanding of Buddhism in the medieval period as it summarizes the doctrinal views of the major lineages. Gyōnen was highly regarded in his own lifetime and without precedent received the title of "national master" (Jpn. *kokushi*) while still living.[125] Gyōnen actively promoted the Pure Land movement of Hōnen.[126]

Both of the figures responsible for the establishment of sectarian Pure Land Buddhism lineages in Japan practiced at Zentsū ji (no. 75). Hōnen (1133–1212), founder of the Jōdo sect, and Shinran (1173–1262), founder of the Jōdo Shin sect, originally trained as Tendai monks on Hieizan. Claiming to be disillusioned with the Tendai sects' assertions of political power, both abandoned their affiliation with the mountain in preference for the practice of reciting the mantra of Amida. While Hōnen remained a monk, Shinran is known for having abandoned that status, calling himself "neither monk nor layman."

One of the leading figures of medieval Tendai esoteric Buddhism is Enchin (posthumous title: Chishō Daishi, 814–891). In 851, he traveled to China, studying at Tiantaishan—the main center in China of Tiantai Buddhism, which is the lineal antecedent of Tendai in Japan. He was the fifth abbot of Enryakuji, the main Tendai temple on Hieizan, and considered to be the founder of the Jimon sect based at Miidera on Lake Biwa. Enchin is said to have expanded Shiramine ji (no. 81).

122 Ann Gleig, "Enacting Social Change Through Buddhist Meditation," in *The Oxford Handbook of Meditation*, ed. Miguel Farias, David Brazier, and Mansur Lalljee, n.p. (New York: Oxford University Press, online 2020: doi.org/10.1093/oxfordhb/9780198808640.013.38), 15 of 21.

123 Griffiths, *Tracing the Itinerant Path*, 1.

124 Gyōnen, *The Essentials of the Eight Traditions*, trans. Leo M. Pruden (Berkeley, CA: Numata Center for Buddhist Translation and Research, 1994).

125 Bowring, *The Religious Traditions of Japan*, 364.

126 Mark Blum, *The Origins and Development of Pure Land Buddhism: A Study and Translation of Gyōnen's* Jōdo Hōmon Genrushō (New York: Oxford University Press, 2002), 132.

Such sedimentation of significance is, of course, not peculiar to Japan, but it is an important aspect of the way that the Shikoku pilgrimage was institutionalized. The conceptual framework of continuity accommodates an historiography of sedimentation more readily than the rhetoric of rupture can. The sequential sedimentation of associations can also be understood as an instance of localizing the tradition following the decline of Buddhism in India. According to Jovan Maud, the loss of India as the "central pilgrimage landscape" shared by everyone across the Buddhist cosmopolis meant that "Buddhist geography and cosmology, and corresponding pilgrimage trails ... became increasingly localized."[127] Processes of localization

> took many forms. One was the overlaying and fusing of Buddhist with indigenous sacred sites associated with specific geographical features such as mountains, lakes, and caves that were considered to be the abode of deities or other powerful entities.[128]

The pilgrim journeys through this complex landscape, and while they need not be consciously aware of it, the history and culture are as much a part of that landscape as are the rivers, mountains, and forests. The unifying thread for the Shikoku pilgrimage, however, is the figure of Kūkai, Kōbō Daishi. "The pilgrimage involves the pilgrim in a close relationship with the saint; indeed Kōbō Daishi is believed to travel spiritually with each and every pilgrim, and it is common for pilgrims to wear a white pilgrimage shroud with four Japanese ideograms written on it, with the meaning 'two people, one practice' (*dōgyō ninin*), representing the notion that the pilgrim is not alone but traveling with the saint."[129]

The Shikoku pilgrimage is an important dimension of the praxis centered on the figure of Kūkai. The route begins and ends at Kūkai's mausoleum on Kōyasan, where he is said to be in eternal meditation.[130] Indicative of the way that practices can develop independently of texts, the pilgrimage does not derive from any particular tantric text, but rather from the travels by ascetics and pilgrims from the Heian era on into the present. Created through

[127] Jovan Maud, "Buddhist Relics and Pilgrimage," in *The Oxford Handbook of Contemporary Buddhism*, ed. Michael Jerryson, 421–435 (Oxford: Oxford University Press, 2017), 427.

[128] Maud, "Buddhist Relics and Pilgrimage," 427.

[129] Tanabe, "Legends, Miracles, and Faith," 361.

[130] Some pilgrims apparently begin at Tōji Temple in Kyoto, rather than starting from Okunoin in Kōyasan. See Pamela Winfield, "Kyoto Pilgrimage Past and Present," *Crosscurrents* 59.3 (Sept. 2009): 349–357, 351.

practice, the pilgrimage itself is a tantric institution both by self-designation, through the extensive use of tantric components, and as contextualized by the praxis centered on Kūkai.

Summary

Seeing dhāraṇī as the centripetal focus of some praxes highlights ideas regarding the autonomous agency of language, both spoken and written. These ideas reflect Indic conceptions of language, constituting the conceptual supports for the use of extraordinary language.[131] Widespread throughout tantra—Buddhist, Hindu, and Jain—these ideas are found wherever Indic religious culture has been influential. Understanding the power of extraordinary language continues into the present, becoming visible on the global horizon through the spread of yogic traditions of various kinds.[132]

As with other praxes, dhāraṇī praxes have long histories, reaching down through various layers of sedimented ideas about the powers of speech. Resting atop those layers, many dhāraṇī, such as the Great Compassion dhāraṇī, continue to be popular into the present.[133] Similarly, mantra recitation, such as the Clear Light Mantra (Jpn. *kōmyō shingon*), are also popular in the present day.[134] Given their centrality for much of Buddhist practice, it comes as no surprise that dhāraṇī recitation and dhāraṇī praxes endure into the present. Ho notes that "To this day, most, if not all, monasteries in China and other parts of Asia, including Hong Kong, Taiwan, and Vietnam where the Chinese Buddhist tradition dominates, continue to begin the morning with the recitation of the SD [Śūraṃgama Dhāraṇī]."[135] The role of dhāraṇī as central to present-day praxes is evidenced by some practitioners making use of contemporary media to propagate dhāraṇī practices, including electronic media such as YouTube.[136] Dhāraṇī praxes have been enduring components

131 Payne, *Language in the Buddhist Tantra of Japan.*

132 See, for example, Amanda Lucia, "Innovative Gurus: Tradition and Change in Contemporary Hinduism," *Journal of Hindu Studies* 18.2 (August 2014): 221–263, 240.

133 See Richard D. McBride II, "*Dhāraṇī* and Mantra in Contemporary Korean Buddhism: An Ethnography of Spell Materials for Popular Consumption," *Journal of the International Association of Buddhist Studies* 42 (2019): 361–403.

134 See for example, "Buddha Vairocana (Kunrig) Maha Mantra—The Mantra of Light: Meaning and Benefits," https://www.awakeningstate.com/spiritual-awakening/buddha-vairocana-maha-mantra-light. On the Clear Light Mantra more generally, see Unno, *Shingon Refractions.*

135 Ho, "The Śūraṃgama Dhāraṇī in Sinitic Buddhist Context," 3.

136 Ungern Sternberg, "Komyo Shingon (Mantra of Light)," https://www.youtube.com/watch?v=jxTeTcWkL4Q, March 9, 2017.

transmitted over the networks connecting the Buddhist cosmopolis. They were part of the early transmission of Buddhist praxes to East Asia, forming some of the groundwork in the cultural milieu into which more extensive tantric praxes entered.

Dhāraṇī praxes are one institutional form of tantric praxis. The Shikoku pilgrimage is another. The circuit of eighty-eight temples around the island is a prominent instantiation of the praxis centered on Kūkai. Pilgrims' feet—and cars and buses, and as I saw at one temple, helicopters—all follow a path that is understood to be Kūkai's path. Established gradually over several centuries, it requires an historiography that frames change in terms of the *longue durée*, instead of the rhetoric of rupture found so frequently in religious studies. Each site, each temple has its own significance and history—histories that in some cases predate Kūkai, but all of which continue long after. The significance and history of each temple contribute to the route as a whole, while the route as a whole contextualizes the significance of each temple.

There is a delightful ambivalence about the route. It is just exactly what it is, fixed in those specific locations and paths through mountains and valleys, into small villages and modern cities, along that specific coastline. And, at the same time, it can be reproduced in other locations an indefinite number of times. Sand taken from each site, gathered and transported elsewhere, can set up the pilgrimage in miniature, making the significance of the route a reflected presence in its new location.

Like the image of 84,000 doors through which practitioners can pass to encounter the dharma, in addition to the Shikoku pilgrimage, there are many other sites of Buddhist history that are felt to be potent locations. We do not know how many of these have been lost due to dynastic and imperial changes, warfare and conquest, sectarian conflicts, and reformation movements. But some others have been recovered. Constructed as part of state formation, connecting Java to the entire Buddhist cosmopolis across Asia, Borobudur is one such monumental site.

IV
Southeast Asia
State Formation and Monuments

The *Kāraṇḍavyūha sūtra*, or the *Sūtra of the Basket's Display*, draws less attention in contemporary religious studies literature than do several other Mahāyāna sutras. Its role in the transmission of tantric praxes into Southeast Asia means, however, that it has historical significance for our inquiry here.[1] It was also important as part of the praxis of Avalokiteśvara that connects Southeast Asia with Inner Asia.

Avalokiteśvara is central to the text. While in other sources Avalokiteśvara is a bodhisattva whose predominant characteristic is compassion, in this sutra he is a fully awakened buddha whose body is the vast cosmos in the pores of which exist world realms containing uncounted living beings.

The sutra is a transitional text, bridging Mahāyāna sutra literature and the tantras, and is estimated to date from approximately the fifth century.[2] Like many Mahāyāna texts, it evidences the cult of the book. For example, in the second section the Buddha's primary interlocutor is the bodhisattva "Dispeller of all Hindrances" (Sarvanīvaraṇaviṣkambhin). Upon being told of the miracles that follow from simply thinking the name of the sutra, he exclaims that he is astonished because

> "then those who listen to, cause to be written out, possess, recite, study, and have their minds completely focused on the precious king of the Mahāyāna sūtras, *The Sūtra of the Basket's Display*, will have happiness.
>
> "Those who write a single letter from the precious king of the Mahāyāna sūtras, *The Sūtra of the Basket's Display*, will have happiness and will not see these sufferings of saṃsāra. They will not be reborn as an untouchable

[1] Phillip Scott Ellis Green, "The Many Faces of Lokeśvara: Tantric Connections in Cambodia and Campā Between the Tenth and Thirteenth Centuries," *History of Religions* 54.1 (Aug. 2014): 69–93, at 74.

[2] Peter Alan Roberts and Tulku Yeshe, eds., *The Basket's Display: Kārandavyūha* (2013. Rev. 84,000, https://84000.co/translation/toh116, 2020), i.2. (Text is unpaginated, but it is marked by section notations.)

Tantra Across the Buddhist Cosmopolis. Richard K. Payne, Oxford University Press. © Oxford University Press 2025.
DOI: 10.1093/9780197825105.003.0004

or of mixed caste; they will not be reborn as someone with defective senses; they will not be reborn as lame, hunchbacked, with a deformed nose, a goiter, or a cleft lip, nor with leprosy. Their bodies will not be afflicted by illness. They will have health, great strength, and clear faculties."[3]

A more explicitly tantric quality is that Avalokiteśvara's name and the six-syllable mantra, OṂ MANI PADME HŪṂ, are identical. While explaining how difficult it is to obtain the mantra, the Buddha informs Dispeller that "Noble son, it is difficult to obtain his name. Those who remember the name that is the six-syllable vidyāmantra will be reborn in those pores. They will no longer continue to be in saṃsāra. They will go from one pore to another, living within those pores until they reach the level of nirvāṇa."[4] And as with the *Vairocanābhisaṃbodhi tantra*, initiation into the mandala assembly of the chief deity is required. In this section of the *Kāraṇḍavyūha sūtra*, Avalokiteśvara is in conversation with Amitābha, to whom he gives a description of the initiatory mandala that the aspirant must enter to obtain the mantra.

Avalokiteśvara describes to Amitābha how the mandala should be created with the figure of Amitābha in the center formed from the powder of precious gems, gold, and silver. A variety of attendant deities are to be drawn using the same materials, and in the four corners jars filled with precious gems are to be placed. But, Amitābha objects, what if an aspirant is poor and cannot make a mandala out of the powder of precious gems, gold, and silver?

Avalokiteśvara replies that the aspirant can then make it out of colored powders, flowers, and incense. But Amitābha again objects, asking what if the aspirant is in a foreign land and cannot even manage to obtain colored powders, flowers, and incense? Then, Avalokiteśvara explains, the aspirant can form the mandala as a mental image, and the aspirant's teacher is to then teach the mudras and mantras needed.

But Dispeller doesn't just want to hear about the mantra; he wants to have it himself. The Buddha tells him that in Varanasi there is a preacher of the dharma (Skt. *dharmabhanaka*), "who possesses, recites, and is completely focused on the six-syllable mahāvidyā. . . . [Such a teacher] is rare. He should be seen as being equal to the tathāgatas; seen as being the life of the world;

[3] *The Basket's Display*, 2.20–21.

[4] *The Basket's Display*, 2.34. The description here seems to parallel the function ascribed to Sukhāvatī that one born there will only go on to nirvana, not to another rebirth.

seen as a mass of merit; seen as being like the Ganges and all sacred places; seen as one who speaks that which is not false; seen as one who speaks the truth; seen as a heap of jewels; seen as a wish-fulfilling jewel; seen as a Dharma king; and seen as a savior of beings."[5]

It is noteworthy that this preacher of the dharma is a disreputable figure who does not follow the monastic rules, and thus similar to the mahāsiddhas. Despite this, the Buddha advises Dispeller, saying, "Noble son, you should have no doubts when you see this dharmabhāṇaka. Noble son, do not fall from a bodhisattva bhūmi to be reborn in the lower existences. This dharmabhāṇaka's conduct is poor, and his behavior is poor. He is surrounded by his wife, sons, and daughters. His orange robes are filled with feces and urine; he has not followed the noble path."[6]

Dispeller does indeed go to Varanasi, and there finds the disreputable preacher of the dharma. After describing the powers of the mantra, the preacher of the dharma hesitates to respond to Dispeller's request for it. However,

> Then a voice came from the sky saying, "Give him the six-syllable queen of mahāvidyās!"
>
> The dharmabhāṇaka wondered where this voice had come from. Again there came the voice from the sky, saying, "This bodhisattva has undergone many hardships. Give him the six-syllable queen of mahāvidyās!"
>
> The dharmabhāṇaka looked up into the sky and saw someone who had a body white as the autumn moon, a crown of coiled hair, an omniscient buddha upon his head, and a beautiful lotus in his hand, and was adorned with the splendor of lotuses.
>
> Then the dharmabhāṇaka said to [Dispeller], "Noble son, the Bodhisattva Mahāsattva Avalokiteśvara has given permission for the six-syllable queen of mahāvidyās to be given to you."[7]

Dispeller reverently placed his palms together and received the mantra.

Avalokiteśvara is the centripetal deity, who, along with his mantra *oṃ maṇi padme huṃ* and the *Kāraṇḍavyūha sūtra*, constituted a tantric praxis transmitted from India to Southeast Asia. It has been argued that after more than a decade of study there, Atiśa then brought that praxis to Tibet, where

[5] *The Basket's Display*, 2.63.
[6] *The Basket's Display*, 2.64.
[7] *The Basket's Display*, 2.75–2.76

Avalokiteśvara (Tib. Chenrezig) is identified with the Dalai Lama. And, as indicated by the sutra, the mantra is widely and ceaselessly recited, and it is also inscribed on stones, walls, prayer wheels, and cliffs across the countryside.

Orienting to the Study of Tantra in Southeast Asia

This chapter explores the history of tantric Buddhism in Southeast Asia, a field of inquiry that has only recently been made accessible, largely by archeological and art historical studies. While the study of tantra elsewhere has large bodies of texts to draw on, in Southeast Asia this is not the case because the textual record for this history is very scant. Archeological and art historical records are largely the work of state actors, and therefore the perspective of state formation (creation, maintenance, and protection) provides access to that history.[8] Since premodern states do not correspond to modern nation-states, either in organization or geography, this chapter employs the term "mandala." In addition to the symbolic meaning of a buddha surrounded by his retinue, the term also has an explicitly political significance and is used in the historiography of Southeast Asia. The final section of this chapter considers the monument of Borobudur, both in its role toward state formation and as evidencing the transregional networks of tantric Buddhism, which will be explicitly examined in Chapter VI.

Seeing Tantric Buddhism in Southeast Asia

Tantric Buddhism was an important part of the religious world of Southeast Asia for centuries, and many of the royal courts affiliated with the tradition.[9] Much of the early Western scholarship in Buddhist studies has characterized tantra in terms of transgressive practices, particularly sexual ones.[10] A less

[8] Martin Lehnert has noted the importance of state formation for understanding tantric Buddhism, which involved "the appropriation of ritual performance and language in respect of state formation, crisis of social order, and state protection, employing distinct expressions of what may reservedly be categorised as apotropaic ritualism." ("Tantric Threads Between India and China," in *The Spread of Buddhism*, ed. Ann Heirman and Stephan Peter Bumbacher, 247–276 [Leiden: Brill, 2007], 250).

[9] The phrase "Southeast Asia" is used here expansively, to include Sri Lanka.

[10] Such representations also played a role in polemical contestation between Hindus and Buddhists; see James A. Boon, *Affinities and Extremes: Crisscrossing the Bittersweet Ethnology of East Indies History, Hindu-Balinese Culture, and Indo-European Allure* (Chicago: Chicago University Press, 1990).

one-dimensional understanding of tantra, however, reveals a movement often employed in the service of state formation—not only in Southeast Asia, examined in this chapter, but also throughout the Buddhist cosmopolis. For Southeast Asia, however, sectarian historiography, warfare and other conflicts, imperial suppression, colonialism, and modern reform movements have obscured that history. These dynamics have placed tantric Buddhism under erasure—despite attempts to excise the movement from Southeast Asian history, it has left tracks and traces.[11] Over the past few decades, studies of art history, epigraphy, and archeology, together with new textual studies of both canonic and noncanonic texts, have provided additional information making these tracks and traces visible, and thereby revealing the importance of tantric Buddhism in Southeast Asian history.[12]

This chapter focuses on the function of tantra for state formation—that is, the creation, maintenance, and defense of states—for three reasons. First, state formation has been a key function for tantric praxis from its beginnings into the modern era.[13] Second, despite the limitations of textual records, what remains available to us—art, architecture, material culture, and epigraphy—are largely the products of state actors, and therefore evidence the role of tantric Buddhism in state formation.

And third, this close relation between tantra and state formation challenges two modern conceptions regarding the relation between religion and the state. The first is the presumption that nation-states are the natural and unproblematic form of sociopolitical organization. History is then structured by modern nation-states as they exist in the present. Historically, the states of Southeast Asia were not organized in this fashion. Scholars of Southeast Asian history employ the term "mandala" to indicate the political structure of those states. The second modern idea is that religion and the state naturally and unproblematically constitute two distinct categories. The role of tantra

[11] A very important and rich resource on this is the two-volume edited collection *The Creative South: Buddhist and Hindu Art in Mediaeval Maritime Asia*, ed. Andrea Acri and Peter Sharrock (Singapore: ISEAS Publishing, Yusof Ishak Institute, 2022).

[12] Archeological research continues to uncover physical remains that deepen and extend our understanding of the role of tantric Buddhism in Southeast Asia. A report on recent research was presented by Eko Bastiawan, Mathilde Mechling, and Emma Natalya Stein, "A Javanese Bronze Buddhist Mandala," Smithsonian Museum, National Museum of Asian Art, online January 14, 2025.

[13] One phrase for this function is "state protection Buddhism." Hiram Woodward, "Esoteric Buddhism in Southeast Asia in the Light of Recent Scholarship," *Journal of Southeast Asian Studies* 35.2 (June 2004): 329–354, 331. This usage should not be taken as identifying a kind of Buddhism separate from others, such as a kind characterized as the individual search for nirvana, but rather as one function to which tantric practices were used.

in premodern state formation, however, is one instance that demonstrates that this artifact of Enlightenment-era European culture is not universal.[14]

One impediment to seeing tantra in Southeast Asia is that, almost without qualification, the modern representation of the Buddhist world portrays Southeast Asia as the domain of Theravāda Buddhism—as if this had always simply been the case, and as if geography and religious affiliation are somehow coterminous.[15] Although these ideas linger in popular representations, they are inaccurate and outdated. Both tantric and Mahāyāna Buddhist praxes were at times central to the states of Southeast Asia. And Buddhism was only part of the rich Indic culture influential in the region. Frits Staal has pointed out that when

> Buddhist practices and ideas went from India to *Southeast* Asia, they were not only connected with many non-religious ideas and techniques, but they were also linked with the expansion of Hinduism [i.e., Śaivite and Vaiśnava traditions]. In most of Southeast Asia, Hindu expansion preceded the advent of Mahāyāna Buddhism. The two merged to some extent . . . and then, in countries such as Burma and Thailand, were replaced by Sinhalese Theravāda Buddhism after the twelfth century.[16]

The current meaning of the category "Theravāda" to identify a pure transmission of original Buddhism dating in unbroken lineage from the Buddha Śākyamuni is of modern origin. Ashley Thompson summarizes the research on this issue, noting that the image of Theravāda as uniquely legitimate, "pristine, conservative and orthodox" form of Buddhism was created out of the encounter of European and Buddhist cultures. It was reified in 1950 at the first World Fellowship of Buddhists conference in Sri Lanka, a representation that has since been naturalized in Western religious studies discourse.[17] She goes on to point out that the construct sought to

[14] Timothy Fitzgerald, *The Ideology of Religions Studies* (New York: Oxford University Press, 2000).

[15] For a more complex version relating specifically to ritual practices, see Donald K. Swearer, *The Buddhist World of Southeast Asia*, 2nd ed. (Albany: State University of New York Press, 2010), x.

[16] Frits Staal, *Rules Without Meaning: Ritual, Mantras and the Human Sciences* (New York: Peter Lang Publishing, 1989), 403–404.

[17] This terminological issue is complicated by the use of the same term, Theravāda, with significantly different meanings. See, for example, Anālayo, "The Name Theravāda in an Eighteenth-Century Inscription: Reconsidering the Problematization of the Term," in *Śāntamatiḥ: Manuscripts for Live, Essays in Memory of Seishi Karashima*, ed. Noriyuku Kudo (Tokyo: International Research Institute for Advance Buddhology, Soka University, 2023), 1–25. Anālayo's attempt to insulate the term from problematization, however, does not address the issues identified by Thompson.

> efface the invention itself: a coherent singular body of contemporary Buddhist practices strictly tied to a set of texts in the Pali language was to be seen as having its roots in the very earliest consolidation of the historical Buddha's teachings. . . . The invention of "Theravada" thus arose in the colonial period in which Buddhism was studied and labeled and, in the process, transformed by European and Asian scholars and practitioners.[18]

Thompson further points out that in the present a conceptual shift is taking place: "from considering Buddhism as a religion essentially embodied in Sanskrit and Pali texts to understanding 'Buddhism' as a more general word for a wide range of associated practices, some but not all of which may be explicitly textual."[19] The emphasis on praxes taken in this work makes this shift methodologically explicit.

An additional problem is that the entire region is often represented as marginal and as the culturally passive recipient of outside influences. As Andrea Acri notes, "much of previous scholarship has tended to . . . perceive [the region] as a consumer rather than a 'generator' of Esoteric Buddhism."[20] This colonial narrative has continued to influence the way the region is understood, and this representation of passivity obscures the active role of those in the region who contributed to ongoing developments of tantric Buddhism.

Mandala: A Social, Political, and Religious Category

Southeast Asian historiography uses the term "mandala" to identify polities, that is, organized societies, and it will be used here to organize the evidence for the importance of tantric Buddhism throughout Southeast Asia. Widely familiar today are painted or sculpted mandalas: symmetrical diagrams showing a central deity and four attendant deities—though the number of deities and the complexity of the diagrams can spiral upward dizzyingly. But this understanding of the mandala appears to have been borrowed from Indic political theory regarding the structure of polities. In other words, mandalas

[18] Ashley Thompson, "Contemporary Cambodian Buddhist Traditions: Seen from the Past," in *The Oxford Handbook of Contemporary Buddhism*, ed. Michael Jerryson (New York: Oxford University Press, 2017; DOI: 10.1093/oxfordhb/9780199362387.013.32), 237.

[19] Thompson, "Contemporary Cambodian Buddhist Traditions," 237.

[20] Andrea Acri, "Introduction: Esoteric Buddhist Networks Along the Maritime Silk Routes, 7th–13th Century AD," in *Esoteric Buddhism in Medieval Maritime Asia: Networks of Masters, Texts, Icons*, ed. Andrea Acri (Singapore: ISEAS Yusof Ishak Institute, 2016), 11.

are at the intersection of the social, the political, and the religious.[21] And cosmological, as Julie Gifford explains—

> semi-autonomous chiefdoms that surround the royal seat at the center were smaller satellites, each of which replicated the cosmological symbolism, so that the whole was characterized by the "replication of like entities on a decreasing scale." Thus, the galactic polity as a whole was a system of overlapping spheres of power in which each satellite participates in the power radiated *from* the center, but also radiates power *to* its own even smaller satellites.[22]

Thus, the social and political significance of mandalas also reflected this conception of the cosmos. Focusing on the political dimension Prapod Assavavirulhakarn states that

> overlords had to attract loyal followers, and that was done by establishing a central court filled with large, beautiful buildings with enclosed sacred precincts that served as the foci for rituals, ceremonies, and display. Added to this was the ability to deploy military force. Some overlords succeeded in manipulating all of these factors and thus established political units whose sphere of influence expanded beyond the boundary of chiefdom. The result was not, however, a state with a central capital or clearly defined boundaries, but rather, a political unity which was fluid in terms of territory and the ability to endure.[23]

Rather than clearly demarcated nation-states, where geographic and political boundaries coincide, these states were based on the extent of the ruler's influence—political, religious, and military. Not coterminous with the modern political states of Southeast Asia, it is these premodern center-periphery structures of power and authority that are referred to as mandalas.

[21] Ronald Davidson, *Indian Esoteric Buddhism: A Social History of the Tantric Movement* (New York: Columbia University Press, 2002), 2.

[22] Julie A. Gifford, *Buddhist Practice and Visual Culture: The Visual Rhetoric of Borobudur* (New York: Routledge, 2011), 174. Internal quote is from Stanley Tambiah, *World Conqueror and World Renouncer: A Study of Buddhism and Polity in Thailand against a Historical Background* (Cambridge: Cambridge University Press, 1976), 113–114.

[23] Prapod Assavavirulhakarn, *The Ascendancy of Theravāda Buddhism in Southeast Asia* (Chiang Mai, Thailand: Silkworm Books, 2010), 18.

Assavavirulhakarn identifies three broad periods of premodern Southeast Asian history: "the early *maṇḍala*s from circa first to ninth century CE . . . , the great *maṇḍala*s from circa ninth to thirteenth century; and the premodern *maṇḍala*s of the Burmese and the Thai from the twelfth century until the era of Western colonization."[24] Compared to those of the later periods, the early mandalas across the region were small. Some of these early mandalas, such as Zhenla in the upper Mekong Delta and Tonle Sap plains, were important in the history of tantric Buddhism in the region.[25]

The three mandalas of the second period were larger and more complexly organized.[26] Angkor extended across the Mekong Delta, modern Cambodia, and through central and northeast Thailand. Srivijaya incorporated the earlier mandalas of the Malay Peninsula, covering its lower southern part and Sumatra, with centers in Thailand, and Palembang in Sumatra. Śailendra was in central Java.

The premodern Burmese and Thai mandalas developed into the modern nation-states on the mainland of Southeast Asia. "Their advent is believed to have coincided with the expansion and the adoption of Sri Lankan Theravāda Buddhism."[27] These modern relations between Theravada Buddhism and state formation indicate that such a relation has not been unique to tantric Buddhism, instead being an integral aspect of Buddhist history.

Characterizing the religious culture of premodern Southeast Asia is made complicated by different and shifting patterns of religious affiliation. Some kingdoms were actively pluralistic in their religious affiliations. This pattern was true of the "Buddhist" dynasties of eastern India, such as the Pālas (750–1161),[28] and of the Southeast Asian kingdoms of the Khmers, Chams, and Javanese. In such cases, royal support was given in some combination to Buddhist, Śaiva, and Vaiśnava institutions. Sometimes, however, affiliation shifted with a change of dynastic ruler—from one tradition to another, or from a plural to an exclusive affiliation.[29]

[24] Assavavirulhakarn, *The Ascendancy of Theravāda Buddhism in Southeast Asia*, 19.

[25] See Chapter VI on Punyodaya's travels from the subcontinent, to China, and Zhenla as evidence of the networks of the Buddhist cosmopolis.

[26] Assavavirulhakarn, *The Ascendancy of Theravāda Buddhism in Southeast Asia*, 20.

[27] Assavavirulhakarn, *The Ascendancy of Theravāda Buddhism in Southeast Asia*, 21.

[28] Romila Thapar, *The Past Before Us: Historical Traditions of Early North India* (Cambridge, MA: Harvard University Press, 2013), 496–506.

[29] For a further discussion of these issues as related to the Khmer maṇḍala state and the dominance of Śaivism, see Daniel Michon, "Pre-Angkor Khmer Religion and State," *Religion Compass* 5.1 (2011): 28–36, DOI: 10.1111/j.1749-8171.2010.00261.x.

The study of tantric Buddhism in Southeast Asia has developed even more recently than the study of tantric Buddhism as a whole. Since the last decade of the twentieth century, however, an increasing amount of detailed evidence has been compiled by experts in the field—so much so that a comprehensive detailed review is beyond the scope of this work. Instead, state formation—that is, the creation, maintenance, and protection of the state—provides the interpretive lens by which to identify the tracks and traces left by tantric Buddhism through Southeast Asian history.

As demonstrated by Davidson, the connection between tantric Buddhism and the state is foundational to the Indian origins of tantra.[30] And, citing Zanning in ninth-century China, Orzech points out that in some instances the practitioner's body is equated with the body politic, "The role of the practice of the body—the 'esoteric' teaching—*is to protect the body politic*."[31]

Adapting Assavavirulhakarn's analysis, we focus the following discussion on two of his three major historical and cultural periods: the early mandalas and the three great mandalas, sampling specific sites within these domains. Tantric Buddhism was already displaced by the third period, that of the premodern mandalas.

Early Mandalas: Circa First to Ninth Century

Between approximately 250 and 550 CE, Indic religiopolitical influences enter the societies of Southeast Asia. In several cases, kings adopt names declaring their devotion to Hindu deities such as Viṣṇu, Śiva, or Rudra,[32] but extensive influence of Buddhism is also evident. The clearest indication of tantric Buddhism at this early period is from the kingdom of Srivijaya, located in southern Sumatra. Because of the extent of archeological findings there, one site is particularly important. That key site is referred to as "Palembang," since it is near that present-day city.

[30] Davidson, *Indian Esoteric Buddhism*, 113–168.

[31] Charles Orzech, "The 'Great Teaching of Yoga,' the Chinese Appropriation of the Tantras, and the Question of Esoteric Buddhism," *Journal of Chinese Religions* 34 (2006): 29–78, 67.

[32] Charles F. W. Higham, "Ritual and Religion in South-East Asia," in *The Oxford Handbook of the Archaeology of Ritual and Religion*, ed. Timothy Insoll (New York: Oxford University Press, 2011; DOI: 10.1093/oxfordhb/9780199232444.013.0031), 470–481, 475.

Palembang in Southern Sumatra: Early Srivijaya

Important to the development of Palembang as a center of Buddhism was its location. Swati Chemburkar explains that "Palembang lay halfway between India and the Chinese capital of Changan (Xian today), where international scholars congregated and consolidated the growing Buddhist network."[33] Several inscriptions dating from the seventh century, the early period of the kingdom of Srivijaya, provide evidence of familiarity with the dual categories of the "perfection path" (Skt. *pāramitāyāna*) and the tantric or "mantra path" (Skt. *mantrayāna*). According to Hiram Woodward, the "Śrivijayan inscriptions, when taken together, evoke a realm familiar with the teachings of Perfection Path Buddhism, the ancillary magical powers those at the end of the path acquire, and the use of *mantra* and *yantra* as instruments of war."[34]

On a less combative, but still religiopolitical note, Miksic calls attention to an inscription dated 684 dedicating a garden or park to the benefit of all living beings. Known as the Talang Tuwo inscription, Miksic says that it "contains the most information on religious beliefs of any Srivijayan inscription: the wish that the thought of Bodhi [*bodhicitta*] will be born in all, references to the three jewels and the diamond body of the *mahasattvas*, and ends with the wish that all will attain enlightenment."[35] In addition to the sentiment, Reichle points out that the inscription is noteworthy because it identifies itself as a *praṇidāna*, "a vow taken by an individual to help all sentient creatures achieve enlightenment before doing so oneself (also known as a bodhisattva vow)."[36] There is a key phrase that shifts the valence of the inscription from a Mahāyāna orientation to a tantric one. That is the term "diamond body" (Skt. *vajraśarīra*)—in some tantric systems attaining a diamond body is a necessary step for the practitioner to realize full awakening.[37] Other inscriptions also include key terms indicative of tantric praxis.[38]

[33] Swati Chemburkar, "*Stūpa* to *Maṇḍala*: Tracing a Buddhist Architectural Development from Kesariya to Borobudur to Tabo," *Pacific World: Journal of the Institute of Buddhist Studies* 3rd series, no. 20 (2018): 169–221, 193.

[34] Woodward, "Esoteric Buddhism in Southeast Asia in the Light of Recent Scholarship," 336. Also indicating a connection between conflict and tantric praxis, see Natasha Reichle, *Violence and Serenity: Late Buddhist Sculpture from Indonesia* (Honolulu: University of Hawai'i Press, 2007), 17.

[35] John Miksic, "The Buddhist-Hindu Divide in Premodern Southeast Asia," Nalanda-Sriwijaya Centre Working Paper Series no. 1. (Singapore: Institute of Southeast Asian Studies, 2010), 12.

[36] Reichle, *Violence and Serenity*, 18.

[37] Reichle, *Violence and Serenity*, 19.

[38] Reichle, *Violence and Serenity*, 17.

Miksic goes on to suggest that the concepts being put to political use in the inscription "can be connected with Vajrayana or Tantrayana which arose at Nalanda . . . not long before this date."[39] More concretely, Reichle points out another important part of the record. Of the several Buddhist monks and teachers known by name to have come to Srivijaya, either to stay or in passage between India and China, one is particularly significant for the movement of tantric Buddhism to the kingdom. As the head of Nālandā, when Dharmapāla went to Srivijaya in the early seventh century, "he would have been well-versed in the developments of esoteric Buddhism."[40] In other words, teachers, practices, and teachings moved rapidly across the networks connecting Nālandā in India and Srivijaya in southern Sumatra. Indic culture, including tantric Buddhism, continued to expand into Southeast Asia in the following period as well.

The Great Mandalas: Circa Ninth to Thirteenth Century

Shifting to the middle period, there are three prominent mandalas—each of which is affiliated with tantric Buddhism during its history. First, we consider the Khmer Empire in peninsular Southeast Asia, and then the two kingdoms in insular Southeast Asia—the Śailendra and Srivijaya mandalas.

Peninsular Southeast Asia

The Khmer Empire dominated much of Southeast Asia for several centuries, and it reached a high point with the Angkorian period. The Khmer Angkor mandala exemplifies the complexity of the relations between tantric Buddhist, Vaiśnava, and Śaiva traditions in the history of Southeast Asia. Alexis Sanderson explains that

> records of the Khmer principalities of the fifth to eighth centuries and of the unified kingdom of Angkor that emerged thereafter and endured into the fourteenth, show that religion throughout that time comprised three . . . faiths of Indian origin: Śaivism, the Pāñcarātrika Vaiṣṇavism of the

[39] Miksic, "The Buddhist-Hindu Divide in Premodern Southeast Asia," 12.
[40] Reichle, *Violence and Serenity*, 16.

> Bhāgavatas, and Mahāyāna Buddhism in the developed form that includes the system of ritual and meditation known as the Mantranaya, Mantrayāna or Vajrayāna.[41]

Sanderson goes on to explain that this threefold pattern of Śaivism, Vaiṣṇavism, and Vajrayāna was common throughout Southeast Asia. East of the Khmers was a confederation of Chams, who also evidenced this threefold pattern from the fifth to seventeenth centuries, and similarly in Sumatra and Borneo in the fourteenth century. This same threefold pattern was found in East Java from the eighth century until the early sixteenth century, in West Java until the late sixteenth, and it continued in Java until the eighteenth century.[42] It remains active in Bali, where intermixed rituals of Śaivite and Buddhist priests continue to be practiced.[43]

The Mandala of Angkor: Khmer Buddhism

The Khmer king Jayavarman II (c. 770 to 835) established the Angkor Empire (late ninth to fifteenth century) in the plains of what is today Cambodia. Woodward suggests that tantric involvement in state formation is evident in 1080 when Jayavarman VI of the Mahidharapura lineage seized power.[44] Further, Woodward says that the Mahidharapura "had many ties to a Buddhism that by then incorporated not only Mantrayāna texts but also Yoginī Tantras."[45] Of the Yoginī tantras, the *Hevajra tantra* is the most clearly attested.[46] In the twelfth century, following a period in which Buddhist tantra was out of favor, Jayavarman VII (r. 1181 to 1218) shifted state affiliation from Vaiśnava and Śaiva to Mahāyāna Buddhist.

Peter Sharrock speaks of the "rapid international expansion of tantric Buddhism in the eighth century" as a second period of tantric Buddhist

[41] Alexis Sanderson, "The Śaiva Religion Among the Khmers, Part I," *Bulletin de l'École française d'Extrême-Orient* 90–91 (2003–2004): 349–462, 349.

[42] Andrea Acri, *Dharma Pātañjala: A Śaiva Scripture from Ancient Java* (Groningen: Egbert Forsten, 2011), and Andrea Acri, "Revisiting the Cult of 'Śiva-Buddha' in Java and Bali," in *Buddhist Dynamics in Premodern and Early Modern Southeast Asia*, ed. Christian Lammerts, 261–282 (Singapore: Institute of Southeast Asian Studies, 2015).

[43] Sanderson, "The Śaiva Religion Among the Khmers, Part I," 351. See also Tyra de Kleen, *Mudrās: The Ritual Hand-Poses of the Buddha Priests and Shiva Priests of Bali* (1924. Reprint. New York: University Books, 1970).

[44] Charles F. W. Higham, "The Origins of the Civilization of Angkor," in *Proceedings of the British Academy, Volume 121, 2002 Lectures*, ed. P. J. Marshall, 41–89 (London: British Academy Online, 2012; DOI: 10.5871/bacad/9780197263037.001.0001), 47.

[45] Woodward, "Esoteric Buddhism in Southeast Asia," 349.

[46] Woodward, "Esoteric Buddhism in Southeast Asia," 349–350.

dominance across Asia, the first having been a century earlier.[47] This was, for example, that same period that Śubhākarasiṃha, Vajrabodhi, and Amoghavajra were active in Tang dynasty China, and it is referred to by some scholars as the "second wave" of tantric transmission out of India. The *Sarvatathāgatatattvasaṃgraha* is a primary text for this period, during which Vajrapāṇi (also Vajrin, "possessor of the vajra") and his wrathful form, Trailokyavijaya (the "conqueror of the three worlds"), were particularly important. In mid-tenth-century Angkor, Vajrapāṇi is found together with the Buddha Vairocana and Divyadevī (that is, Prajñāpāramitā) in the first Buddhist temple to be built in Angkor, Bat Cum (953 CE). The importance of Vajrapāṇi in Angkor is evidenced also by other epigraphic material from the tenth century, which further indicates the centrality of the *Sarvatathāgatatattvasaṃgraha* to the form of tantric Buddhism active there. Vajrapāṇi's function in state formation reflects the potential for violence in the Buddha's society such that Śākyamuni is often represented with a bodyguard. The figure of Vajrapāṇī has been traced back to representations of this bodyguard, found in early artwork.[48] As a protective guardian, Vajrapāṇī plays an important role in the praxes for state formation.

Outlining the history of Khmer involvement with Buddhism, Sharrock notes that there were periods in the seventh, tenth, and eleventh centuries when Buddhism was influential in the court.

> [From] Jayavarman VII's reign [1181–1218] until today, however, Khmer regimes have all been Buddhist (except for a brief, destructive resurgence of Śaivism perhaps under Jayavarma Parameśvara [Jayavarma VIII, r. 1243–1295]). Khmer Buddhism at some as yet undetermined point subsequently switched from the northern to the southern vehicle, but the fundamental shift from state Śaivism to state Buddhism was made under Jayavarman VII, and it is this turn that stands out as one of the most abrupt and decisive in the country's religious history.[49]

[47] Peter Sharrock, "Garuḍa, Vajrapāṇī and Religious Change in Jayavarman VII's Angkor," *Journal of Southeast Asian Studies* 40.1 (February 2009): 111–151, 129.

[48] I-Tien Hsing and William G. Crowell, "Heracles in the East: The Diffusion and Transformation of His Image in the Arts of Central Asia, India, and China," *Asia Major* 18.2 (2005): 103–154, 118–120.

[49] Sharrock, "Garuḍa, Vajrapāṇī and Religious Change," 119–120.

Subjugation and State Formation

Trailokyavijaya, Vajrapāṇi's wrathful form, may have originated in the contestation between Buddhist and Śaivite religious groups in India, but then continued as a key Buddhist figure wherever the two were in contact, such as in tenth-century Angkor.[50]

As one subjugation narrative goes, Vairocana is in his vajra-jeweled palace at the summit of Mount Sumeru assembling the retinues of the *vajradhātu* mandala, that is, an imperial project bringing together his own retinue of followers and in turn their retinues as well. Vajrapāṇi arrives and explains that he cannot bring his clan because Śiva together with his own retinue has refused to accept the authority of the Buddha Vairocana. Vairocana then empowers Vajrapāṇi and causes Śiva and his retinue to be present at the assembly. In their wrathful forms—Trailokyavijaya for Vajrapāṇi, and Mahābhairava for Śiva—the two engage in combat. Trailokyavijaya tramples Mahābhairava and his consort Umādevā, killing them both. In this way, Vajrapāṇi/Trailokyavijaya triumphs over Śiva (Maheśvara, "great lord"), who had refused to convert to the buddhadharma. Śiva is then resuscitated and, now named Tathāgata-bhasmeśvara-nirghosa, takes up a place within the vajradhātu mandala; that is, he becomes part of the Buddha Vairocana's retinue.[51] Similar stories of violent subjugation are also told regarding Rudra,[52] and

[50] The *Vairocanābhisaṃbodhi tantra* locates Trailokyavijaya in the northwest corner of the mandala, and it is portrayed as "surrounded by fearsome flames, has a jeweled diadem, and holds a *vajra*. With no regard for his own life, he devotes himself to requesting and receiving instructions." *The Vairocanābhisambodhi Sutra*, trans. Rolf Giebel (Berkeley, CA: Numata Center for Buddhist Translation and Research, 2005), 35. In the *Sarvatathāgatatattvasaṃgraha*, Trailokyavijaya vanquishes Rudra, another manifestation of Maheśvara, that is, Śīva. See Ronald Davidson, "Reflections on the Maheśvara Subjugation Myth: Indic Materials, Sa-skya-pa Apologetics, and the Birth of Heruka," *Journal of the International Association of Buddhist Studies* 14.2 (1991): 197–235. On the pervasive character of this theme in tantric Buddhism, see Jacob Dalton, *The Taming of the Demons: Violence and Liberation in Tibetan Buddhism* (New Haven, CT: Yale University Press, 2011), 32. Woodward calls attention to Khmer epigraphy recording gifts being given to Trailokyavijaya, in 979. Woodward, "Esoteric Buddhism in Southeast Asia," 349.

[51] Sharrock, "Garuḍa, Vajrapāṇī and Religious Change," 130.

[52] Dalton, *The Taming of the Demons*, 21. The subjugation of Rudra is also the creation myth for the eight great charnel grounds (*aṣṭamahāśmaśāna*). To paraphrase Georgios T. Halkias: The eight great charnel grounds in tantric lore are sacred physical sites imbued with potency, where visionary encounters and revelations of teachings take place. Symbolically, they refer to the different body parts of Rudra, the archetypal violator of the tantric precepts, spread across the sites. They are both external and internal sites, fearsome places where life and limb are in danger. They are places where the most secret teachings are transmitted and where feasts and hierogamy took place in group settings (personal communication via email, Nov. 6, 2023). The eight sites correspond to the locations of Rudra's head, heart, intestines, and genitals (cardinal directions) and his four limbs (intercardinal directions) when he was thrown by Vajrakīla from the top of Mount Malaya (Boord,

Maheśvara,[53] and are continuous with stories of religious violence from early Buddhism.[54]

This narrative of subjugation reveals two important aspects of tantric Buddhism. The first is the political organization implicit in Vajrapāṇi's relations to Vairocana as his overlord and to Śiva as his own recalcitrant retainer, who is, in turn, unwilling to swear fealty to Vairocana. Vairocana's strategy is to provide his willing chieftain with the additional resources necessary to bring that chieftain's subordinates into line. Second, the contest between Trailokyavijaya and Maheśvara reflects the conflict between Buddhist and Śaivite traditions, in this case portraying Buddhism triumphant.[55] Given that Jayavarman VII shifted the state's religious affiliation from a Śaivite to a Buddhist, Vajrapāṇi's triumph over Śiva is a powerful symbol of success, especially when displayed publicly in temple artworks. Dalton notes that "Literary and oral narratives of demon subjugation... represented a popular strategy for establishing the superiority of one's own tradition over the demonic other."[56]

Insular Southeast Asia

The relation between tantric activity in insular Southeast Asia and the sources of tantra in India is evidenced by a variety of sources—archeological, institutional, textual, epigraphic, and art historical. Andrea Acri notes that these "all conjure up the role of insular Southeast Asia as a recognized seat of esoteric cults in a highly interconnected Buddhist cosmopolis rather

"Vajrakīla Tantras," in *The Oxford Encyclopedia of Buddhism*, ed. Richard K. Payne and Georgios T. Halkias [Oxford: Oxford University Press, online 2019: https://doi.org/10.1093/acrefore/9780199340378.013.555]). See also Gudrun Bühnemann, "Bhairava and the Eight Charnel Grounds: On the History of a Monumental Painting at the Jayavāgīśvarī Temple, Kathmandu," *Berlin Indological Studies* 21 (2013): 307–326.

53 Davidson, "Reflections on the Maheśvara Subjugation Myth." See also D. L. Snellgrove's Introduction to *Sarva-Tathāgata-tattva-saṅgraha: Facsimile Reproduction of a Tenth Century Sanskrit Manuscript from Nepal*, ed. Lokesh Chandra and D. L. Snellgrove, 5–67 (Delhi: Sharada Rani, 1981). And see David Snellgrove, *Indo-Tibetan Buddhism: Indian Buddhists and Their Tibetan Successors* (Boston: Shambhala Publications, [1987] 2002), 134–141.

54 Richard K. Payne, "Lethal Fire: The Shingon Yamāntaka Abhicāra Homa," *Journal of Religion and Violence* 6.1 (2018): 11–31.

55 This significance of such motifs needs to be contextualized as an interpretation relevant to one time and place that may be irrelevant to another. See Rob Linrothe, "Beyond Sectarianism: Toward Reinterpreting the Iconography of Esoteric Buddhist Deities Trampling Hindu Gods," *Indian Journal of Buddhist Studies* 2.2 (1990): 16–25.

56 Dalton, *The Taming of the Demons*, 11.

than a remote and backward periphery."[57] Not only was it not peripheral, but Buddhist teachers and practitioners there were active participants in ongoing development of tantric Buddhist praxis. Like Sharrock, Acri highlights the creative contributions of "Maritime Asia," emphasizing that

> Far from being a mere southern conduit for the maritime circulation of Indic religions, in the period from ca. the 7th to the 14th century those regions transformed across mainland and island polities the rituals, icons, and architecture that embodied these religious insights with a dynamism that often eclipsed the established cultural centers in Northern India, Central Asia, and mainland China.[58]

There were two mandalas of insular Southeast Asia—the Srivijaya (seventh to twelfth century) and the Śailendra (eighth to eleventh century). Both played important roles in the history of tantric Buddhist praxis and were part of the wide-ranging networks of the tantric cosmopolis.

Srivijaya Dynasty, Sumatra: Dharmakīrtiśri and Atiśa

In contrast to land-based empires, Srivijaya was a maritime empire, that is, one whose expanse was based on long-distance trade and control of sea routes. Importantly, for the period that Srivijaya controlled the Strait of Malacca and the Sunda Strait, it participated in "the lucrative international trade between West Asia, India and China."[59] Buddhist monks came to Srivijaya over this maritime network, and some of them stayed there for extended periods of time.[60]

Appreciation for the sophisticated tantric Buddhist culture of Srivijaya is recorded in Tibetan sources and is evident in the life story of Atiśa. Miksic notes that by early in the eleventh century "Sumatra was known far and wide as a great centre of Buddhist practice. The 'Golden Island', almost certainly

[57] Andrea Acri, "Introduction," in *Esoteric Buddhism in Medieval Maritime Asia: Networks of Masters, Texts, Icons*, ed. Andrea Acri (Singapore: ISEAS Yusof Ishak Institute, 2016), 11. See also Andrea Acri and Peter Sharrock, "Introduction, Volume I: Intra-Asian Transfers and Mainland Southeast Asia," in *The Creative South: Buddhist and Hindu Art in Medieval Maritime Asia*, ed. Andrea Acri and Peter Sharrock, 1–6 (Singapore: ISEAS–Yusof Ishak Institute, 2022). See also Hudaya Kandahjaya, "A Study on the Origin and Significance of Borobudur," PhD diss. (Graduate Theological Union, 2004).

[58] Acri and Sharrock, "Introduction, Volume I," 1.

[59] Hermann Kulke, "Śrīvijaya Revisited: Reflections on State Formation of a Southeast Asian Thalasoccracy," *Bulletin de l'École française d'Extrême-Orient* 102 (2016): 45–96, 47.

[60] Kulke, "Śrīvijaya Revisited," 48.

denoting Sumatra, is mentioned in Tibetan sources of this period such as the *Hevajra Tantra* and the *Yogaratnamala*."[61] At this time, northeast India was under threat of Muslim invasion, and Miksic suggests that this is why Atiśa (982–1054), then twenty-nine years old, "went to Srivijaya, where there lived a famous teacher named Dharmakirti[śri]."[62] Before being invited to western Tibet, where he helped in the reestablishment of monastic Buddhism and founded the Kadampa lineage,[63] he studied and practiced with Dharmakīrtiśri in Suvarṇadvīpa (Sumatra, Java). Although this period of Atiśa's life is often passed over in silence, or only mentioned in extreme brevity,[64] his stay lasted twelve years—equal to the amount of time he spent in Tibet. His time in Sumatra was so important for him that he referred to his most important teacher, Dharmakīrtiśri, by the place name Suvarṇadvipa. One Tibetan source suggests that Dharmakīrtiśri himself was a Sumatran prince who had traveled to India and visited Bodhgaya. After he returned to Sumatra, "several students went to Srivijaya to study with Dharmakirti[śri]. . . . There is therefore reason to believe that when Atisha went to Tibet, in order to 'purify' Buddhism there (according to Tibetan sources), he replicated much of what he was taught in Sumatra."[65]

Atiśa's biography indicates the importance of Java as an interregional center of tantric Buddhism and the importance of tantric Buddhism for Atiśa. Because of Atiśa's role in the "Tibetan Renaissance," however, he is most frequently associated with Tibet and studied in the context of a reformist movement there.[66] And, given the privileged status of philosophy in Western academia, he has largely been remembered for his contributions to the transmission of Madhyamaka thought to Tibet.[67]

[61] Miksic, "The Buddhist-Hindu Divide in Premodern Southeast Asia," 23.

[62] Miksic, "The Buddhist-Hindu Divide in Premodern Southeast Asia," 23. To avoid confusion with Dharmakīrti the epistemologist (fl. c. sixth or seventh century), we will refer to the Javanese teacher as Dharmakīrtiśri, by which he is also known. The similarity between the two names has been the source of some confusion in Tibetan histories, such as the Blue Annals; see Jean Naudou, *Les Bouddhists Kaśmīriens au Moyen Age* (Paris: Presses Univesitaires de France, 1968), 105.

[63] See Ulrike Roesler, "The Kadampa: A Formative Movement in Tibetan Buddhism," in *The Oxford Encyclopedia of Buddhism*, ed. Richard K. Payne and Georgios T. Halkias, 1393–1415 (New York: Oxford University Press, 2024).

[64] For example, although treated more extensively than in other instances, Atiśa's time with Dharmakīrtiśrī is covered in four short paragraphs in "The Life of Atisha," by Ngawang Dhargyey, http://www.berzinarchives.com/web/en/archives/approaching_buddhism/teachers/lineage_masters/life_atisha.html.

[65] Miksic, "The Buddhist-Hindu Divide in Premodern Southeast Asia," 24.

[66] See, however, Ronald M. Davidson, *Tibetan Renaissance: Tantric Buddhism in the Rebirth of Tibetan Culture* (New York: Columbia University Press, 2005), 108–115.

[67] David Seyfort Ruegg, *The Literature of the Madhyamaka School of Philosophy in India* (A History of Indian Literature, vol. VII, fasc. 1. Wiesbaden: Otto Harrassowitz, 1981), 110–113.

In 1025, the Chola, a Tamil dynasty from southern India (BCE 300s to 1279 CE), conquered Srivijaya, shifting the center of Sumatran Buddhism from Palembang to more central and northern locales. Miksic notes that there were several "esoteric Buddhist sites" in these regions dating from the eleventh century.[68] Along with Srivijaya, the neighboring Śailendra dynasty of Central Java was an important node in the widespread network of tantric Buddhism.

Śailendra Dynasty in the Tantric Buddhist Network: Classical Central Java

Like Srivijaya, the Śailendra dynasty played a role in the history of Buddhist tantra in insular Southeast Asia.[69] According to Anton Zakharov, the dynasty was of Javanese origin, and it was established in central Java in the eighth century.[70] This is the period that also saw the rise of the Pāla dynasty in northwest India, the return of the Tang dynasty in China, and the beginning of the Heian period in Japan. As with the Śailendra, tantric Buddhism played an important role in all of them. The dynasty was connected to other realms in South and Southeast Asia through maritime links, including Śri Lanka, and the tantric tradition of the Abhayagiri Vihāra that was located there.

Connecting the tantric Abhayagiri lineage (Skt. *vihāra*, lit. "abode"[71]) in Śri Lanka and the Śailendra dynasty in Central Java is a delegation of Abhayagiri monks who arrived in Java in 792.[72] Although attempts were made to erase the Abhayagiri lineage from Sri Lankan history, we now know that it was one of two main lineages during the medieval period in the Sri Lankan kingdom of Anurādhapura (377 BCE to 1017 CE).

Jeffrey Sundberg argues that the tantric Abhayagiri lineage was so widely known and respected that by the middle of the eighth century "they merited an invitation to an important foreign court a thousand miles away,"[73] that is, the Śailendra. Both the Sri Lankan Second Lambakaṇṇa dynasty (691–1017) and the Śailendra did not merely consume tantric teachings and practices.

[68] Miksic, "The Buddhist-Hindu Divide in Premodern Southeast Asia," 25.

[69] Anton O. Zakharov, "The Śailendras Reconsidered" (Singapore: The Nalanda–Sriwijaya Centre, Institute of Southeast Asian Studies, 2012), 24.

[70] Zakharov, "The Śailendras Reconsidered," 27.

[71] Although not literal, "lineage" seems to more accurately portray the relations among monks than does the more literal "abode." As such, it allows for easier comparisons with other lineal relations in the history of Buddhism.

[72] Jeffrey Sundberg, "The Abhayagirivihāra's *Pāṃśukūlika* Monks in Second Lambakaṇṇa Śrī Laṅka and Śailendra Java: The Flowering and Fall of a Cardinal Center of Influence in Early Esoteric Buddhism," *Pacific World: Journal of the Institute of Buddhist Studies* 3rd series, no. 16 (2014): 49–185.

[73] Sundberg, "The Abhayagirivihāra's *Pāṃśukūlika* Monks," 49.

They were instead active agents in further developing and propagating those teachings and practices.[74]

Much of this history was lost, however, because of shifting imperial affiliations following wars between Sri Lanka and the Tamil Pandyan dynasty. Sri Lankan losses were (conveniently) attributed to the Abhayagiri lineage, which was suppressed "as part of the royal campaign to impose a Theravāda orthodoxy on the Sinhalese monasteries. . . . The result of this campaign of orthodoxy was the imposition of a historical amnesia that is very difficult for a historian to pierce."[75] The Theravādin orthodox tradition in Sri Lanka at that time was the Mahāvihāra, the "Great Monastery."

Disappearing the "esoteric experiment" involved not just erasure from the historical records of Sri Lanka, such as "The Shorter Chronicle" (*Cūḷavaṃsa*), but also the destruction of libraries of texts, including the Abhayagiri's own historical records (Skt. *vaṃsas*), the destruction of inscriptions, and the discarding of statuary. Steven Collins notes that the chronicles of the Mahāvihāra "tell of repeated book-burnings by pro-Mahāvihārin kings."[76] As the textual materials appear to be beyond recovery, establishing the shared Abhayagiri identity of monastic institutions in Sri Lanka and Java depends on the material record, both art historical and archaeological.

Matching dual platforms found both in Sri Lanka and in Java demonstrate the common religious history of the two states. The first is located at Tiriyāy in Sri Lanka, where a large cache of Mahāyāna and Vajrayāna statuary was found buried, and the other is on the Ratu Baka (also, Ratu Boko) plateau in Java.[77] The platform at Ratu Baka was constructed in 792 specifically for the Abhayagiri monks who had traveled there from Sri Lanka. In Sundberg's interpretation, "the foundation of this branch of the Abhayagirivihāra on the top of the Ratu Baka plateau must have been one of the culminating points of a deliberate attempt on the part of the Śailendra kings to couple their court monks into the most current trends of thought and practice of monasteries in the cosmopolitan Buddhist world, likely in order to gird their realm with crisis-averting supernatural power."[78]

[74] Sundberg, "The Abhayagirivihāra's *Pāṃśukūlika* Monks," 50.

[75] Sundberg, "The Abhayagirivihāra's *Pāṃśukūlika* Monks," 74–75.

[76] Steven Collins, "On the Very Idea of the Pāli Canon," *Journal of the Pali Text Society* XV (1990): 89–126. Reprint: 78.

[77] See Andrea Acri, "Once More on the 'Ratu Boko Mantra': Magic, Realpolitik, and Bauddha-Śaiva Dynamics in Ancient Nusantara," in *Esoteric Buddhism in Medieval Maritime Asia: Networks of Masters, Texts, Icons*, ed. Andrea Acri, 323–348 (Singapore: ISEAS Yusof Ishak Institute, 2016).

[78] Sundberg, "The Abhayagirivihāra's *Pāṃśukūlika* Monks," 93.

Sundberg suggests that these distinctive dual platforms were used for initiation, probably both monastic and royal.[79] In this regard, we can point out that this dual-platform structure parallels the dual-altar initiatory setting that Kūkai describes he experienced in Tang and which continues in use today on Kōyasan for initiations into the Shingon lineage. Each of the two altars employed in Shingon initiations is one of the two mandalas in the dual-mandala system widespread through East Asian tantric praxis.[80]

As maritime dynasties, exchange with India, China, and other areas throughout South, Southeast, and East Asia enabled Śailendra and its neighbor Srivijaya to prosper. Just as the Silk Road was the vehicle not only for commercial but also cultural exchanges, the sea route between India and China moved both goods and monks, rituals, texts, and cultural knowledge between South Asia and East Asia. The reach of these cultural exchanges extended as far as the Philippines, another location in which later religious traditions—in this case Catholic—worked to place earlier Buddhist forms under erasure.

Two epigraphic findings from the Philippines with tantric significance are a copper plate and a gold foil amulet, both containing the dhāraṇi for the "textual deity" Mahāpratisarā.[81] Roderick Orlina explains that this dhāraṇī was part of a praxis that spread across maritime Buddhist Asia.[82] It was, for example, promoted by Amoghavajra who visited Java twice (in 718 and between 741 and 746), and who translated the "Great Wish-Fulfilling Spell" (*Mahāpratisarāmahāvidyārājñī*) into Chinese.[83] Indicative of the spread and popularity of the dhāraṇī, the earliest record of it are fragmentary birch-bark records dating from the first half of the seventh century recovered from Gilgit in Kashmir.[84] In addition to two more Chinese translations, the Mahāpratisarā dhāraṇī text was translated into Tibetan, Uigur, and

[79] For Sundberg's speculations on the double platform's function, see Sundberg, "The Abhayagirivihāra's *Pāṃśukūlika* Monks," 104.

[80] These similarities suggest directions for future research on the networks connecting South Asia, Southeast Asia, and East Asia that combines art historical and archeological methods.

[81] Cruijsen, Thomas, Arlo Griffiths, and Marijke J. Klokke, "The Cult of the Buddhist *Dhāraṇī* Deity Mahāpratisarā Along the Maritime Silk Route: New Epigraphical and Iconographic Evidence from the Indonesian Archipelago," *Journal of the International Association of Buddhist Studies* 35.1–2 (2012 [2013]): 71–157, 73.

[82] Roderick Orlina, "Epigraphical Evidence for the Cult of Mahāpratisarā in the Philippines," *Journal of the International Association of Buddhist Studies* 33.1–2 (2012/2013): 159–169.

[83] Da suiqiu tuoluoni 大随求陀罗尼,T. 1153. For a complete review of the sources, see Gergely Hidas, *Mahāpratisarā-Mahāvidyārājñī: The Great Amulet, The Great Queen of Spells* (New Delhi: International Academy of Indian Culture and Aditya Prakashan, 2012), 7–12.

[84] Hidas, *Mahāpratisarā-Mahāvidyārājñī*, 7.

Mongolian.[85] The gold amulet is recorded in a script known to have been used in the tenth and eleventh centuries. Taken together, the copper plate and the amulet demonstrate some presence of tantric Buddhism in the Philippines, which is perhaps the farthest reach of the sea routes connecting maritime Buddhism across South and Southeast Asia.

As noted by Kandahjaya, "Java, or more generally the archipelago, lies geographically in the middle of [the] sea-route Buddhist transmission line between South Asia and East Asia."[86] Again, far from being passive, derivative and peripheral, these were active centers in the tantric Buddhist cosmopolis. The importance of both Indic culture expanding across Southeast Asia and local cultural creativity is evident in the now internationally renowned Buddhist monument, Borobudur.[87]

Borobudur: Monumental Presencing of the Realm of the Buddhas

While the importance of translocal exchange has been emphasized repeatedly by scholars of Borobudur, the monument is at the same time Javanese. The interpretation of Borobudur has long been a matter of debate, particularly whether its mandalic quality indicates that it was constructed within a tantric context. Implicit within this debate are different methodological assumptions regarding not only the function and meaning of such monuments but also the nature of tantric Buddhism.

The Śailendra dynasty constructed Borobudur around the end of the eighth or beginning of the ninth century. It is not simply an awe-inspiring monumental construction but is part of a cultural dynamic that transformed

[85] The Tibetan name for the Mahāpratisarā dhāraṇī text is "'phags pa rig pa'i rgyal mo so sor 'brang ba chen mo," rendered as "The Noble Queen of Incantations: The Great Amulet." For a translation of the Tibetan version of this text (Toh. 561), see the 84000 website at https://84000.co/translation/toh561. The summary there explains that the text "prescribes the use of amulets into which the incantation is physically incorporated. These devices are then worn around the neck or arm, attached to flags, interred in stūpas and funeral pyres, or otherwise used anywhere their presence is deemed beneficial. Wearing or encountering the incantation promises a range of effects, including the prevention and healing of illness, the conception and birth of male offspring, and control over the world of nonhuman spirit entities. The text also protects against consequences of negative deeds, delivering evildoers from negative rebirths and ensuring their place among the gods. The promise of augmenting merit even extends in one passage to an increase of mindfulness and liberation from saṃsāra."

[86] Kandahjaya, "Origin and Significance of Borobudur," 45.

[87] Borobudur has been designated by UNESCO as a World Heritage Site, https://whc.unesco.org/en/list/592.

the landscape, constructed buildings, and installed statues and narrative panels as assertions of power, authority, and identity.[88] What is known as the Kayumwungan inscription has been augmented by recent discoveries of additional parts of the inscription. Now more complete, the inscription has also been complemented by other archeological findings. These demonstrate a relation between the inscription and both Borobudur and the ancient Javanese Buddhist text, *the Sang Hyang Kamahāyānikan*. With these additional sources, the inscription is now understood to record the royal consecration of Borobudur.[89]

Constructed on top of a small hill, Borobudur appears to have originally had a lake in front of it, at least seasonally. The site was probably chosen to reflect the imagery of Sumeru, the central mountain of the Indic cosmos. Located at the center of the cosmic ocean, on Sumeru's peak is the fabulous palace of Indra, while Jambudvīpa, the continent upon which we are thought to reside, is one of four continents surrounding its base.[90] This symbolism is widely employed in Buddhist Asia, perhaps as a consequence of the widespread influence of the *Avataṃsaka sūtra*.[91] The imagery from that text is often the symbolic reference for the design of features in Japanese temple gardens, for instance, as well as contributing to the symbolism of the Mahābodhi temple in Bodhgaya, India.

Julie Gifford suggests that the "architects appear to have artfully selected a location that would allow them to use a combination of built form and natural landscape to represent the *cakravāla* cosmos."[92] In Indic cosmology, the *cakravāla* (Skt. var. *cakravāda*) is the ring of metal mountains that surround our realm of desire (Skt. *kāmaloka*), but it is used to refer to the cosmos as a whole.[93]

[88] Cf. Anne M. Blackburn, "Writing Buddhist Histories from Landscape and Architecture: Sukhotai and Chiang Mai," *Buddhist Studies Review* 24.2 (2007): 192–225, 193–194.

[89] Hudaya Kandahjaya, "The Lord of All Virtues," *Pacific World: Journal of the Insititute of Buddhist Studies* third series, no. 11 (2009): 1–24, 1–2.

[90] Eric Huntington, "Buddhist Cosmology," in *The Oxford Encyclopedia of Buddhism*, ed. Richard K. Payne and Georgios T. Halkias, 478–493 (New York: Oxford University Press, print version 2024, online 2022: https://doi.org/10.1093/acrefore/9780199340378.013.1050).

[91] On the role of the Avataṃsaka sūtra and tantric Buddhism in state formation in China and Japan, see Dorothy C. Wong, "The Art of *Avataṃsaka* Buddhism in the Courts of Empress Wu and Emperor Shōmu/Empress Kōmyō," in *Avataṃsaka (Huayan, Kegon, Flower Ornament) Buddhism in East Asia: Origins and Adaptation of a Visual Culture*, ed. Robert Gimello, Frédéric Girard, and Imre Hamar, 223–260 (Wiesbaden: Harrassowitz Verlag, 2012).

[92] Gifford, *Buddhist Practice and Visual Culture*, 150.

[93] Buswell and Lopez, *Dictionary of Buddhism*, s.v. "cakravāḍa," 163.

Borobudur: Palace, Mandala, Stupa, Mountain, or What?

Kandhajaya has pointed out that modern Western scholars have interpreted Borobudur as modeled on a variety of different "possible architectural prototypes—monastery (vihāra), memorial (stūpa), cosmic mountain (sumeru), cosmic diagram (maṇḍala), palace (*prāsāda*), or penthouse (*kūṭāgāra*)."[94]

Woodward adds to this complexity by suggesting a symbolic relation between the architecture of Borobudur and "yogic anatomy," that is, esoteric physiology.[95] This physiological symbolism is either modeled on chapter five of the *Saṃvarodaya tantra*, or—in a reversal of the ordinary academic privileging of text—provided the model for that text "and perhaps for other aspects of the Yoginī Tantra as well."[96] Thus, Woodward's analysis calls into question the presupposition that the relation is always from texts as determinative and foundational, to other aspects of traditions. Geri H. Malandra makes the same point regarding another Buddhist temple complex, Ellora, in the western peninsular region of India. She describes Ellora as "a kaleidoscopic expression of religious architecture on a monumental scale, its mile long basaltic scarp punctuated by thirty four major rock-cut temples."[97] Asserting that "many of its images have no clear relationship to texts that might explain their meaning or record iconographical details,"[98] she says that "what makes a place like Ellora so fascinating and important is that [it] does *not* conform in every detail to what we know from religious texts."[99]

In the absence of any specific text that can be identified as the model for the monument, Gifford concludes that Borobudur is not a mandala.[100] Gifford, however, largely considers Borobudur in isolation, rather than as part of a circulation of tantric architecture and imagery from Pala to Java and back across the subcontinent to Tabo. Swati Chemburkar, however, places Borobudur in relation to several other Buddhist sites across South and

[94] Kandahjaya, "A Study on the Origin and Significance of Borobudur," 6.

[95] See Chapter II.

[96] Woodward, "Esoteric Buddhism in Southeast Asia," 343.

[97] Geri H. Malandra, *Unfolding a Maṇḍala: The Buddhist Cave Temples at Ellora* (Albany: State University of New York Press, 1993), xvii.

[98] Malandra, *Unfolding a Maṇḍala*, xviii.

[99] Malandra, *Unfolding a Maṇḍala*, xix. In this regard, see also Gregory Schopen, "On the Buddha and His Bones: The Conception of a Relic in the Inscriptions of Nāgārjunikoṇḍa," *Journal of the American Oriental Society* 108.4 (Oct.–Dec. 1988): 527–537; see also Gregory Schopen, "Archaeology and Protestant Presuppositions in the Study of Indian Buddhism," *History of Religions* 31.1 (Aug. 1991): 1–23.

[100] Gifford, *Buddhist Practice and Visual Culture*, 33–34.

Southeast Asia, demonstrating a consistent mandalic pattern.[101] Further, the particular issue of whether Borobudur is a mandala highlights the need to question some presumptions. First is the presumption that there is a close correlation between text and monument. Second is that a text is the primary source from which the monument is to be explained. And, third, that the major tantric texts are the sources from which symbolism and meaning derive.[102] Chemburkar calls attention instead to the known movement of mandalic diagrams, sculptural models, and artwork along the maritime routes between Pala and Tang, as well as architectural models of the Mahābodhi temple that were conveyed "from eastern India to Nepal, Tibet, Arakan, and Myanmar."[103] Thus, sources of mandalic models for Borobudur need not have only been key tantras, but they could well also have been portable shrines, diagrams used in ritual, or other artwork.[104] Sam van Schaik argues that portable shrines representing the Mahābodhi temple "allowed the ritual act of veneration of the Vajrāsana Buddha[105] to be carried out in places other than Bodhgayā itself, making possible the performance of offerings, circumambulation of the temple and other devotional acts."[106] As valued ritual objects transported by pilgrims, these models of the Mahābodhi temple would have been available as models for what a Buddhist monument should look like.[107]

In addition, we should not rule out the role of artisans and craftsmen who may have carried mandalic models in memory, or in handbooks or sketchbooks that have been lost to history because they were not "canonic." In other words, cultural knowledge such as the importance of mandalic

[101] Swati Chemburkar, "Tantra and Temple Architecture in Buddhist Southeast Asia," in *The Oxford Handbook of Tantric Studies*, ed. Richard K. Payne and Glen A. Hayes, 581–677 (Oxford: Oxford University Press, 2024).

[102] This can be a bit slippery, since a scholar might reasonably maintain that these texts are the only ones available to us today, but that slides over into treating them as the actual sources for people of the time.

[103] Chemburkar, "Stūpa to Maṇḍala," 193.

[104] Chemburkar, "Stūpa to Maṇḍala," 190–192.

[105] ["Vajrāsana" refers to the site of Śākyamuni's awakening, commemorated by the Mahābodhi temple.]

[106] Sam van Schaik, "The Internalisation of the Vajrāsana," in *Precious Treasures from the Diamond Throne: Finds from the Site of the Buddha's Enlightenment*, ed. Sam van Schaik et al. (London: The British Museum, 2021), 70.

[107] Transforming a fixed location such as the Mahābodhi temple into a portable object for ritual practice employs the same kind of logic as the construction of miniature Shikoku pilgrimages discussed in Chapter III on East Asia. Not only was the sanctity of Buddhism portable in the form of teachers, teachings, and texts, but the sanctity of Buddhist sites was made portable as well. As noted in Chapter III, this makes the distinction between fixed and portable more complex than it might first appear.

organization can be conveyed by many different means, not just by major canonic texts. There is also a distinction between saying that Borobudur is a mandala and saying which mandala it is. It is entirely possible that it is in an important sense unique, what might be called the "Borobudur mandala," as it were.

Important to the symbolic impact of Borobudur are its narrative panels. Gifford emphasizes the ritual and embodied experiential aspects of an encounter with the narrative panels. "The narrative relief panels contribute to an enduring programmatic ritual venue that demands to be encountered in part through bodily movement. This is something that architecturally situated narrative art does *better* than written texts can."[108] In other words, the important stories of the Buddhist tradition may be known by experiencing artistic representations of the stories found along the route leading up to the top of Borobudur, instead of from texts.[109]

Related to the suggestion that the symbolism of esoteric physiology contributed to the construction of Borobudur is a vision of the human body as a stupa on the outside and a palace on the inside. This symbolism engages the five-element stupa (Jpn. *gorintō*): the cubic base for the earth element, then a sphere for water, a pyramid for fire, cresent for air, and a drop for empty space.[110] This stupa is homologized with the human body, as for example in funerary monuments on Mt. Kōya in Japan.[111] This equation appears to go back to the origins of stupa as memorial mounds for the Buddha Śākyamuni—the stupa being an enduring bodily presence in the symbolic form of the five elements.[112]

Embodying a buddha, stupas make a buddha present in a mandala. Similar to the "nesting" of stupa and palace (Skt. *prāsāda*) suggested for Borobudur, a nesting relation between stupa and mandala is exemplified by the altar of Chion-in, the Shingon temple on Kōyasan where I studied. Like many Shingon temples, the altar there comprises a mandala with a stupa in

[108] Gifford, *Buddhist Practice and Visual Culture*, 49. Emphases in original.

[109] See also Victor Mair, *Painting and Performance: Chinese Picture Recitation and Its Indian Genesis* (Honolulu: University of Hawai'i Press, 1988).

[110] An interesting discussion in relation to funerary memorials in Japan is in Helmut Brinker, "Facing the Unseen: On the Interior Adornment of Eizon's Iconic Body," *Archives of Asian Art* 50 (1997/1998): 42–61, 43–44.

[111] The representation is a cube at the base representing earth, a sphere representing water, a triangle representing fire, a demilune representing air, and a drop representing empty space. These five elements constitute the cosmos, including both humans and buddhas. This "elemental" identity of humans and buddhas informs the ritual practice of the threefold mystery.

[112] Adrian Snodgrass, *The Symbolism of the Stupa* (Ithaca, NY: Cornell Southeast Asia Program, 1985), 360.

the center. The explanation that I was given, an "oral transmission," was that inside the stupa was another mandala, at the center of which was another stupa, and so on indefinitely. This alternate nesting of mandala and stupa is also reminiscent of the kind of imagery associated with the jewelled net of Indra, described in the *Avataṃsaka sūtra*. Each node of the net being a jewel, each jewel reflects all of the others—an infinite series of reflections such as when two mirrors are placed facing one another.

Referring to an earlier perspective that examined Borobudur in isolation, Swati Chemburkar notes that Borobudur's "stepped pyramid structure and maṇḍalic arrangement of deities in circular form has hitherto been considered unique and without precedent."[113] However, the monument's significance emerges by comparing it with other sites, that is, when it is not viewed as an isolated instance, or only in relation to texts. J. L. Moens provided a more complex context when he placed Borobudur in relation to two other monuments, Mendut and Pawon, which are close to Borobudur.[114] Moens argues that Borobudur itself was not originally tantric, but that with the addition of Pawon and Mendut about a quarter century after Borobudur was finished, the entire complex was imbued with tantric imagery and used for royal rituals. Thus, like the Shikoku pilgrimage discussed in the previous chapter, the tantric character of Borobudur resulted from changes over time, rather than from some single founding act—continuity rather than rupture. And its tantric nature is established by the broader context and the ritual use of the monument.

Providing an even larger context by looking further afield from Borobudur in Java, Chemburkar looks to the Tabo monastery. Now located in an isolated region in the far north of India, Tabo was visited by Atīśa in 1042 when it was being renovated. The monastery contains "a complete sculptural *maṇḍala* of the life-size clay figures of the Vajradhātu Maṇḍala deities. . . . An exactly contemporaneous set of Vajradhātu Maṇḍala bronzes survives from East Java."[115] By considering Borobudur in relation to other architecturally similar monuments from across the subcontinent, Chemburkar avoids the methodological pitfall of considering the monument in isolation, that is, in too narrow a cultural context.

[113] Swati Chemburkar, "Borobudur's Pāla Forebear? A Field Note from Kesariya, Bihar, India," in *Esoteric Buddhism in Mediaeval Maritime Asia: Networks of Masters, Texts, Icons*, ed. Andrea Acri (Singapore: ISEAS-Yusuf Ishak Institute, 2016), 191–192.

[114] J. L. Moens, "Barabudur, Mendut and Pawon and their mutual relationship," trans. Mark Long (privately published, www.borobudur.tv, 2007). While Moens saw the complex of temples as tantric, his argument remains unconvincing for some present specialists, such as Hudaya Kandahjaya (personal communication, via email, Sept. 19, 2020).

[115] Chemburkar, "*Stūpa* to *Maṇḍala*," 171–172.

Chemburkar sketches a sequence that begins with the monument at "Kesariya in east Champāran, Bihar, India (ca. seventh to eighth centuries CE); Borobudur in Central Java, Indonesia (ca. eighth to ninth centuries CE); and the main temple of Tabo Monastery (founded in 996 CE and renovated in the eleventh century [during the period that Atiśa visited]) in the Indo-Tibetan sphere, Spiti Valley India."[116] These three monuments present "a body of evidence in support of inter-Asian connections. These sites reflect a consistent pattern of religious, cultural, and ritual ideas that defy geographical boundaries."[117] The Vajradhātu mandala of the *Sarvatathagatatattvasaṃgraha tantra* is central to the analysis of the conceptual complex that was transmitted.

In Chemburkar's understanding, Borobudur is an instance of a more general shift in Buddhist architecture that served as the ritual center for Buddhist kings. That shift is from stupa to mandala, and it is found in the mandalic structure of Kesariya, Borobudur, and Tabo. These royal centers reflect the facets of mandalas—the functional plurality of organizing a social polity, legitimating royalty, localizing the cosmic order, providing an initiatory and ritual space, and yogic identification with buddhas, bodhisattvas, and protectors.[118]

Summary

Both historical events and climactic degradation have eradicated most, though not all, of the Southeast Asian textual record regarding forms of Buddhism other than those strains that developed into modern Theravāda.[119] Our historical understanding of tantric Buddhism in Southeast Asia largely depends, therefore, on the material record—art history, archeology, epigraphy—and on textual sources from outside the area, such as those from China and Tibet. The material record found in the wide range of archeological sites throughout Southeast Asia also highlights the actions of kings who engaged in construction projects, sometimes on a monumental

[116] Chemburkar, "*Stūpa* to *Maṇḍala*," 173–175.
[117] Chemburkar, "*Stūpa* to *Maṇḍala*," 175.
[118] Chemburkar, "*Stūpa* to *Maṇḍala*," 220.
[119] Sven Bretfeld, "Theravāda Buddhism," in *The Oxford Encyclopedia of Buddhism*, ed. Richard K. Payne and Georgios Halkias (Oxford: Oxford University Press; https://doi.org/10.1093/acrefore/9780199340378.013.561), n.p. Also, Nathan McGovern, "Esoteric Buddhism in Southeast Asia," in *The Oxford Encyclopedia of Buddhism*, ed. Richard K. Payne and Georgios Halkias (Oxford: Oxford University Press; https://doi.org/10.1093/acrefore/9780199340378.013.617), n.p.

scale. For this reason, the perspective of state formation—creation, maintenance, and defense—provides a methodological window for studying the history of tantric Buddhism in Southeast Asia.

Like other strains within Buddhism, tantra plays an important role in state formation—not only in Southeast Asia but across the entire range of the Buddhist cosmopolis. Although the modern, post-Enlightenment division between state and religion seems to often be simply presumed in popular discourse and religious studies, the role of tantra in state formation turns out to be much more typically the case.

Interpreting the material record requires Buddhist scholars continue to embrace methodologies beyond the constraints of textual studies. Such an embrace does not replace the textual, but instead complements and contextualizes the textual record by reference to other records of Buddhist history. Rather than presuming that the textual is primary, and the material derivative, textual and material approaches mutually augment one another. The same methodological complementarity can bring ritual, economic, and sociopolitical methods into play as well.

A different aspect of the prominence of the material record for the history of tantric Buddhism in Southeast Asia is the necessity to balance local and translocal perspectives. This dual perspective frames Borobudur as a Javanese monument contextualized by the other two temples of Mendut and Pawon, and as a transregional instance of mandalic architecture found across the Buddhist cosmopolis. The expanse of networks that made it possible for tantric masters, teachings, texts, and practices to move throughout the Buddhist cosmopolis stretched across the whole of Buddhist Asia, and therefore it is that whole that needs to be taken into account as the context for interpretation.

Maritime trade routes that connected South, Southeast, and East Asia had complements in overland routes that connected South, Inner, and East Asia—the better known "Silk Route."[120] Dominating Inner Asian Buddhism is Tibet, which received some Buddhist praxes from along the Silk Route, some from China and some from India.

[120] A third trade route, sometimes called the "Rice Route" connected northeast India with southwest China. The significance of these connections for the spread of tantric Buddhism is still in need of further research. Regarding the complexity of the study of this area, see Megan Bryson, "Mahākāla Worship in the Dali Kingdom (937–1253): A Study and Translation of the *Dahei tianshen daochang yi*," *Journal of the International Association of Buddhist Studies* 35.1–2 (2012/2013): 3–69. She shows that the emphasis on Indic imagery for Mahākāla is a reflection of political strategics, rather than evidence of India as a source more direct than China.

V

Inner Asia

Decaying Corpses and Hungry Ghouls

Introduction

Abhirūpā Nandā was a young woman much taken with her own beauty. Once she attended a discourse by the Buddha Śākyamuni, and he created an illusory woman standing next to him, one that only he and Nandā were able to see. This visionary beauty seems to Nandā like a golden goose in comparison to whom she herself is more like a crow. Over the course of his teaching, the Buddha gradually changes the vision, making the illusory woman appear older and older, until finally

> the old woman is gripped by a disease so terrible that she screams in agony, falls to the ground, rolls in her own urine and feces, and eventually dies. Her body then bloats, and pus and worms soon leak out of every orifice and festering sore. Finally, crows and dogs descend on the body and devour it. The visual display works in ways that the Buddha's words could not. Rūpa Nandā now understands her own body's impermanence with an immediacy that would not have been possible had she merely listened to a sermon on the topic.[1]

In lived Buddhist praxis, impermanence is not an abstract philosophical concept. Despite often being treated as a metaphysical or ontological claim in much of the Western literature on Buddhist thought, for the Buddhist adherent it is an immediate confrontation with the inevitability of sickness, old age, and death. Despite modernizing attempts to place happiness

[1] Sarah McClintock, "Compassionate Trickster: The Buddha as a Literary Character in the Narratives of Early Indian Buddhism," *Journal of the American Academy of Religion* 79.1 (March 2011): 90–112, 104–105.

Tantra Across the Buddhist Cosmopolis. Richard K. Payne, Oxford University Press. © Oxford University Press 2025.
DOI: 10.1093/9780197825105.003.0005

at the center of Buddhism, various expressions of impermanence thread through the entirety of Buddhist history, and they constitute an important strand of tantric Buddhist praxis. More explicitly, the mindfulness of death (Skt. *maraṇānusmṛti*, Pali *maraṇānusatti*) is a meditative practice found throughout the Buddhist tradition.[2]

Although some commentators have tended to characterize tantra in terms of horrific representations of death and decay, these themes are not inherently tantric, much less can they serve to define tantra. Since death, decay, and impermanence are found across Buddhist praxis, what makes some instances tantric? Components of Buddhist thought and practice, whether abstract ones such as impermanence or concrete ones such as sickness, old age, and death, have tantric inflections by context, use, and designation. The Inner Asian tradition of the Severance (Tib. *Chöd*) employs ritual practices and visualizations focusing on death and decay, and used in that context, those components of the broader Buddhist tradition can be designated tantric.

A focus on death and decay transgresses against widely shared social norms oriented toward growth and life. Historically, much of both scholarly and popular literature has identified transgressive practices, such as those focusing on death and decay, wrathful deities and hungry ghosts, as the hallmark of tantra—its defining characteristic.[3] Transgression, however, is itself contextual—it depends on the norms being transgressed. "Transgression" is a three-term relation, one that includes not just the quality of transgressing, and that which transgresses, but also the cultural standards that determine what is a transgression.

Buddhism, for example, has usually transgressed orthodox Brahmanical rules—contravening rules of purity and pollution, and denying caste identity. Charnel grounds, where corpses were discarded to decay in the open air, and cremation grounds, where corpses were burnt, were used as sites for meditation by Buddhist monks. Purposely encountering corpses is a particularly striking instance of a Buddhist practice that transgresses Brahmanical norms of purity.

[2] Sarah Shaw, "Buddhist Meditation and Contemplation," in *The Oxford Encyclopedia of Buddhism*, ed. Richard K. Payne and Georgios T. Halkias, 506–527 (New York: Oxford University Press, 2024), 518.

[3] See David B. Gray, "Eating the Heart of the Brahmin: Representations of Alterity and the Formation of Identity in Tantric Buddhist Discourse," *History of Religions* 45.1 (August 2005): 45–69.

Other yogic practitioners were also transgressing Brahmanical rules of purity by frequenting charnel grounds.[4] Among these, the Kāpālika ascetics were particularly focused on charnel ground practices. The Kāpālikas followed a twofold ascetic practice: identification and penance. David N. Lorenzen explains this double asceticism, saying that "the Kāpālikas in fact ritually modeled their lives on a divine archetype, on the god Śiva-Kapālin who must endure a lengthy penance to atone for the sin of having cut off one of the five heads of Brahmā."[5] Gavin Flood glosses the name Kāpālikas as "skull-men," from the skull-topped staff (Skt. *khaṭvāṅga*) and skull bowl that they carry as part of their great vow (Skt. *mahāvrata*) to identify with Śiva, who in his wrathful form, Bhairava, had murdered Brahman.[6] Regarding their practices, Flood explains that

> The Kāpālika ascetic lived in the cremation grounds, imitating his fierce deities and appeasing these deities with offerings of blood, meat, alcohol and sexual fluids from ritual intercourse unconstrained by caste restrictions. . . . The goal of the Kāpālika was power (*siddhi*) which he thought he could achieve through breaking social taboos, appeasing his deities with offerings which would be anathema to the vedic practitioner, and harnessing the power of his deities through controlled possession.[7]

The Kāpālikas and similar tantric groups developing alongside Buddhist tantra are generally associated with the medieval period.[8] However, practices that breached Brahmanical purity, including charnel ground practices, constitute part of the wide spread of Indic religious culture, and were present from much earlier.[9] Being based on practices that both predate the time of

[4] For a full discussion, see Gavin Flood, *An Introduction to Hinduism* (Cambridge: Cambridge University Press, 1996), 148–173. See also Wendy Doniger, *The Hindus: An Alternative History* (New York: Penguin Press, 2009), 406–444.

[5] David N. Lorenzen, "New Data on the Kāpālikas," in *Criminal Gods and Demon Devotees: Essays on the Guardians of Popular Hinduism*, ed. Alf Hiltelbeitel (Albany: State University of New York Press, 1989), 231.

[6] Flood, *An Introduction to Hinduism*, 165.

[7] Flood, *An Introduction to Hinduism*, 165.

[8] See also Shaman Hatley, "Converting the Ḍākinī: Goddess Cults and the Tantras of the Yoginīs Between Buddhism and Śaivism," in *Tantric Traditions in Transmission and Translation*, ed. David Gray and Richard Ryan Overbey, 37–86 (Oxford: Oxford University Press, 2016; DOI: 10.1093/acprof:oso/9780199763689.003.0003).

[9] In this regard, see in particular Ronald M. Davidson, "More Pre-Tantric Sources of Tantrism: Skulls and Skull-Cups," in *Tantra, Magic, and Vernacular Religions in Monsoon Asia: Texts, Practices, and Practitioners from the Margins*, ed. Andrea Acri and Paolo E. Rosati, 12–39 (London: Routledge, 2023).

Śākyamuni, and which were integrated into the Buddhist tradition in its earliest formations, charnel ground practices develop within Buddhism and are not a breach from Buddhist norms. They cannot, therefore, be explained away as later corruptions of a putatively pure early Buddhist tradition.[10]

The *Satipaṭṭhana sutta*,[11] an early Buddhist text, prescribes charnel ground practices, and these are also known from such wide-ranging sources as the orthodox and respected Theravādin teacher Buddhaghosa's *Visuddhimagga* (dating from the fifth century), inscriptions from Sumatra dating from 1024,[12] and the writings of Kūkai, founder of the tantric Shingon tradition, in ninth-century Japan. These examples are not intended to suggest a single developmental line from pre-Buddhist and early Buddhist charnel ground meditations to Buddhist tantra, extending from South Asia to East Asia and Inner Asia. It is instead intended to highlight that Buddhist monks adhering to orthodox practices were in charnel grounds, meditating on corpses and skeletons, or were replicating such practices in more symbolic ways, and that these ideas and practices can be traced across the entirety of the Buddhist cosmopolis. This chapter explores the varieties of such practices, demonstrating that neither transgressive practices *per se* nor a focus on death and decay is a defining characteristic of tantric Buddhism. It then turns to examine the Severance (*Chöd*) tradition in Tibet to uncover the importance of context, use, and designation in creating a specifically tantric inflection of these practices. To see both the continuity of these practices and how they come to have a tantric inflection, several will be described as part of lived practice.

Meditations on the Foulness of the Decaying Human Body

Predating Śākyamuni Buddha, charnel ground meditation was practiced by members of various traditions of renunciates (Skt. *śramaṇas*). These practices, and belief in their efficacy, were already part of the cultural milieu

[10] This is a rhetorical strategy found in some contemporary secular Buddhists who equate original, pure, and authoritative, and reject Mahāyāna and tantric traditions as not original, impure, and inauthentic. See Richard K. Payne and Casey Alexandra Kemp, "Secular Buddhism," in *The Oxford Encyclopedia of Buddhism*, ed. Richard K. Payne and Georgios T. Halkias, 2125–2152 (New York: Oxford University Press, 2024), 2138–2140.

[11] MN 10. For a translation and commentary, see Thānissaro, "The Establishing of Mindfulness Discourse Satipaṭṭhāna Sutta (MN 10)," https://www.dhammatalks.org/suttas/MN/MN10.html.

[12] John Miksic, "The Buddhist-Hindu Divide in Premodern Southeast Asia" (Nalanda-Sriwijaya Centre Working Paper Series no. 1. Singapore: Institute of Southeast Asian Studies, 2010), 28.

within which the Buddhist tradition arose. Śākyamuni's quest leading to the extinction of mistaken conceptions (Skt. *jñeyāvaraṇa*) and misplaced affections (Skt. *kleśāvaraṇa*) was famously initiated by the four sights, which along with an aged man, a sick man, and a mendicant, included a corpse. While Buddhism is at times reduced to rather abstract and "bloodless" philosophic concepts such as impermanence (Skt. *anitya*), emptiness (Skt. *sunyatā*), and conditioned coproduction (Skt. *pratītyasamutpāda*), confrontation with a corpse is an immediate, visceral encounter revealing the truth of impermanence. The founding narrative of Buddhism suggests that directly encountering sickness, old age, and death creates an awareness of impermanence, and it was this awareness that motivated Śākyamuni to leave his life of luxury.

Unexpectedly confronting the reality of death and personal impermanence can be transformative. Several years ago, a colleague recounted her encounter with a funeral procession in South India. Rather than being hidden in a coffin, the corpse had been strapped into a chair that was carried by members of the procession. She clearly recalled the feelings of shock and dismay that this encounter instilled in her, likening the effect of her experience to Śākyamuni's. While my colleague's experience had not been intentional, actively seeking out such experiences in charnel grounds was part of the early yogic milieu. These practices were integrated into the Buddhist meditative tradition as a means of directly perceiving the immediate reality of bodily impermanence, and thereby overcoming attachments.

Pāli literature, both canonic and paracanonic, not only mentions such practices, but actively advocates them. For example, according to the rules of the order (Skt./Pāli *vinaya*), the robes that a monk wears (Skt. *kāṣāya*, Pāli *kāsāya*) are to be made from pieces of cloth that have been discarded as useless, tattered, defiled—including cloths stained by menstrual blood, urine, feces, or mucus, and the shrouds in which the dead have been wrapped.[13] The *vinaya* includes guidelines for how to take cloth from corpses in a respectful manner, and how and when the cloth gathered in this way is to be shared with other monks.[14] Superficially this is a confrontation with attachments to fine clothing, but perhaps more importantly it simultaneously confronts the monk with the dualistic conceptions of attachment and rejection, purity

[13] Willa Jane Tanabe, "Robes and Clothing," in *Encyclopedia of Buddhism*, ed. Robert E. Buswell, Jr. 731–735 (New York: Macmillan, 2004).

[14] Ṭhānissaro, *The Buddhist Monastic Code, II: The Khandhaka Rules* (Valley Center, CA: Metta Forest Monastery, 2001), ch. 2, "Cloth Requisites" (unpaginated, pdf p. 21).

and pollution, and, most profoundly, the personal physicality of bodily death and decay.[15] As George Bond has expressed it in his study of meditations on death in the Theravāda tradition, "Death, as the pivot on which *saṃsāra* turns and the archetype of *dukkha*, represents a basic datum for the wisdom (*paññā*) that rends the veil of ignorance."[16]

One sequence of the systematic training program found in the *Satipaṭṭhana sutta*, foundational for many in the contemporary insight meditation movement, is a ninefold contemplation of a decaying corpse. The practitioner is told to visualize as

> though he were to see a corpse thrown aside in a charnel ground—one, two, or three days dead, bloated, livid, and oozing matter . . . being devoured by crows, hawks, vultures, dogs, jackals, or various kinds of worms . . . a skeleton with flesh and blood held together with sinews . . . a fleshless skeleton smeared with blood, held together with sinews . . . a skeleton without flesh and blood, held together with sinews . . . disconnected bones scattered in all directions . . . bones bleached white, the colour of shells . . . bones heaped up, more than a year old . . . bones rotten and crumbling to dust—he compares this same body with it thus: "this body too is of the same nature, it will be like that, it is not exempt from that fate."[17]

The same list of stages of decay appears in other suttas as well, such as the *Kayagata-sati sutta*, the sutta on mindfulness immersed in the body.[18] More generally, meditation on decaying corpses forms part of the contemplation of the foulness and impurity of human bodies (Skt. *aśubhabhāvanā*).

Lists of the stages by which a corpse decays appear repeatedly in Buddhist literature, suggesting the importance placed on the contemplation. Bhikkhu Analayo explains that the "exercise highlights two things: the repulsive

[15] The white garb of Shikoku pilgrims is similarly said to be a death shroud, so that the pilgrim is immediately confronted with their own mortality by the very clothing they wear.

[16] George D. Bond, "Theravada Buddhism's Meditations on Death and the Symbolism of Initiatory Death," *History of Religions* 19.3 (Feb. 1980): 237–258, 241.

[17] MI 58, summary from Anālayo, *Satipaṭṭhāna: The Direct Path to Realization* (Cambridge: Windhorse Publications, 2003), 153. Also, Soma, "The Way of Mindfulness: The Satipatthana Sutta and Its Commentary," Access to Insight, 1998; https://www.accesstoinsight.org/lib/authors/soma/wayof.html#cemetery.

[18] Thanissaro, "Kayagata-sati sutta, the Sutta on Mindfulness Immersed in the Body," Access to Insight, 1997 (https://www.accesstoinsight.org/tipitaka/mn/mn.119.than.html; updated version: https://www.dhammatalks.org/suttas/MN/MN119.html).

nature of the body as revealed during the stages of decay, and the fact that death is the inescapable destiny of all living beings."[19]

The "disadvantage" of bodily existence is that no matter how attractive or well-maintained, the body inevitably succumbs to old age, sickness, death, and decay through the stages observed in charnel ground contemplation. Meditating on the putrid qualities of the human body—particularly evident in the decay of a corpse—was considered to usually be effective not only in overcoming conceit regarding one's own body but also in counteracting sexual desire. It appears, however, to have not always been effective.

The "Verses of the Elder Monks" (*Theragātha*) tells an anecdote about two monks meditating on the decaying bodies of women, though with different results. "While one monk was able to gain insight, the other was unable to develop the contemplation, since the sight of the body provoked sensual desire in him."[20] Thus, although not always effective, the contemplation of decaying corpses was employed to overcome sensual desire by emphasizing the foul and disgusting nature of the body, to overcome conceit in one's own body by realizing it, too, is subject to decay, and to create an awareness that one's own death is inevitable.

The Path of Purification (*Visuddhimagga*) is one of the classic meditation texts of Indian Buddhism. Authored by Buddhaghosa (ca. fifth century), the text is organized according to a threefold framework widely used throughout Buddhism—virtue (Pāli *sīla*, Skt. *śīla*), concentration (Pāli/Skt. *samādhi*), and understanding or wisdom (Pāli *paññā*, Skt. *prajñā*).[21] In the *samādhi* section of his text, Buddhaghosa lists forty different objects of meditation. Not every meditation object is equally appropriate for all practitioners; rather, the meditation object is to be assigned by the meditation teacher according to the practitioner's temperament.[22]

Buddhaghosa's manual develops a diagnostic and prescriptive approach for meditation teachers working with different practitioners. Diagnoses are made according to which of the three poisons (Skt. *triviṣa*) or primary afflictions (Skt. *mūlakleśa*)—greed (Skt./Pāli *lobha*), hatred (Skt. *dveṣa*, Pāli *dosa*), and delusion (Skt./Pāli *moha*), or their opposites, faith or confidence,

[19] Analayo, *Satipaṭṭhāna*, 153.
[20] Analayo, *Satipaṭṭhāna*, 154.
[21] Buddhaghosa, *The Path of Purification (Visuddhimagga)* (Bhikkhu Ñāṇamoli, trans. 1975. Reprint. Seattle: BPS Pariyatti Editions, 1991).
[22] Buddhaghosa, *The Path of Purification*, 101 (III.75).

intelligence, and speculation[23]—predominates in the practitioner's temperament. Prescriptions that follow from the diagnosis include the location and type of meditation hut, the nature of the practitioner's servants, the type of food and utensils provided, and so on. Suitable for a practitioner with a greedy temperament are mindfulness of the body and mindfulness of the "ten kinds of foulness,"[24] that is, contemplation of a decaying corpse organized by Buddhaghosa into ten, rather than nine, stages of decay.

The ten stages of a decaying corpse is an appropriate meditation object for those motivated by desire or lust. These ten are bloated, livid, festering, cut up, gnawed, scattered, hacked and scattered, bleeding, worm infested, and a skeleton. The meditator is instructed to consider the corpse in great detail, by its color, shape, and location, considering as well such details as its joints, openings, concavities, and convexities.[25] Each of the ten varieties of corpses is further identified as to specific subdivisions of greed for which its contemplation is appropriate. Thus, while a bloated corpse "suits one who is greedy about shape since it makes evident the disfigurement of the body's shape," a skeleton "suits one who is greedy about fine teeth since it makes evident the repulsiveness of the bones in the body."[26]

Buddhaghosa gives very explicit and detailed instructions on how the practitioner is to conduct this meditation on foulness. Charnel grounds are dangerous places he tells us, places where there are vicious animals, ghouls, and bandits. Consequently, a practitioner intent on doing a meditation of this kind should not rush off to some spot where a corpse is reported to be, but instead inform members of his community and set out purposely, with attention to his route. As with the instructions for other meditation objects, the practitioner only gazes on the corpse long enough to form a clear mental image of it, and then returns to his dwelling and meditates on that image.

About three centuries after Buddhaghosa, Śāntideva (late seventh to mid-eighth century) composed his famous instruction manual, the "Introduction to the Practices of Awakening" (Skt. *Bodhicaryāvatāra*). The eighth chapter

[23] These terms for the opposites differ from other renderings, but reveal Buddhaghosa's interpretation, as translated. The group of three is also known as "roots of virtue" (*kuśalamūla*) and alternatives to the renderings of Buddhaghosa's list are nonattachment (*alobha*) or generosity (*dāna*), nonhatred (*adveṣa*) or loving-kindness (*mettā*), and nondelusion (*amoha*) or wisdom (*prajñā*). A view of human consciousness as dynamic would appear to be shared by both this idea that the three poisons have beneficial opposite forms and the tantric conception that negative emotions can be transmuted into positive ones through practice.

[24] Buddhaghosa, *The Path of Purification*, 113.

[25] Buddhaghosa, *The Path of Purification*, 178–180.

[26] Buddhaghosa, *The Path of Purification*, 187–188.

concerns meditation (Skt. *dhyana*) and includes a section on charnel ground practices. Śāntideva seems to see attachment to one's own body and lust for the body of another as afflictions integral to one another. His antidote to both these afflictions is contemplation of the foulness of living and dead bodies.

> 30. When shall I go to the local charnel ground and compare my own rotting body with other corpses?
>
> 31. For this body of mine will also turn putrid in that way, its stench so vile even the jackals will not slink near.

Following these reflections on one's own body, Śāntideva shifts to recollections of a desired other.

> 49. They produce both spit and shit from the single source of food. You do not want the shit from it. Why are you so fond of drinking the spit?
>
> 53. You have plenty of filth of your own. Satisfy yourself with that! Glutton for crap! Forget her, that other pouch of filth!
>
> 70. Apparently you were horrified when you saw a few corpses in the charnel ground. Yet you delight in your village, which is a charnel-ground thronging with moving corpses.[27]

In some cases, greater attention was given to the later stages of decay, with skeletons being more emphasized. The "Great Exegesis of Abhidharma,"[28] for example, gives instructions that match Buddhaghosa's regarding meditating on a mental image one has formed by gazing on a decaying corpse, but gives greater detail about skeletal remains than other stages of decay. The relevant section of this text, which we cite fully as it gives additional details for the practice of this kind of meditation practice, reads:

> The practitioner first goes to a charnel ground and contemplates the image of the bruised corpse of the others. Having well grasped the image, he goes back [to his abode] and sits in a single place and again contemplates that

[27] Śāntideva, *The Bodhicaryāvatāra*, trans. Kate Crosby and Andrew Skilton (Oxford: Oxford University Press, 1995), 90–94.

[28] *Abhidharmamahāvibhāṣa*, a Vaibhāṣika commentary on the Sarvāstivāda abhidharma teachings.

> [mental] image. If the mind is scattered and [the image] does not appear clearly, he should go back to the charnel ground and again contemplate and grasp the image. When [the image] is clear and his mind is focused, he should quickly return to his place of dwelling. He washes his feet, approaches his seat, and then sits with crossed legs, calming his body and mind, separating from all obstacles, and contemplating the previously acquired image. Through the power of his resolve, he then transfers the image to his own body. [The procedure is the same for all nine stages of decay,] from the bruised corpse up to the skeleton. When contemplating the skeleton, he first contemplates the foot bone, then the ankle bone, then the calf bone, then the knee bone, then the thigh bone, then the hip bone, then the waist bone, then the spine, then the ribs, then the shoulder blade, then the upper arm, then the lower arm, then the wrist, then the hand, then the shoulder, then the neck, then the jaw, then the teeth, then the skull.[29]

Identifying one's own body with a decaying corpse from the beginnings of decay to the collapse of a heap of bones makes impermanence and the foul nature of the human body immediate and personal. It is not just others who die and decay, but myself as well.

Corpse Meditation on the Silk Road

Across Inner Asia along the Silk Road in its various branchings, Buddhist caves contain depictions of corpses, skeletons, and skulls. From Tape Shotor in present-day eastern Afghanistan to the Kizil caves in Xinjiang, at Toyok, and at Yungang, Longmen, and the Mogao caves at Dunhuang, Buddhists built monastic residences and funerary temples in caves.[30] Frequently, however,

[29] Eric Greene, "Death in a Cave: Meditation, Deathbed Ritual, and Skeletal Imagery at Tape Shotor," *Artibus Asiae* 83.2 (2013): 265–294, 269.

[30] While archeologists had previously designated many of these as "meditation caves," any blanket application of terms such as meditation and visualization has been questioned. See Sunkyung Kim, "Seeing Buddhas in Cave Sanctuaries," *Asia Major* 24.1 (2011): 87–126, 88; see also Robert Sharf, "Art in the Dark: The Funerary Context of Buddhist Caves in Western China," in *Art of Merit: Studies in Buddhist Art and Its Conservation*, ed. David Park, Kuenga Wangmo, and Sharon Cather, 38–65 (London: Archetype Publications, Courtauld Institute of Art, 2013), 44. Sharf's broader claims have been subject to detailed critical examination. See Angela F. Howard, "On 'Art in the Dark' and Meditation in Central Asian Buddhist Caves," *The Eastern Buddhist* 46.2 (2017): 19–39; and Henrik H. Sørensen, *Light on "Art in the Dark": On Buddhist Practice and Worship in the Mogao Caves*, Buddhist Road Paper 5.6 (Bochum, Germany: Center for Religious Studies, Ruhr-University Bochum, 2022).

decorations of these caves include depictions of monks meditating on corpses, skeletons, or skulls, or pointing to skeletons as if instructing the observer.[31]

Eric Greene identifies two meditations on the foulness of the body, one external and the other internal. The external is the one described above, in which a monk uses an actual corpse as the object of meditation, including forming a mental, eidetic image to be contemplated after returning from the charnel ground. The internal was known in Chinese as "white bone contemplation." Greene explains that rather "than going to a charnel ground, the practitioner of the white bone contemplation simply imagines his or her own body transforming into a skeleton, and it is this imagined skeleton, rather than any external object, that serves as the object of contemplation."[32]

Greene elicits additional evidence of the continuity of corpse meditation practices from a careful consideration of texts from the second and third century. Earlier scholarship had considered breath meditation to be the most popular form of Buddhist meditation in China at this time. Greene shows, however, that contemplation of impurity, of the foulness of the body, is "often presented as the most basic and prototypical form of practice."[33] An early Chinese meditation text called the "Scripture on the Twelve Gates,"[34] has recently been recovered from Kongō-ji temple in Japan. Rather than breath contemplation, it emphasizes the contemplation of bodily impurity. Greene says that the section explaining "the method of actually practicing meditation (*chan*) [only gives] a detailed description of the contemplation of impurity."[35] In other words, the only meditation presented in this early text is contemplation of the decay of the body after death. The prescription dwells particularly on the foulness of the body as an antidote for sexual desire:

> One who desires to sit in meditation and practice the Way must always analyze and contemplate the thirty-six impure things within the body—such as the head, eyes, hands, feet, bones, teeth, skin, flesh, entrails, stomach, liver, kidney—as each scattered about in a different place. When one's thoughts

[31] Greene, "Death in a Cave," 285.

[32] Greene, "Death in a Cave," 270. Greene suggests that one particular painting of a skeleton at Tape Shotor is plausibly explained as an object of meditation—though he considers the evidence to be insufficient to firmly establish either that this was indeed its function or what particular kind of meditation might have been practiced in relation to it. Greene, "Death in a Cave," 286.

[33] Eric Greene, "Healing Breaths and Rotting Bones: On the Relationship Between Buddhist and Chinese Meditation Practices During the Eastern Han and Three Kingdoms Period," *Journal of Chinese Religions* 42.2 (Nov. 2014): 145–184, 154.

[34] Attributed to An Shigao (fl. c. 148–180 CE), it had previously only been known from catalogues.

[35] Greene, "Healing Breaths and Rotting Bones," 157.

> crave the beautiful white of a woman's body, one should think of the deep white bones of a corpse. When one's thoughts crave the beautiful flesh of a woman's skin, one should think of the swollen [skin] of a corpse. When one's thoughts crave the beautiful red of a woman's lips, one should think of the deep red of the blood [coming from] a rotting corpse. When one's thoughts crave the beautiful black of a woman's eyebrows, one should think of the deep blue-black of a rotting corpse. Everything is empty—it is but the workings of the mind.[36]

The emblematic quality of a rotting corpse as indicating emptiness and impermanence also carries over to Japan, where the imagery becomes aestheticized in poetic form.

The Nine Faces of Death: Japan

Meditations on the foulness of the human body, particularly as displayed by decaying corpses in charnel grounds, and the teaching of impermanence are also found in Japan. In Japanese culture one frequently encounters the aestheticized imagery of cherry blossoms being scattered in the wind, after blooming so beautifully for such a brief time. During my own time in Japan, I realized that this is not just a poetic stereotype, a dead metaphor—when the cherry trees were blooming in Maruyama Koen, a park near our house in Kyoto, people not only visited the park, but many of them spent the night there to savor this ephemeral beauty.

From Kūkai there is a set of nine poems on the "Contemplation of the Nine Appearances" (Jpn. *Kusōkan*), that is, the nine stages of the decay of a corpse. Just as with the sequences already discussed, these run from the appearance of the just recently deceased, through the discoloration, bloating, bursting open, scattering by wild animals, decay down to bones, bleaching of the bones, falling apart of the bones, and final disappearance like ashes.[37] The ninth poem references the practice of erecting a memorial stupa:

> 9. The Appearance of Becoming Ashes.
> Mountains and rivers endure thousands of generations.

[36] Greene, "Healing Breaths and Rotting Bones," 157.
[37] Ron Green, "The Mysterious Mirror of Writing: Kūkai's Poetry and Literary Theory," http://ww2.coastal.edu/rgreen/kukaipoetry.htm.

A person's affairs are shorter than a century.
One's skull and knees become exhausted and destroyed.
A casket and vault become like dust.
The spirit and the corpse have no place for dependency.
What is entrusted to the deity of the [memorial] mound?
The monument above bears a temporary name.
Instead, you are at the bottom of the mound.
Suns and moons[38] yellows and whitens[39] the earth.
In the end, the wind returns the blackness to the mountain.
There is only the treasure of the Three Vehicles.
Without cultivation, this person has eight kinds of suffering.[40]
The six consciousnesses, now where are they?
In the four elements only a worthless name remains.
In the winter the surrounding moss is green and fertile.
In the summer grass bores into the mound and thrives.
(The body is) a sack in which provisions still exist.
Beneath the pine, it is like green hair.
Green, green, uniting mound and clouds.
Shh, shh,[41] the voice of the evening pine.[42]

While Kūkai uses many metaphors from nature in his set of poems on the nine stages of death, he does not use the metaphor of cherry blossoms blown by the wind. This motif is found in a related collection, the "Poems of the Nine Stages"—an illustrated collection of poems that was influenced by Kūkai's set of poems. James Sanford notes that though Kūkai's "poems survive, and, like all of Kūkai's writings, are an important part of the Japanese literary tradition, they were probably always restricted to a relatively small circle of readers and do not seem to have made any substantial impact on later generations."[43] The "Poems of the Nine Stages," however, brought the

[38] Time.
[39] Weather.
[40] Jpn. *Hakku*, traditional categorization: birth, old age, sickness, death, separation from loved ones, contact with those one despises, deprivation, attachment to the five aggregates.
[41] Onomatopoetic for the sound of the wind in the pines.
[42] Green, "The Mysterious Mirror of Writing." M.m.: translation slightly revised for presentation here.
[43] James H. Sanford, "The Nine Faces of Death: 'Su Tung-po's' *Kuzō-shi*," *The Eastern Buddhist* n.s., XXI.2 (Autumn 1988): 54–77, 58.

same contemplation of the stages of decay of a corpse to a wider audience.[44] The work comprises four parts. In addition to a preface emphasizing familiar Buddhist themes, and the Chinese-style poems, there are also Japanese-style poems (Jpn. *waka*) and illustrations. The *waka* poem included at the start of the process of decay reads:

Just at their peak
the fresh, young blossoms go;
scattering, drifting.
How painful, how beautiful—
This evening of Spring.

Blossoms scattering,
and Spring going dark,
beneath the trees;
Life itself has slipped away:
Tolling twilight bell.[45]

The poems proceed in the familiar order through the first eight stages: newly dead, bloated, spattered blood, dismembered, chewed and gnawed, flesh decayed, skeleton, bones scattered. "Then, in the very last scene, even the bones are gone and only a memorial *stūpa* survives—presumably until with time it too will erode into nothingness."[46]

Charnel ground practices, meditating on decaying corpses, using skeletal images as the object of meditation, and aestheticized imagery of death and decay—this variety reveals a consistent pattern by which the teaching of impermanence became viscerally immediate to practitioners and adherents. Rather than being unique to the tantric tradition, they pervade the Buddhist tradition as a whole. This originary and pervasive character demonstrates that like transgression more generally, death and decay are not definitive of tantric Buddhism, nor are they somehow inherently tantric. It is through context, use, and designation that these components become tantric.

[44] While it is attributed to the famous Song poet Su Shi (Su Dongpo; 1036–1101), "it seems virtually certain that all segments of the text were of Japanese provenance, that they developed independently of each other for a time, and were then brought together to form the extant composite version, perhaps as late as the Ashikaga period" (1336–1573). Sanford, "The Nine Faces of Death," 59.

[45] Sanford, "The Nine Faces of Death," 65.

[46] Sanford, "The Nine Faces of Death," 62.

The practice of severance (Tib. *chöd*[47]) found in many Tibetan lineages is an example of a tantric practice that employs these themes and images.

Offering One's Own Corpse: Chöd

Introduction

Based on the Perfection of Wisdom teachings of emptiness and impermanence, Severance is a tantric praxis by which practitioners "sever" their obscurations (Skt. *kleśa*). Sarah Harding explains that "the term used to describe the process is *chöd* (*gcod*, 'to sever or cut'), not in the sense of cutting up a corpse but of attaining definite resolution of one's fears and obstacles—the 'object' or 'field' (*yul*) to be severed—through the profound realization of emptiness and compassion."[48]

In tantric practice of *chöd*, cemeteries are important locations in which severing one's obscurations can be pursued. Demons are thought to come to feast on corpses, and practitioners of *chöd* visualize cutting up their own bodies as offerings to these demons.[49] While this "body donation practice" (Tib. *lus byin*) is the best-known aspect of *chöd*, in Harding's presentation of the history of Severance, it is a later development.

According to Jamgön Kongtrul (1813–1899), practicing severance "is a radical method for cutting through the inflation of self-fixation to the willingness to accept what is undesirable, the direct subjugation of adverse circumstances, the realization that gods and demons are in your own mind, and the knowledge that you and everyone else are utterly equal."[50] Body donation practice is "the path of solitary yogic practitioners of the *chöd* practice, who visualize offering their body to the worldly deities and to Tantric deities as training in radical nonattachment."[51]

[47] Semantically related is the Tibetan *chöd* (*mchod*, *mchod-pa*), which has the general meaning of making an offering or giving a gift. Nicolas Sihlé, "Towards a Comparative Anthropology of the Buddhist Gift (and Other Transfers)," *Religion Compass* 9.11 (2015): 352–385, 357. We distinguish here between *chöd* as practice and Chöd as the lineage.

[48] Sarah Harding, "Translator's Introduction," in *Chöd: The Sacred Teachings on Severance*, ed. Jamgön Kongtrul, trans. Sarah Harding, xi–xix (Boulder, CO: Snow Lion, 2016), xvii.

[49] See Jérôme Edou, *Machig Labdrön and the Foundations of Chöd* (Ithaca, NY: Snow Lion, 1996).

[50] Jamgön Kongtrul, "Beloved Garden: Brief Notes on the Offering and Gift of the Body," in *Chöd: The Sacred Teachings on Severance*, ed. Jamgön Kongtrul, trans. Sarah Harding, 483–501 (Boulder, CO: Snow Lion, 2016), 484.

[51] Geoffrey Samuel, *Civilized Shamans: Buddhism in Tibetan Societies* (Washington, DC: Smithsonian Institution Press, 1993), 175.

The modern Nyingma master Dudjom Lingpa (1835–1904)[52] discusses body donation, explaining that

> Finally, in order to collapse the cave of fixations on hopes and fears,
> visualize your body, speech, and mind as the three vajras,
> and with the vital points of the pith instructions on the three great principles,
> rove about in haunted places
> and make the supreme offering of your cherished body.
> By the power of this, the false cave of hopes and fears will collapse.[53]

Machik Labdron—Founder and Deity

Machik Labdron (Ma gcig lap sgron, 1062–1149) is credited with establishing Severance practice in Tibet. According to Tibetan sources, she is "the most important disciple of the Indian yogin Pha dam pa sangs rgyas [Padampa Sanggye], who is said to have founded both the *Zhi byed* [Tib. *Zhije*: "pacification"] and the *gCod* [Tib. *Chöd*: "severance"] school of Tibetan Buddhism."[54] Machig is, however, the most preeminent figure for the Severance tradition, and her renown is such that she is said to have given a teaching, *The Great Speech Chapter*, to three Indian scholars, making it the only teaching to have gone from Tibet to India.[55] She is "the only female lama to found a major teaching lineage, although women in Tibet have regularly taken up yogic practice,"[56] and her cultural importance as the founder of Severance in Tibet is reflected by her being considered an incarnation of Tārā.[57]

[52] See Ron Garry, "Dudjom Lingpa," https://treasuryoflives.org/biographies/view/Dudjom-Lingpa/9688.

[53] B. Alan Wallace, trans., *Heart of the Great Perfection: Düdjom Lingpa's Visions of the Great Perfection*, vol. I (Somerville, MA: Wisdom Publications, 2015), 32.

[54] Karénina Kollmar-Paulenz, "Ma gcig lab sgron ma—The Life of a Tibetan Woman Mystic between Adaptation and Rebellion," *The Tibet Journal* 23.2 (Summer 1998): 11–32: 11.

[55] Michelle J(anet) Sorensen, "Mahāmudrā Chöd? Rangjung Dorjé's Commentary on *The Great Speech Chapter* of Machik Labdrön," in *Wading into the Stream of Wisdom: Essays in Honor of Leslie Kawamura*, ed. Sarah F. Haynes and Michelle J. Sorensen, 129–160 (Berkeley, CA: Institute of Buddhist Studies and BDK America, 2013), 129.

[56] Samuel, *Civilized Shamans*, 478.

[57] Donald S. Lopez, Jr., "A Prayer Flag for Tārā," in *Religions of Tibet in Practice*, ed. Donald S. Lopez, Jr., 548–552 (Princeton, NJ: Princeton University Press, 1997), 549.

Like the practices of Severance, the Pacification of Suffering taught by Padampa Sanggye (eleventh century to 1117) was framed as a praxis conjoining its yogas with the Perfection of Wisdom. The "name Pacification of Suffering is usually identified with the similar phrase that introduces the mantra in the *Heart Sutra*: 'the mantra that utterly pacifies all suffering.'"[58] The two dimensions of Pacification praxis are perfection vehicle doctrines and tantric methods.[59] Broadly speaking, this means that practitioners embrace a worldview marked by the emptiness of all things, that is, all dharmas, and practice toward making their own buddha nature real. Severance is considered a subsidiary to Pacification, and it is likewise rooted in the Perfection of Wisdom teachings of emptiness and impermanence. Harding indicates, however, that despite similarities, "the two systems of practice are quite separate."[60]

The association with the Perfection Vehicle suggests a gradual conception of the path, involving improving oneself over a long period of practice. As early as the fourteenth century, however, Severance also interacted with Dzokchen (*rdzogs chen*). While the Perfection of Wisdom is associated with a gradual path of the practice, the Dzokchen teachings assert that the practitioner is already "in reality indistinguishable from the three dimensions [body, speech, mind] of the Buddha," and indeed, "it is the very concept that there is something to modify that distances the *yogi* from the possibility of experiencing that state."[61] The practitioner is, in other words, always and already awakened, and the very thought that one is imperfect and in need of change is the obstacle to realizing that fact.

In addition to being Machik's teacher, Padampa Sanggye "is remembered for his support of women practitioners, and he was keenly aware of the specific mundane difficulties they had to overcome in order to devote their lives to practice."[62] There were other women who also became leaders and contributed to the development of Buddhism in Tibet. Three and half centuries after Machik, Samding Dorje Phagmo (commonly known as

[58] Sarah Harding, "Translator's Introduction," in *Zhije: The Pacification of Suffering*, ed. Jamgön Kongtrul, trans. Sarah Harding, xi–xxiii (Boulder, CO: Snow Lion, 2019), xiii.

[59] Michelle Janet Sorensen, "Making the Old New Again and Again: Legitimation and Innovation in the Tibetan Buddhist Chöd Tradition," PhD diss. (Columbia University, 2013), 103–104.

[60] Harding, "Translator's Introduction," in *Chöd*, xiii.

[61] Fabian Sanders and Margherita Pansa, "On Some *rDzogs chen* Aspects in a *gCod* Text from the *Bla ma dgongs 'dus*, a *gTer ma* Collection Discovered by Sangs rgyas gling pa (1341–1396)," *Revue d'Études Tibétaines* 35 (2016): 169–202, 182.

[62] Michelle Sorensen, "Padampa Sanngye," *Treasury of Lives* BDRC 1243 (2011), https://treasuryoflives.org/biographies/view/Padampa-Sanggye-/2510.

Chokyi Dronma, 1422–1455 or 1467) exemplifies the prominence to which some women rose. She is "one of the few Tibetan women historically to receive full monastic ordination and to spawn an incarnation lineage."[63] In contrast to the way that the Severance tradition developed outside a specific monastic lineage, Chokyi Dronma established the Samding monastery and founded a "religious dynasty," that is, an institutional lineage.[64] A similar monastic establishment is traced to the fourteenth-century figure Sönam Pelden, considered to be the founder of Ya Nga Jamda Ganden Khachö Ling nunnery.[65]

In contrast, the Chöd lineage of Machik is not constrained to any one monastic institution. Chöd was more widely accessible, and it was "taken up by most of the other major traditions as a supplementary practice, as well as having some followers outside Tibet."[66] As Harding notes,

> Despite the success and popularity of the Severance practice, and perhaps because of its particular yogic character emphasizing the wandering lifestyle, the tradition never developed monastic institutions with successions of lineage holders like the other major traditions. Thus it was "available" to be adopted by other schools when their affiliated masters made connection with it.[67]

Today, for example, *chöd* practice is found in the Nyingma, Kagyu, and Bon traditions. In addition, scholarly treatments have moved beyond both earlier exoticized or sensationalized presentations and theoretically problematic comparative studies.[68] At the same time, the practice is being more openly offered with a psychological interpretation to practitioners.[69]

[63] Hildegard Diemberger, "The First Samding Dorje Pakmo, Chokyi Dronma," *Treasury of Lives* BCRC P2CZ7891 (2014), https://treasuryoflives.org/biographies/view/First-Samding-Dorje-Pakmo-Chokyi-Dronma/13205.

[64] Hildegard Diemberger, *When a Woman Becomes a Religious Dynasty: The* Samding Dorje Phagmo *of Tibet* (New York: Columbia University Press, 2007).

[65] Suzanne M. Bessenger, *Echoes of Enlightenment: The Life and Legacy of Sönam Peldren* (New York: Oxford University Press, 2016), 1.

[66] Samuel, *Civilized Shamans*, 478.

[67] Harding, "Translator's Introduction," in *Chöd*, xv.

[68] For instances of the first, see, L.(aurence) Austine Waddell, *Tibetan Buddhism: With Its Mystic Cults, Symbolism, and Mythology* (New York: Dover, 1972); and Alexandra David-Neel, *Magic and Mystery in Tibet: Discovering the Spiritual Beliefs, Traditions and Customs of Tibetan Buddhist Lamas* (1929 or 1932?. Several reprints). On the latter, see Mircea Eliade, *Shamanism: Archaic Techniques of Ecstasy* (Princeton, NJ: Princeton University Press, 1964).

[69] See for instance, Tsultrim Allione, *Feeding Your Demons: Ancient Wisdom for Resolving Inner Conflict* (New York: Little Brown, 2008).

Severing Attachments, Severing Delusions

Severance is perhaps best known today for the practice of "body donation," that is, first visualizing one's own corpse, and then visualizing dismembering it and feeding it to hungry ghouls. In the early Chöd texts that can be attributed to Machik, this practice is "barely and only indirectly mentioned."[70] Whether it was always important, but held secret, or was only developed and made public by later proponents is not clear. Since its early textual records, however, body donation is the practice for which Severance is best known today.[71]

One of these more recent texts describing body offering practice is the "Beloved Garden" by Jamgön Kongtrul (1813–1900). Like other tantric visualization rituals, this employs a complex set of objects, syllables, and deities in an unfolding sequence. It begins with a set of preliminaries to the main practice, such as going for refuge, arousing the intent to awaken (*bodhicitta*), meditating on the four immeasurables (Skt. *apramāṇa*: loving kindness, compassion, empathetic joy, and equanimity), and the ritual consecration of visualized offerings. Following these preliminaries, the practitioner first visualizes the syllable *trāṃ* appearing in front of oneself and then the syllable transforming into a jeweled throne. Another series of syllables appears on that throne, including the syllable *hūṃ*, which dissolves into light, becoming Machik—who is the chief deity of the ritual and is at one point identified with the *dharmakāya*.[72] This sequence is notably similar to visualization sequences in Shingon tantric rituals.

Following additional visualizations, the offering of the body turns one's own corpse into the cosmos. Projecting one's consciousness into Machik, one emerges as the female Buddha Vajravārāhī, the "Adamantine She-Boar."

[70] Harding, "Translator's Introduction," in *Chöd*, xvi.

[71] The prominence of body donation may largely result from the influence of Eliade's *Shamanism* on the field of religious studies during the second half of the twentieth century. Eliade's comparativist and evolutionary framework interpreted *chöd* as an instance of shamanic initiation (436, see also Anya Bernstein, *Religious Bodies Politic: Rituals of Sovereignty in Buryat Buddhism* [Chicago: University of Chicago Press, 2013], 158). Although now dated, Eliade's works continue to be in publication, and they have retained currency in popular understanding. Here we simply want to add to the critiques of Eliade that his approach uncritically employs the practice/doctrine dichotomy. For example, when he says that "the transformation that a shamanic schema can undergo when it is incorporated into a complex philosophical system, such as tantrism" (437). One of the theoretical goals we seek to accomplish here is pointing out that this dichotomy between practice and doctrine is an inaccurate representation of human cognition based on intellectualist fallacy that thought causes action.

[72] Kongtrul, "Beloved Garden," 490.

This is the epithet for the ferocious aspect of Vajrayoginī, also considered to be an emanation of Tārā.[73] In this form the practitioner is instructed to

> gesture toward your corpse with the curved knife in your right hand. The skin of the corpse is flayed whole and spread out, and the corpse is piled on top of it. The skin is the golden foundation of the ground; the blood and pus are an ocean of scented water; the fingers and toes are the iron mountain rings; the torso is Supreme Mountain [Sumeru]; the four limbs are the four continents [e.g., Jambudvipa] and islands; the head is the gods' abode; the eyes are the sun and moon; the heart is the wish-fulfilling gem; and the inner organs are the eight auspicious signs, the seven emblems of royalty, the precious treasure, the five desirable qualities, and so forth. All of this is arranged in great abundance with nothing left out, like Samantabhadra's offering cloud. In extent, it totally fills the sky. In terms of time, it lasts as long as cyclic existence. It transcends number and measure. When you offer it, meditate on all sentient beings perfecting the accumulations and purifying obscurations. Afterward, rest within the state of total purity of the three spheres.[74]

Kongtrul then gives a series of additional visualizations. These are classified either as white, that is, peaceful; or red, that is, wrathful. In one version, the corpse is visualized as cosmic in scope and then chopped into small pieces and poured into a skull cup. Other visualizations convert the corpse into an elixir, and when this elixir is offered, the "sufferings of each of the six realms are quelled, and those beings develop an interest in liberation and the practice of the holy dharma."[75]

During a training program that I attended many years ago, the lama who was giving the teachings recounted a childhood exploit. When he was a young monk in training himself, one of his teachers was a practitioner of body donation *chöd*, going out at night to the cemetery to visualize dismembering his own body and offering the pieces to hungry ghouls and demons. One night this young monk and some compatriots quietly sneaked down to the cemetery, hiding behind their teacher. Waiting until the ritual visualization had reached the point where the practitioner calls on hungry ghosts and demons

[73] Miranda Shaw, *Buddhist Goddesses of India* (Princeton, NJ: Princeton University Press, 2006), 342–343, 371.
[74] Kongtrul, "Beloved Garden," 490–491.
[75] Kongtrul, "Beloved Garden," 492.

to come eat his flesh, drink his blood, and suck the marrow from his bones, the young lamas jumped up behind their teacher, shrieking in a bloodthirsty fashion.

The lama recalled this story with quite evident nostalgia, but the point he made to us was that if you are going to undertake such a practice, you must be serious in your intent. In other words, such visualizations must be done not as a simple matter of pretending, that is, acting "as if," but rather with full willingness to give over the pieces of one's own body to feed demons and hungry ghouls.

Another text in Kongtrul's collection is the "Essence of Auspicious Renown: A Ritual of Offering and Supplication to All the Gurus of the Holy Dharmas of Pacification and Object Severance Together."[76] In contrast to body severance, object severance refers to severing the practitioner's own fears and obstacles "through the profound realization of emptiness and compassion."[77] The subtitle indicates that this practice brings together the teachings of both Pacification and Severance.

Following the common preliminaries, the main practice opens with the visualization of the palace of great liberation in the center of a pure buddhaland. Inside the palace is an eight-petaled lotus with countless outer petals. On the lotus is a throne, and on the throne is Dampa, that is, Machik's teacher Padampa Sangye, whose appearance is described in detail. Above his head one visualizes several groups of gurus, totaling 130. To Dampa's left is Machik, while around them on the eight petals of the lotus, in the cardinal and intercardinal directions, are visualized another set of masters and lineage teachers arranged on the outer lotus petals. All of space is then seen as filled with multitudes of deities, buddhas, bodhisattvas, gods, and dharma protectors.

This is followed by recitations of invitation and homage. A visualized mandala, the practitioner's own body, and then several other material and mental offerings are visualized, and formulae of confession, homage, and supplication follow. The communal feast offerings are ritually purified and the feast offered. The ritual closes with reciting prayers, requesting forgiveness for any errors in the ritual performance, and a request for empowerment

[76] Jamgön Kongtrul, "Essence of Auspicious Renown: A Ritual of Offering and Supplication to All the Gurus of the Holy Dharmas of Pacification and Object Severance Together," in *Chöd: The Sacred Teachings of Severance*, ed. Jamgön Kongtrul, trans. Sarah Harding, 503–535 (Boulder, CO: Snow Lion, 2016).

[77] Harding, "Translator's Introduction," in *Chöd*, xvii.

and blessings. The closing stanza of the ritual mentions hungry ghosts as intended beneficiaries of the instructions leading to awakening and never-ending happiness.[78]

Feeding Hungry Ghosts

While offering one's own corpse as food and drink to ghouls haunting charnel grounds seems to be unique to the Chöd tradition, feeding hungry ghosts is rooted in praxes of Indic Buddhism and is today widespread through East Asian Buddhism. Hungry ghosts are similar to the ghouls and demons who haunt charnel grounds. They are described as having insatiable appetite and unquenchable thirst, and they are often portrayed with immense bellies and tiny necks.[79] Additionally, their mouths emit flames when they try to eat something, and they are therefore also known as the "flaming mouths." Feeding hungry ghosts is only possible by appropriate ritual activity, as they cannot swallow ordinary food and drink. As a practice of compassion, this is found in the Pāli Khuddaka Nikāya, the Collection of Short Discourses. The first text in the collection is the Khuddakapāṭha, comprised of nine short texts, apparently "designed as a primer for novice monks and nuns."[80] One of these nine is the Tirokuḍḍa Kaṇḍa, which describes the destitute condition of "hungry ghosts outside the walls," and how the living can offer food and drink to their dead relations with the simple expression

"May this be for our relatives.
May our relatives be happy."[81]

In gratitude, the hungry ghosts of the deceased extend a blessing for long life to the living. This idea is congruent with Vedic conceptions of the post-mortem state dating from prior to the widespread acceptance of the idea of rebirth. According to this early idea, the dead continue to dwell in the

[78] Kongtrul, "Essence of Auspicious Renown," 535.

[79] See, for example, Color plate 8, "Detail of Hungry Ghosts from the Womb World Mandala," Elizabeth ten Grotenhuis, "Collapsing the Distinction Between Buddha and Believer: Human Hair in Japanese Esotericizing Embroideries," in *Esoteric Buddhism and the Tantras in East Asia*, ed. Charles D. Orzech, Henrik H. Sørensen, and Richard K. Payne, 876–892 (Leiden: Brill, 2011), 883.

[80] Thānissaro, "Khuddaka Nikāya: The Short Collection," https://www.dhammatalks.org/suttas/KN/index_KN.html.

[81] Thānissaro, "Khp 7. Tirokuḍḍa Kaṇḍa — (Hungry Ghosts) Outside the Walls," https://www.dhammatalks.org/suttas/KN/Khp/khp7.html.

heavens only so long as their descendants continue to offer food for their benefit. If such offerings are discontinued, then they experience a second and final death.[82]

Hungry ghosts are mentioned in the Severance literature as both a cosmological category, one of the six realms of rebirth in the desire realm (Skt. *kamaloka*), and as a kind of impediment to meditation. In the "White Crystal Mirror," one of the sections of offerings is directed to the six realms of beings, and the practitioner is to imagine that innumerable offering goddesses carry the multicolored elixir of the gods in skull cups. "For the hungry ghosts, imagine that a rain of divine elixir falls with the substances, food, and drink that quells their hunger and thirst and they gain excellent, fine forms."[83] In a text attributed to Machik, "The Essential Bundle," an obstacle to meditation is dullness from hungry ghosts, experienced as "due to great drowsiness, due to muddled consciousness, or else because your heart is just not in it, and breathing becomes difficult."[84] The remedies recommended include bringing to mind the guru, and also vigorous exercise while naked.

Throughout East Asian tantric Buddhism, hungry ghosts were fed in more elaborate ritual practices than the simple offering noted above from the Tirokuḍḍa Kaṇḍa, one example being Amoghavajra's "Hungry Ghost Dhāraṇī Scripture."[85] And rituals for feeding hungry ghosts are found in the esoteric practices associated with Zen and Tiantai.[86]

For much of East Asia, the roots of popular practices of feeding hungry ghosts are in stories regarding the arhat Mulian (Mahāmaudgalyāyana). He is described as being able to see hungry ghosts, and upon inquiring of the Buddha Śākyamuni, he learns that they are condemned to this condition because of greed, such as denying alms offerings to monks. The Buddha advises

[82] Carlos Lopez, "Food and Immortality in the Veda: A Gastronomic Theology?" *Electronic Journal of Vedic Studies* 3.3 (1997): 11–19.

[83] Tenzin Namdak, "White Crystal Mirror," in *Chöd*, ed. Jamgön Kongtrul, trans. Sarah Harding, 257–296 (Boulder, CO: Snow Lion, 2016), 272.

[84] Machik Lapdron, "The Essential Bundle," in *Chöd*, ed. Jamgön Kongtrul, trans. Sarah Harding, 143–156 (Boulder, CO: Snow Lion, 2016), 152.

[85] *Pretamukhāgnijvālayaśarakāra dhāraṇī*, T. 1313. See Henrik H. Sørensen, "On Esoteric Buddhism in China: A Working Definition," in *Esoteric Buddhism and the Tantras in East Asia*, ed. Charles D. Orzech, Henrik H. Sørensen, and Richard K. Payne, 155–175 (Leiden: Brill, 2011), 167.

[86] For Tiantai, see Hun Y. Lye, "Feeding Ghosts: A Study of the *Yuquie Yankou* Rite," PhD diss. (University of Virginia, 2003); Hun Y. Lye, "Song Tiantai Ghost-Feeding Rituals," in *Esoteric Buddhism and the Tantras in East Asia*, ed. Charles D. Orzech, Henrik H. Sørensen, and Richard K. Payne, 521–524 (Leiden: Brill, 2011); and Hun Y. Lye, "*Yuquie Yankou* in the Ming-Qing," in *Esoteric Buddhism and the Tantras in East Asia*, ed. Charles D. Orzech, Henrik H. Sørensen, and Richard K. Payne, 562–567 (Leiden: Brill, 2011). For Zen, see William M. Bodiford, "Zen and Esoteric Buddhism," in *Esoteric Buddhism and the Tantras in East Asia*, ed. Charles D. Orzech, Henrik H. Sørensen, and Richard K. Payne, 924–935 (Leiden: Brill, 2011).

Mulian to make a communal offering to the Buddha and to the community of monks, which will allow the hungry ghosts to feed. The Buddha preaches to the assembly of hungry ghosts, and abandoning greed they are reborn in the Heaven of the Thirty-three (Trāyastrimśa Heaven).[87] Stories like these gave rise to the popular "ghost festivals" (Ch. *yulanben*, Jpn. *urabon*, or more popularly, *o-bon*), which is celebrated in mid- to late summer.[88] In contemporary Japan, trays of food are placed at the family altar to feed ancestral spirits, while hungry ghosts are also fed, but with a tray of food placed outside the home. In her study of domestic dharma in Japan Paula Arai notes that "Obon is not only a time to have the ancestors home for meals—it is also a season in which most people go to the family grave site and clean it extra well and make enhanced offerings."[89]

There are significant similarities between the Essence of Auspicious Renown visualization practice described above and the ritual feeding of hungry ghosts in the Shingon tradition. Although the individual ritual acts are not identical, the overall logic of the Essence of Auspicious Renown and the Shingon hungry ghost rituals proceeds in the same fashion. Both open, for example with the practitioner giving rise to an intention to awaken (Skt. *bodhicitta*), and then consecrating the offerings. The Chöd ritual involves visualizing a palace in which the gurus, masters, and teachers are gathered. In the Shingon ritual, however, the offerings are to hungry ghosts, and the practitioner visualizes all of them from throughout the entire cosmos, the *dharmadhātu*, gathering at the ritual site. Ritually, they are freed from their imprisonment in the earth, and their throats are opened. Empowering the food and drink, the practitioner then invites all the tathāgatas to attend to the ritual. Visualizing food, ambrosia, and water being consumed by countless hungry ghosts, all are satisfied, and then homage is offered to the Five Tathāgatas. The ritual closes with again producing the intention for awakening, affirming the *samaya* precepts, reciting the Clear Light mantra and the Heart Sutra, leave taking, and the transfer of merit.[90]

[87] Stephen Teiser, *The Ghost Festival in Medieval China* (Princeton, NJ: Princeton University Press, 1988), 129.

[88] For similar practices in contemporary Southeast Asia, see John Clifford Holt, *Theravada Traditions: Buddhist Ritual Cultures in Contemporary Southeast Asia and Sri Lanka* (Honolulu: University of Hawai'i Press, 2017), ch. 5.

[89] Paula Arai, *Bringing Zen Home: The Healing Heart of Japanese Women's Rituals* (Honolulu: University of Hawai'i Press, 2011), 103.

[90] Richard Karl Payne, "Shingon Services for the Dead," in *Religions of Japan in Practice*, ed. George J. Tanabe, Jr., 159–163 (Princeton, NJ: Princeton University Press, 1999).

Summary

It is sometimes suggested that the fear of death is what motivates the religious "impulse" and is perhaps the origin of religion as such.[91] Archeologists, for example, generally find it unproblematic to assume that any time they find skeletons that have been treated in some special fashion—such as being buried with shells or arrowheads, or the bones marked with red minerals—it indicates the existence of religion.

Death provides a unifying theme in the history of Buddhist practice, one that links the Pāli suttas, Buddhaghosa's *Path of Purification* (*Vissudhimagga*), cave meditations in Central Asia, Tibetan tantric practices, and the aestheticization of death in the form of poems on the decaying corpse of the beloved in Japan. Although not identical, these constitute variations on the theme of death as a universal concern for living humans.

As variations on that theme, some of the artificial divisions that obscure our understanding of the ways in which Buddhist practice developed as a common enterprise are broken down. Now outdated representations of tantra associate it with offensive and horrific images of sex and death. Despite these stereotypical images, meditating on a decaying corpse is found throughout the Buddhist tradition, and while there is nothing intrinsically tantric about it, as with other aspects of tantric Buddhism it is context, use, and designation that create the tantric quality of the practice. The integration of deities and deified teachers, such as Machik, with seed syllables, such as *trāṃ* and *hūṃ*, and with visualized objects, such as jeweled thrones, into a systematic visualization ritual, together with an emphasis on awakening through developing insight into emptiness and compassion, construct this as a tantric version of the threads shared across the entire range of Buddhist praxis. That practitioners of *chöd* designate the practice as tantric is key to considering its praxes to be a tantric inflection of widespread practices of viewing corpses and contemplating one's own impermanence. Thus, contrary to the usual rhetoric of rupture in which tantra is cast as distinctly separate from other forms of Buddhism, what we find are rituals and visualizations, shared beliefs and practices valorized as tantric by use, context, and designation.

[91] I am noting here that these are not infrequently encountered claims, while not implying that they are coherent. Usually, the notion of a religious impulse is left undefined, while given the socially constructed nature of the category religion, it is problematic as to what would constitute its origin.

Across the Buddhist tradition, there are a variety of forms of meditation, visualization, and cultural practices that focus on decaying corpses and skeletons as a means of teaching the truth of impermanence, and on ghouls and hungry ghosts as appropriate recipients of compassionate action. In some forms this involves viewing the corpse of another, while in practices that seem more directly confrontive, it is the practitioner's own body that is viewed as a corpse or skeleton. Like so many of the components that scholars have suggested define tantra, meditating on decaying corpses and skeletons, an aesthetic sensibility valuing the awareness of impermanence, or feeding hungry ghosts is not inherently tantric in nature. What constitutes a tantric inflection of these practices and ideas is context, use, and designation. A clearly tantric version is the Tibetan praxis of "severance," *chöd*. Visualizing oneself as a corpse plays a central role in the "body offering" form of *chöd*, the practice of severance, but the practice is distinguished by the fact that the ritual offering is one's own visualized corpse. The use of visualization, mantra, and mudra to accomplish these offerings to ghouls and hungry ghosts combines specific ritual components with the tantric context to frame these ritual performances as tantric, matching their designation as such in Tibetan discourse.

These practices and imagery spread through the Buddhist cosmopolis along the networks connecting nodes in India with those in Inner and East Asia. It is a misleading commonplace to talk about abstract entities such as Buddhism or tantric Buddhism as being transmitted. Instead, it was components, such as visualizations of decaying corpses and hungry ghouls, and the understandings that informed their use in practice that were carried by monks and yogis along those routes.

VI
Networks
Travelers and Praxes

Buddhists travel. They travel from here to there, along routes that connect those places. This obvious fact needs to be given equal status with the common tendency to think in terms of fixed locations—whether capital cities, big important monasteries, or small mountain hermitages.

Like all travelers, Buddhists carry things that are important with them. And, should they return to where they came from, they bring back other important things. And the same is true for texts, statues, implements, paintings, practices and rituals, styles of art and architecture, and teachings—all travel, from here to there, along the routes that connect those places.

One of the foundational metaphors for the Buddhist tradition is that of the path. The starting point is the ground, the route traveled is the path, and at the end of the path is the goal. Ground, path, and goal—from a deluded ordinary person, to a practitioner, to a person who has awakened—understood variously in different strains of Buddhism as an end of rebirth (Skt. *arhat*), uniting compassion and wisdom (Skt. *bodhisattva*), or mastery through realizing emptiness (Skt. *siddhas*). Although some say that you can complete this journey while sitting quietly on your meditation cushion safely at home, that has not kept Buddhists from traveling.

Some Buddhist travelers are well-known, being part of the pantheon of figures famous in the contemporary Buddhist *imaginaire*: figures such as Xuanzang, Atiśa, Dōgen, and Gendun Chopel. All of these are extraordinary—great translators, founders of new sects, or explorers who ventured outside their personal and cultural comfort zone. Other travelers are much less well-known today and are, therefore, more typical, more representative of the many thousands of largely anonymous Buddhist monks, aspirants, adherents, and tourists who traveled from here to there. "For the academic study of translocated Buddhism . . . there is perhaps at least as much, if not more, to be learned from those who did not make such successful translocations, did not establish lasting institutions, and who

Tantra Across the Buddhist Cosmopolis. Richard K. Payne, Oxford University Press. © Oxford University Press 2025.
DOI: 10.1093/9780197825105.003.0006

remain invisible on the global mediascape."[1] This chapter first examines the metaphor of networks and then introduces two lesser-known Buddhist travelers, Punyodaya (fl. mid-seventh century) and Yogi Chen (1906–1987). Separated by a span of some thirteen centuries, the travels of these two demonstrate the enduring importance of networks in the Buddhist cosmopolis. Following this, the praxis of Mañjuśrī is introduced as an example of how a praxis moved through the networks of the Buddhist cosmopolis.

A View from a Different Perspective: Methodological Implications of Networks

The regional organization of the preceding chapters has been useful for examining a variety of issues in the study of tantric Buddhism. It is not that any specific issue is only relevant to some particular region, but rather that a region creates a manageable scope. For example, relations between tantric Buddhism and state formation did not only play an important role in Southeast Asia but were characteristic of the societal role of tantric praxis across the Buddhist cosmopolis.[2] Likewise, in addition to the Shikoku pilgrimage, there are many other pilgrimage routes to locations that loom large in Buddhist stories and histories.

Shifting perspective from regions to networks avoids two possible misinterpretations of a regional organization. The first is thinking of regions as closed containers—a metaphor that would artificially limit our understanding of the scope of what actors and institutions can effect. Second, perhaps more subtle, is the treatment of regions as having agency of some kind. Historical events are not caused by the location in which they take place. Not only are regions porous, rather than bounded, but regional cultures are generalizations over variety, rather than homogenous and uniform. In other words, regions are simply heuristic categories, and while they may

[1] Richard K. Payne, "Self-Representation and Cultural Expectations: Yogi Chen and Religious Practices of Life-Writing," *Entangled Religions: Interdisciplinary Journal for the Study of Religious Contact and Transfer* 3 (2016): 33–82, 35.

[2] For example, state formation (creation, maintenance, and protection) was central to much of Amoghavajra's work under the Chinese emperors Suzong and Daizong. See Charles Orzech, *Politics and Transcendent Wisdom: The Scripture of Humane Kings in the Creation of Chinese Buddhism* (University Park: Pennsylvania State University Press, 1998).

be of use in organizing information, they are not causal and therefore not explanatory.[3]

In contrast, thinking in terms of networks requires looking to specific locations and the connections between those locations—what in the terminology of networks are called nodes and strands. The metaphor of networks is an increasingly popular way to describe the patterns by which people, trade, cultures, and religions move.[4] Its current prominence, however, simply highlights the utility of what is a long-standing and widespread metaphor. The image of Indra's net, which is the array of stars above Indra's palace on top of Mount Sumeru, is a prominent metaphor for networks from Buddhist literature. Each star is a node in the net, connected by the net's strands to every other, each reflecting all the others.[5] Unilinear and unidirectional transmissions from one political center to another, or from one culture to another, are more established academic models of Buddhist history. In contrast, the network metaphor provides a more nuanced way of conceptualizing the history of Buddhism, as one of flows moving along multiple pathways back and forth across cultural, linguistic, and political boundaries.

The familiar image of Buddhism flowing out of India in a series of one-directional transmissions is at best an initial representation. It is overly simplistic, obscuring the actual complexity of the ways in which concepts and practices, monks and teachings and rituals, and texts and symbolic motifs moved through networks of the Buddhist cosmopolis. Rather than one-directional flows, the strands connecting nodes allow not only for movement in both directions, but for movement in multiple directions—Tang to Srivijaya to Sri Lanka, Pala to Srivijaya to Tibet, Sri Lanka to Śailendra Java, and so on. These complex networks across which traffic flowed in multiple directions were both land-based and maritime.[6]

[3] An important instance of a regional study of contemporary Buddhism is Jeff Wilson, *Dixie Dharma: Inside a Buddhist Temple in the American South* (Chapel Hill: The University of North Carolina Press, 2014).

[4] It is worth noting right at the start that like "region," "network" is at best an explanatory metaphor of the form "If you think about it this way, it makes sense." Networks are not causal explanations, that is, not theories. They do, however, point to constraints. A network facilitates movement along its strands, while at the same time discouraging movement elsewhere. See Jason Neelis, *Early Buddhist Transmission and Trade Networks: Mobility and Exchange Within and Beyond the Northwestern Borderlands of South Asia* (Leiden: Brill, 2011), 10.

[5] Imre Hamar, "Deconstructing and Reconstructing Yogācāra: Ten Levels of Consciousness-Only/One-Mind in Huayan Buddhism," in *Avataṃsaka (Huayan, Kegon, Flower Ornament) Buddhism in East Asia: Origins and Adaptation of a Visual Culture*, ed. Robert Gimello, Frédéric Girard, and Imre Hamar, 53–71 (Wiesbaden: Harrassowitz Verlag, 2012), 61.

[6] A modern instance is the complex movements of what Cody Bahir labels "Neo-Zhenyan." Cody R. Bahir, "From China to Japan and Back Again: An Energetic Example of Bidirectional Sino-Japanese Esoteric Buddhist Transmission," *Religions* 12: 675 (2021), https://doi.org/

Like region, network is a heuristic metaphor. In other words, using the metaphor of networks is not the one correct way to write history, in contrast to which other historiographies are wrong. Historiographies are neither right nor wrong, but rather ways of organizing information into coherent patterns.[7] Organizing principles, such as regions, countries, and lineages, are simply ways to delimit a field of study. At the same time, such principles identify what is important to look at in that field. Long-standing organizing principles have served the field well—nation-state (e.g., Burmese Buddhism), school (e.g., Yogācāra), historical era (e.g., Kamakura Buddhism), life and works (e.g., Longchenpa), and so on. Now well-worn, what more they enable us to see has in some instances decreased over time. Initial studies may be large and therefore vague, and the passage of time sees an increasing number of corrections and emendations to the standard, received understanding. Conversely, however, these increasingly detailed refinements constitute diminishing returns.[8]

The use of networks as an organizing principle is relatively new as an historiography and therefore opens fresh perspectives and allows us to see both novel things and familiar things in new ways. This, again, does not mean that the metaphor of networks is the only way to write the history of Buddhism. Other structuring metaphors, organizing themes, and previously unconsidered topics will continue to add to our understanding of the tradition.

Networks: Well-Known and Little-Known

Two well-known networks important for the history of Buddhism are the Silk Route through Inner Asia and the "Spice Route" through maritime Southeast Asia. Less well-known but also important for Buddhist history is the network connecting northeast India and southwest China, known as the Southern Silk Route.

10.3390/rel12090675. Another modern instance is provided by Michiro Ama, *Immigrants to the Pure Land: The Modernization, Acculturation, and Globalization of Shin Buddhism, 1898–1941* (Honolulu: University of Hawai'i Press, 2011).

[7] See Hayden White, *Metahistory: The Historical Imagination in Nineteenth-Century Europe* (Baltimore: Johns Hopkins University Press, 1973).

[8] This characterization of the cyclic nature of knowledge creation reflects the pattern described by Thomas Kuhn for the history of science. Thomas S. Kuhn, *The Structure of Scientific Revolutions*, 4th ed. (Chicago: University of Chicago Press, 2012).

As frequently noted, although the Inner Asian routes are conventionally identified with silk, they developed for trade of many different goods and facilitated the transmission of cultural knowledge and Buddhist praxes. Discussing the extension of the Silk Road to Japan, George Keyworth concludes that

> The recitation of *dhāraṇīs* to female and male *kami* and goddesses, bodhisattvas, and buddhas in Japan can be connected to the material and intellectual world of the medieval Silk Road(s). That culture is not necessarily one focused on silk or fine textiles from Persia or India or even China. Instead, this was the transmission of Indic sounds, phonetics, rituals, and religion.[9]

The romantic association with silk was fixed in popular imagination in the second half of the nineteenth century when Ferdinand von Richthofen coined the term, in German, "Seidenstrasse." And, while sometimes referred to as "roads," they actually comprise multiple interconnected routes. Describing the routes followed by Buddhist monks, Jason Neelis notes that they

> followed various itineraries, including major arteries, minor capillary routes, and "middle paths" to travel back and forth between destinations. Their roads frequently overlapped and intertwined with those of merchants and traders in pursuit of both religious and economic goals.[10]

In other words, the "strands" of the network metaphor need to be understood as themselves comprising multiple threads.

Although Rome and China have been privileged in many of the representations of the Silk Route, it should not be thought of simply as a conduit between "the West and the East." Susan Whitfield has argued that these routes should instead be seen in their fullness. "The concept of a road can be a distraction, concentrating attention on the beginning and end at the expense of the stops *en route* and the lands between the stops. Far from being

[9] George A. Keyworth, "Did the Silk Road(s) Extend from Dunhuang, Mount Wutai, and Chang'an to Kyoto, Japan?" in *Buddhism in Central Asia II—Practices and Rituals, Visual and Material Transfer*, ed. Yukiyo Kasai and Henrik H. Sørensen, 17–67 (Leiden: Brill, 2022), 67.

[10] Neelis, *Early Buddhist Transmission and Trade Networks*, 1.

an ocean of emptiness, the middle of the Silk Road consisted of thriving and fascinating countries and cultures."[11]

Though not as well-known, a third route connected northeast India to southwest China, with further links to Tibet and Southeast Asia. In keeping with the names given to the other two, the historian Bin Yang has referred to this latter route as the "Southern Silk Road."[12] Yang notes that in 1074 a visitor to the Dali Kingdom (present-day Yunnan Province in southern China) recorded the road directions at a local post station, including east to Rongzhou and northeast to Chengdu—both in Sichuan—west to India, southeast to Vietnam, north to the "Big Snow Mountain," and south to the sea.[13] The networks crossing at this site in the Buddhist cosmopolis connected locations not only in South, Inner, and East Asia, but in Southeast Asia as well.

Prior to the modern era, Southeast Asian Buddhism was both more interconnected and more integrated into the rest of the Buddhist community than modern representations might suggest. John Miksic characterizes the place of Southeast Asian Buddhism in that wider community, saying that although

> many texts have been lost, especially those composed in Southeast Asia, the names and some of the doctrines of the teachers from this region have survived in documents found elsewhere. We can therefore reconstruct an ancient Southeast Asian Buddhist culture which was seen as a pillar of the worldwide edifice of the religion. Parochialism was not one of the characteristics of this ecumene.[14]

The networks that facilitated the transmission of tantric Buddhism to and from Southeast Asia were both land-based and ocean-based. Speaking of the latter, Andrea Acri has said:

[11] Susan Whitfield, "Introduction: A Part of All Our Histories," in *The Silk Road: Trade, Travel, War and Faith*, ed. Susan Whitfield, 13–18 (Chicago: Serindia Publications, 2004), 13. See also Imre Hamar, "The Mañjuśrī Cult in Khotan," *Studies in Chinese Religions* 5.3–4 (2019): 343–352.

[12] Bin Yang, *Cowrie Shells and Cowrie Money: A Global History* (London: Routledge, 2019), 109. Earlier Bin Yang had referred to it as the "Southwest Silk Road," see Bin Yang, "Horses, Silver, and Cowries: Yunnan in Global Perspective," *Journal of World History* 15.3 (2004): 281–322, 281. My thanks to Megan Bryson for these references.

[13] Yang, *Cowrie Shells and Cowrie Money*, 109.

[14] John Miksic, "The Buddhist-Hindu Divide in Premodern Southeast Asia" (Nalanda-Sriwijaya Centre Working Paper Series no. 1. Singapore: Institute of Southeast Asian Studies, 2010), 8.

> Cutting across the natural boundaries and barriers of continental topography, sea-based routes formed a network of conduits that led to the formation of a mediaeval global Buddhist Asia. . . . By the middle of the 7th century AD, factors such as a radical expansion of commercial maritime routes connecting South with East Asia contributed significantly to the exchange not only of mercantile goods but also, and more importantly, of ideas, beliefs and ritual practices, and artistic styles.[15]

These maritime relations constitute an important part of the wide-ranging networks that connected medieval Buddhist communities in all the regions, thus constituting the Buddhist cosmopolis as both a geographic entity and a social one. An example, discussed in a preceding chapter, is that of the Tang-era tantric masters such as Vajrabodhi and Amoghavajra who traveled along these maritime routes, stopping in and studying at Buddhist centers in insular Southeast Asia. They were not just traveling through "peripheral" regions. Although identified with Tang, and discussed in Chapter III of this volume, these two and many other tantric teachers and practitioners were moving through the networks that comprise the Buddhist cosmopolis. Similarly, Miksic identifies three teachers who moved through the networks connecting Southeast Asia with India and Tibet. One is the seventh-century abbot of Nalanda, Dharmapala, who retired to Suvarnadvipa (the "land of gold"). The second is Dīpaṃkara Śrijñana, who went there specifically to learn tantra. And the third is Atiśa, who also learned tantra there, before transmitting those teachings to Tibet.[16] Nodes in those networks include the monastic centers throughout Southeast Asia that were important destinations in their own right, not simply transit points between India and China.

The complexity of networks also provided for multiple contemporaneous influences. For example, Woodward suggests that there were possibly two distinct sources of Indic influence on eleventh-century esoteric Buddhism in Cambodia. "There may have been two different strands in eleventh-century esoteric Buddhism: one from northern India, as the presence of Pala-type tasselled crowns on a few bronze sculptures indicates, and the other southern

[15] Andrea Acri, "Introduction: Esoteric Buddhist Networks along the Maritime Silk Routes," in *Esoteric Buddhism in Mediaeval Maritime Asia: Networks of Masters, Texts, Icons*, ed. Andrea Acri (Singapore: ISEAS Yusof Ishak Institute, 2016), 2.

[16] Miksic, "The Buddhist-Hindu Divide in Premodern Southeast Asia," 16. Internal references elided.

Indian . . . involving Srivijaya and Chola realms."[17] This is another instance of the tracks of tantric Buddhist history running in several different directions, creating a network of relationships between royal centers.

Woodward also discusses the movement of tantric Buddhism from Srivijaya to India, contrary to the common image of a unidirectional flow of Buddhism out of India. He identifies two specific travelers who exemplify this flow from insular Southeast Asia to India. First, "In the 850s or 860s, Balaputra, an exiled Javanese prince, established a monastery at Nalanda in India."[18] Epigraphic evidence links a stupa at this monastery in Nalanda in India to Borobudur in Java. Woodward suggests that this interpretation is further reinforced by the symbolic similarity of the circular arrangement of deities in the Yoginī tantras and the circular arrangement of deities on the topmost terrace of Borobudur.[19]

Second, Atiśa not only transmitted what he had learned in Southeast Asia to India but also to Tibet.[20] Indicative of Atiśa's role in the transmission of teachings from Srivijaya is the Tibetan translation of his teacher Dharmakīrtiśri's commentary on a Perfection of Wisdom text, the "Illuminating the Unfathomable" (*Durbodhāloka*).[21] In addition, both Dharmakīrtiśrī and Atiśa promoted the praxis of Tārā, who became a very popular devotional figure in Tibet. Woodward indicates that another link is the six-syllable mantra associated with the bodhisattva Avalokiteśvara (oṃ maṇi padme huṃ)—widely recognized today as the most popular mantra in Tibet. This mantra is proclaimed in the *Kāraṇḍavyūha sūtra*, which "was more important in Indonesia than has been hitherto recognised."[22] Woodward suggests that Atiśa would have been introduced to the praxis of Avalokiteśvara during his studies in Java. Familiar with both the *Kāraṇḍavyūha sūtra* and the six-syllable mantra of Avalokiteśvara, Atisa transmitted this practice to Tibet where it rooted deeply into the religious culture.

[17] Hiram Woodward, "Esoteric Buddhism in Southeast Asia," *Journal of Southeast Asian Studies* 35.2 (June 2004): 329–354, 350.
[18] Woodward, "Esoteric Buddhism in Southeast Asia," 346.
[19] Woodward, "Esoteric Buddhism in Southeast Asia," 346.
[20] Woodward, "Esoteric Buddhism in Southeast Asia," 347.
[21] Swati Chemburkar, "*Stūpa* to *Maṇḍala*: Tracing a Buddhist Architectural Development from Kesariya to Borobudur to Tabo," *Pacific World: Journal of the Institute of Buddhist Studies* 3rd series, no. 20 (2018): 169–221, 171. See also Swati Chemburkar, "Tantra and Temple Architecture in Buddhist Southeast Asia," in *The Oxford Handbook of Tantric Studies*, ed. Richard K. Payne and Glen T. Hayes (Oxford: Oxford University Press, 2023).
[22] Woodward, "Esoteric Buddhism in Southeast Asia," 347.

The murals at Tabo, a monastery that Atiśa visited in 1042, provide a more material indication of his role in transmitting tantric Buddhism from Srivijaya to India. The visual narrative program of the murals resonates both with that at Borobudur and with one at Samye in Tibet. As mentioned in Chapter IV, Chemburkar also calls attention to "a complete sculptural *maṇḍala* of the life-size clay figures of the Vajradhātu Maṇḍala deities" displayed at Tabo.[23] Surviving from East Java, there is an "exactly contemporaneous set of Vajradhātu Maṇḍala bronzes."[24] It is no doubt too speculative to attribute these parallels to Atiśa personally. But as Atiśa traveled between these locations, his itinerary highlights the strands made up of many travelers who link these three sites—Borobudur in Indonesia, Tabo in India, and Samye in Tibet. The networks that Atiśa traveled over also carried tantric praxes, including artistic motifs and architectural styles.

Where Strands Meet: Nodes

The routes that made up the strands of networks were always malleable—old paths abandoned, new ones being opened. For example, some trading routes followed a northern path around the Takla Makan Desert—the middle of the Silk Route—while others followed a southern one. Nodes also underwent changes, and what were at one time locations that were key to networks could later become almost forgotten despite their previous importance. An instance of this kind of social, political, and economic change is the kingdom of Derge, which was at one time literally central to networks connecting Inner and East Asia.

Derge

In what is now southwest China, the kingdom of Derge compiled and printed one of the important Tibetan Buddhist canons, now commonly referred as the Derge canon. Derge today is a small city in a rather remote location in the Ganzi Tibetan Autonomous Prefecture in southwestern Sichuan (or Kham). In the seventeenth and eighteenth centuries, however, the Derge clan ruled

[23] Chemburkar, "*Stūpa* to *Maṇḍala*," 171.
[24] Chemburkar, "*Stūpa* to *Maṇḍala*," 172.

a much larger area, and sitting roughly equidistant from Lhasa in Tibet, Chengdu in China, and Kokonor in Mongolia, its location made it a natural node for the networks running between these important cities. "Lhasa sits over 650 kilometers (404 miles) to the west behind a rocky landscape challenged by breathtaking mountain passes. The closest Chinese population center is Chengdu, which lies roughly the same distance to the east, and across a very rough ride over precipitous passes. The eighteenth-century Mongolian stronghold of Kokonor, present-day Qinghai, lies roughly the same distance—600 kilometers—to the north."[25]

Tenpa Tsering (1678–1738), considered the most eminent of the Derge clan, founded a printing house, known as the Parkhang, for the production of Buddhist canonic texts. Production of printing blocks for the Kanjur (Tib. bka' 'gyur, sutra) began in 1729, and for the Tenjur (Tib. bstan 'gyur, śāstra) eight years later in 1737. The kingdom had a variety of motivations for producing the canon. Just as for Buddhist studies scholars today, there was certainly the desire for an accurate record of what was understood to be the teachings of the Buddha, as well as the authoritative commentaries on those teachings. This project of producing the Derge canon did not mean simply reproducing or copying some other canon, however. This was instead a scholarly project involving translators and editors tasked with assuring the accuracy of individual texts and of the canon as a whole. The Derge canon was a printing project and therefore differs from the scribal context examined by Daniel Veidlinger; however, the scholastic virtues are consistent with his assertion that "all scriptural copying processes . . . are designed to maintain the highest standards of fidelity and discourage innovation."[26] Thus, the canon was a scholarly resource, used by monastic intellectuals both for training in the conceptual world of Buddhist thought and practice and for maintaining that conceptual world.

At the same time, as embodiments of the awakened one, the texts were objects of veneration—many of them prescribing how such veneration should be conducted, such as copying the text, and the merit gained by such veneration. This is an instance of the now familiar "cult of the book."[27]

[25] Cynthia Col, "Picturing the Canon: The Murals, Sculpture, and Architecture of the Derge Parkhang," PhD diss. (Berkeley, CA: Graduate Theological Union, 2009), 6–7.

[26] Daniel M. Veidlinger, *Spreading the Dhamma: Writing, Orality, and Textual Transmission in Buddhist Norther Thailand* (Honolulu: University of Hawai'i Press, 2006), 165–166.

[27] Gregory Schopen, "The Phrase '*sa pṛthivīpradeśaś caityabhūto bhavet*' in the *Vajracchedikā*: Notes on the Cult of the Book in Mahāyāna," *Indo-Iranian Journal* 17.3/4 (Nov./Dec. 1975): 147–181.

Physical books themselves were often treated as "objects of talismanic efficacy."[28] More than simply containing information, these texts make present the word of the Buddha (Skt. *buddhavacana*) and make available the teachings, dharma, even in the absence of Śākyamuni Buddha. Making the Buddha's power present meant that the physical books could "grant protection, health, long life, and merit, and can do so even when no attempt to understand their contents is made."[29] Thus, the project of editing the text, carving the blocks, preparing the paper and ink,[30] and printing the Buddhist canon initiated at Derge resounded with both intellectual and dharmic significance.

In addition to scholastic and devotional functions, by gifting copies of the canon to other kingdoms, Derge asserted its own authority and legitimacy. The printing house produced high-quality books that were well-edited and finely printed at a time when printing was a newly adopted technology in Tibet. The quality of the Derge editions was "a crucial factor in Derge's rise to prominence in the Tibetan cultural sphere."[31] Cultural capital was being generated in the "complex web of cultural, political, and military concerns that were very much specific to Eastern Tibet in the 18th century."[32] Given its physical location, the kingdom of Derge was an important node in the networks of the Buddhist cosmopolis for four centuries. The Parkhang printery is an embodiment of this centrality and a focal point of the tantric Buddhist culture of Derge.

The physical structure of the Parkhang directly links the Derge printing project to key components of tantric Buddhism. Mandalic patterns served as an organizing principle for architecture throughout the tantric Buddhist cosmopolis.[33] However, not all tantric temples match the regularity of an idealized mandala, nor is there always a clear textual precedent that can be identified as the source of a particular architectural form.[34] Cynthia Col's analysis of the Parkhang places the Buddha Śākyamuni at the symbolic "center of the array of deities that rise up throughout the Parkhang,"[35]

[28] Richard Nance, "Indian Buddhist Preachers Inside and Outside the Sutras," *Religion Compass* 2.2 (March 2008): 134–159, 134, doi.org/10.1111/j.1749-8171.2007.00057.x.
[29] Nance, "Indian Buddhist Preachers Inside and Outside the Sutras," 134.
[30] Regarding the paper and ink used, see Col, "Picturing the Canon," 54.
[31] Joseph Scheier-Dolberg, "Treasure House of Tibetan Culture: Canonization, Printing, and Power in the Derge Printing Hourse," PhD thesis (Harvard University, 2005), 5.
[32] Scheier-Dolberg, "Treasure House of Tibetan Culture," 6.
[33] Chemburkar, "Tantra and Temple Architecture in Buddhist Southeast Asia."
[34] See discussion of the relation between Borobudur and textual models in Chapter IV of this work.
[35] Col, "Picturing the Canon," 18.

making it symbolically analogous to the mandala palace of Śākyamuni Buddha. Col argues that the Parkhang mandala serves to place "Derge at the center, commanding respect from its powerful surrounding neighbors."[36] In other words, although little-known today, Derge was a key node of the tantric Buddhist network, both geographically and symbolically.

Architecture and tantric symbolism interact with one another, but they develop in their own ways—that is, they are semiautonomous traditions. Architecture in Derge had its own native traditions, materials, and style, along with the demands of the specific location, local concerns, and the ongoing history of the building that housed the printing project. Anne M. Blackburn has noted that the motivations of Buddhist patrons, in this case the kings of Derge, are complex and not segregated by modern conceptions of politics and religion as distinct and separate. "An analysis of the production of space that moves between sites, the objects established there and the frames of reference articulated by inscriptions and local histories reveals with particular clarity the ways in which the creation of Buddhist landscapes served interests that *we* might identify as political and devotional, but which were not so clearly distinguished from one another within past worlds of Buddhist patronage."[37]

Mandalas constitute one kind of tradition, different from local building practices, though mandalas explicitly reference architecture in symbolically portraying a palace in which a buddha and their retinue dwell.[38] Employed in ritual, mandalas are then refracted back as models for art and architecture, as an organizing principle for the display of pantheons, in illustrated texts, and in visualization practices. In doing so, they can be seen to establish a relation between each entity that is portrayed mandalically—from the cosmic mandala, to a political mandala, to a building, to the body.[39] Neither architecture nor tantric symbolism is entirely closed (autonomous) nor entirely open. Each has its own ongoing developmental trajectory while interacting with the other, and hence they are "semiautonomous" to one another. Derge portrayed itself as more than simply one node in the network of the Buddhist cosmopolis. With the cultural capital gained by preserving and propagating the teachings of the buddhas, and constructing the Parkhang as the mandalic

[36] Col, "Picturing the Canon," 21.

[37] Anne M. Blackburn, "Writing Buddhist Histories from Landscape and Architecture: Sukhotai and Chiang Mai," *Buddhist Studies Review* 24.2 (2007): 192–225, 222.

[38] See discussion of the political significance of the term "mandala" in Chapter IV of this work.

[39] Col, "Picturing the Canon," 18.

center, Derge symbolically located itself as the central court of the Buddhist cosmopolis.

Buddhist Travelers: Puṇyodaya and Yogi Chen

The vast majority of Buddhist travelers through the networks of the Buddhist cosmopolis remain unknown and anonymous to us. But a few fall into a mid-range of having left traces without becoming major figures in Buddhist religious culture. Two of these less-well known travelers, of whom we do have records, provide us with examples of how complex, interconnected, and widespread the networks of the Buddhist cosmopolis have been.

Puṇyodaya

About a century before Śubhakarasiṃha, Vajrabodhi, and Amoghavajra, the monk Puṇyodaya traveled from India to Chang-an, arriving there in 655.[40] Having brought a large quantity of texts from India to China, Puṇyodaya attempted to introduce tantric teachings. At this time, however, Xuanzang (602–664), himself already famous for his own travels to India and back, was a dominating figure at the court and was promoting the Yogācāra (or Vijñaptimātratā) teachings that he had made his own. Given his dominant position, he was able to influence the court against supporting Puṇyodaya. Emperor Gaozong (r. 649–685) treated Puṇyodaya as an "employee" rather than as a religious teacher.[41]

An important source for information about Puṇyodaya is the monk Yijing (635–713), himself an active traveler through the Buddhist cosmopolis. Yijing spent almost a quarter century in India and Sumatra, and his records continue to be a valuable historical resource.[42] According to Yijing's accounts, Puṇyodaya was not unique in being treated as an employee of the

[40] Chou Yi-liang, "Tantrism in China," *Harvard Journal of Asiatic Studies* 8.3/4 (March 1945): 241–332, 244. Reprinted in *Tantric Buddhism in East Asia*, ed. Richard K. Payne, 33–60 (Boston: Wisdom Publications, 2006), 35.

[41] Lin Li-kouang, "Punyodaya (Na-t'i), Un Propagateur du Tantrism en Chine et au Cambodge à l'Époque de Hiuan-tsang," *Journal Asiatique* 227 (1935): 83–100, 85.

[42] Max Deeg, "Chinese Buddhist Travelers: Faxian, Xuanzang, and Yijing," in *The Oxford Research Encyclopedia of Asian History* (New York: Oxford University Press, online 2019), n.p.

court—other monks were also "recruited by the court to undertake tasks on behalf of the emperor."[43]

The quest for longevity, both medicinal and alchemical, was one of the prominent motivations for contacts between the Tang court and Buddhist communities in South and Southeast Asia.[44] Emperor Gaozong sent Puṇyodaya to Zhen-la in peninsular Southeast Asia in search of medicinal herbs, part of what Pierce Salguero has described as "one of the most extensive and well-documented cases of cross-cultural medical exchange in world history."[45] Puṇyodaya's first mission to Zhen-la lasted four years, after which he returned to the Tang capital.

Xuanzang took advantage of his absence to move Puṇyodaya's texts out of the capital. Consequently, only three translations into Chinese are attributed to Puṇyodaya.[46] Later, "a Zhen-la delegation of Buddhist elders travelled to the T'ang capital in 663 to plead for his return. [Receiving permission to depart,] the Indian Tantric master spent the rest of his days in Zhen-la."[47] Peter Sharrock considers this "early exposure to the emergent Tantric form of Buddhism . . . [as having] had a lasting effect on the Khmers."[48] Despite the intervening century and a half when Buddhism was suppressed and Śaivite practices were given precedence by the Khmer Angkor state, "we can discern clear Tantric traits when it re-emerges in the 10th century."[49]

Sharrock further concludes that the Khmer were quite expert in medicinal herbs, a fact that was known in China through trade. Thus, the network built of trade exchanges, including trade in medicinal herbs, also provided movement for tantric Buddhism—the teacher and teachings being imported at the

[43] Tansen Sen, "Yijing and the Buddhist Cosmopolis of the Seventh Century," in *Texts and Transformations: Essays in Honor of the 75th Birthday of Victor H. Mair*, ed. Haun Saussy, 345–368 (Amherst, MA: Cambria Press, 2018), 354.

[44] Jinhua Chen, "A Chemical 'Explosion' Triggered by an Encounter Between Indian and Chinese Medical Sciences: Another Look at the Significances of the Sinhalese Monk Śākyamitra's (567?–668+) Visit at Mount Wutai in 667," in *What Happened After Mañjuśrī Migrated to China? The Sinification of the Mañjuśrī Faith and the Globalization of the Wutai Cult*, ed. Jinhua Chen, Guang Kuan, and Hu Fo, 3–18 (London: Routledge, 2022).

[45] C. Pierce Salguero, "Buddhist Medicine and Its Circulation," *Oxford Research Encyclopedias, Asian History*, online 2018; doi.org/10.1093/acrefore/9780190277727.013.215, n.p.

[46] Chou, "Tantrism in China," 244. These include the "Eight Part Maṇḍala" (T 486, "Maṇḍalāṣṭasūtra," Skt title reconstructed from Tibetan), the "Method for Worshipping the Buddha" (T. 487), and the Āṭānāṭiya sutta (Dīgha Nikāya), 32. See Maurice Walshe, *The Long Discourses of the Buddha* (1987. Reprint. Boston: Wisdom Publications, 1995), 471–478.

[47] Peter Sharrock, "The Buddhist Pantheon of the Bàyon of Angkor: An Historical and Art Historical Reconstruction of the Bàyon Temple and Its Religious and Political Roots," PhD diss. (School of African and Oriental Studies, University of London, 2006), 45.

[48] Sharrock, "The Buddhist Pantheon of the Bàyon of Angkor," 9.

[49] Sharrock, "The Buddhist Pantheon of the Bàyon of Angkor," 9.

initiative of the Khmer themselves. In the seventh century, Puṇyodaya traveled networks connecting India to China to Southeast Asia, back to China, and ultimately returning to Southeast Asia. In the twentieth century, another tantric practitioner, Yogi Chen, traveled networks even more widespread through the Buddhist cosmopolis.

Yogi Chen

Yogi Chen's life story[50] reveals networks of the twentieth-century Buddhist cosmopolis—networks that cross the usual nationally defined boundaries between "Chinese Buddhism" and "Tibetan Buddhism." While there is no single, authoritative biography of Yogi Chen, he recounted parts of his life story at different times to different audiences. The most complete such recounting is based on a series of conversations that Yogi Chen had with Sangharakshita while residing in Kalimpong.[51] Although the life story is structured into the four categories used in Tibetan life writing—outward, inward, secret, and most secret—here we are concerned primarily with events that trace his movements along networks in the mid-twentieth-century Buddhist cosmopolis.[52]

"Young Chen," as he calls himself, was originally trained in the Confucian classics. A wealthy neighbor had hired a teacher and allowed Chen to participate in the instruction. Formal education then followed, including six years at the Normal School in Changsha, the capital city of the province of Hunan. Chen read both Daoist texts and the works of Venerable Taixu (1890–1947), the early twentieth-century reformer and modernizer of Buddhism in China,[53] which the provincial library had in its holdings. Chen contacted

[50] On the use of the terminology of "life writing" (here as "life story") in preference to "autobiography," see Payne, "Self-Representation and Cultural Expectations," 37–38.

[51] Jianmin Chen, "Buddhist Meditation: Systematic and Practical, CW 35 Introduction," first published 1967, now online: http://www.yogichen.org/cw/cw35/bm00.html.

[52] See also Yutang Lin, Forever in Our Hearts, http://www.yogichen.org/gurulin/efiles/mb/mbk02.html.

[53] Eric Goodell, "Taixu," in *The Oxford Encyclopedia of Buddhism*, ed. Richard K. Payne and Georgios Halkias, 2277–2301 (Oxford: Oxford University Press; online 2022: https://doi.org/10.1093/acrefore/9780199340378.013.1018); and Mario Poceski, "Contemporary Chinese Buddhist Traditions," in *The Oxford Handbook of Contemporary Buddhism*, ed. Michael Jerryson, 79–99 (Oxford: Oxford University Press, 2017; online 2106: DOI: 10.1093/oxfordhb/9780199362387.013.15), 83–85. Taixu was a leading proponent of modernizing Chinese Buddhism by integrating Japanese esoteric Buddhism to recreate the Tang school that was no longer extant at the end of the nineteenth century. Wei Wu, *Esoteric Buddhism in China: Engaging Japanese and Tibetan Traditions, 1912–1949* (New York: Columbia University Press, 2024), 31.

Taixu for some local monks who wanted him to come to Changsha, which led eventually to Chen working at the new Buddhist College that Taixu had founded. During this period, Chen also met a Gelug master called Gelu Rinpoche, under whose guidance he completed the first of the three foundation trainings—prostrations, refuge, and recitation of the one-hundred-syllable mantra of Vajrasattva. Chen then also sought out a Nyingma teacher, Lola Hutuktu (evidently a Mongolian lama), from whom he learned the Atiyoga practices of Mahāmudrā and Dzokchen.

Following a series of visions, Chen went to Derge in Sichuan to obtain further initiations and teachings not available in Hunan. His practice was interrupted by the Second World War, during which he helped to relocate his family to a safer place and then engaged in solitary meditation in a cave. With the assistance of a wealthy patron, Chen traveled to India, eventually settling in Kalimpong. In 1972, he moved to the United States and developed a following among the Chinese community in the East San Francisco Bay Area (Oakland, Berkeley, and Emeryville). Active in the community for fifteen years, Yogi Chen passed away in 1987 in Berkeley, California. His disciple, Lin Yutang, continues the work of Yogi Chen. Yogi Chen's travels through the Buddhist cosmopolis took him from Hunan to Sichuan within China, then to Kalimpong in India, and ultimately to the East Bay of Northern California in the United States.

The travels of these two tantric masters show us some of the strands of the networks connecting widely separated parts of the Buddhist cosmopolis. Like texts, artworks, architectural expertise, and rituals, masters such as Punyodaya and Yogi Chen are an answer to the question "What moved through the networks?" From a different perspective, however, it is tantric praxes that moved through the networks. As integrated systems of thought and practice, praxes are why texts, artworks, rituals, implements, and so on moved, and it was mastery of the practices, doctrines, texts, and rituals that made monks into masters whose biographies trace their movements through the networks of the Buddhist cosmopolis.

Praxes: Instantiations of Tantric Buddhism

Despite ordinary usage, it was not "tantric Buddhism" that moved along the strands between the nodes that together constitute the Buddhist cosmopolis. "Tantric Buddhism" is only a retrospectively constructed abstraction, too vague and most likely not what masters or adherents themselves thought they were doing. Instead, we could look for more definite, concrete, and portable components, that is, texts, masters, statues, rituals, implements, and so on that were transported from one place to another. As noted previously, however, in isolation such components are not tantric. But, as components of a praxis, the parts constitute an integrated whole and become tantric through the three signifiers we have been working with to identify tantra: designation, context, and use. The argument here is that the various components were transported because of their role in praxes. Praxes then serve as an analytic category in the middle ground between the abstract category "tantric Buddhism" and individual components that in isolation are not tantric. For example, the miniatures of the Mahābodhi temple discussed in the previous chapter were not simply mementos, but rather employed as objects of veneration practices. From this perspective, we can reasonably reframe what is called "Buddhism" in Western discourse as the praxis of Śākyamuni. Praxes were formed and reformed out of a variety of portable components, together with local components put to use in the system of thought and practice in its new locale, forming a new constellation of components and reconstituting the praxis.[54] Taking praxis as our perspective shifts from looking at individual components to looking at the relations between components, evidenced by context, use, and designation.[55]

The Praxis of Mañjuśrī Bodhisattva

From the introduction of the figure of Mañjuśrī in early Mahāyāna texts during the first or second centuries, he has become one of the most widely revered of the bodhisattvas. Also known as Mañjughoṣa, he is a literary presence from the beginnings of the Mahāyāna into the present. Here we are concerned with the praxis of Mañjuśrī, which is tantric in some of its forms, and with the movement of that praxis through the networks of the Buddhist cosmopolis. Paul Harrison argues for an historical distinction between the

[54] See, for example, Nicolas Sihlé, "Written Texts at the Juncture of the Local and the Global: Some Anthropological Considerations on the Local Corpus of Tantric Ritual Manuals (Lower Mustang, Nepal)," in *Tibetan Ritual*, ed. José Ignacio Cabezón, 35–52 (New York: Oxford University Press, 2010).

[55] This difference is analogous to that between biology and ecology.

bodhisattva who becomes increasingly prominent in Mahāyāna literature and the bodhisattva who is the centripetal figure of the Mañjuśrī praxis.

From Literary Figure to Chief Deity

Focusing on an early corpus of translations of Mahāyāna texts into Chinese, those done by Lokakṣema (late second century CE), Harrison asks what would the textual record show if a praxis is present at the time that texts were being written, compiled, or translated? His answer is that the texts should evidence "explicit injunctions to worship Mañjuśrī or his image, to bring him to mind or engage in visualization practice directed towards him, or to call on his name for help and assistance."[56] While absent in the early texts Harrison examines, just these kinds of injunctions for bodhisattvas are to be found in later Mahāyāna texts.

The absence of such indications of a praxis of Mañjuśrī or other bodhisattvas in these early translations of Mahāyāna texts indicates that they were literary figures rather than the centripetal figure for a praxis of their own. While Śākyamuni and other buddhas, stupas, and books are central figures for praxes, it is only in later texts, and later versions of the same texts, that such treatments of Mañjuśrī and other bodhisattvas appear.[57] In other words, in this case, it was other praxes—those of the Buddha Śākyamuni, and of buddhas, of stupas, and of books—that traveled from the Indian subcontinent to continental East Asia. Once there, they provided models of what such praxes would look like and models for constructing such a praxis, as well as some of the components for a system focused on Mañjuśrī.

David Quinter examines one of these later texts, the *Mañjuśrī parinirvāṇa sūtra*, which he groups with other visualization sutras and dates to the period from the late fourth through fifth century—two to two-and-a-half centuries later than Lokakṣema's translations.[58] These texts evidence the range of practices involved in bodhisattva praxes and how those components were employed.

[56] Paul Harrison, "Mañjuśrī and the Cult of Celestial Bodhisattvas," *Chung-Hwa Buddhist Journal* 13.2 (2000): 157–193, 178.
[57] Harrison, "Mañjuśrī and the Cult of Celestial Bodhisattvas," 180.
[58] David Quinter, "Visualizing the *Mañjuśrī Parinirvāṇa Sūtra* as a Contemplation Sutra," *Asia Major* 23.2 (2010): 97–128, 128.

The specifically visualization part of the sutra is enmeshed with other practices. If, after performing the visualization, Mañjuśrī does not appear to the practitioner, then the practitioner is enjoined to recite the *Śūraṃgama sūtra* and Mañjuśrī's name. If wanting to make offerings, and cultivate merit, the practitioner brings Mañjuśrī to mind, then Mañjuśrī will manifest as "an impoverished, solitary, or afflicted sentient being, and appear before the practitioners. When people call Mañjuśrī to mind, they should practice compassion. Those who practice compassion will thereby be able to see Mañjuśrī."[59] Within this wider frame, practices include not only the visualization per se but also sutra recitation, reciting the name and acts of compassion toward the needy. Although the Mañjuśrī sutra does not provide a mantra as such, the emphasis on receiving, retaining, reading, and reciting the name of the bodhisattva is congruent with understandings of the power of reciting the names of buddhas, bodhisattvas, and protectors that informs mantra practice.[60]

The transition from the absence of a Mañjuśrī praxis in the late second century to an established praxis in the late fourth to fifth century raises the question of the origin of the Mañjuśrī sutra, which records such practices. Does this indicate a change in Indian Buddhism after the period of the texts translated by Lokakṣema, or does this reflect a development of bodhisattva praxes in China? The history of Buddhism and Buddhist texts does not fall neatly into these two categories, however. Central Asian Buddhists also played an active role—as with Southeast Asia, Central Asia was not merely a conduit but an active contributor to the history of Buddhist tantra. Quinter suggests Jonathan Silk's concept of a "mixed origin" as appropriate for the visualization sutras—or what we could call hybrids. Whether the texts were written in Chinese or not, their contents were compiled from Indian, Central Asian, and Chinese components.[61]

Mañjuśrī's Many Functions

Mañjuśrī is prominent in several of the best known Mahāyāna texts, such as the Lotus Sutra, the *Gaṇḍavyūha sūtra*, the *Vimalakīrti nirdeśa sūtra*, and several Perfection of Wisdom texts. Several perhaps less familiar texts focus

59 Quinter, "Visualizing the *Mañjuśrī Sutra*," 112–113.
60 Cf. Quinter, "Visualizing the *Mañjuśrī Sutra*," 119.
61 Quinter, "Visualizing the *Mañjuśrī Sutra*," 124.

specifically on the figure of Mañjuśrī, such as the *Mañjuśrī buddhakṣetra guṇavyūha sūtra*, the already mentioned *Mañjuśrī parinirvāṇa sūtra*, the *Nāmasaṃgiti*, and the *Mañjuśrī nirdeśa nāma mahāyāna sūtra*.[62] Based on his review of that literature, Anthony Tribe describes Mañjuśrī as having several functions; these include being one of the interlocutors in a sutra narrative, as a spokesperson presenting teachings, as compassionately bringing living beings onto the path, and as a spiritual friend. Mañjuśrī also plays a role in state formation, having been identified with the rulers of Khotan and Tibet in early, founding periods of those polities.[63] As a centripetal figure, Mañjuśrī is also identified as an object of meditation and devotion, and as a protector. He is variously described as a tenth-stage bodhisattva, a fully awakened buddha, and as the teacher of buddhas.

Laura Harrington identifies three texts as particularly central to the tantric form of Mañjuśrī's praxis. These are the *Mañjuśrīmūlakalpa*,[64] the *Nāmasaṃgīti* (or *Mañjuśrīnāmasaṃgīti*), and the *Kālacakra tantra*. These three texts reveal a range of ways in which the praxis of Mañjuśrī was entextualized. Mañjuśrī is the central teacher of the extensive collection of ritual manuals, the *Mañjuśrīmūlakalpa*. Having been compiled over half a millennium—from the seventh to twelfth centuries—it is both an "expansive visionary text" (Skt. *mahāyānavaipulyasūtra*) and, at the same time, organizes a large array of ritual practices into a single comprehensive resource for practice (Skt. *kalpa*).[65] Since at least some of the ritual practices recorded in the text necessarily preexisted the text, and texts that would become sections of the larger compilation circulated independently,[66] we can speculate the existence of practices that contributed to the development of the tantric praxis of Mañjuśrī perhaps as early as the sixth century.

Much shorter is the *Nāmasaṃgitī*, a liturgical text dating from the late seventh or early eighth century. Monks and laymen have recited it daily in India

[62] On this last, see Peter Skilling, "How the Unborn Was Born: The Riddle of Mahāyāna Origins," in *Setting Out on the Great Way: Essays on Early Mahāyāna Buddhism*, ed. Paul Harrison, 31–71 (Sheffield, UK: Equinox, 2018), 44.

[63] Lewis Doney, "Early Bodhisattva-Kingship in Tibet: The Case of Tri Songdétsen," *Cahiers d'Extrême-Asie* 24 (2015): 29–47, 31–32.

[64] On the title of this work, and a detailed study of sources, see also Martin Delhey, "The Textual Sources of the *Mañjuśrīyamūlakalpa* (*Mañjuśrīmūlakalpa*), with Special Reference to Its Early Nepalese Witness NGMPP A39/4," *Journal of the Nepal Research Center* XIV (2012): 55–75.

[65] Glenn Wallis, *Mediating the Power of the Buddhas: Ritual in the Mañjuśrīmūlakalpa* (Albany: State University of New York Press, 2002), 12–13.

[66] Wallis, *Mediating the Power of the Buddhas*, 61, 172.

and Tibet,[67] reflecting the importance for tantric praxis of the understanding that names, mantra, and deities constitute an identity. Rather than a resource for ritual practices, like the *Mañjuśrīmūlakalpa*, the *Nāmasaṃgīti* is itself used in conducting the praxis of Mañjuśrī.

While the *Mañjuśrīmūlakalpa* is one of the earliest tantric Buddhist texts, the *Kalacakra tantra* is one of the last to be produced in India. It draws on the vast resources of the tantric movement available at the time, and it went on to provide a basis for tantric practice in Nepal and Tibet. Today it is considered by many practitioners and scholars to be the pinnacle of the tantric teachings.[68] These three are not primarily doctrinal texts, but rather include doctrinal explanations in conjunction with ritual practices. In stratifying the text of the *Nāmasaṃgīti*, for example, Davidson identifies the early core of the text to be "a basic meditative form complete with devotional homage in the final five verses."[69]

For our inquiry of tantra as a lived tradition, these three texts need to be understood as part of the range of texts that Anne Blackburn has called the "practical canon," which she distinguishes from the "formal canon."[70] While Blackburn gives a detailed definition (see Chapter I), a practical canon can be understood as those texts that practitioners actually use. For tantric practitioners, these texts formed part of the practical canon, along with "an ever-shifting circle of ritual manuals—*sādhanas* for accomplishing ritual transformations, but also assorted liturgical works, *kalpas* for constructing the ritual spaces, *vidhis* for granting initiations or making offerings, and so on. This genre of locally produced manuals served as a primary point of contact between the tantric subject and their ritual tradition."[71] In other words, these include texts like the newly compiled Mañjuśrī homa manual discussed below.

[67] Ronald Davidson, "The *Litany of Names of Mañjuśrī*: Text and Translation of the *Mañju śrīnāmasaṃgīti*," in *Tantric and Taoist Studies in Honour of R.A. Stein*, ed. Michel Strickmann (Brussels: Institut Belge des Hautes Études Chinoises, 1981), 1–69, 1.

[68] For additional information, see Vesna Wallace, "Kālacakra-Maṇḍala: Symbolism and Construction," in *The Oxford Encyclopedia of Buddhism*, ed. Richard K. Payne and Georgios T. Halkias, 1416–1433 (New York: Oxford University Press, 2024).

[69] Davidson, "The *Litany of Names of Mañjuśrī*," 3.

[70] Anne Blackburn, "Looking for the *Vinaya*: Monastic Disciplines in the Practical Canons of the Theravāda," *Journal of the International Association of Buddhist Studies* 22.2 (1999): 281–309.

[71] Jacob P. Dalton, *Conjuring the Buddha: Ritual Manuals in Early Tantric Buddhism* (New York: Columbia University Press, 2023), 1–2.

Locations

Contrasting with the portable components of a praxis, such as masters and texts, are those that are fixed.[72] "Fixed elements are those which are not only in some way unique, but more importantly are only relevant to a particular locale."[73] For the praxis of Mañjuśrī, two locations that display its movement through the networks of the Buddhist cosmopolis are Wutai shan and Dunhuang.

Wutai Shan

Religious, mercantile, and governmental networks may often coincide, but not always, and Wutai shan ("five-terraced mountain") is "not obviously at a nodal point of any major transport networks."[74] It is, however, an important node in Buddhist networks of pilgrimage. Pilgrims from many different domains—Tibet, Mongolia, China, and Inner Asia—sought out the mountain.[75] Many hoped to perhaps have a vision of Mañjuśrī, who was thought to dwell there, or at least to see the miraculous display of five-colored clouds, multicolored radiance, the sound of chimes, or unusual fragrances—all

[72] This builds upon the fixed/portable distinction introduced by Lionel Rothkrug, "Religious Practices and Collective Perceptions: Hidden Homologies in the Renaissance and Reformation," *Historical Reflections/Réflexions Historiques* (1980) 7: 1–251. See also Lewis Lancaster, "Fixed, Portable, Measurable Sanctity: Buddhism and the Mountains of China," unpublished essay, n.d. (https://www.academia.edu/44112072/Fixed_Portable_Measurable_Sanctity_Buddhism_and_the_Mountains_of_China); and Richard K. Payne, "On the Ritual Culture of Japan: Symbolism, Ritual, and the Arts," in *The Nanzan Guide to Japanese Religions*, ed. Paul L. Swanson and Clark Chilson, 235–256 (Honolulu: University of Hawai'i Press, 2006). The distinction between fixed and portable seems simple and straightforward—the bodhi tree under which Śākyamuni awoke is a specific site, unique and fixed in the geography of India. The Shikoku pilgrimage comprises the eighty-eight temples that encircle the island of Shikoku. Yet such literal geographies do not correspond to religious geographies, imaginal realities in which locations are potentially indefinitely reproducible. Is a *ficus religiosa* growing at a temple in the United States, propagated from a seed gathered by a devoted traveler from Bodhgaya in India, somehow not significantly "the same"? Are the miniature Shikoku pilgrimages recreated in Hawai'i out of sand drawn from each of the eighty-eight temples somehow not significantly "the same" as the pilgrimage route around the island? While locations are fixed, they are also reproducible, and the locational presencing of the cult is made present in a new location.

[73] Payne, "Ritual Culture Japan," 236.

[74] T. H. Barrett, "Northern Wei Wutaishan: An Outside View of Centres and Peripheries," in *What Happened After Mañjuśrī Migrated to China? The Sinification of the Mañjuśrī Faith and the Globalization of the Wutai Cult*, ed. Jinhua Chen, Guang Kuan, and Hu Fo, 77–88 (London: Routledge, 2022), 77.

[75] On Uyghur pilgrims from Inner Asia, see Yukio Kasai, *The Bodhisattva Mañjuśrī, Mt. Wutai, and Uyghur Pilgrims*, Buddhist Road Paper 5.4 (Bochum, Germany: Center for Religious Studies, Ruhr-University Bochum, 2020).

signs of the bodhisattva's presence.[76] Consequently, several routes of travel connected it to other nodes in the tantric Buddhist cosmopolis.[77] This broader network also connected continental East Asia to Japan.[78]

"When Buddhism came to Wutaishan we do not know, for the sense of the presence of Mañjuśrī tended so to overwhelm later writers as to eclipse all human agency in the creation of the mountains as a Buddhist place."[79] Despite this concealing radiance, T. H. Barrett suggests that it is the Northern Wei emperor Xiaowendi (r. 471–499), who engaged the mountain in such a fashion as to give it a Buddhist identity.[80] The Northern Wei (386–535) had also been responsible for the creation of the Buddhist Yungang caves. In addition, they appear to have been responsible for transforming Wutai shan from a local abode of dragons into a Buddhist locale by bringing a multitude of small stone pagodas to the mountain and founding a monastery there.[81]

One of several "Buddhist mountains" in East Asia, Wutai shan's name, five "terraces" indicating five peaks, links this location with others associated with Mañjuśrī, particularly the five mountains surrounding the famous lake Anavatapta from which the Ganges, Indus, and Oxus Rivers flow.[82] Another name by which Wutai shan was known is "Mount Clear and Cool" (Ch. Qingliang shan), which was equated with the "Mountain of Snows"—which the *Mañjuśrī parinirvāṇa sūtra* identifies as Mañjuśrī's dwelling place.[83]

Wutai shan was both a geographic node in the networks of East Asian Buddhism and a node in the tantric networks. Susan Andrews notes that the

[76] Wei-cheng Lin, "Relocating and Relocalizing Mount Wutai: Vision and Visuality in Mogao Cave 62," *Artibus Asiae* 73.1 (2013): 77–136, 84.

[77] George A. Keyworth lists Tibetans, Tanguts, Mongolians, Manchurians, Koreans, southern Chinese, Nepalese, and Indian pilgrims. "How the Mount Wutai Cult Stimulated the Development of Chinese Chan in Southern China at Qingliang Monasteries," in *What Happened after Mañjuśrī Migrated to China? The Sinification of the Mañjuśrī Faith and the Globalization of the Wutai Cult*, ed. Jinhua Chen, Guang Kuan, and Hu Fo, 89–112 (London: Routledge, 2022), 91, 104.

[78] David Quinter, "Moving Monks and Mountains: Chōgen and the Cults of Gyōki, Mañjuśrī, and Wutai," in *What Happened After Mañjuśrī Migrated to China? The Sinification of the Mañjuśrī Faith and the Globalization of the Wutai Cult*, ed. Jinhua Chen, Guang Kuan, and Hu Fo, 133–156 (London: Routledge, 2022).

[79] Barrett, "Northern Wei Wutaishan," 79.

[80] Barrett, "Northern Wei Wutaishan," 80.

[81] See also Raoul Birnbaum, "Secret Halls of the Mountain Lords: The Caves of Wu-t'ai shan" *Cahiers d'Extrême-Asie* 5 (1989): 115–140, https://doi.org/10.3406/asie.1989.945.

[82] Anthony Tribe, "Mañjuśrī: Origins, Role and Significance (Parts 1 & 2)," *The Western Buddhist Review* 2 (1997): 1–47, 5. We also note in passing that Kōyasan was founded by Kūkai in a valley surrounded by five mountains.

[83] David Quinter, "Mañjuśrī in East Asia," in *Brill's Encyclopedia of Buddhism*, Vol. II: Lives, ed. Jonathan A. Silk (Leiden: Brill, 2019), 591–599, 592. See also Michelle Wang, "Dunhuang Art," in *The Oxford Encyclopedia of Buddhism*, ed. Richard K. Payne and Georgios T. Halkias, 781–806 (New York: Oxford University Press, 2024).

association with Mañjuśrī is not the "sole understanding of Mount Wutai's significance."[84] Perhaps from as early as the Northern Wei dynasty (386–535), the mountain held associations with healing and longevity—a realm of immortals, hermits, and both botanical and alchemical medicines. The praxis of Mañjuśrī did not displace, but instead added to this preexisting set of associations, creating an additional resonance and an appeal to court and literati as well as recluses and those seeking relief from bodily decline and aging.

Dunhuang

Dunhuang was another node linked with Wutai shan, the praxis of Mañjuśrī being shared by these two locations. Most prominent in this regard is Cave 61, which is known as the Mañjuśrī Cave. Across the back wall of the cave is a mural depicting Wutai shan, identifying its temples and displaying the landscape of the territory. As Michelle C. Wang notes, this portrayal of the landscape of Wutai shan is not derived from texts, but rather from the actual geography as experienced by a pilgrim—though stylized for representation in mural form.[85]

The importance of Mañjuśrī's role in several Mahāyāna texts is made evident in artwork from Dunhuang that displays Mañjuśrī paired with various interlocutors. Mañjuśrī is paired, for example, with the layman Vimalakirti (*Vimalakirti nirdeṣa sūtra*) and with Samantabhadra (*Gaṇḍavyūha sūtra*). The representation pairing him with Samantabhadra shows Mañjuśrī riding a lion, a motif now widely known as Mañjuśrī's "true presence form," which originated on Mount Wutai in 710–711.[86] This image of Mañjuśrī riding a lion highlights the importance of the strand between Wutai where the image is said to have originated in a visionary experience and Duhuang where it was employed in other caves as well. In her study of the one thousand armed Mañjuśrī figures at Dunhuang, Michelle Wang notes that paintings such as these were not simply visual aids for texts, but rather that "their innate

[84] Susan Andrews, "Gathering Medicines Among the Cypress: The Relationship Between Healing and Place in the Earliest Records of Mount Wutai," in *What Happened After Mañjuśrī Migrated to China? The Sinification of the Mañjuśrī Faith and the Globalization of the Wutai Cult*, ed. Jinhua Chen, Guang Kuan and Hu Fo, 37–49 (London: Routledge, 2022), 37.

[85] Wang, "Dunhuang Art," 793.

[86] Michelle C. Wang, "The Thousand-Armed Mañjuśrī at Dunhuang and Paired Images in Buddhist Visual Culture," *Archives of Asian Art* 66.1 (2016): 81–105, 86.

pictorial logic in turn shaped the composition" of texts.[87] In this instance, the imagery derives from a visionary experience and does not derive from texts.[88] Both texts and art are semiautonomous traditions in interaction with one another.

A Mañjuśrī Homa in California

As discussed in Chapter I, the homa is a ritual in which votive offerings are made into a fire. Having roots in the Vedic tradition, today it is widespread throughout tantric traditions, including Hindu, Jain, and Buddhist. It is one of the components that can be employed in tantric praxes, and there are versions of the homa that have Mañjuśrī as the chief deity of the ritual. Ritual identification is an indicator of the historical transformation of the homa from a Vedic style of ritual to a tantric one. While Vedic rituals involved making offerings to the deities by means of the fire, in tantric versions the practitioner becomes the deity and performs the offerings. In Shingon interpretations, the practitioner also identifies with the fire, which represents the transformative power of wisdom. The offerings are identified with the practitioner's own mistaken conceptions (Skt. *jñeyāvaraṇa*) and misplaced affections (Skt. *kleśāvaraṇa*), and, offered into the fire, are transformed and purified by the practitioner's own wisdom.

After Yogi Chen passed away, his dharma lineage heir, Dr. Yutang Lin, has continued to maintain and propagate the teachings and practices of his teacher. Lin has added many texts to the already rich ritual corpus found on the Yogi Chen website, including a Mañjuśrī homa manual. This ritual is based on those homa previously compiled by Yogi Chen, and it is similar to those manuals in both structure and content. Dr. Lin created the Mañjuśrī homa at the request of a member of his community, but he waited for signs indicating that it was appropriate for him to undertake such a project. Only when he had received such signs did he create and perform the homa.

The manual lays out a ritual that is recognizably similar to other homas, beginning with a series of invocations and praises, and then proceeding to the offerings as such.[89] There are several differences from Shingon homas,

[87] Wang, "The Thousand-Armed Mañjuśrī," 81.
[88] On visionary experience in relation to Wutai Shan, see Lin, "Relocating and Relocalizing Mount Wutai," 86–87.
[89] Yutang Lin, "Homa Ritual Honoring Manjusri," http://yogichen.org/gurulin/efiles/e0/e0070.html.

but the key tantric component—identification of the practitioner with the deity—is present at the start of the ritual. Identified with Mañjuśrī, the practitioner makes two sets of offerings, one set to Agni, identified as "the golden god of fire," and one to Mañjuśrī.

Thus, we can say that the praxis of Mañjuśrī was part of the tantric Buddhist tradition supported by a largely Chinese sangha in the greater San Francisco Bay Area. The course of Yogi Chen through the Buddhist cosmopolis of the late twentieth century brought the necessary components of a praxis of Mañjuśrī—belief in the efficacy of Mañjuśrī for benefits or protection, existing homas as models for a new homa manual, a qualified master, and transmission to a dharma heir qualified to compile a new manual and perform this ritual—to twenty-first century El Cerrito, California, where the praxis of Mañjuśrī could be recreated or perhaps reactivated.

As Tribe notes, Mañjuśrī's "popularity continues today, not only within traditional Buddhist communities but also in contemporary 'western' Mahāyāna Buddhist traditions. American, European and Australasian Buddhists visualize Mañjuśrī, recite his name and depict his form as part of their practice, seeing these as effective means of developing the insightful awareness (*jñāna*) that is at the heart of the Mahāyāna Buddhist perspective."[90] With Mañjuśrī as its centripetal deity, the praxis integrates beliefs, visualization practices, recitation, images and graphic representations, homa, ritual objects, canonic and ritual texts, teachers, and so on. As we have noted previously throughout this work, there is nothing uniquely or inherently "tantric" about the figure of Mañjuśrī, or the beliefs, practices, objects, texts, teachers, and so on considered in isolation. Organized into a coherent whole, however, some instances of the praxis become tantric by designation, context, and use.

Summary

The regional organization of previous chapters provided a convenient way of delimiting a geographic and cultural scope within which to examine facets of the tantric Buddhist tradition, facets that help us to understand that tradition as a complex and self-recreating movement. Regions are, however, only

[90] Tribe, "Mañjuśrī: Origins, Role and Significance," 1.

heuristic categories, and because of the limitations that they themselves can entail, this chapter shifted perspective to networks.

The metaphor of a network refocuses our vision of the Buddhist cosmopolis from geopolitical regions into a system of strands connecting nodes. In some cases, strands were mercantile or governmental routes, and sometimes nodes were more primarily of religious significance.[91] Some of the most famous figures of Buddhist history were travelers through the networks of the Buddhist cosmopolis. But those are only a small fraction of the Buddhist travelers—monastic and lay, pilgrims and tourists—who, by traveling, create the networks. Being lesser-known figures, Punyodaya and Yogi Chen are indicative of those thousands of anonymous travelers.

"Tantric Buddhism" is too abstract an entity to be usefully considered as an answer to the question of "What moved through the networks?" However, more concrete entities, such as rituals, teachers, texts, and artwork, are not inherently tantric. Praxes provide the context, use, and designation required to configure such components as tantric. And at the same time, they are more integral and coherent than the abstract category of tantric Buddhism. We are, therefore, better served by thinking of tantric praxes, such as that of Mañjuśrī, as what moved from node to node along the strands of networks connecting the nodes of the Buddhist cosmopolis. While, as noted previously, all academic categories are conventional—that is, constructed and social—the systemic organization of praxes, which allows for their enduring over time and across cultural boundaries, is such that they approach being "natural" objects for inquiry.

[91] The travels of the Buddha Śākyamuni were themselves along established trade routes. Abhishek Singh Amar, "The Buddhakṣetra of Bodhgaya: Saṅgha, Exchanges, and Trade Networks," in *Religions and Trade: Religious Formation, Transformation and Cross-Cultural Exchange Between East and West*, ed. Peter Wick and Volker Rabens, 117–138 (Leiden: Brill, 2014).

VII
Closing Reflections
Tantric Buddhism and Religious Studies

The path goes ever on, but this journey has reached its end.

Introduction

Two goals have motivated this work. The first is to support three interrelated claims regarding tantric Buddhism, and the second is to identify methodological issues that the tantric tradition of Buddhism raises for religious and Buddhist studies.

The three claims are that tantric Buddhism is pervasive in the history of Buddhism, that it is often invisible, and that it constitutes a coherent and continuous movement. From its beginnings in South Asia (Chapter II), tantric Buddhist praxis has moved throughout the Buddhist world—East Asia (Chapter III), Southeast Asia (Chapter IV), Inner Asia (Chapter V), and via networks (Chapter VI) to become a globalized presence today.[1] Tantric Buddhism has been rendered invisible by a number of historical factors (such as sectarian conflicts and environmental degradation of the textual record), as well as by the prejudice that it is solely characterized by transgressive practices, particularly sexual ones, and was therefore not worthy of serious scholarly attention. It had for long, therefore, fallen into an academic blind spot. In addition, tantra can be understood to exist in different ways—as an independent institution, as an unrecognized form within a larger institution, or, as an established alternative within a larger tradition, which may or may not be explicitly designated as tantric.[2]

[1] Richard K. Payne, "Globalizing Tantric Buddhism," in *The Oxford Encyclopedia of Buddhism*, ed. Richard K. Payne and Georgios T. Halkias (Oxford: Oxford University Press, 2024; online 2021: https://doi.org/10.1093/acrefore/9780199340378.013.1043).

[2] Based on analysis by Tony K. Stewart, see Richard K. Payne and Glen A. Hayes, "Tantric Studies: Issues, Methods and Scholarly Collaborations," in *The Oxford Handbook of Tantric Studies*, ed. Richard K. Payne and Glen A. Hayes, 5–6 (Oxford: Oxford University Press, 2023).

Tantra Across the Buddhist Cosmopolis. Richard K. Payne, Oxford University Press. © Oxford University Press 2025.
DOI: 10.1093/9780197825105.003.0007

The academic study of Buddhism and religions more generally operates with a set of intellectual understandings, that is, ideas regarding what religion is (theory) and ideas regarding how to study it (method). Those understandings are themselves not neutral, transcendent, or ahistorical, not a "view from nowhere." Instead, they are themselves the consequence of the history of religious studies, which developed both within the Western intellectual tradition and from the theologically informed beginnings of comparative religions in the nineteenth century.[3] Although a variety of such issues have been discussed in the preceding chapters, the concluding reflections here focus on four topics that provide opportunities for the field of religious studies to revise its existing preconceptions and expand the ways in which traditions can be conceived and studied. The four specific issues examined here broaden this work's methodological relevance beyond Buddhism, toward the field of religious studies more generally.

Important to this analysis is the intellectual process by which the concepts, categories, and concerns of Protestant religious culture are "raised up out of" their sociohistorical context and abstracted as universally appropriate for the study of all religions—a process known as sublation. This involves a dynamic discursive relation of expectation, selection, and overdetermination. Next, an important issue is the rhetoric of decadence and its historiographic consequences, including the narrative of disappearing traditions. The concept of praxis is the third topic. As the dialectic relation between doctrine and practice, it challenges the presumptions that thought causes action, and that doctrine is determinative of practice. The last topic is the benefit of taking praxis as the object of study, rather than more vague abstractions such as "religion" or "Buddhism."

Protestant Presuppositions: The Dynamics of Sublation and of Overdetermination

The discourse of religious studies structures representations of Buddhism in terms of the concepts, categories, and concerns of a religious tradition other than itself, largely those of Protestant Christianity. Two of the conceptual dynamics by which this happens are by raising concepts, categories,

[3] An important critique on this development is provided by Talal Asad, *Genealogies of Religion: Discipline and Reasons of Power in Christianity and Islam* (Baltimore: Johns Hopkins University Press, 1993).

and concerns up out of that historico-religious context as characteristic of religion as an abstract, overarching category, and the selection of particular aspects of a tradition being studied because they match expectations already implicit in the idea of what religion is, thus overdetermining those characteristics.

Sublation

For Buddhism the process of sublation begins when it is called a "religion." As Brent Nongbri has said, the pervasive use of the term "religion" creates an intuitive understanding before its definition, as "religion is anything that sufficiently resembles modern Protestant Christianity."[4]

In the field of religious studies, aspects of the Protestant religious culture have been lifted up out of their context of origin and applied universally to identify apparently similar phenomena from a wide variety of religious cultures.[5] When the concepts, categories, and concerns native to Protestant thought are treated as if they are unproblematically descriptive of any "religion," then they have been sublated.[6] Sublating a concept, category, or concern out of a particular historico-religious context is not an intellectually neutral act. Applying those sublated concepts, categories, and concerns implicitly constrains how traditions can be understood. While not neutral, this is a common conceptual process, which is all the more reason for Buddhist scholars to be attentive to their own use of Western language religious and philosophic terminology. When two apparently similar phenomena are discussed under the same cover term, it is assumed that characteristics of one will be found in the other. Those characteristics are then "smuggled into" the conceptualization, whether appropriate or not, even in the face of stipulative definitions that attempt to restrict such connotations. In considering the study of the religions of Japan, for example, Edmund Gilday has written:

[4] Brent Nongbri, *Before Religion: A History of a Modern Concept* (New Haven, CT: Yale University Press, 2013),18.

[5] Recognition that the Protestant tradition determines the categories, concepts, and concerns of religious studies is increasingly commonplace in critical reflection on the field. An important case of such reflection is Gregory Schopen, "Archaeology and Protestant Presuppositions in the Study of Indian Buddhism," *History of Religions* 31.1 (Aug. 1991): 1–23. Critique of the field of religious studies by examining the history of its development out of Protestant thought is distinct from any imputed criticism of the Protestant tradition—a clarification made necessary as a consequence of some students' confusion of the two.

[6] We should note that not all sublation in religious studies employs the concepts, categories, and concerns of Protestant Christianity. Mircea Eliade, for example, drew on different sources, such as yoga.

> Dyadic patterns, polarities between the "sacred" out there and us "humans" here, are so patently presumptive, so evidently determined by our own culture's religious and philosophical assumptions, that to accept so handily their validity as models for the Japanese worldview is tantamount to precluding the possibility of discovery altogether.[7]

Similarly, in methodological comments introducing an essay on "Religion and Popular Beliefs in Southeast Asia Before c. 1500," J. G. de Casparis and I. W. Mabbett identify one of the essential characteristics of modern conceptions of religion as being separate and distinct from other social institutions. As they put it,

> In Western societies religion is generally felt to be clearly separated from other fields of social and political life, so that it can be studied for its own sake. This is also the case in modern Southeast Asia. In pre-modern Southeast Asia, however, it is hardly possible to separate religion from other fields of socio-economic and cultural life, with which it is closely interwoven. There is not even a real equivalent of our term religion in the pre-modern languages of the area. To study religion one has, as it were, to detach from their social and political contexts those elements that we subsume under religion. These include, for example, various rituals and other forms of the worship of God, of deities or superhuman spirits and powers, as reflected in art and architecture, in literature and inscriptions.[8]

Although their concern is the study of religions in Southeast Asia, we can mutatis mutandis apply the same considerations to the study of tantric Buddhism prior to modernity.[9] "Detaching" religious elements from their social and political contexts is not some kind of pristine intellectual process of repurifying the spiritual jewel by washing off the dirt of social, political, or economic associations. It is an act of interpretive violence conducted in the mode of intellectual colonialism. As indicated by Gilday, and by Casparis and

[7] Edmund T. Gilday, "Power Plays: An Introduction to Japanese Festivals," *Journal of Ritual Studies* 4.2 (Summer 1990): 263–295, 266.

[8] J. G. De Casparis and I. W. Mabbett, "Religion and Popular Beliefs in Southeast Asia Before c. 1500," in *The Cambridge History of Southeast Asia*, vol. 1: From Early Times to c. 1800, ed. Nicholas Tarling, 276–339 (Cambridge: Cambridge University Press, 1992), 276–277.

[9] These concerns are actually more generally applicable to the study of all premodern traditions outside of the three Western monotheisms.

Mabbett, such a "religion" is constructed on the model of modern Western conceptions of religion.

More specifically, the structure of Protestant Christianity as a tradition established by a founder who gave a reformist teaching, which is recorded in a sacred book and propagated by a church, is abstracted as universal. These categories are then utilized in presenting Buddhism as a religion. In the version found in Buddhist modernism, Śākyamuni is the founder, countering Vedic sacrificial rituals with a psychologized emphasis on meditation, as recorded in the Pali canon and maintained by the Theravāda lineage.

Overdetermination: Expectation and Selective Representation

Many representations of tantric Buddhism—and other traditions more generally—are formed by a two-part dialectic process in which expectation and selection interact in a mutually reinforcing manner.[10] Such representations are "overdetermined." In its barest sense, to be overdetermined simply means to have more than one cause, as introduced by Sigmund Freud in his analysis of dreams.[11] Rather than this barest of meanings, however, the term is used here to identify the closely interrelated way in which background expectations—assumptions, beliefs, desires—work to highlight particular aspects of a tradition, with the result that those aspects are chosen to exemplify that tradition. This already selected characterization is then experienced as convincing because it is congruent with the background assumptions, beliefs, and desires—expectations having already selectively highlighted certain aspects.[12] In other words, because of the template provided by expectations about human nature, about religion, about the Other (whether despicable or desirable), both the idea that the Other necessarily has a religion, and the representation of that religion is created by selecting particular aspects of culture.[13] These formulations of the religion of

[10] This is true, of course, not only for tantric Buddhism, but for other religious traditions as well.

[11] "An event is overdetermined if there exist more than one antecedent events, any of which would be a sufficient condition for the event occurring. Analogously, a conclusion is overdetermined if it can be proved in any of a number of independent ways. The concept is employed by Freud to describe the possibility of multiple causes and interpretations of dreams." *Oxford Dictionary of Philosophy*, s.v. "overdetermination" (New York: Oxford University Press, 2008; online 2016: https://www.oxfordreference.com/display/10.1093/acref/9780199541430.001.0001/acref-9780199541430-e-2285).

[12] A particularly valuable study of this process is David Chidester, *Savage Systems: Colonialism and Comparative Religion in South Africa* (Charlottesville: University Press of Virginia, 1996).

[13] Although the concept is heuristically useful, we note that, originating with the rise of the field of anthropology, the idea of culture as a coherent unity of belief and action is itself a formulation

the Other are consequences of presuming that religion is a human universal, rather than it being a modern cultural formation specific to European and American societies.[14]

These highlighted aspects are then constellated into a pattern that appears comparable to the already familiar, because of the expectations that selected the elements to be highlighted in the first place. This process of selective representation is overdetermined because those aspects are actually there, and not mere fantasies of the representation's creator. To the extent then that the representation in turn matches the template provided by the expectations of its audience, it will be experienced as unproblematically plausible, easily acceptable, and indeed authoritative.[15] Being accepted as authoritative and accurate, the representation then serves to reinforce the expectations, creating a *relatively* closed cycle. I emphasize that the cycle is only *relatively* closed because new knowledge is possible, and indeed that is the purpose of scholarship. Despite the problems created by what has been called the "inevitable pre-understanding of religion,"[16] this is *simply* an epistemological problem created by the social dynamics of knowledge.[17]

Two familiar instances from religious studies representations of Indian religions exemplify overdetermination. One is "Nāsadīya," the "creation myth" (Ṛg Veda 10.129[18]), and the other is the sacrifice of Puruṣa (the *Puruṣasūkta*, RV 10.90). The cultural template of the Bible creates the expectation that a religious teaching begins with a founding story of creation. This motivates the selection of RV 10.129 as the first Vedic text to be examined in religious studies texts and its being labeled the "creation hymn"

that is selectively projected onto other societies. Cf. Susan J. Rasmussen, "Cultural Anthropology," in *The Oxford Handbook of Culture and Psychology*, ed. Jean Valsiner, 96–115 (New York: Oxford University Press, 2012).

[14] See Timothy Fitzgerald, *The Ideology of Religious Studies* (New York: Oxford University Press, 2000). See also Chidester, *Savage Systems*.

[15] An example is how Huston Smith's ability to appeal, or rather, pander to the prejudices, preconceptions, and prejudgments of his audience make his work popularly authoritative. See my "How Not to Talk About Pure Land Buddhism," in *Path of No-Path: Contemporary Studies in Pure Land Buddhism Honoring Roger Corless*, ed. Richard K. Payne, 147–172 (Berkeley, CA: Institute of Buddhist Studies and Numata Center for Buddhist Translation and Research, 2009).

[16] Gavin Flood, *Beyond Phenomenology: Rethinking the Study of Religion* (London: Cassell, 1999), 65.

[17] This understanding that the hermeneutic circle is not firmly closed is in line with Gadamer's. See Hans Georg Gadamer, *Truth and Method*, trans. Joel Weinsheimer and Donald G. Marshall (rev. 2nd ed. 2004. London: Bloomsbury, 2013).

[18] Vedic annotations refer first to one of the four Vedas, in this case the Ṛg, and then identify the "cycle" (Skt. *maṇḍala*) and last the number of the "hymn." Thus, the "creation hymn" is the 106th hymn in the tenth cycle, or "book," of the Ṛg Veda.

of Hinduism. Thus, selections from the Vedas often start with this "creation myth." However, this "is a cultural construct due to religious prejudice."[19]

This is similarly the case with what is known as the "sacrifice of Puruṣa,"[20] the myth of the cosmic primordial man from whom the universe and its inhabitants are created when he is cut into parts. The hymn recounting the sacrifice of Puruṣa is frequently prominent in presentations of the Vedas. The factors here are threefold, and such multiple reinforcement gives an interpretation greater plausibility. One factor is the reading backward of modern Hindu concerns with caste onto the Vedic literature. In this reading, four parts of Puruṣa are said to be the source from which the four castes (Skt. *varna*) originate: the highest caste, priests (Skt. *brāhmaṇa*), originate from his mouth; while the next, warriors (Skt. *kṣatriya*), from his arms; the third, merchants and farmers (Skt. *vaiśya*), from his thighs; and the lowest caste, serfs and servants (Skt. *śūdra*), from his feet. This is taken as a charter myth justifying modern practices related to caste.[21] Second is the centrality of sacrifice in the Christian tradition, making a seemingly natural point of comparative contact. The third is the Romantic and neo-Romantic adoption of an organic conception "that the world is 'a single visible living being', 'a living being that contains within itself all living beings.'"[22] Given authority by Plato's conception that "all of nature should be conceived on analogy with a human being, so that it is a *macroanthropos*," the Vedic hymn of Puruṣa further justified this organicism.[23] These two instances exemplify overdetermination because, while the selections and interpretations are motivated by extraneous factors, the object of interpretation is actually there. In just this fashion, the writing of tantric Buddhist history within the framework of the Christian pattern of founder, teaching, book, and church can be overdetermined—but doing so selectively highlights those aspects of tantric

[19] Frits Staal, *Discovering the Vedas: Origins, Mantras, Rituals, Insights* (London: Penguin, 2008), 90.

[20] Recounted in the "Song of the Person" (Puruṣa sukta) in the tenth book of the Ṛg Veda. E. J. Michael Witzel, *The Origins of the World's Mythologies* (New York: Oxford University Press, 2013), 118. See also Matthew I. Robertson, *Puruṣa: Personhood in Ancient India* (New York: Oxford University Press, 2023), 32–37.

[21] Staal, *Discovering the Vedas*, 66. See also Nicholas B. Dirks, *Castes of Mind: Colonialism and the Making of Modern India* (Princeton, NJ: Princeton University Press, 2001).

[22] Frederick Beiser, *Hegel* (New York: Routledge, 2005), 87. Internal quote is from Plato's Timaeus, 30d and 33b.

[23] Beiser, *Hegel*, 87. For a more general treatment of the Romantics' engagement with India, see Wilhelm Halbfass, *India and Europe: An Essay in Understanding* (Albany: State University of New York Press, 1988), esp. chs. 5–8.

Buddhism that match those categories, rather than attempting to reflect on the historical patterns by which the movement has been organized.

Strikingly, when juxtaposed with the Protestant presumptions informing religious studies, tantric Buddhism is lacking—lacking a single founding figure, lacking a reformist impulse in its teachings, lacking a single authoritative text, lacking an individualized meditative program of moral reform and self-betterment, lacking a church. It is, however, just in these lacunae that tantra constitutes a critical perspective for religious studies.

Historiography

One of the long-standing ways that tantra has been characterized is that it is decadent. This characterization plays on a narrative arc found widely in religious studies, that religions go from an original purity through a process of decay until reformed, and then again fall into decay. Decadence is not, however, a straightforward characteristic. It is, rather, one term of a two-term relation, reflected in the way the historical narrative contrasts the mythic purity of origins with the decadence of later times.

The application of the rhetoric of decadence has not been limited to the tantras, or to the history of Buddhism more generally, but has been widespread in the study of Indian religious cultures by Western scholars. As early as 1805 in the Western study of India, H. T. Colebrooke presented an idealized view of Vedic India, one which now in retrospect appears to suspiciously mirror Victorian English ideals. As described by David Kopf,

> The new view romanticized the virtues of the Aryan inhabitants of north India in the second millenium B.C. Instead of being introspective and other-worldly, the Aryans were thought to have been outgoing and nonmystical. They were pictured as a robust, beef-eating, socially equalitarian society. Instead of Oriental despotism, scholars discerned tribal republics.... There were no temples, and there was not the slightest evidence to suggest that Aryans concretized idolatrous images of their gods. And to round out the picture, also absent were the fertility goddesses, the evil personification of Kali, and the rites and rituals of later Tantrism.[24]

[24] David Kopf, *British Orientalism and the Bengal Renaissance: The Dynamics of Indian Modernization, 1773–1835* (Berkeley: University of California Press, 1969), 41.

Against this idealized golden age of Vedic India, Colebrooke contrasted contemporary Indian religious practices, finding them decadent. In his "On the Vedas or the Sacred Writings of the Hindus," Colebrook wrote, "Most of what is there taught, is now obsolete; and in its stead new orders of religious devotees have been instituted; and new forms of religious ceremonies have been established. Rituals founded in the Puranas and observances borrowed from a *worse* source, the *Tantras*, have in great measure . . . [replaced] the Vedas."[25] Thus, at the beginning of Western study of Indian religions, the rhetoric of decadence with its contrastive polarity between ancient golden age and present-day decadence was in place. Whether the positively valued terms of the opposition were Vedic India or the Buddhism of Śākyamuni,[26] the rhetorical structure remains the same, and it is this rhetorical structure that has largely framed the historiography.[27]

The Decadence of Tantra

As noted by many scholars, the modern Western reaction to the tantras was largely one of abhorrence, disdain, or rejection.[28] Because that image continues to play a prominent role in some popular representations of Buddhist tantra, it is worthwhile to review the sources of it here. The characteristic of "decadent" is a comparative one, therefore requiring a second term against which something is judged to be decadent. The rhetoric of decadence implies, therefore, the existence of some other form that is purer. For much of contemporary discourse on Buddhism, this role is played by Buddhist modernist representations of an original, pure, and authoritative form of Buddhism that continues unbroken from the time of Śākyamuni to the present.

The view that tantra is decadent is already in place at the earliest stage of Western Buddhist studies scholarship. Published four decades after Colebrooke, in 1844, Eugène Burnouf's *Introduction to the History of Indian*

25 Quoted in Kopf, *British Orientalism*, 41.

26 Or, indeed, the Protestant notion of a "primitive Christianity."

27 Although not directly adhering to Hayden White's analyses of historiography, this analysis is itself influenced by the kind of critical reflection on historiography embodied in White's *Metahistory: The Historical Imagination in Nineteenth-Century Europe* (Baltimore: Johns Hopkins Press, 1975).

28 Hugh Urban, *Tantra: Sex, Secrecy, Politics and Power in the Study of Religion* (Berkeley: University of California Press, 2003), and Hugh Urban, *The Power of Tantra: Religion, Sexuality and the Politics of South Asian Studies* (London: I.B. Tauris, 2009).

Buddhism set the popular perceptions and intellectual agenda for generations thereafter. Burnouf's secularist and humanist attitude contributes to his evaluation that tantra is not worthy of attention, since its "importance for the history of human superstitions does not compensate for its mediocrity and vapidity. It is certainly not without interest to see Buddhism, which in its first organization had so little of what makes a religion, end in the most puerile practices and the most exaggerated superstitions."[29] This evidences the Victorian characterization of religion as unscientific, irrational, and emotional, a characterization that in turn contributed to modernist rhetorics in which Buddhism is not a common, superstitious sort of religion,[30] but a scientific form of religion, or a lifestyle, or a philosophy of life, or a psychology.[31] Burnouf similarly dismisses tantric practice. Quoting at some length:

> Nowhere, indeed, is Buddhism reduced to more human proportions and to conditions of practice more easy, in general, than in these books. It is no longer a matter, as in the ancient sūtras, of preparing oneself through the exercise of all virtues, in order to one day fulfill the duties of a buddha. It suffices to trace a figure, to divide it into a certain number of compartments, to draw here the image of Amitābha, the buddha of a world as fabulous as he is, there that of Avalokiteśvara, the famous bodhisattva, the tutelary saint of Tibet; somewhere else those of some female divinities with singular names and terrible forms; and the devotee assures himself the protection of these divinities, who arm him with the magical formula or spell that each possesses. For coarse and ignorant minds, such books certainly have more value than the moral legends of the early days of Buddhism. They promise temporal and immediate advantages; in the end, they satisfy this need for superstitions, this love of pious practices by which the religious sentiment expresses itself in Asia, and to which the simplicity of primitive Buddhism responded but imperfectly.[32]

[29] Eugène Burnouf, *Introduction to the History of Indian Buddhism*, trans. Katia Buffetrille and Donald S. Lopez, Jr. (Chicago: University of Chicago Press, 2010), 483.

[30] Jack L. Graham, "Nonreligious Buddhism: Understanding Secular Buddhism as the Result of a Dialogue Between Victorian Constructions of 'Buddhism' and the Discourse of Non-Religion," Postgraduate diss. (University of Oxford, 2018).

[31] On the first, see David McMahan, "Modernity and the Early Discourse of Scientific Buddhism," *Journal of the American Academy of Religion* 72.4 (Dec. 2004): 897–933.

[32] Burnouf, *Introduction to the History of Indian Buddhism*, 480.

Here we see the rhetoric of decadence being reinforced by an appeal to the problematic theory of "religious needs" in the assertion of a need for ease of practice, and for superstition and a "love of pious practices by which the religious sentiment expresses itself in Asia." Alex Wayman has pointed out, however, that tantric practice is not particularly easy—

> it is passing strange that anyone would bother with the Tantra to justify his "degenerate" practice, for who so bent among worldly persons would divert his energies by muttering a *mantra* a hundred thousand times at dawn, noon, sunset, and midnight, with fasting and other inhibitions to engage in a "degenerate" practice, when, as we know so well, people at large engage in degenerate practices without bothering to mortify themselves at dawn, noon, sunset, and midnight![33]

Perhaps with this in mind, Christian Wedemeyer suggests that

> The notion that Tantric Buddhism was created to accommodate degenerate tendencies in the Buddhist monastic community, whose members sought pleasures of the flesh prohibited to them by the disciplinary rules of the order, is perhaps the easiest to dismiss.[34]

Wedemeyer describes the idea that tantra is a way of legitimating monastic degeneracy as a "just so story," a fanciful and simplistic story about how something came to be, rather than a conclusion based on evidence.

The Rhetoric of Decadence as the Narrative Structure of Religious History

The "rhetoric of decadence" is a common structure for writing the history of religions.[35] This historiography presumes that religious traditions follow a consistent pattern, a narrative arc: an initially pure teaching, which in the

[33] Alex Wayman, *The Buddhist Tantras: Light on Indo-Tibetan Esotericism* (1973. Reprint. London: Routledge, 2008), 6.

[34] Christian Wedemeyer, *Making Sense of Tantric Buddhism: History, Semiology, and Transgression in the Indian Traditions* (New York: Columbia University Press, 2013), 23.

[35] Kevin Trainor uses the term "degeneration" to identify this trope. Kevin Trainor, *Relics, Ritual, and Representation in Buddhism: Rematerializing the Sri Lankan Tradition* (Cambridge: Cambridge University Press, 1997), 9–10.

case of Buddhism is characterized as an ethical and rational program of personal self-improvement, followed by an ongoing decay caused by a variety of factors—becoming institutionalized and codified, rigid and ossified, ritualized and professionalized, and corrupted and exploited for material benefit. This leads to a reform, a purification of the religious tradition often accompanied by declarations of returning to the purity of the origins, but in its turn, this is followed by another period of decline and decay.

This rhetoric is rooted in the Protestant Reformation and, setting aside any questions regarding the validity of the Protestant Reformers portrayal of the Catholicism of their time, what is important is that the rhetoric and the pattern of the narrative itself have structured religious historiography, leading to the presumption that it is in fact a universal historical pattern, which religious histories of any kind, anywhere all follow.[36] These presumptions came to be rooted in the new "science of religion" originating in the Victorian era, which was the context for most of the early academic studies of Buddhism, and many of these presumptions continue into the present. Christopher Clausen has noted the connection between an ahistorical essentialism, Perennialism, philological and comparative methods, and the rhetoric of decadence.

> The chief method of this new discipline would be the study of ancient religious documents, both comparatively and philologically; this technique would enable the student to peel away the layers of accretion and priestly corruption that hid the original form of the religion from view, and also assist in restoring his own faith to its original purity. If one looked deeply enough in any religion, something spiritually valuable, even worthy of imitation, could be found where all had seemed to be darkness and superstition. The Protestant assumptions that the essential truth about religion lies in its earliest scriptures, that a priesthood inevitably shackles and degrades it, and (in seeming contradiction to the Darwinian impulse) that the historical development of a religion is a process of corruption, were widely influential.[37]

[36] As with other interpretive processes, there is a dialectic here in that the designation of historical events as "religious," and as constituting a religious history, already implicates the presumption that those events will follow a familiar pattern. This same narrative structure was applied to Kamakura-era Buddhism as well; see Richard K. Payne, "Introduction," in *Re-Visioning "Kamakura" Buddhism*, ed. Richard K. Payne, 1–23 (Honolulu: University of Hawai'i Press, 1998).

[37] Christopher Clausen, "Victorian Buddhism and the Origins of Comparative Religion," *Religion* 5.1 (1975): 4.

What makes the rhetoric of decadence work is the dichotomy by which it structures history. This is familiar to us from the way in which reform movements frequently claim the authority of an ancient, glorious, idealized past. As noted previously, in contemporary Western religious studies, this organizing narrative is rooted in the rationale of the Protestant Reformation, which claimed to be a return to the purity of the original teachings of Jesus and a rejection of later corruptions of those teachings. The rhetoric of decadence creates a dichotomy between a "golden age"—that of the founder's lifetime as an idealized past when the teacher was present and the teachings available directly—and a present infected by corruption and the failure to adhere to traditional standards of proper belief and proper behavior.[38]

In other words, the semiotic pair of pure past and decadent present provides the rhetorical point of contrast motivating the desire for a return to the purity of that original state. In this pair the original, pure, rational, moralistic teaching of the Buddha Śākyamuni is itself a characterization of Śākyamuni modeled on nineteenth-century liberal Protestant conceptions of Jesus. The rhetoric of decadence informs the repeated notion that somehow tantra "weakened" Buddhism so that it could not survive the onslaughts of the Muslim invasions and is responsible for the putative disappearance of Buddhism from the subcontinent.[39]

The Narrative of the Disappearing Tradition

Complementing the rhetoric of decadence is the "disappearing tradition" narrative. For example, one of the grand organizing tropes structuring the writing of Indian Buddhist history is that it disappeared "from the land of its birth."[40] According to this historiography, the reason is that it became decadent. The tantric tradition is not uncommonly identified as either the

[38] Interpreting the history of Buddhism along these lines is overdetermined by the presence of similar ideas in Buddhist thought. It has been argued, for example, that motivating the rise of Mahāyāna is the felt need for alternatives to direct contact with Śākyamuni Buddha after his death. This interpretation, however, sometimes obscures the idea that buddhas in other realms were important because they could provide prophecies of future awakening, including the name of the future buddha and the name of his buddhaland, and not simply direct access to the teachings.

[39] See, for example, Constantin Regamey, "Motifs Vichnouites ed Śivaïtes dans le Kāraṇḍavyūha," in *Études tibétaines: dédieés à la mémoire de Marcelle Lalou*, ed. Ariane Spanien, 411–432 (Paris: Librairie d'Amerique et d'Orient, 1971), 411.

[40] We can speculate that this is another sublation from the historiographic narrative that Christianity disappeared from the Holy Land.

effect or the cause of that decadence and the consequent disappearance of Buddhism from India.

The explanatory value of the narrative of "disappearing traditions" has become increasingly problematic for the historiography of both South and East Asia. Stephen Berkwitz summarizes some of the rationales that had been offered in support of the narrative:

> The reasons offered by scholars for the decline of Buddhism in late medieval India include the withdrawal of royal patronage, hostility and persecution by Hindu Brahmins, the destruction of monasteries by invading Muslim armies, internal schisms and moral laxity within Buddhist monasticism, suppression by Hindu kings, absorption into Hinduism, and estrangement from the laity. Many such theories contribute plausible factors in the decline of Buddhism's vitality in late medieval India, although no single factor can account for the collapse of the religion by the early thirteenth century.[41]

David Gellner has challenged this narrative of the "collapse of the religion" in South Asia, pointing to the continuous tradition found in Nepal.[42] But the trope of collapse and disappearance is so widespread and enduring that it should be considered not simply as a question of fact, but as an interpretive rhetoric. There is, no doubt, something appealingly nostalgic about the sense of tragic loss, the image of a great world's religion being driven out of its place of origin by Muslim invaders.[43] Additionally, this image of a tragically lost homeland resonates with the Christian narrative of the loss of the "Holy Land" familiar to many nineteenth- and twentieth-century European and American scholars of Buddhism.

The disappearing tradition narrative is also enmeshed with the rhetoric of decadence, which moralistically attributes the "decline and eventual destruction" of Buddhism in its homeland to the moral corruption of members

[41] Stephen C. Berkwitz, *South Asian Buddhism: A Survey* (London: Routledge, 2010), 140.

[42] Buddhism in Nepal, like Korea, has become an important area of study relatively recently. Both had been neglected, and continue to be marginalized, due to the rhetoric of center–periphery, which treats the Buddhism of the center as normative, while that of the periphery is suspect.

[43] On the role of nostalgia in Buddhist studies, see Natalie Quli, "Western Self, Asian Other: Modernity, Authenticity, and Nostalgia for 'Tradition' in Buddhist Studies," *Journal of Buddhist Ethics* 16 (2009): 1–38. This sense of recovering lost glories seems to give meaning to the antiquarianism that characterizes some aspects of Buddhist studies. The disappearing tradition narrative has also served claims of authority based on sectarian assertions of being the sole authentic form of that absent original.

of the tradition who abandoned the austere purity of the vinaya for the seductive enticements of tantra. In this way it also plays to the sectarian claims of Theravāda apologists that their own tradition is the only pure, continuous lineage reaching back to the founder, Śākyamuni. And for scholarship, it leaves a convenient vacuum in which accounts of the Indian phase of Buddhist history could be constructed in the absence of a living tradition.[44]

That there is a continuous tradition of Buddhism on the subcontinent requires rethinking Buddhist history, a project which in the face of the well-established and authoritative history is difficult. But a continuous tradition of Buddhism does exist in the kingdoms of Nepal, Bhutan, and Sikkim—a fact that connects with the theme of tantric invisibility.[45] That a tantric tradition continued and thrived for centuries is awkward counterevidence to the rhetoric of decadence as the cause of decline and disappearance.

This is also an instance where the dichotomizing historiographic structure of center and periphery distorts the historical record by marginalizing what is considered peripheral. Because the conceptual structure of center and periphery values what is central, in this case Indian Buddhism, it allows for forms on the periphery to be ignored. Alternatively, Nepal and the other kingdoms are equally easily cast as a peripheral subset of Tibetan Buddhism, which dominates contemporary scholarship as another center. Benefiting in part from the media image of the Dalai Lama in popular religious culture, Tibetan Buddhism is treated as authentic and authoritative. And, last, it also is no doubt easy to ignore Nepalese Buddhism because, with its married priesthood, it does not fit easily into preconceptions of authentic Buddhism as a monastic praxis.

On this history, Todd Lewis explains that

> by 1192 when most Indian monasteries were abandoned or in ruins, Nepal became a great textual repository, where scholars, tantric teachers, scribes, and artists preserved and elaborated on the culture of late Indic Mahāyāna Buddhism. Unlike in the lower Gangetic plain, Buddhism in the Kathmandu Valley was never extinguished, and its vast material culture—in texts, icons, architecture, sacred sites, and its distinctive Mahāyāna

[44] See Donald Lopez, Jr., "Foreigner at the Lama's Feet," in *Curators of the Buddha: Buddhism under Colonialism*, ed. Donald Lopez, Jr., 251–295 (Chicago: University of Chicago, 1995): 251.

[45] One clear instance is the close continuity of ritual practices that can be traced from the eleventh-century *Kriyāsaṁgrahapañjikā* by Kuladatta to present-day Newar Buddhist practice in the Kathmandu Valley. See Igor Kokhan, "The 'Ten Rites' (*Daśakriyā*) in Kuladatta's *Kriyāsaṁgrhapañjikā*," PhD diss. (University of the West, 2020).

> rituals and festivals—endures until the present day. . . . Newar Buddhist tradition shares some similarities with Nyingma Tibetan Buddhism, although on the popular level, Buddhists in Nepal like Buddhists everywhere are concerned with making merit and performing rituals for both this life's material blessings and better next-life rebirth.[46]

Lewis's comparison of Newar and Nyingma traditions indicates that there is no sharp distinction between "late Indic Mahāyāna Buddhism" and tantric Buddhism, the one shading into the other. The relation between Buddhist and Brahmanic traditions in Nepal is similarly complex.

Like Southeast Asian dynasties during roughly the same period, the Licchavi dynasty in Nepal (ca. 400–750 CE) patronized both Brahmanic and Buddhist institutions, establishing the foundations for the ongoing traditions of Newar Buddhism. The following transitional period between the Licchavis and the Malla dynasty saw an increasing tantric Buddhist presence in the Kathmandu Valley, eventually leading to "the acceptance of Vajrayāna as the dominant form of Buddhism" there.[47]

As in Southeast Asia, worship of Avalokiteśvara, "the Buddhist deity of compassion who was also known as Lokeśvara (Lord of the World) and Karuṇāmaya (Compassionate)," was popular in ninth- and tenth-century Nepal.[48] Berkwitz has suggested that this popularity may have resulted from "the conflation of his identity with Śiva and with a deified Nātha yogin named Macchendra."[49] Other deities with tantric associations who were worshipped in Nepal during this period included Hevajra, Heruka, Tārā, Vasudhāra, Prajñāpāramitā, and Vajrapāṇī.

The period of the Malla dynasty (ca. 1201–1779) in Nepal saw transformations of Buddhist institutions that created a system more congruent with the Hindu caste system of social organization. Tantric ritual specialists (Skt. *vajrācāryas*) and ordinary monastics (Skt. *śākyabhikṣus*, caste name Śākyas) developed into two castes. This meant that birth and heredity determined one's social position and identity. Vajrācāryas "assumed responsibility for performing the fire sacrifices [homa] needed for major life-cycle rituals and for worshipping Buddhist tantric deities. The Śākyas

[46] Todd Lewis, "*Avadānas* and *Jātakas* in the Newar Traditions of the Kathmandu Valley: Ritual Performances of Mahāyāna Buddhist Narratives," *Religion Compass* 9.8 (2015): 235.
[47] Berkwitz, *South Asian Buddhism*, 158.
[48] Berkwitz, *South Asian Buddhism*, 158.
[49] Berkwitz, *South Asian Buddhism*, 158.

retained a nominal identity as *bhikṣus*, and qualified to perform day-to-day domestic rites, including worship of conventional Buddhist deities."[50] Nepalese tantric Buddhism does not fit into idealized preconceptions of monastic austerity. This is perhaps one reason that the Buddhism that continued unbroken on the subcontinent in the sub-Himalayan regions has been marginalized for much of the history of Buddhist studies. The romantic nostalgia of the disappearing tradition narrative for India and the disregard of "peripheral" regions also contributed to this neglect.

The disappearing tradition narrative also characterizes the historiography of tantric Buddhism in East Asia. According to this narrative, the tantric tradition, Zhenyan (Skt. *mantranaya*, Jpn. *shingon*), disappeared from Tang religious culture after the death of Amoghavajra (Ch. Bukong) and did not survive into the Song.[51]

Charles Orzech describes the disappearing tradition as "the common historical narrative" according to which a "few decades after Kūkai's departure from China the school apparently vanished."[52] Orzech suggests that terminological issues play a significant part in the apparent disappearance of Buddhist tantra. The terminology employed in the histories of Buddhism written by Zanning (919–1001) during the Song (960–1279)[53] include two phrases, the "Wheel of Instruction and Command" and the "Great Teaching of Yoga," to identify the substance of what was taught and practiced by the three founders. Zanning says elsewhere in his work that "the Esoteric Teaching is the method of Yoga: the *abhiṣeka* of the five divisions, the *homa*, the three secrets, and the methods for the mandala."[54] Amoghavajra's own terminology includes phrases such as "the vajra vehicle of yoga," which if back-translated into Sanskrit could be rendered as "vajrayāna yoga."[55] Amoghavajra uses the "great teaching of yoga" frequently to refer to "those teachings based on the template of the STTS [*Sarvatathāgatatattvasaṃgraha*], both as a *supplement*

[50] Berkwitz, *South Asian Buddhism*, 159.

[51] For one example of this, see Richard C. Foltz, *Religions of the Silk Road: Overland Trade and Cultural Exchange from Antiquity to the Fifteenth Century* (New York: St. Martin's Press, 1999), 53.

[52] Charles D. Orzech, "The 'Great Teaching of Yoga,' the Chinese Appropriation of the Tantras, and the Question of Esoteric Buddhism," *Journal of Chinese Religions* 34 (2006): 29–78, 29. See also Geoffrey C. Goble, *Chinese Esoteric Buddhism: Amoghavajra, the Ruling Elite, and the Emergence of a Tradition* (New York: Columbia University Press, 2019), 211.

[53] See Chou Yi-Liang, "Tantrism in China," in *Tantric Buddhism in East Asia*, ed. Richard K. Payne, 33–60 (Boston: Wisdom Publications, 2006), 37–39.

[54] Translation from *T.* 2061, 50:724b18 by Orzech, quoted from "Great Teaching," 44.

[55] The phrase "great teaching of yoga" would seem to suggest a contemporaneous and transregional understanding, not something uniquely concocted in the Tang. Cf. Buddhaguhya's discussion of the status of the Vairocanābhisaṃbodhi tantra, Hodge, trans., *Mahāvairocana*, 43.

to the Mahāyāna and as the pinnacle of all Buddhism."[56] For Amoghavajra the great teaching of yoga was not, therefore, a separate sect or a displacement of the Mahāyāna.[57]

The smooth historiographic arc of the disappearing tradition narrative has found its way into modern scholarship for Buddhism across Asia. Orzech says, however, that despite appearing to be a satisfying explanation, the disappearing tradition narrative has created its own explanatory problems. When contrasted with the long history of Shingon in Japan and Vajrayāna in Central Asia, the seemingly short history of the tradition in China had been taken to indicate that it had somehow "failed" there.[58] Like the rationales for the "disappearance" of Buddhism from India indicated by Berkwitz, Orzech summarizes several different theories that have been suggested to explain this apparent failure in China.[59] One is that the tradition was only supported by the court and could not therefore survive the persecution of 845.[60] Another suggestion is that the transgressive character of tantric Buddhism offended the rather puritanical sensibilities of Chinese intellectuals, so that it did not extend beyond the court elites. A third suggestion is that it was already in decline in the late Tang, and a resurgence of Confucianism then and in the following Song era led to an eclipse of tantric lineages. In Orzech's analysis, these purported explanations follow from presumptions about the kinds of institutional forms that religious traditions take.

> Having assumed that institutionalized schools were the natural form of religion, scholars posit that if no Esoteric "school" can be found or was

[56] Orzech, "Great Teaching," 48. For the *Sarva tathāgata tattva saṃgraha sutra/tantra*, see Do-Kyun Kwon, "Sarva Tathāgata Tattva Saṃgraha, Compendium of all the Tathāgatas: A Study of its Origin, Structure and Teachings," PhD diss. (School of Oriental and African Studies, 2002); and Steven Weinberger, "The Significance of Yoga Tantra and the *Compendium of Principles* (*Tattvasaṃgraha Tantra*) Within Tantric Buddhism in India and Tibet," PhD diss. (University of Virginia, 2003).

[57] Nor does the usage of the phrase "vajra vehicle" (*vajrayāna*) indicate that he thought of this as a third "vehicle" as in the categorization of "three vehicles" frequently encountered in Western treatments of Buddhism in which the three vehicles are represented as a progression from Hīnayāna (or less polemically Theravāda), to Mahāyāna, to Vajrayāna. Those representations seem to partake in the "rhetoric of rupture" found in almost the same fashion as the concept that Jesus brought a "new dispensation" is used in Christian theology, that is, that the new religion displaced the old.

[58] Orzech, "Great Teaching," 31.

[59] See, for example, Holmes Welch, *The Practice of Chinese Buddhism, 1900–1950* (Cambridge, MA: Harvard University Press, 1967), 185–187. See also Kenneth Ch'en, *Buddhism in China: A Historical Survey* (Princeton, NJ: Princeton University Press, 1972), 404–405, 445–447.

[60] This is structurally similar to an explanation offered for the "disappearance" of Buddhism from the Indian subcontinent (a narrative that itself ignores the continuity of Buddhism in the sub-Himalayan regions). Buddhism was supposedly so monastery-centered that there was no support for it in villages when the monasteries were destroyed by the Moghals.

> sustained, there can have been no interest in the texts, deities, or rituals in question. A new historiographical paradigm emerging in the last two [now three] decades has shown that these assumptions have skewed our understanding of East Asian religion and have rendered a flourishing interest in esoteric texts, practices and images from the Tang onwards all but invisible.[61]

The persistence of the disappearing tradition narrative, however, reveals several of the themes recurrent in the Western presentation of tantric Buddhism. These themes have a ready-made appeal to contemporary Western audiences and, as such, need to be interrogated. First, there is the problematic distinction between popular and elite. Second, there is the implication that as an elite form of Buddhism, tantra is inherently only an artificially sustained religiosity. In the botanical metaphor, tantric Buddhism is like an exotic tropical flower that may be sustained in a hothouse, but which would wither and die when exposed to the rigors of the real world, unlike hardier, native species. This creates a dichotomy that legitimates some forms of Buddhist praxis as "native," and which then further allows them to be considered "more authentic."[62] Despite these rhetorical assertions, as both Orzech and Goble have shown, the claim that tantric Buddhism simply disappeared from Chinese religious history after the death of Amoghavajra is not supported. More broadly, despite the several rationales formulated to justify the disappearing tradition narrative for Buddhism across Asia, contemporary research demonstrates that it is an overly simple and fundamentally misleading characterization of much more complex historical realities.

Institutional Designations

In addition to the rhetorical power of the disappearing tradition narrative, the implicit universalization of the categories of Western religious

61 Orzech, "Great Teaching," 31.

62 A third, given by Foltz, is the curious but unexamined notion that there was some undefined "natural affinity" between tantra and Tibet, which was somehow "particularly receptive to Tantrism," an affinity that did not exist in China. Foltz, *Religions of the Silk Road*, 53. Theories that employ concepts of natural affinity, like those employing the idea of "religious needs," are inherently problematic as such concepts are offered as explanations, without being adequately theorized as to how they effect causal relations.

institutions has also distorted the writing of tantric Buddhist history. This assumption has formed some of the familiar representations of the history of tantra in East Asia. Charles Orzech has noted that the problem of institutional categories is "*part of the fabric of historical and religious developments throughout history*."[63] This indicates two issues: designating institutions and sublating categories.

The first issue is how institutions have been identified over the history of the tantric Buddhist movement—important because of the role of designation for delineating tantra. For example, solely focusing on the Zhenyan (*mantra* school) as the name of a *sect* of Chinese Buddhism—while overlooking less familiar historical designations, such as the "Wheel of Instruction and Command," and the "Great Teaching of Yoga"—necessarily circumscribes too small a boundary around our understanding.[64]

Second, it is problematic to universalize those institutional categories that are commonly employed within the academic fields of religious studies and the sociology of religion—categories such as church, sect, and cult. Despite having been abstracted out of Western academic and religious history, these categories continue to entail connotations based on that history. Such connotations become preconceptions, which limit the scope of inquiry and consequently distort our understanding. One such preconception is that the *normal* form of affiliation is exclusive membership in a religious institution whose membership is typically "closed." Generally, this means both that it is for members only, and that it claims to offer a comprehensive set of religious services—in other words, a "church." Orzech explains that

> [n]ineteenth- and twentieth-century Western scholars tended to see religion through the lens of the binary opposition of Religion or syncretism. Sects, schools, or religions were characterized by exclusive membership and were thought to represent natural and pure categories. All else was a

[63] Charles Orzech, "The 'Great Teaching of Yoga,' the Chinese Appropriation of the Tantras, and the Question of Esoteric Buddhism," *Journal of Chinese Religions* 34 (2006): 29–78, 35. Emphasis in original.

[64] During the Song dynasty, the scholar Zanning (919–1001) authored several important works on the history of Buddhism in China, including on the tantric tradition in the Tang and Song dynasties. He refers to institutionalized forms of tantra as the "Wheel of Instruction and Command," and he explains that "Thereafter the lineage divided into many sects . . . and [they] all claim to teach the Great Teaching of Yoga" (cited from Orzech's translation of Zanning, "The 'Great Teaching of Yoga,'" 30). These terms—Wheel of Instruction and Command and the Great Teachings of Yoga—are key to understanding the history of the tantric movement in China.

> blend or hybrid (but without the cachet accorded the category in recent theory). The metaphorical basis of such taxonomies is one of purity versus pollution and miscegenation, and it should be understood in light of contemporary racial theories as well as the history and development of religious taxonomies.[65]

Two institutional categories employed in our examination of Buddhist tantra are movement and praxis. Movement is an intentionally vague and broad category, pointing to the historical continuities connecting the many different and overlapping forms of tantric Buddhist thought and practice, and the category can remain largely untheorized.[66] In contrast, as used here, praxis is a more specific institutional category, with clearer boundaries and identity.

The common categories of the sociology of religion—such as church, sect, and cult—have their own histories in Western religious discourse, histories that are separate from those of the variety of institutions in the Buddhist cosmopolis. The difference between those histories makes applying the sociological categories to tantric Buddhism at least problematic, or even entirely inappropriate. For example, in contrast to exclusive membership in a church, affiliation with several different praxes is possible, depending on interests and needs.[67]

In contrast to institutions based on exclusive membership and institutionalized authority, praxes tend toward more fluid forms of participation and affiliation. Organizing concepts and practices as an integral system, praxes have an enduring identity over time and across cultural boundaries. Praxes are organized around some central figure, toward which practices and doctrines are oriented. Like a centripetal force, the central figure holds the system together. The centripetal figure may be a buddha, a bodhisattva, a guardian deity, or a nonanthropomorphic figure, such as a dhāraṇī.

[65] Orzech, "The 'Great Teaching of Yoga,'" 35.

[66] Use of the term "movement" here follows on the precedent set by the subtitle of Ronald Davidson's groundbreaking work, *Indian Esoteric Buddhism: A Social History of the Tantric Movement* (New York: Columbia University Press, 2002).

[67] See, for example, Barbara Ambros, *Emplacing a Pilgrimage: The Ōyama Cult and Regional Religion in Early Modern Japan* (Cambridge, MA: Harvard University Press, 2008), 4. In the twenty-first century, the expectation of exclusive adherence to a particular church is not as strong as it once was, though it remained a point of criticism for putative "new-age" religiosity.

Praxis: Dialectic of Thought and Action

The consequence of nineteenth-century categories locating Buddhism as one of the "world religions"—to be studied by the then-nascent field of religious studies—and of defining religions as belief systems is that the primary frame for understanding Buddhism continues to be doctrine and doctrinal texts, or the selectively doctrinal portions of texts. As others have asked, Why are *these* texts—whether the *Satipaṭṭhāna sutta*, or the *Mūlamadhayamaka kārikā*, or the Lotus Sutra—taken as representative of "Buddhism"?[68] These same presumptions also lead to highlighting selected portions of texts as doctrinal and then examining those portions in isolation from other textual components, such as devotion and practice, even if found in the same text. Most Buddhist texts, however, are better understood as complex wholes.

Even further, religious studies scholars often select specific instances of Buddhist doctrine on the basis of their similarity to the concerns, categories, and concepts of Protestant Christianity.[69] In some instances, a second level of abstraction is created when the selected doctrines are then framed in the context of Western philosophy of religion. In other words, those aspects that look like doctrine are first extracted from a text and then treated in the abstract as ideas separate from their religio-historical place (dehistoricized), separate from their relations with other aspects of the text (decontextualized), and separate from their connections to the living tradition (deracinated).

Contemporary Western religious culture's dualistic value system regarding the goals of practice—material goals, judged to be of lesser moral value; and spiritual goals, judged to be of greater moral value—is often imposed on tantric Buddhist practice. The dualistic value system is colloquially codified as the naturalized distinction between "this-worldly" and "other-worldly." In the context of scholarship on Buddhism, this is also sometimes framed as a distinction between "kammatic" and "dhammic" forms of Buddhism.

This value system reflects the foundational role of mind–body dualism—or thought–action, or spirit–matter dualism—in contemporary Western

[68] Jonathan Silk, "The Most Important Buddhist Scripture?," paper presented at the 12th Conference of the International Association of Buddhist Studies, Université of Lausanne, Lausanne, Switzerland, August 27, 1999; see also Jan Nattier, *A Few Good Men: The Bodhisattva Path According to* The Inquiry of Ugra (Ugraparipṛcchā) (Honolulu: University of Hawai'i Press, 2003), 7; and Richard K. Payne, "Aparimitāyus: 'Tantra' *and* 'Pure Land' in Medieval Indian Buddhism?" *Pacific World: Journal of the Institute of Buddhist Studies*, third series, no. 9 (2007): 277–278.

[69] See, for example, Martin Baumann, "Culture Contact and Valuation: Early German Buddhists and the Creation of a 'Buddhism in Protestant Shape,'" *Numen* XLIV (1997): 270–295.

religious culture. Judgments based on this value system immediately privilege what the value system considers to be properly "religious" goals. To use this in our understanding of tantric Buddhist practice and thought constructs a normative version of Buddhism, in this case based not on the values of the tradition itself, but rather on those of modern Western religious culture.[70] The tantric Buddhist movement itself, of course, includes its own kinds of value judgments. However, an effective academic understanding of tantric Buddhist praxis would not employ value judgments from either tradition, but rather treat all goals of practice neutrally in the context of a specific ideology.

The focus on doctrine implicitly suggests that it has been the primary driving factor of Buddhist history—in the same way and to the same extent that it has been for Christendom, whose historiography often seems to be structured by theological disputes. Decentering doctrine does not mean abandoning the study of texts, but instead treating doctrines in their appropriate contexts. This would mean rethinking Buddhist history as a stream of praxis—one that is an ongoing dialectic relation between practices and doctrines. As the dialectic interaction between practice and ideology, "praxis" integrates both ideas and actions without giving primacy to either and avoids presuming a one-directional causal relation.[71]

From a slightly different perspective, in place of the long-standing focus on what Buddhists should think (doctrine abstracted from practice), there is value in attending to what practitioners and adherents actually do.[72] Rather than privileging thought/doctrine and treating action/practice as derivative, this change of focus calls for a nondual understanding of the dialectic integrity of thought and action. There are two obstacles to this shift. First, the presumption that thought causes action, and second, the presumption that what it means to be a Buddhist is to meditate.

The belief that doctrine is foundational for practice is a corollary to the belief that thought causes action. Consequently, understanding action is

[70] The relation between normative and descriptive is itself not a simple one, easily demarcated. See Richard Nance, "Indian Buddhist Preachers Inside and Outside the Sūtras," *Religion Compass* 2.2 (2008): 134–159, 139.

[71] For a discussion of the dialectic of practice and doctrine, see Nance, "Indian Buddhist Preachers Inside and Outside the Sūtras," 135.

[72] For an expansive exposition of what this means in terms of valorizing emotion, experience, and embodiment in the study of Buddhism, see Kevin Trainor and Paula Arai, "Introduction: Embodiment and Sense Experience," in *The Oxford Handbook of Buddhist Practice*, ed. Kevin Trainor and Paula Arai, 1–18 (New York: Oxford University Press, 2022; https://doi.org/10.1093/oxfordhb/9780190632922.013.40).

given less importance than understanding doctrine—or not given much attention at all. In the conceptual framework of "world religions," each religion is thought to be unique and distinct from all others, and therefore the most important doctrines are those unique doctrines that most clearly distinguish one religious tradition from another. Rupert Gethin has called attention to the privileging of doctrine, describing

> a modern tendency to understand religion as principally a kind of belief system—usually revolving around a God who is both creator and savior—that an individual takes on board and which then provides him or her with a way of looking at the world. Probably the reduction of religion to this kind of belief system should be seen as a relatively recent phenomenon—the legacy of the Reformation and Enlightenment.[73]

As Gethin notes, this conception of religion is rooted in the Protestant Reformation, when proper belief (ortho-doxy) was promoted as more important to one's salvation than proper action (ortho-praxy).[74] The primacy given to belief in the academic study of Buddhism is, therefore, not an empirical generalization based on the study of religions, but is instead itself an implicitly religious claim.[75] Buddhism, however, is not heir to the Protestant Reformation.[76] At least into late modernity, the main concern of many adherents would have been effective practice.

The organizing schema of ground, path, and goal is widely employed in Buddhist thought, and it can be adapted to discuss tantric Buddhist praxis. This schema describes the conditions of human existence as unsatisfactory (ground), the actions and practices to be taken to change that unsatisfactory

[73] Rupert Gethin, *The Foundations of Buddhism* (Oxford: Oxford University Press, 1998), 64–65.

[74] The ways in which ritual is conceived to be effective was a central issue in this distinction. Dale Wright notes that the primary intent of the Protestant "critique of ritual as a way of engaging in religious practice [was] to challenge the link between ritual and magic—the view that if you do the ritual then, magically or in recompense, the gods or angels will do something favorable for you." "Introduction: Rethinking Ritual Practice in Zen Buddhism," in *Zen Ritual: Studies of Zen Theory in Practice*, ed. Steven Heine and Dale Wright, 3–20 (Oxford: Oxford University Press, 2007), 14.

[75] This is even more sharply evident when one critically examines the philosophy of religion. With a few rare exceptions, general treatments of the philosophy of religion are concerned with religious ideas that derive directly from the Western religious tradition. For even those few that do make some serious attempt to integrate religious ideas from outside that narrow range, the organizing structures of inquiry are codified by the concerns of Christian theology. This is equally the case for "religion and science," which is also almost entirely structured by the issues of Christian theology. See Richard K. Payne, "Why 'Buddhist Theology' Is Not a Good Idea," *The Pure Land: Journal of the International Association of Shin Buddhist Studies* n.s., no. 27 (2012–2013): 37–71.

[76] Though, of course, in the modern era, Buddhism in its Western interpretations has been reframed in accord with the concepts, categories, and concerns of Protestant Christianity.

condition (path), and what is to be attained by undertaking those practices (goal). In this summary form, it does not presume the dualistic value system that would privilege "awakening" over other humanly relevant goals. As an analytic tool, the structure of ground, path, and goal points to the integral character of ideas and practices, that is, praxis. Talking about ideas, that is, ideology, is broader than doctrine. A practitioner may have a conception of the goal, and a desire for an effective practice to attain that goal, without being concerned with doctrinal issues *per se*.

Secondary to effective practice is a concern with proper lineage, which answers the question, How can I be assured that the practice I undertake is going to be effective? Lineage establishes a teacher–student relation that claims to trace back to an authoritative source, such as Śākyamuni Buddha or Mahāvairocana Tathāgata. Knowing that a practice comes from someone who did achieve that goal is the assurance of efficacy. "The category that is least important in Buddhism is the category of belief."[77]

From the perspective of Buddhist thought, effective practice requires right view (Skt. *samyak dṛṣṭi*), which is important as the first of the eight aspects of the path. This foundational role of right view is not, however, the same as the idea that proper belief is itself salvific. Right view is interdependent with the other seven aspects of the eightfold path. The representation of the eightfold path as an eight-spoked wheel indicates the mutual support each aspect provides the other.

In many Indic Buddhist conceptions of the path, knowledge (Skt. *vidyā*) is essential to awakening, while ignorance (Skt. *avidyā*) is its main obstacle. Right view is at times explained as comprehending of "how things actually are" (Skt. *tathatā*), whether on the basis of the authority of a teacher, or realized by reasoned reflection, or experienced directly through contemplative insight.[78] In this pragmatic interpretation, right view is necessary, but

[77] Frits Staal, *Rules Without Meaning: Ritual, Mantras and the Human Sciences* (New York: Peter Lang Publishing, 1989), 399. The three-part hierarchy given here is based on my recollection of Staal's presentation at the second Buddhist-Christian Dialogue Conference in 1984.

[78] Buddhist epistemology is a vast area of specialist expertise, and the sources of valid knowledge (*pramāna*) are one of the central issues of contention. The school of Buddhist epistemologists (Dignaga, Dharmakīrti, and their followers) argued that there are only two sources: reason and insight. Arguments are also made, however, for the authority of the Buddha's teachings. See Dan Arnold, "The Philosophical Works and Influence of Dignāga and Dharmakīrti," in *The Oxford Encyclopedia of Buddhism*, ed. Richard K. Payne and Georgios Halkias, n.p. (Oxford: Oxford University Press, 2017; https://doi.org/10.1093/acrefore/9780199340378.013.198); Roger Jackson, *Is Enlightenment Possible?: Dharmakīrti and Rgyal Tshab Rje on Knowledge, Rebirth, No-Self and Liberation* (Boston: Snow Lion, 1993); and Richard K. Payne, "Authority of the Buddha: The Limits of Knowledge in Medieval Indian Buddhist Epistemology," *Acta Orientalia Vilnensia* 11.1 (2010): 13–36.

not sufficient for awakening. Abstracted in this way, doctrines can communicate right view, that is, an understanding of how things work, and at the same time form a dialectic with practices. Doctrine informs (guides, structures) practice, and practice informs (corrects, modifies) doctrine.

An instance of this dialectic integrity of doctrine and practice is the relation between the practice of ritual identification and the idea (doctrinal claim) that there is a fundamental identity between the practitioner and the deity. These two form a dialectic—the practice and the concept support and reinforce each other. Not all praxis, however, is as closely integrated as ritual identification is with the idea of inherent awakening. The relations may be much looser. In some cases, the ideology may have been appended later as justifying a practice already in use, or a practice may have been disjoined from its "native" or at least earlier ideological context and a different justification provided as appropriate to a new context.

The modern image of Buddhist practice is dominated by individual, seated, silent meditation of one kind or another. Zen, insight, mindfulness, and several other modern forms of Buddhist practice share this basic model, despite the different details of what one is directed to focus attention on—or not.[79] More importantly, this modern view has tended to dismiss other possible kinds of practice, particularly ritual, as either not really Buddhist or not really effective—a view that distinguishes meditation and ritual as fundamentally different activities.[80]

The common distinction between meditation and ritual is, however, an artifice—though one that is so familiar that its artifactual status is made invisible, being taken for granted. Rather than being opposites, meditation and ritual are two different ways of thinking about practice. In most modern discourse, to describe a practice as a meditation is to privilege the mental perspective of that practice. Conversely, foregrounding the embodied activity of that same practice means that it can be described as ritual. The value judgments that the two terms often carry in present-day English—meditation is positive and beneficial, but ritual is pointless and ineffective—are a

[79] Even the quasi-tantric practices of the "old meditation" (*borān kammaṭṭhāna*) found in Southeast Asia have in the modern period been subject to the pressures of conforming to this model. Kate Crosby, *Esoteric Theravada: The Story of the Forgotten Meditation Tradition of Southeast Asia* (Boulder, CO: Shambhala, 2021), 222. On nonconceptual realization, see Klaus-Dieter Mathes, *A Fine Blend of* Mahāmudrā *and Madhyamaka: Maitripa's Collection of Texts on Non-Conceptual Realization* (Amanasīkara) (Vienna: Austrian Academy of Sciences, 2015).

[80] Richard K. Payne, "Ritual, Rituals, and Ritualizing in American Buddhism," in *The Oxford Handbook of American Buddhism*, ed. Scott Mitchell and Ann Gleig (Oxford: Oxford University Press, forthcoming).

consequence of cultural history, not an accurate characterization of different practices.[81] All practices are simultaneously both physical and mental, and whether a practice is described as meditation or ritual is a consequence of which aspect is highlighted, of which perspective is taken. To explain, as the first chapter of the *Vairocanābhisambodhi tantra* does, that tantric practice arises because of the intention toward awakening (Skt. *bodhicitta*), is rooted in compassion (Skt. *karuṇā*), and expressed as expedient means (Skt. *upaya*) does not give primacy to either physical or mental aspects of our existence, instead addressing the practitioner as an organically integral whole.

While Buddhist meditative practices constitute a complex, and rich, subject matter, they are part of a much larger category of practice, which includes ritual. As a more comprehensive category, practice offers a perspective from which ritual is not separate from meditation but is simply a different way of thinking about practice. As widely employed in both popular and academic discourse, labeling a practice "meditation" means framing it as a mental activity; it is equally possible to label that same practice "ritual" by framing it as a physical one. The two are simply different perspectives, but each entails very different interpretations and valuations.

Praxis as the Object of Study

The field of religious studies has had little success in defining its object of study: religion.[82] This consequence is inevitable, given that there is no object that can be studied, only instances that we label collectively as religion. The category "religion" identifies an intersubjective entity, one located between people and given meaning by use. Not only is religion an abstraction, but, equally so, "Buddhism" is also an intersubjective entity given meaning by use. In both cases, it is the linguistic habits of observers, scholars, and practitioners that hold the pieces together. There are no clear demarcations identifying what's in the category and what's out. For example, is the devotion some people feel toward Elvis Presley religious? If they travel to Graceland, is that a pilgrimage?[83] With one list of criteria, the answer is yes; with a different list, it is no.

[81] See Catherine Bell, *Ritual Theory, Ritual Practice* (Oxford: Oxford University Press, 1992).

[82] Malcolm David Eckel, "The Ghost at the Table: On the Study of Buddhism and the Study of Religion," *Journal of the American Academy of Religion* 62.4 (Winter 1994): 1085–1110.

[83] These are not (entirely) facetious questions. These topics were examined in a number of papers presented at the American Academy of Religion meeting, when it was held in Nashville in 2000.

While abstract terms such as "religion" and "Buddhism" may be convenient ways of talking about a field of study, they are not adequate as objects of study. The concept of praxes, as systems integrating thought and action, and centering on an integrating figure, offers a more productive object of study. Specific praxes are coherent systems organized around the centripetal figure. When refracted through the lens of a praxis, actions, beliefs, settings, artwork, and objects take on significance that they may not otherwise have; that is, context, use, and designation change the meaning of components of the praxis. There is, therefore, a praxis of Elvis, whether categorized by religious studies scholars as religious or not. For adherents, travel to Graceland is pilgrimage, and portraits of the King on black velvet are icons.[84]

The centripetal figure acts as a unifying force, forming an organized whole. The praxis is more than simply a collection of components; it is a system integrating practices and meanings. While in many, if not most cases the central figure is anthropomorphic—a buddha, bodhisattva, guardian deity, teacher—this is not always the case. From the early medieval period, the Buddhist tradition has included praxes of stupas, and of sutra texts, and these praxes were related to each other as well. As David McMahan explains, "Certain Mahāyāna sūtra manuscripts were considered sacred objects with the power to consecrate places, thereby establishing sacred sites and Mahāyāna centers of worship that are similar to, and modeled on, stūpa cults that were already prevalent."[85] While praxes are systemic wholes, they may be identified conventionally by reference to a centripetal figure.[86] Praxes having a buddha or bodhisattva as its chief deity are identified as the praxis of that figure, such as the praxis of Avalokiteśvara. It is therefore more appropriate to identify a "stupa praxis" or a "praxis of the book" by reference to some specific stupa, such as that at Sanchi, or in relation to some specific book, such as the Lotus Sutra. It is not that there is some general "stupa praxis" or "praxis of the book," but those categories generalize over a large set of specific, actual instances. As seen in Chapter III, there are praxes in which the central figure is a dhāraṇī, the empowering verbal formula said to contain the essence of a

[84] Juan E. Campo, "Religious Pilgrimages in the United States," in *Oxford Research Encyclopedias, Religion*, ed. John Barton (New York: Oxford University Press, online 2017; https://doi.org/10.1093/acrefore/9780199340378.013.483).
[85] David McMahan, "Orality, Writing, and Authority in South Asian Buddhism: Visionary Literature and the Struggle for Legitimacy in the Mahāyāna," *History of Religions* 37.3 (Feb. 1998): 249–274, 256.
[86] The Japanese term "chief deity" (Jpn. *honzon*) refers to the organizing center or centripetal figure of praxis, one that is not necessarily anthropomorphic.

teaching, such as the Śūraṃgama dhāraṇī, and there are also praxes in which anthropomorphized forms of ritual implements, such as *Vajrakīla*, act as the chief deity.[87]

Far from being fixed, static, or "timeless," praxes are malleable, fluid, and changing. One example has been discussed by David Quinter in his study of the Mañjuśrī praxis in the Shingon Ritsu school founded by Eison (or Eizon, 1201–1290) in medieval Japan. The character of the chief deity itself transforms in response to changing conditions. In medieval Japan, Mañjuśrī, usually cast as being representative of wisdom, became identified with the quality of compassion—usually associated with the figure of Avalokiteśvara. This change was part of the medieval Shingon Ritsu school's involvement with social service activities for the benefit of outcasts (Jpn. *hinin*). This association is not unique to Japan, despite having been emphasized by the Shingon Ritsu monks. "Traditions extolling Mañjuśrī's benefits for the poor and afflicted extend from the circa fifth-century Chinese scripture known as the *Mañjuśrī Parinirvāṇa Sutra*."[88] In a similar fashion, although not portrayed in particularly wrathful form, Mañjuśrī was also invoked for state protection and success in warfare—thus appealing also to political elites and warriors.[89] "The Mañjuśrī cult blurs the lines between popular and elite, this-worldly and otherworldly, and public and private."[90]

Closing Summary

Looking across the regions of Buddhist history, several different topical issues have been deployed to examine facets of the tantric Buddhist movement. The background of Vedic ritual, the importance of initiation as explained in the early tantric Buddhist work the *Vairocanābhisaṃbodhi tantra*, the dynamics of interiorization, and the group of practitioners known

[87] Martin Boord, "The Vajrakīla Tantras," in *The Oxford Encyclopedia of Buddhism*, ed. Richard K. Payne and Georgios Halkias (Oxford: Oxford University Press, 2019; DOI: 10.1093/acrefore/9780199340378.013.555).

[88] David Quinter, *From Outcasts to Emperors: Shingon Ritsu and the Mañuśrī Cult in Medieval Japan* (Leiden: Brill, 2015), 3. For further on this sutra, see David Quinter, "Visualizing the *Mañjuśrū Parinirvāṇa Sutra* as a Contemplation Sutra," *Asia Major*, third series, 23.2 (2010): 97–128; and more generally, David Quinter, "Visualization/Contemplation Sutras (*Guan Jing*)," in *The Oxford Encyclopedia of Buddhism*, ed. Richard K. Payne and Georgios T. Halkias (New York: Oxford University Press, 2021; doi.org/10.1093/acrefore/9780199340378.013.770).

[89] Quinter, *From Outcasts to Emperors*, 10–11.

[90] Quinter, *From Outcasts to Emperors*, 3.

as mahāsiddhas introduced the South Asian roots of tantric Buddhism. Institutions supporting tantric Buddhist praxis, particularly dhāraṇī and pilgrimage, were examined in relation to East Asia. In Southeast Asia, the history of tantric Buddhism is recorded in its role of state formation and evidenced by monuments, such as Borobudur. The themes of death and decay that run throughout the Buddhist tradition as a whole took a particular tantric form in Inner Asia as the practice of Severance (Tib. *Chöd*). Buddhist history, however, is not compartmentalized by region, but instead has taken place through networks across regions. That history is one of praxes, such as the praxis of Mañjuśrī, being carried by masters through those networks.

In addition to tantric Buddhism as a pervasive, if sometimes invisible, part of Buddhist history, this work has been concerned with challenging the preconceptions of religious studies that constrain the field in dysfunctional ways. This closing chapter, therefore, made explicit four areas in which the study of tantric Buddhism can serve to shift the field of religious studies toward more inclusive conceptions and accurate understandings.

The dynamics by which Protestant presuppositions have been sublated as universally appropriate for the understanding of all religions opened these reflections to clear the air. One of the dominant ways of writing religious history is according to the narrative arc of original purity that decays over time—the rhetoric of decadence. Implicated by this style of historiography is also the narrative of the disappearing tradition, an overly simplified image of Buddhist history. Decontextualizing doctrine from its dialectic relation with practice and privileging it as foundational has created a distorted understanding of tantric Buddhism as simply a kind of ritual technology.[91] And, while general abstract terms such as religion and Buddhism may be of use in organizing an academic field, they are too vague to be adequate objects of study. The alternative being proposed here is praxes, which are systematically organized around a centripetal figure, and which cohere and endure over time and across cultural and linguistic boundaries.

Tantric Buddhism can, therefore, be understood as a movement comprised of overlapping praxes originating in South Asia and spreading via networks throughout the Buddhist cosmopolis. Identifying tantric Buddhism can best be done by context, use, and designation—that is, what does it exist in relation to, how is it employed, and what is it called? These

[91] Richard K. Payne, "Practicing the 'Three-Fold Mystery': Rethinking a Shingon Ritual from Dichotomy to Dialectic," *Journal of Contemplative Studies* 19.4 (2024): 1–29, https://doi.org/10.57010/XNID2516.

praxes are not fixed objects, but instead everchanging and self-organizing patterns of components—the components change, but the pattern is ongoing. The enduring metaphor, the one to remember, is a standing wave: the wavering ripples that form around a rock in a stream do not move downstream away from the rock—despite water constantly flowing through the ripple, the ripple remains.

Glossary

A

abhidharma (Skt.), third "basket" of the Buddhist canon, "higher" teachings

abhiṣeka (Skt.), initiation

abridged version of a tantra, (Skt.) *laghu-tantra*

Acalanātha Vidyārāja (Skt.), Immovable Wisdom King, Jpn. Fudō Myōō (不動明王)

ācārya (Skt., Jpn. ajari 阿闍梨)

adamantine songs (Skt. *vajragīti*)

ādibuddha (Skt.), primordial buddha

ādyanutpāda (Skt.), originally unborn: "original non-arising"

Agni, Jpn. Katen (火天, lit. "fire god")

agnicayana (Skt.), the "piling up of Agni," a Vedic ritual

already awakened buddha mind (Jpn.) *bodai*, 菩提; *bodaishin* 菩提心

Amoghavajra, Ch. Bukong, Jpn. Fukū, 不空

anitya (Skt.), impermanence

anuttarayoga tantras (Skt.), "supreme yoga" tantras

apramāṇa (Skt.), four immeasurables: loving kindness, compassion, empathetic joy, and equanimity

apratiṣṭhā-nirvāṇa (Skt.), remaining in the world as an awakened being

argha (Skt.), perfumed water

asanas (Skt.), bodily postures

aśubhabhāvanā (Skt.), contemplation of the foulness and impurity of human bodies

austerities, (Jpn.) *shugyō*, 修行

Avalokiteśvara (Skt.,) (Tib.) Chenrezig, (Ch.) Guanyin, (Jpn.) Kannon, 観音

āvaraṇa (Skt.), obscurations

Avataṃsaka sūtra, (Jpn.) Kegon gyō, 華厳経

avidyā (Skt.), ignorance

awakened ones (Skt. *tathāgatas*)

awakening (Skt. *bodhi*, Jpn. *bodai*, 菩提)

B

"banners" (Ch.), *chuang*, 幢, dhāraṇī pillars

bardo (Tib.), state between death and rebirth

"becoming awakened in this body," (Jpn.) *sokushin jōbutsu* 即身成仏

Bhaiṣajya guru (Skt.), Medicine Buddha

bodhicitta (Skt.), *bodhi*-mind, the intention to become awakened

bodhi-mind, (Skt.) *bodhicitta*, the intention to become awakened

bodily postures, (Skt.) *asanas*

body donation practice, (Tib.) *lus byin*

brāhmaṇa (Skt.), highest caste, priests

breath, or "winds," (Skt.) *prana*; (Tib.) *lung*

buddhavacana (Skt.), word of the Buddha

Bukong (Ch.), see Amoghavajra

C

cakravāla (Skt., var. *cakravāda*), ring of metal mountains, cosmos

caryagīti (Skt.), collection of vernacular songs by Saraha

caste, (Skt.) *varna* (lit. color or outward appearance)

caturmahārāja (Skt.), four great kings

celestial musicians, (Skt.) *gandharva*

central deity, see chief deity

cessation, (Skt.) *nirvana*, (Jpn.) *nehan*, 涅槃

Chang'an, (Ch.) 長安

channels, (Skt.) *nāḍī*

chief deity, or central deity, (Jpn.) *honzon* 本尊

chingo kokka (Jpn. 鎮護国家), state protection

chöd (Tib.), severance

"circulatory pilgrimage," reflecting the Japanese term *meguri* (廻), meaning "going round"

cold water austerities , (Jpn.) *suigyō*; also *mizugori* (using buckets of water when a waterfall is not available)

collections of dhāraṇī practices (Skt. *dhāraṇīsaṃgraha*)

Compassionate Honored One, (Jpn.) Jison 慈尊

comprehensive resource for practice, (Skt.) *kalpa*

concentration (Pāli & Skt.) *samādhi*

conditioned coproduction (Skt.) *pratityasamutpada*

conditioning habits (Skt.) *saṃskāra*

contemplation of the foulness and impurity of human bodies, (Skt.) *aśubhabhāvanā*

"Contemplation of the Nine Appearances," (Jpn.) *Kusōkan*, 九想観; Kūkai's poem

D

Da Guan-ding jing (Ch.), 大灌頂經 TITAL. 1331

Dainichi Nyorai 大日 如来 (Mahāvairocana Tathāgata)

Daizong (Ch.) 代宗 emperor (r. 762–779)

ḍākinī (Skt.), female deity

dana-parāmitā (Skt.), perfection of generosity

deity yoga

delusion (Skt./Pāli), *moha*

Derge (Tib.), Sde dge; also Ch. Dege 德格

dhāraṇī (Skt.), verbal formula used ritually

dhārānī pillar, pillar on which a *dhāraṇī* is inscribed, the shadow of which conveys the *dhāraṇī*'s power

dhāraṇīsaṃgraha (Skt.), collections of dhāraṇī practices

dharmabhāṇaka (Skt.), Buddhist orator or preacher, more generally practitioners

dharmadhāraṇī (Skt.), dhāraṇī to remember the teachings

dhyana (Skt.), (Ch.), *chan*, 禪, meditation

diamond body, (Skt.) *vajraśarīra*

dīkṣā (Skt.), initiation, ordination

discriminative consciousness, (Skt.) *vijñāna*

dohā (Skt.), songs, poems

dual-occupancy sites, (Jpn.) *Jingūji*; 神宮寺

dukkha (Pali), (Skt.) *duḥkha*, suffering

dveṣa (Skt.), (Pāli) *dosa*, hatred

E

Eison (or Eizon), 1201–1290; 叡尊

emptiness (Skt.) *sunyatā*

Ennin, 793 or 794–864, 圓仁

En no Ozunu (b. 634), 役小角, or En no Gyoja

"entering me, me entering" (Jpn.), *nyūga–ganyū* 入我我入, summarizing the visualization of an interpenetration of Buddha and practitioner that culminates in a ritual identity

esoteric, esoteric Buddhism, (Ch.) *mijiao, mizung*, 密宗 (Jpn.) *mitsu*, 密, and *himitsu*, 秘密.

esoteric treasury, (Ch.) *mizang* 密藏

expansive visionary text, (Skt.) *mahāyānavaipulyasūtra*

expedient means, (Skt.) *upaya*

F

festival, (Jpn.) *matsuri* 祭

feudal system of vassal relations, (Skt.) *samanta*

five-element stupa, (Jpn.) *go rin tō* 五輪塔

four immeasurables, (Skt.) *apramāṇa*: loving kindness, compassion, empathetic joy, and equanimity

four great kings, (Skt.) *caturmahārāja*

Fudō Myōō (Jpn.), (Skt.) Acalanātha Vidyārāja 不動明王, Immoveable Wisdom King

G

gandharva (Skt.), celestial musicians

garbhadhātu (Skt.), womb or matrix realm

garbhadhātu maṇḍala, also garbhakośadhātu maṇḍala, (Jpn.), taizōkai mandara, 胎藏界曼荼羅

gatha (Skt.), verses

generosity, perfection of, (Skt.) *dana-parāmitā*

gods, also spirits, (Jpn.), kami, 神

goma (Jpn.), 護摩, see homa

gongen (Jpn.), 権現, (Skt.) avatar

gorintō (Jpn.), 五輪塔, five-element stūpa, lit. "five cakras"

"great monasteries," (Skt.) *mahāvihara*

"great seal," (Skt.) *mahāmudrā*

Great Teaching of Yoga, (Ch.) *yuqie dajiao* 瑜伽大教

great vow, (Skt.) *mahāvrata*

great yoga tantras, (Skt.) *mahāyoga tantras*

greed, (Skt. & Pāli) *lobha*

gṛhya (Skt.), domestic rites

gtum mo (Tib.), inner heat

guardian deity, (Skt.) *lokapāla*

Gyōgi (Jpn.), 行基, 668–749

H

hatred, (Skt.) *dveṣa*, (Pāli) *dosa*

Heaven of the Thirty-three, (Skt.) Trāyastriṃśa Heaven

hinin (Jpn.), 非人, outcasts

holy men of Kōyasan, (Jpn.) *Kōya hijiri*, 高野聖

homa (Skt.), (Jpn.) *goma*, 護摩, votive offerings made into fire

honzon (Jpn.), central deity of a ritual, mandala, or temple

hosshin (Jpn.) 發心, arising of the mind, intent or thought to awaken, i.e., *bodhicitta*

"how things actually are," (Skt.) *tathatā*, (Tib.) *de bshin nyid*, or *de kho na nyid*, (Ch.) *zhen ru*, (Jpn.) *shinnyo*, 眞如

Huiguo (Ch.), 746–805; (Jpn.) Keika, 惠果

human person, (Skt.) *jiva*

hungry ghosts, (Skt.), *preta*, (Ch.) *egui*, (Jpn.) *gaki*, 餓鬼, (Tib.) *yi dwags*

I

ignorance, (Skt.) *avidyā*

Immovable Wisdom King, (Skt.) Acalanātha Vidyārāja, (Jpn.) Fudō Myōō 不動明王

impermanence, (Skt.) *anitya*

impure, (Jpn.) *edo*, 穢土

initiation (Skt.) *dīkṣā*, also *abhiṣeka*, also ordination

"inner heat," (Tib.) *gtum mo*

insightful awareness, (Skt.) *jñāna*

intention toward awakening, (Skt.) *bodhicitta*

Ippen shōnin (Jpn.)一遍, 1239–1289

J

jingūji (Jpn.) 神宮寺, "dual-occupancy" temples

Ji-shū (Jpn.) 時宗, a Pure Land sect

jiva (Skt.), human person

jñāna (Skt.), insightful awareness

K

Kaiyuanzong (Ch.), school of the Kaiyuan era [713–741], 開元宗

Kalingga, (Ch.) Heling, 訶陵

kalpa (Skt.), comprehensive resource for practice

kāmaloka (Skt.), realm of desire

Kanjur (Tib.) bka' 'gyur), sutra section of the Tibetan canon

kāṣāya (Skt.), (Pāli) *kāsāya*, (Ch.) *jiasha*, (Jpn.) *kesa*, 袈裟, robes worn by a monk

khaṭvāṅga (Skt.), skull-topped staff

king of kings, (Skt.) *rājādhirāja*

knowledge, (Skt.) *vidyā*

Kokubun ji (Jpn.) 国分寺, national or imperial temples

kōmyō shingon (Jpn.) 光明真言, Clear Light Mantra

Kōya hijiri (Jpn.) 高野聖, "holy men of Kōyasan"

Kōya Myōjin (Jpn.) 高野明神

kṣāntilābābhāya dhāraṇī (Skt.), dhāraṇī bestowing patient acceptance

kṣatriya (Skt.), warriors

Kūkai (Jpn.), 774–835, 空海, posthumous title: Kōbō Daishi, 弘法大師

kūṭāgāra (Skt.), penthouse

L

laghu-tantra (Skt.), abridged version of a tantra

lay practitioners, (Jpn.), *ubasoku*, 優婆塞

lineage, (Skt.) *vihāra*, lit. "abode"

liu (Ch.) 流, (Jpn.) *ryū*, lineage, sect, school

"Lives of Eminent Monks Composed in the Song," (Ch.) Sung gaoseng zhuan, 宋高僧傳; *T.* 2061

lobha (Skt. & Pāli), greed

lokapāla (Skt.), guardian deity

lus byin (Tib.), body donation practice

M

Madhyamaka (Skt.), "middle way" system of thought

Mahākalparāja, Ch. *Da jiaowang* 大教王, "Great King of the Teaching."

Mahāmayūrī -rājñi-saṃyuktāṛddhidhāraṇī sūtra, 大金色孔雀王咒經 various translations: T. 986, 987?

mahāmudrā (Skt.), "great seal"

mahāsiddhas (Skt.), "greatly accomplished," advanced yogic practitioners

Mahātantrarāja, Ch. *Da jiaowang* 大教王, "Great King of the Teaching"

mahāvihara (Skt.), great monasteries

mahāvrata (Skt.), great vow

mahāyānavaipulyasūtra (Skt.), expansive visionary text

mahāyoga tantras (Skt.), great yoga tantras

Maitreya, (Jpn.) Miroku, 彌勒

mantra (Skt.), Ch. zhenyan, Jpn. shingon 真言, verbal formulae used ritually

mantradhāraṇī (Skt.), dhāraṇī with magical power

mantranaya (Skt.), the mode of mantra, mantra recitation

mantraśāstra (Skt.), the practice of mantras, tantric practices

mantrayāna (Skt.), the mantra vehicle, or mantra path, contrasted with the sutra vehicle (Skt. sūtrayāna), also known as the perfection mode (Skt. pāramitānaya)

mantrin (Skt.), one who has mantra

maraṇānusmṛti (Skt.), (Pāli) *maraṇānusatti*, mindfulness of death

material aspects of existents, (Skt.) *rūpa*

Medicine Buddha, (Skt.) Bhaiṣajya guru, (Tib.) Sman bla, (Ch.) Yaoshi rulai, (Jpn.) Yakushi nyorai, 薬師如来

meditation, (Skt.) *dhyana*, (Ch.) *chan*, 禪

meditative concentration, (Skt.) *samādhi*

merchants and farmers, (Skt.) *vaiśya*

"methods of recalling and reciting," (Ch.) *niansongfa* 念誦法

mgur (Tib.), "songs of awakening" or "songs of realization" *mikkyō* (Jpn.) 密教, esoteric teaching

mind of awakening, (Skt.) *bodhicitta*, (Jpn.) *hosshin*, 発心

mindfulness of death, (Skt.) *maraṇānusmṛti*, (Pāli) *maraṇānusatti*

Minobusan (Jpn.), 身延山

misplaced affections, (Skt.) *kleśavāsanā*, those emotional attachments (both clinging and rejecting) we have to things that will not satisfy us

mistaken conceptions, (Skt.) *jñeyavāsanā*, those consistently mistaken ways in which we think about the world

"mixed" esoteric Buddhism, (Jpn.) *zōmitsu*, 雑密; sometimes rendered in English as proto-tanta, or heteroprax

mizong (Ch.) 密宗, esoteric school

moha (Skt./Pāli), delusion

mudra (Skt.), hand gestures employed in ritual (also in paintings, statuary, and dance)

mūlakleśa (Skt.), primary afflictions

N

nāḍī (Skt.), channels

"national master," (Jpn.) *kokushi*, 國師

Ningai (Jpn.), 仁海, 951–1046

nirupadhiśeṣa-nirvāṇa (Skt.), nirvana without remainder

nirvana (Skt.), (Jpn.) nehan, 涅槃

nirvana without remainder, (Skt.) *nirupadhiśeṣa-nirvāṇa*

Niutsuhime no kami (Jpn.), 丹生都比売の神

O

obscurations, (Skt.) *āvaraṇa*, also *kleśa*, (Tib.) *sgrib pa*, (Ch.) *zhang*, (Jpn.) *shō*, 障

Okunoin (Jpn.), 奥院, mausoleum on Mt. Kōya

oral transmission texts, (Jpn.) *kuden*, 口伝

ordinary monastics, (Skt.) *śākyabhikṣus* (Nepal)

ordination, (Skt.) *dīkṣā*, also initiation

originally unborn, (Skt.) *ādyanutpāda*: "original non-arising"

outcasts, (Jpn.) *hinin*, 非人

P

pacification, (Skt.) *śāntika*

paradise of a saving buddha, (Jpn.) *gongu jōdo* 欣求浄土

parāmitā (Skt.), perfections

pāramitāyāna (Skt.), "perfection path"

paritta (Pāli), verses of protection

perception, (Skt.) *samjñā*

"perfection path," (Skt. *pāramitāyāna*)

perfections, (Skt.) *parāmitā*

perfumed water, (Skt.) *argha*

phowa (Tib.), "transfer of consciousness"

poems in the Japanese style, (Jpn.) *waka* 和歌

pollution, (Jpn.) *kegare* 穢れ

power/potency, (Jpn.) ki 気, (Ch.) chi; comparable to (Skt.) prāṇa, also rei 霊

practice, (Skt.) *sādhana*, (Jpn.) *shugyō*, 修行), religious, yogic, ritual

prajñā (Skt.), (Pāli) *paññā*, wisdom

prāṇa (Skt.), (Tib.) *lung*, breath, or "winds"

praṇidāna (Skt.), a vow

prāsāda (Skt.), palace

pratītyasamutpāda (Skt.), conditioned coproduction

priests, highest caste, (Skt.) *brāhmaṇa*

primary afflictions, (Skt.) *mūlakleśa*

primitive, (Jpn.) *shugenja*, 修験者

pūjā (Skt.), offertory ritual, worship

"pure" esoteric Buddhism, (Jpn.) *junmitsu*, 純密; sometimes rendered into English as "orthoprax"

Q

R

rājādhirāja (Skt.), king of kings

ratnatraya (Skt.), three jewels: buddha, dharma, sangha

realm of desire, (Skt.) *kāmaloka*

religious practices in the mountains, (Jpn.) *sangaku shugen*, 山岳修験

remaining in the world as an awakened being, (Skt.) *apratiṣṭhā-nirvāṇa*

renunciates, (Skt.) *śramaṇas*

right view, (Skt.) *samyak dṛṣṭi*

ritual specialists, (Skt.) *vajrācāryas* (Nepal)

robes that a monk wears, (Skt.) *kāṣāya*, (Pāli) *kāsāya*, (Ch.) *jiasha*, (Jpn.) *kesa*, 袈裟

rules of the order, (Skt.) *vinaya*

rūpa (Skt.), material aspects of existents

S

sacred diagrams, (Skt.) *maṇḍala*, also *yantra*

sādhana (Skt.), lit. "method" or "technique"; religious, yogic, or ritual practice

Saichō, (Jpn.) 最澄 (767–822), posthumous title: Dengyō Daishi, 傳教大師

saitō goma (Jpn.) 柴灯護摩, large outdoor fire ritual

śāktization, Sanderson's term for appropriation from Śaiva tantra

śākyabhikṣus (Skt.), ordinary monastics (Nepal)

samādhi (Pāli & Skt.), meditative concentration

samanta (Skt.), feudal system of vassal relations

samaya (Skt.), vows, particularly tantric

samjñā (Skt.), perception

saṃskāra (Skt.), conditioning habits

samyak dṛṣṭi (Skt.), right view

sangha, a community of Buddhist practitioners, from *saṃgha* (Skt.) which has a more limited meaning, such as, either ordained monks and nuns, or ordained monks and nuns, and male and female lay disciples

śāntika (Skt.), pacification

school, (Ch.) *zong*, (Jpn.) *shū*, 宗

"secret" or "esoteric" teachings, (Ch.) *mijiao*, (Jpn.) *mikkyō*, 密教

self-ordained, (Jpn. *shido*), 私度, or *shidosō* 私度僧

sensation, (Skt.) *vedanā*

"separation of kami and buddhas," (Jpn.) *shinbutsu bunri*, 神佛分離

serfs and servants, (Skt.) *śūdra*

Severance, (Tib.) *Chöd*, the school

severance, (Tib.) *chöd*, the practice

Shikoku (Jpn.), four (shi 四) "countries" (koku 国)

Shingon (Jpn.) pron. of (Ch.) Zhenyan, that is, mantra school, 真言

shinbutsu bunri (Jpn.), 神佛分離, "separation of kami and buddhas"

Shugendō practitioners, (Jpn.) Shugensha, also *yamabushi*

shugyō, (Jpn.) 修行, practice, esp. of austerities

siddhas (Skt.), accomplished practitioners, yogis and yoginis

siddhi (Skt.), "realization" or "attainment"

sīla (Pāli), (Skt.) *śīla*, virtue

single charismatic figure pilgrimage, (Jpn.) *seiseki junrei* 聖跡巡礼

single deity pilgrimage, (Jpn.) *honzon junrei* 本尊巡礼

Śīva (Skt.), Hindu deity associated with yogic austerities and destruction

skull-topped staff, (Skt.) *khaṭvāṅga*

soma (Skt.), liquid offering in Vedic ritual, "drink of the gods"

"songs of awakening," or "songs of realization," (Tib.) *mgur*

Soshitchikara kyō (Jpn.), (Skt.) Sussidhikara), T. 893:, 蘇悉地羯羅經

śramana (Skt.), renunciates

śrauta (Skt.), solemn. rites, communal rites

state protection, (Jpn.) *chingo kokka* 鎮護国家

sthaṇḍila (Skt.), ritual site, earthen domestic fire altar

stupa (Skt. *stūpa*), memorial (see also Jpn. *gorintō*)

Śubhākarasimha (Skt.), (Ch.) Shan wu wei, (Jpn.) Zenmui, 善無畏

śūdra (Skt.), serfs and servants

suffering (Pāli), *dukkha,* (Skt.) *duḥkha*

sunyatā (Skt.), emptiness

supreme yoga tantras, (Skt.) *anuttarayoga tantras*

T

taimitsu (Jpn.) 台密, the esoteric dimension of Tendai

Taixu (Ch.), 太虚, 1890–1947

Taizong (Ch.), 太宗 (r. 976–997), Song emperor

Taizu (Ch.), 太祖, r. 960–976

tathāgatas (Skt.), awakened ones

tathatā (Skt.), "how things actually are"

"teaching of yoga" (Ch.) *yujiajiao* 瑜珈教

Tendai (Jpn. 天台), Japanese tradition established by Saichō, which though based on Chinese Tiantai with its Lotus Sutra emphasis; also includes a tantric dimension

Tenjur (Tib.), *bstan 'gyur, śāstra* section of the Tibetan canon

"three countries" (Jpn.) *sankoku*, 三国, model of Buddhist history

three evil paths, (Jpn.) *sanzu no kokyō* 三途の故郷: hell beings, animals, hungry ghosts

three jewels, (Skt.) *ratnatraya*: buddha, dharma, sangha

three poisons, (Skt.) *triviṣa*

tōmitsu (Jpn.), 東密, esoteric teaching of the Eastern Temple (Tōji), i.e., Shingon

transfer of consciousness, (Tib.) *phowa*

Trāyastrimśa Heaven (Skt.), Heaven of the Thirty-three

triple refuge, (Skt.) *triśaraṇa*

triśaraṇa (Skt.), triple refuge

triviṣa (Skt.), three poisons

"true word," (Ch.) *zhenyan*, (Jpn.) *shingon*, 真言

U

upaya (Skt.), expedient means

V

vaiśya (Skt.), merchants and farmers

Vajra (Skt.), diamond or thunderbolt, (Jpn.) *kongō* (金剛)

vajra holders, (Skt.) *vajradharas*

vajrācāryas (Skt.), ritual specialists (Nepal)

vajradharas (Skt.), vajra holders

vajrayāna (Skt.), the diamond or thunderbolt path

"the vajra vehicle of yoga," (Ch.) 金剛乘瑜伽

Vairocanābhisambodhi tantra (*T.* 848), (Jpn.) Dainichi kyō, 大日経

Vajrabodhi, (Ch.) Chin kang chih, (Jpn.) Kongōchi 金剛智

vajradhātu (Skt.), diamond realm, or "thunderbolt" realm

vajradhātu maṇḍala, (Jpn.) *kongōkai mandara*, 金剛界曼荼羅

vajragīti (Skt.), vajra songs, adamantine songs, songs of awakening *vajraśarīra* (Skt.), "diamond body"

Vajraśekhara tantra (*T.* 865), (Jpn.) Kongōchō kyō, 金剛頂教 (there is reason to believe that the proper reconstruction of the Sanskrit name of this work is Vajra-usniṣa)

varna (Skt.), caste (lit. color or outward appearance)

vedanā (Skt.), sensation

verses, (Skt.) *gatha*

vidyā (Skt.), knowledge

vidyārājas, (Ch.) *ming wang,* (Jpn.) *myōō,* 明王, "lords of light," "kings of wisdom"

vihāra (Skt.), lineage, or monastery, lit. "abode"

vijñāna (Skt.), discriminative consciousness

vinaya (Skt. & Pāli), rules of the order

virtue, (Pāli) *sīla,* (Skt.) *śīla*

vows, (Skt.) *samaya,* "sacramental commitments"

W

waka (Jpn.), 和歌, Japanese-style poems

warriors, (Skt.) *kṣatriya*

"we two traveling, or practicing together," (Jpn.) *dōgyō ninin,* 同行二人

Western direction pure land, (Jpn.) *saihō jōdo* 西方浄土

"Wheel of Instruction and Command," (Ch.) *jiao ling lun* 教令輪

wisdom, (Skt.) *prajñā,* (Pāli) *paññā*

womb, (Jpn.) *taizō* 胎蔵

word of the Buddha, (Skt.) *buddhavacana*

Wuzong (Ch.), 武宗 (r. 841–846), Tang emperor

X

Y

yantra (Skt.), geometric diagrams, for ritual use

Yixing (Ch.), 673–727, 一行

yoga tantras (Skt.), tantras that focus on yogic practices

Yogācāra (Skt., lit. "accomplishment of yoga"), school of medieval Indian Buddhist systematic thought

yulanben (Ch.), ghost festivals, (Jpn.) *urabon* 盂蘭盆, or more popularly, *o-bon*

Z

Zhiyi (Ch.) 538–597, 智顗

zong (Ch.), 宗 (Jpn.) *shū*

Bibliography

Note: When Japanese names are given in the literature in traditional form, that is, family name first, followed by given name, the family name is indicated by small caps.

A

Abé, Ryuichi. "Saichō and Kūkai: A Conflict of Interpretations." *Japanese Journal of Religious Studies* 22.1–2 (1995): 103–137.

Abé, Ryuichi. *The Weaving of Mantra: Kūkai and the Construction of Esoteric Buddhist Discourse*. New York: Columbia University Press, 1999.

Abhayadatta, *Buddha's Lions: The Lives of the Eighty-Four Siddhas*. Translated by James B. Robinson. Berkeley, CA: Dharma Publishing, 1979.

Achard, Jean-Luc. *L'Essence Perlée du Secret: Recherches philologiques et historiques sur l'origine de la Grande Perfection dans la tradition rNying ma pa*. Turnhout, Belgium: Brepols, 1999.

Acri, Andrea. *Dharma Pātañjala: A Śaiva Scripture from Ancient Java*. Groningen: Egbert Forsten, 2011.

Acri, Andrea, ed. *Esoteric Buddhism in Medieval Maritime Asia: Networks of Masters, Texts, Icons*. Singapore: ISEAS Yusof Ishak Institute, 2016.

Acri, Andrea. "Introduction: Esoteric Buddhist Networks along the Maritime Silk Routes, 7th–13th Century AD." In *Esoteric Buddhism in Medieval Maritime Asia: Networks of Masters, Texts, Icons*, edited by Andrea Acri, 1–25. Singapore: ISEAS Yusof Ishak Institute, 2016.

Acri, Andrea. "Once More on the 'Ratu Boko Mantra': Magic, Realpolitik, and Bauddha-Śaiva Dynamics in Ancient Nusantara." In *Esoteric Buddhism in Medieval Maritime Asia: Networks of Masters, Texts, Icons*, edited by Andrea Acri, 323–348. Singapore: ISEAS Yusof Ishak Institute, 2016.

Acri, Andrea. "Revisiting the Cult of 'Śiva-Buddha' in Java and Bali." In *Buddhist Dynamics in Premodern and Early Modern Southeast Asia*, edited by Christian Lammerts, 261–282. Singapore: Institute of Southeast Asian Studies, 2015.

Acri, Andrea, and Peter Sharrock, eds. *The Creative South: Buddhist and Hindu Art in Medieval Maritime Asia*. 2 vols. Singapore: ISEAS Yusof Ishak Institute, 2022.

Acri, Andrea, and Peter Sharrock. "Introduction, Volume I: Intra-Asian Transfers and Mainland Southeast Asia." In *The Creative South: Buddhist and Hindu Art in Medieval Maritime Asia*, 2 vols., edited by Andrea Acri and Peter Sharrock, 1–6. Singapore: ISEAS Yusof Ishak Institute, 2022.

Albanese, Catherine L. *A Republic of Mind and Spirit: A Cultural History of American Metaphysical Religion*. New Haven, CT: Yale University Press, 2007.

Allione, Tsultrim. *Feeding Your Demons: Ancient Wisdom for Resolving Inner Conflict*. New York: Little Brown, 2008.

Almond, Philip C. *The British Discovery of Buddhism*. Cambridge: Cambridge University Press, 1988.

Ama, Michiro. *Immigrants to the Pure Land: The Modernization, Acculturation, and Globalization of Shin Buddhism, 1898–1941*. Honolulu: University of Hawai'i Press, 2011.

Amar, Abhishek Singh. "The Buddhakṣetra of Bodhgaya: Saṅgha, Exchanges, and Trade Networks." In *Religions and Trade: Religious Formation, Transformation and Cross-Cultural Exchange between East and West*, edited by Peter Wick and Volker Rabens, 117–138. Leiden: Brill, 2014.

Ambros, Barbara. *Emplacing a Pilgrimage: The Ōyama Cult and Regional Religion in Early Modern Japan*. Cambridge, MA: Harvard University Press, 2008.

Ambros, Barbara. "Tōzanha Shugendō in the Early Modern Period." In *Esoteric Buddhism and the Tantras in East Asia*, edited by Charles D. Orzech, Henrik Sørensen, and Richard K. Payne, 1018–1023. Leiden: Brill, 2010.

Anālayo. "The Name Theravāda in an Eighteenth–Century Inscription: Reconsidering the Problematization of the Term." In *Śāntamatiḥ: Manuscripts for Live, Essays in Memory of Seishi Karashima*, edited by Noriyuku Kudo, 1–25. Tokyo: International Research Institute for Advance Buddhology, Soka University, 2023.

Anālayo. *Satipaṭṭhāna: The Direct Path to Realization*. Cambridge: Windhorse Publications, 2003.

Andreas, Holger. "Theoretical Terms in Science." In *The Stanford Encyclopedia of Philosophy* (Fall 2017 edition), edited by Edward N. Zalta. https://plato.stanford.edu/archives/fall2017/entries/theoretical-terms-science/.

Andreeva, Anna. *Assembling Shinto: Buddhist Approaches to Kami Worship in Medieval Japan*. Cambridge, MA: Harvard University Asia Center, Harvard University Press, 2017.

Andreeva, Anna, and Dominic Steavu, eds. *Transforming the Void: Embryological Discourse and Reproductive Imagery in East Asian Religions*. Leiden: Brill, 2016.

Andrews, Susan. "Gathering Medicines Among the Cypress: The Relationship Between Healing and Place in the Earliest Records of Mount Wutai." In *What Happened After Mañjuśrī Migrated to China? The Sinification of the Mañjuśrī Faith and the Globalization of the Wutai Cult*, edited by Jinhua Chen, Guang Kuan, and Hu Fo, 37–49. London: Routledge, 2022.

Anthony, David W. *The Horse, the Wheel and Language: How Bronze-Age Riders from the Eurasian Steppes Shaped the Modern World*. Princeton, NJ: Princeton University Press, 2007.

Apple, James B. "Perfections (Six and Ten) of Bodhisattvas in Buddhist Literature." In *Oxford Research Encyclopedia of Religion*, edited by John Barton. Oxford: Oxford University Press, 2016. DOI: 10.1093/acrefore/9780199340378.013.193.

Appleton, Naomi. "The Story of the Horse-King and the Merchant Siṃhala in Buddhist Texts." *Buddhist Studies Review* 23.2 (2006): 187–201. DOI: 10.1558/bsrv.2006.23.2.187.

Arai, Paula. *Bringing Zen Home: The Healing Heart of Japanese Women's Rituals*. Honolulu: University of Hawai'i Press, 2011.

Ardussi, John A. "Brewing and Drinking the Beer of Enlightenment in Tibetan Buddhism: The *Dohā* Tradition in Tibet." *Journal of the American Oriental Society* 97.2 (1977): 115–124.

Arnold, Dan. "The Philosophical Works and Influence of Dignāga and Dharmakīrti." In *The Oxford Encyclopedia of Buddhism*, edited by Richard K. Payne and Georgios Halkias, n.p. Oxford: Oxford University Press, 2017, https://doi.org/10.1093/acrefore/9780199340378.013.198.

Asad, Talal. *Genealogies of Religion: Discipline and Reasons of Power in Christianity and Islam*. Baltimore: Johns Hopkins University Press, 1993.

Asaṅga. *The Bodhisattva Path to Unsurpassed Enlightenment: A Complete Translation of the* Bodhisattvabhūmi. Translated by Artemus B. Engle. Boulder, CO: Snow Lion, 2016.

Assavavirulhakarn, Prapod. *The Ascendancy of Theravāda Buddhism in Southeast Asia*. Chiang Mai, Thailand: Silkworm Books, 2010.

Awakening State. "Buddha Vairocana (Kunrig) Maha Mantra—The Mantra of Light: Meaning and Benefits." May 25, 2023. https://www.awakeningstate.com/spiritual-awakening/buddha-vairocana-maha-mantra-light/.

B

Bacus, Elisabeth A., Ian C. Glover, and Peter D. Sharrock, eds. *Interpreting Southeast Asia's Past: Monument, Image and Text*. Singapore: National University of Singapore Press, 2008.

Bahir, Cody. "Buddhist Master Wuguang's (1918–2000) Taiwanese Web of the Colonial, Exilic and Han." *Electronic Journal of East and Central Asian Religions* 1 (Autumn 2013): 81–93. http://journals.ed.ac.uk/ejecar/issue/view/63.

Bahir, Cody. "From China to Japan and Back Again: An Energetic Example of Bidirectional Sino-Japanese Esoteric Buddhist Transmission." *Religions* 12 (2021): 675. https://doi.org/10.3390/rel12090675.

Bahir, Cody. "Reenchanting Buddhism via Modernizing Magic: Guru Wuguang of Taiwan's Philosophy and Science of Superstition." PhD diss., Leiden University, 2017.

Bahir, Cody. "Reformulating the Appropriated and Relinking the Chain: Challenges of Lineage and Legitimacy in Zhenyan Revival." In *The Hybridity of Buddhism: Contemporary Encounters Between Tibetan and Chinese Traditions in Taiwan and the Mainland*, edited by Fabienne Jagou, 91–108. Paris: École française d'Extrême-Orient, 2018.

Bahir, Cody. "Replanting the Bodhi Tree: Buddhist Sectarianism and Zhenyan Revivalism." *Pacific World: Journal of the Institute of Buddhist Studies*, third series, no. 20 (2018): 95–129.

Bahir, Cody. "Telecommunicative Transmission: Remotely Resurrecting Chinese Esoteric Buddhism." Conference presentation, American Academy of Religions, Nov. 2018, Denver, Colorado.

Barrett, T. H. "Buddhism and Print Culture in China." In *The Oxford Encyclopedia of Buddhism*, edited by Richard K. Payne and Georgios T. Halkias, 319–332. New York: Oxford University Press, 2024; online 2019: https://doi.org/10.1093/acrefore/9780199340378.013.636.

Barrett, T. H. "Northern Wei Wutaishan: An Outside View of Centres and Peripheries." In *What Happened After Mañjuśrī Migrated to China? The Sinification of the Mañjuśrī Faith and the Globalization of the Wutai Cult*, edited by Jinhua Chen, Guang Kuan, and Hu Fo, 77–88. London: Routledge, 2022.

Barron, Richard, trans. and ed. *The Autobiography of Jamgön Kongtrul: A Gem of Many Colors*. Ithaca, NY: Snow Lion, 2003.

Bassnett, Susan. "The Translator as Cross-Cultural Mediator." In *The Oxford Handbook of Translation Studies*, edited by Kirsten Malmkjær and Kevin Windle, 94–107. New York: Oxford University Press, 2011. DOI:10.1093/oxfordhb/9780199239306.013.0008.

Baumann, Martin. "Culture Contact and Valuation: Early German Buddhists and the Creation of a 'Buddhism in Protestant Shape.'" *Numen* XLIV (1997): 270–295.

Baumann, Martin. "Global Buddhism: Developmental Periods, Regional Histories, and a New Analytical Perspective." *Journal of Global Buddhism* 2 (2001): 1–43.

Beane, Wendell Charles. *Myth, Cult and Symbols in Śākta Hinduism: A Study of the Indian Mother Goddess*. Leiden: E.J. Brill, 1977.

Becerra, Gaston. "Tantric Buddhists in Buenos Aires: A Case Study of Secular Religiosity Among Young People." *The International Journal of Religion and Spirituality in Society* 1.2 (2011): 97–102.

Beckford, James A. *Social Theory and Religion*. Cambridge: Cambridge University Press, 2003.

Beckwith, Christopher I. *Empires of the Silk Road: A History of Central Eurasia from the Bronze Age to the Present*. Princeton, NJ: Princeton University Press, 2009.

Beckwith, Christopher I. *The Tibetan Empire in Central Asia*. Princeton, NJ: Princeton University Press, 1987.

Beckwith, Christopher I. *Warriors of the Cloisters: The Central Asian Origins of Science in the Medieval World*. Princeton, NJ: Princeton University Press, 2012.

Beinorius, Audrius. "Buddhism in the Early European Imagination: A Historical Perspective." *Acta Orientalia Vilnensia* 6.2 (2005): 7–22.

Beiser, Frederick. *Hegel*. New York: Routledge, 2005.

Bell, Catherine. *Ritual Theory, Ritual Practice.* Oxford: Oxford University Press, 1992.

Bell, Christopher. "Tibetan Demonology." In *Oxford Research Encyclopedias.* New York: Oxford University Press, online 2020. https://doi.org/10.1093/acrefore/9780199340378.013.700.

Bell, Sandra. "'Crazy Wisdom,' Charisma, and the Transmission of Buddhism in the United States." *Nova Religio: The Journal of Alternative and Emergent Religions* 2.1 (October 1999): 55–75.

Bentor, Yael. "Interiorized Fire Rituals in India and in Tibet." *Journal of the American Oriental Society* 120.4 (Oct./Dec., 2000): 594–613.

Berkwitz, Stephen C. *South Asian Buddhism: A Survey.* London: Routledge, 2010.

Bernstein, Anya. *Religious Bodies Politic: Rituals of Sovereignty in Buryat Buddhism.* Chicago: University of Chicago Press, 2013.

Bessenger, Suzanne M. *Echoes of Enlightenment: The Life and Legacy of Sönam Peldren.* Oxford: Oxford University Press, 2016.

Beyer, Peter. "The Religious System of Global Society: A Sociological Look at Contemporary Religion and Religions." *Numen: International Review for the History of Religions* 45 (1998): 1–29.

Beyer, Stephan. *The Cult of Tārā: Magic and Ritual in Tibet.* Berkeley: University of California Press, 1973.

Bianchi, Ester. "The Tantric Rebirth Movement in Modern China: Esoteric Buddhism Re-Vivified by the Japanese and Tibetan Traditions." *Acta Orientalia Academiae Scientiarum Hung* 57.1 (2004): 31–54.

Birnbaum, Raoul. "Secret Halls of the Mountain Lords: The Caves of Wu-t'ai shan." *Cahiers d'Extrême-Asie* 5 (1989): 115–140. https://doi.org/10.3406/asie.1989.945.

Bishop, Peter. *Dreams of Power: Tibetan Buddhism and the Western Imagination.* London: The Athlone Press, 1993.

Blackburn, Anne M. "Buddha-Relics in the Lives of Southern Asian Polities." *Numen* 57.3/4 (2010): 317–340.

Blackburn, Anne M. "Looking for the *Vinaya*: Monastic Disciplines in the Practical Canons of the Theravāda." *Journal of the International Association of Buddhist Studies* 22.2 (1999): 281–309.

Blackburn, Anne M. "Writing Buddhist Histories from Landscape and Architecture: Sukhotai and Chiang Mai." *Buddhist Studies Review* 24.2 (2007): 192–225.

Blofeld, John. *The Tantric Mysticism of Tibet: A Practical Guide to the Theory, Purpose, and Techniques of Tantric Meditation.* 1970. Reprint. New York: Arkana, 1992.

Blum, Mark. *The Origins and Development of Pure Land Buddhism: A Study and Translation of Gyōnen's* Jōdo Hōmon Genrushō. New York: Oxford University Press, 2002.

Bodiford, William M. "Zen and Esoteric Buddhism." In *Esoteric Buddhism and the Tantras in East Asia,* edited by Charles D. Orzech, Henrik H. Sørensen, and Richard K. Payne, 924–935. Leiden: Brill, 2011.

Bodman, Richard Wainwright. "Poetics and Prosody in Early Mediaeval China: A Study and Translation of Kūkai's *Bunkyō Hifuron.*" PhD diss., Cornell University, 1978.

Bogel, Cynthea J. "Canonizing Kannon: The Ninth-Century Esoteric Buddhist Altar at Kanshinji." *The Art Bulletin* 84.1 (March 2002): 30–64.

Bolle, Kees W. *The Persistence of Religion: An Essay on Tantrism and Sri Aurobindo's Philosophy.* Studies in the History of Religions, VIII. Leiden: E.J. Brill, 1971.

Bond, George D. "Theravada Buddhism's Meditations on Death and the Symbolism of Initiatory Death." *History of Religions* 19.3 (Feb. 1980): 237–258.

Boon, James A. *Affinities and Extremes: Crisscrossing the Bittersweet Ethnology of East Indies History, Hindu-Balinese Culture, and Indo-European Allure.* Chicago: Chicago University Press, 1990.

Boord, Martin. "The Vajrakīla Tantras." In *The Oxford Encyclopedia of Buddhism,* edited by Richard K. Payne and Georgios T. Halkias, 2635–2656. Oxford: Oxford University Press, 2024; online 2019: https://doi.org/10.1093/acrefore/9780199340378.013.555.

Borchert, Thomas. "The Sangha as an Institution." In *The Oxford Encyclopedia of Buddhism*, edited by Richard K. Payne and Georgios T. Halkias, 2061–2075. New York: Oxford University Press, 2024. https://doi.org/10.1093/acrefore/9780199340378.013.194.

Boucher, Daniel. *Bodhisattvas of the Forest and the Formation of the Mahāyāna: A Study and Translation of the Rāṣṭapālaparipṛcchā-sūtra*. Honolulu: University of Hawai'i Press, 2008.

Bowring, Richard. *The Religious Traditons of Japan, 500–1600*. Cambridge: Cambridge University Press, 2005.

Boyer, Pascal. "Explaining Religious Ideas: Elements of a Cognitive Approach." *Numen* 39.1 (1992): 27–57.

Braitstein, Lara. *The Adamantine Songs:* Vajragitī. New York: American Institute of Buddhist Studies at Columbia University, 2014.

Braitstein, Lara. "The Direct Path: Saraha's Adamantine Songs and the Bka' brgyud Great Seal." In *Mahāmudrā and the Bka'-brgyud Tradition*, edited by Roger R. Jackson and Matthew T. Kapstein. Andiast, Switzerland: International Institute for Tibetan and Buddhist Studies GmbH, 2011. (The title given on the Table of Contents differs, reading "The Extraordinary Path"; however, the author indicates that the title on the first page of the essay itself is the correct one. Personal communication, email, July 27, 2020.)

Braitstein, Lara. "Exploring Saraha's Treasury of Adamantine Songs." *The Tibet Journal* 33.1 (Spring 2008): 40–65.

Braitstein, Lara. "Saraha's Adamantine Songs: Texts, Contexts, Translations and Traditions of the Great Seal." PhD diss., McGill University, 2004.

Brauen, Martin, ed. *Les Dalaï-Lamas: Les 134 réincarnations du bodhisattva Avalokiteśvara*. Lausanne: Éditions Favre, 2005.

Bretfeld, Sven. "Theravāda Buddhism." In *The Oxford Encyclopedia of Buddhism*, edited by Richard K. Payne and Georgios Halkias, n.p. Oxford: Oxford University Press. https://doi.org/10.1093/acrefore/9780199340378.013.561.

Brinker, Helmut. "Facing the Unseen: On the Interior Adornment of Eizon's Iconic Body." *Archives of Asian Art* 50 (1997/1998): 42–61.

Brock, Karen L. "Awaiting Maitreya at Kasagi." In *Maitreya, the Future Buddha*, edited by Alan Sponberg and Helen Hardacre, 214–247. Cambridge: Cambridge University Press, 1988.

Brooks, Douglas Renfrew. *The Secret of the Three Cities: An Introduction to Hindu Śākta Tantrism*. Chicago: University of Chicago Press, 1990.

Brown, Candy Gunther. *Debating Yoga and Mindfulness in Public Schools: Reforming Secular Education or Reestablishing Religion?* Chapel Hill: University of North Carolina Press, 2019.

Brown, Daniel. *Pointing out the Great Way: The Stages of Meditation in the Mahamudra Tradition*. Boston: Wisdom Publications, 2006.

Bryant, Edwin. *The Quest for the Origins of Vedic Culture: The Indo-Aryan Migration Debate*. Oxford: Oxford University Press, 2001.

Bryant, Edwin F., and Laurie L. Patton, eds. *The Indo-Aryan Controversy: Evidence and inference in Indian History*. London: Routledge, 2005.

Bryson, Megan. "Buddhist Geography and Regionalism." In *Oxford Research Encyclopedia of Religion*. New York: Oxford University Press, 2018. DOI: 10.1093/acrefore/9780199340378.013.626.

Bryson, Megan. "Mahākāla Worship in the Dali Kingdom (937–1253): A Study and Translation of the *Dahei tianshen daochang yi*." *Journal of the International Association of Buddhist Studies* 35.1–2 (2013): 3–69.

Buddhaghosa. *The Path of Purification (Visuddhimagga)*. Translated by Bhikkhu Ñāṇamoli. 1975. Reprint. Seattle: BPS Pariyatti Editions, 1991.

Bühnemann, Gudrun. "Bhairava and the Eight Charnel Grounds: On the History of a Monumental Painting at the Jayavāgīśvarī Temple, Kathmandu." *Berlin Indological Studies* 21 (2013): 307–326.

Bühnemann, Gudrun. "Buddhist Deities and Mantras in the Hindu Tantras: I The *Tantrasārasaṃgraha* and the *Īśānaśivagurudevapaddhati*." *Indo-Iranian Journal* 42.4 (1999): 303–334.

Bühnemann, Gudrun. "Buddhist Deities and Mantras in the Hindu Tantras: II The *Śrīvidyārṇavatantra* and the *Tantrasāra*." *Indo-Iranian Journal* 43.1 (2000): 27–48.

Bühnemann, Gudrun, ed. *Maṇḍalas and Yantras in the Hindu Traditions*. Brill's Indological Library, vol. 18. Leiden: Brill, 2003.

Burchett, Patton E. "The 'Magical' Language of Mantra." *Journal of the American Academy of Religion* 76.4 (December 2008): 807–843.

Burnouf, Eugène. *Introduction to the History of Indian Buddhism*. Translated by Katia Buffetrille and Donald S. Lopez, Jr. Chicago: University of Chicago Press, 2010.

Buswell, Robert E., Jr., ed. *Encyclopedia of Buddhism*. 2 vols. New York: Macmillan, 2004.

C

Cabezón, José Ignacio, and Penpa Dorjee. *Sera Monastery*. Boston: Wisdom Publications, 2019.

Campany, Robert F. "Buddhist Revelation and Taoist Translation in Early Medieval China." *Taoist Resources* 4.1 (1993): 1–29.

Campo, Juan E. "Religious Pilgrimages in the United States." In *Oxford Research Encyclopedias, Religion*, edited by John Barton. New York: Oxford University Press, online 2017. https://doi.org/10.1093/acrefore/9780199340378.013.483.

Casparis, J. G. de, and I. W. Mabbett. "Religion and Popular Beliefs in Southeast Asia before c. 1500." In *The Cambridge History of Southeast Asia*, vol. 1: From Early Times to c. 1800, edited by Nicholas Tarling, 276–339. Cambridge: Cambridge University Press, 1992.

Chandler, Jeannine. "Invoking the Dharma Protector: Western Involvement in the Dorje Shugden Controversy." In *Buddhism Beyond Borders: New Perspectives on Buddhism in the United States*, edited by Scott A. Mitchell and Natalie E. F. Quli, 75–91. Albany: State University of New York Press, 2015.

Chandler, Stuart. "Spreading Buddha's Light: The Internationalization of Foguang Shan." In *Buddhist Missionaries in the Era of Globalization*, edited by Linda Learman, 162–184. Honolulu: University of Hawai'i Press, 2005.

Chandra, Lokesh. *The Thousand-Armed Avalokiteśvara*. New Delhi: Indira Gandhi National Centre for the Arts, 1988.

Charters, Ann. *Kerouac: A Biography*. San Francisco, CA: Straight Arrow Books, 1973.

Chemburkar, Swati. "Borobudur's Pāla Forebear? A Field Note from Kesariya, Bihar, India." In *Esoteric Buddhism in Mediaeval Maritime Asia: Networks of Masters, Texts, Icons*, edited by Andrea Acri, 191–209. Singapore: ISEAS Yusuf Ishak Institute, 2016.

Chemburkar, Swati. "*Stūpa* to *Maṇḍala*: Tracing a Buddhist Architectural Development from Kesariya to Borobudur to Tabo." *Pacific World: Journal of the Institute of Buddhist Studies* third series, no. 20 (2018): 169–221.

Chemburkar, Swati. "Tantra and Temple Architecture in Buddhist Southeast Asia." In *The Oxford Handbook of Tantric Studies*, edited by Richard K. Payne and Glen T. Hayes, 581–677. Oxford: Oxford University Press, 2024.

Chen, Jianmin. "Buddhist Meditation: Systematic and Practical, CW 35 Introduction." First published privately by Upasaka Khoo Poh Kong, Malaysia, 1967; online: http://www.yogichen.org/cw/cw35/bm00.html.

Chen, Jinhua. "A Chemical 'Explosion' Triggered by an Encounter Between Indian and Chinese Medical Sciences: Another Look at the Significances of the Sinhalese Monk Śākyamitra's (567?–668+) Visit at Mount Wutai in 667." In *What Happened After Mañjuśrī Migrated to China? The Sinification of the Mañjuśrī Faith and the Globalization of the Wutai Cult*, edited by Jinhua Chen, Guang Kuan, and Hu Fo, 3–18. London: Routledge, 2022.

Chen, Jinhua. "The Construction of Early Tendai Esoteric Buddhism: The Japanese Provenance of Saichō's Transmission Documents and Three Esoteric Buddhist Apocrypha Attributed to Śubhākarasiṁha." *Journal of the International Association of Buddhist Studies* 21.1 (1998): 21–76.

Chen, Jinhua. *Crossfire: Shingon-Tendai Strife as Seen in Two Twelfth-century Polemics, with Special References to Their Background in Tang China*. Tokyo: International Institute for Buddhist Studies, 2010.

Chen, Jinhua. *Legend and Legitimation: The Formation of Tendai Esoteric Buddhism in Japan*. Brussels: Institut Belge des Hautes Études Chinoises, 2009.

Ch'en, Kenneth. *Buddhism in China: A Historical Survey*. Princeton, NJ: Princeton University Press, 1972.

Chetsang, Drikung Kyabgon. *The Practice of Mahamudra*. Translated by Robert Clark. Edited by Ani K. Trinlay Chödron. Ithaca, NY: Snow Lion, 1999.

Chidester, David. *Authentic Fakes: Religion and American Popular Culture*. Berkeley: University of California Press, 2005.

Chidester, David. *Religion: Material Dynamics*. Oakland: University of California Press, 2018.

Chidester, David. *Savage Systems: Colonialism and Comparative Religion in Southern Africa*. Charlottesville: University of Virginia Press, 1996.

Ching, Leo. "Globalizing the Regional, Regionalizing the Global: Mass Culture and Asianism in the Age of Late Capital." In *Globalization*, edited by Arjun Appadurai, 279–306. Durham, NC: Duke University Press, 2001.

Christian, David. "Silk Roads or Steppe Roads? the Silk Roads in World History." *Journal of World History* 11.1 (Spring 2000): 1–26.

Cintula, Petr, Christian G. Fermüller, and Carles Noguer. "Fuzzy Logic." In *The Stanford Encyclopedia of Philosophy* (Fall 2017 edition), edited by Edward N. Zalta. https://plato.stanford.edu/archives/fall2017/entries/logic-fuzzy/.

Clark, Joyce, ed. *Bayon: New Perspectives*. Bangkok: River Books, 2007.

Clausen, Christopher. "Victorian Buddhism and the Origins of Comparative Religion." *Religion* 5.1 (1975): 1–15.

Coedès, G(eorge). *The Indianized States of Southeast Asia*. Edited by Walter F. Vella. Translated by Sue Brown Cowing. Honolulu: University of Hawai'i Press, 1968.

Cohen, Richard. *Beyond Enlightenment: Buddhism, Religion, Modernity*. London: Routledge, 2006.

Col, Cynthia. "Picturing the Canon: The Murals, Sculpture, and Architecture of the Derge Parkhang." PhD diss., Graduate Theological Union, Berkeley, 2009.

Collins, Steven. "On the Very Idea of the Pāli Canon." *Journal of the Pali Text Society* 15 (1990): 89–126.

Copp, Paul. "Altar, Amulet, Icon: Transformation of *Dhāraṇī* Culture, 740–980." *Cahiers d'Extrême-Asie* 17 (2008): 239–264.

Copp, Paul. *The Body Incantatory: Spells and the Ritual Imagination in Medieval Chinese Buddhism*. New York: Columbia University Press, 2014.

Copp, Paul. "Voice, Dust, Shadow, Stone: The Making of Spells in Medieval Chinese Buddhism." PhD diss., Princeton University, 2005.

Cousins, L. S. "Aspects of Esoteric Southern Buddhism." In *Indian Insights: Buddhism, Brahmanism, and Bhakti*, edited by Peter Connolly and Sue Hamilton, 185–207. London: Luzac Oriental, 1997.

Cozort, Daniel. *Highest Yoga Tantra: An Introduction to the Esoteric Buddhism of Tibet*. Ithaca, NY: Snow Lion, 1986.

Crosby, Kate. *Esoteric Theravada: The Story of the Forgotten Meditation Tradition of Southeast Asia*. Boulder, CO: Shambhala, 2021.

Crosby, Kate. "History Versus Modern Myth: The Abhayagirivihāra, the *Vimuttimagga* and *Yogāvacara* Meditation." *Journal of Indian Philosophy* 27 (1999): 503–550.

Crosby, Kate. "Tantric Theravāda: A Bibliographic Essay on the Writings of François Bizot and others on the Yogāvacara Tradition." *Contemporary Buddhism* 1.2 (2000): 141–198.

Crosby, Kate. *Traditional Theravada Meditation and Its Modern-Era Suppression*. Hong Kong: Buddha Dharma Centre of Hong Kong, 2013.

Cruijsen, Thomas, Arlo Griffiths, and Marijke J. Klokke. "The Cult of the Buddhist *dhāraṇī* Deity Mahāpratisarā Along the Maritime Silk Route: New Epigraphical and Iconographic Evidence from the Indonesian Archipelago." *Journal of the International Association of Buddhist Studies* 35.1–2 (2012 [2013]): 71–157.

Csordas, Thomas J. "Introduction: Modalities of Transnational Transcendence." In *Transnational Transcendence: Essays on Religion and Globalization*, edited by Thomas J. Csordas, 1–29. Berkeley: University of California Press, 2009.

D

Dachille, Rae Erin. *Searching for the Body: A Contemporary Perspective on Tibetan Buddhist Tantra*. New York: Columbia University Press, 2022.

Dalton, Jacob P. *Conjuring the Buddha: Ritual Manuals in Early Tantric Buddhism*. New York: Columbia University Press, 2023.

Dalton, Jacob P. "A Crisis of Doxography: How Tibetans Organized Tantra During the 8th–12th Centuries." *Journal of the International Association of Buddhist Studies* 28.1 (2005): 115–181.

Dalton, Jacob P. "The Development of Perfection: The Interiorization of Buddhist Ritual in Eighth and Ninth Centuries." *Journal of Indian Philosophy* 32 (2004): 1–30.

Dalton, Jacob P. *The Gathering of Intentions: A History of Tibetan Tantra*. New York: Columbia University Press, 2016.

Dalton, Jacob P. "How Dhāraṇīs WERE Proto-Tantric: Liturgies, Ritual Manuals, and the Origins of the Tantras." In *Tantric Traditions on the Move*, edited by David B. Gray and Ryan Overbey, 199–229. Oxford: Oxford University Press, 2016.

Dalton, Jacob P. *The Taming of the Demons: Violence and Liberation in Tibetan Buddhism*. New Haven, CT: Yale University Press, 2011.

Dargyay, Eva M. *The Rise of Esoteric Buddhism in Tibet*. Delhi: Motilal Banarsidass, 1977.

Datta, Rajeshwari. "The Religious Aspects of the Bāul Songs of Bengal." *Journal of Asian Studies* 37.3 (May 1978): 445–455. DOI: 10.2307/2053571.

David-Neel, Alexandra. *Magic and Mystery in Tibet: Discovering the Spiritual Beliefs, Traditions and Customs of Tibetan Buddhist Lamas*. French 1929, English 1932. Reprint. New York: Dover Publication, 1971.

Davidson, Ronald M. "Abhiṣeka." In *Esoteric Buddhism and the Tantras in East Asia*, edited by Charles D. Orzech, Henrik H. Sørensen, and Richard K. Payne, 71–75. Leiden: Brill, 2011.

Davidson, Ronald M. "Esoteric Buddhism in the Matrix of Early Medieval India: An Overview." In *On the Regional Development of Early Medieval Buddhist Monasteries in South Asia*, edited by Abhishek Singh Amar, Nicolas Morrisey, and Akira Shimada, 1–40. RINDAS Series of Working Papers, #34. Kyoto: Ryukoku University, 2021.

Davidson, Ronald M. *Indian Esoteric Buddhism: A Social History of the Tantric Movement*. New York: Columbia University Press, 2002.

Davidson, Ronald M. "Initiation (*Abhiṣeka*) in Indian Buddhism." In *The Oxford Handbook of Tantric Studies*, edited by Richard K. Payne and Glen A. Hayes. Oxford: Oxford University Press, 2024.

Davidson, Ronald M. "The *Litany of Names of Mañjuśrī*: Text and Translation of the *Mañj uśrīnāmasaṃgīti*." In *Tantric and Taoist Studies in Honour of R.A. Stein*, edited by Michel Strickmann, 1–69. Brussels: Institut Belge des Hautes Études Chinoises, 1981.

Davidson, Ronald M. "Magicians, Sorcerers and Witches: Considering Pretantric, Non-sectarian Sources of Tantric Practices." *Religions* 8.188 (2017).

Davidson, Ronald M. "More Pre-Tantric Souces of Tantrism: Skulls and Skull-cups." In *Tantra, Magic, and Vernacular Religions in Monsoon Asia: Texts, Practices, and Practitioners from the Margins*, edited by Andrea Acri and Paolo E. Rosati, 12–39. London: Routledge, 2023.

Davidson, Ronald M. "The Place of *Abhiṣeka* Visualization in the *Yogalehrbuch* and Related Texts." In *From Turfan to Ajanta: Festschrift for Dieter Schlinghoff on the Occasion of*

His Eightieth Birthday, edited by Eli Franco and Monika Dix, 185–198. Bhairahawa, Nepal: Lumbini International Research Institute, 2011.

Davidson, Ronald M. "The Problem of Secrecy in Indian Tantric Buddhism." In *The Culture of Secrecy in Japanese Religion*, edited by Bernhard Scheid and Mark Teeuwen, 60–77. London: Routledge, 2006.

Davidson, Ronald M. "Reflections on the Maheśvara Subjugation Myth: Indic Materials, Sa-skya-pa Apologetics, and the Birth of Heruka." *Journal of the International Association of Buddhist Studies* 14.2 (1991): 197–235.

Davidson, Ronald M. "Reframing *Sahaja*: Genre, Representation, Ritual and Lineage." *Journal of Indian Philosophy* 30 (2002): 45–83.

Davidson, Ronald M. "Studies in Dhāraṇī Literature I: Revisiting the Meaning of the Term *Dhāraṇī*." *Journal of Indian Philosophy* 37.2 (April 2009): 97–147. DOI: 10.1007/s10781-008-9054-8.

Davidson, Ronald M. "Studies in *Dhāraṇī* Literature III: Seeking the Parameters of a *Dhāraṇī-piṭaka*, the Formation of the *Dhāraṇīsaṃgrahas*, and the Place of the Seven Buddhas." In *Scripture:Canon::Text:Context: Essays Honoring Lewis Lancaster*, edited by Richard K. Payne, 119–180. Berkeley, CA: Institute of Buddhist Studies and BDK/America, 2014.

Davidson, Ronald M. *Tibetan Renaissance: Tantric Buddhism in the Rebirth of Tibetan Culture.* New York: Columbia University Press, 2005.

Davidson, Ronald M., and Christian K. Wedemeyer, eds. *Tibetan Buddhist Literature and Praxis: Studies in Its Formative Period, 900–1400.* Brill's Tibetan Studies Library, vol. 10/4. Leiden: Brill, 2006.

Davis, Winston. "Pilgrimage and World Renewal: A Study of Religion and Social Values in Tokugawa Japan." 2 parts. *History of Religions* 23.2 (November 1983): 97–116, and 23.3 (February 1984): 197–221.

Dawson, Lorne. "Church–Sect–Cult: Constructing Typologies of Religious Groups." In *The Oxford Handbook of the Sociology of Religion*, edited by Peter B. Clarke, 525–544. New York: Oxford University Press, 2009. doi.org/10.1093/oxfordhb/9780199588961.001.0001.

de Jong, Albert. "Secrets and Secrecy in the Study of Religion: Comparative Views from the Ancient World." In *The Culture of Secrecy in Japanese Religions*, edited by Scheid and Teeuwen, 37–59. Milton Park, UK: Routledge, 2006.

de Kleen, Tyra. *Mudrās: The Ritual Hand-Poses of the Buddha Priests and Shiva Priests of Bali.* 1924. Reprint. New York: University Books, 1970.

Deeg, Max. "Chinese Buddhist Travelers: Faxian, Xuanzang, and Yijing." In *The Oxford Research Encyclopedia of Asian History*, n.p. New York: Oxford University Press, online 2019. https://doi.org/10.1093/acrefore/9780190277727.013.217.

Delhey, Martin. "The Textual Sources of the *Mañjuśrīyamūlakalpa* (*Mañjuśrīmūlakalpa*), with Special Reference to Its Early Nepalese Witness NGMPP A39/4." *Journal of the Nepal Research Center* XIV (2012): 55–75.

Dempster, Lisa. *Neon Pilgrim.* Victoria, Australia: aduki independent press, 2009.

des Jardins, J. F. Marc. *Le sūtra de la Mahāmāyūrī: rituel et politique dans la Chine des Tang (618–907)*. Québec: Les Presses de L'Université Laval, 2011.

Devitt, Michael. "Scientific Realism." In *The Oxford Handbook of Contemporary Philosophy*, edited by Frank Jackson and Michael Smith, 767–791. Oxford: Oxford University Press, 2007. DOI: 10.1093/oxfordhb/9780199234769.003.0026.

Dhargyey, Ngawang. "The Life of Atisha." http://www.berzinarchives.com/web/en/archives/approaching_buddhism/teachers/lineage_masters/life_atisha.html.

Dharmachakra Translation Committee, trans. "Destroyer of the Great Trichiliocosm." *Mahāsāhasrapramardanīnāsūtra*, Toh. 558. 84000: Translating the Words of the Buddha, 2016. https://read.84000.co/translation/UT22084-090-002.html.

Dharmachakra Translation Committee, trans. "The Dhāraṇī 'Essence of Immeasurable Longevity and Wisdom.'" *Aparimitāyurjñānahṛdayadhāraṇī*, Toh. 676. 84000: Translating the Words of the Buddha. https://read.84000.co/translation/toh676.html.

Dharmachakra Translation Committee, trans. "The Dhāraṇī of the Tathāgata Jñānolka." *Jñānolkadhāraṇī*, Toh. 522. 84000 Translating the Words of the Buddha, 2020. https://read.84000.co/translation/toh522.html.

Dharmachakra Translation Committee, trans. "The Discourse of the Dhāraṇī of the Buddha's Essence." *Buddhahṛdayadhāraṇīdharmaparyāya*, Toh. 514. 84000: Translating the Words of the Buddha, 2020. https://read.84000.co/translation/toh514.html.

Dharmachakra Translation Committee, trans. "Great Upholder of the Secret Mantra." *Mahāmantrānudhāriṇī*, Toh. 563. 84000: Translating the Words of the Buddha, 2016. https://read.84000.co/translation/UT22084-090-007.html.

Dharmachakra Translation Committee, trans. "The Queen of Incantations: The Great Peahen." *Mahāmāyūrīvidyārājñī*, Toh. 559. 84000: Translating the Words of the Buddha, 2023. https://read.84000.co/translation/toh559.html.

Dharmachakra Translation Committee, trans. "The Root Manual of the Rites of Mañjuśrī." *Mañjuśrīmūlakalpa*, Toh. 543. 84000: Translating the Words of the Buddha, 2020. https://84000.co/translation/toh543.

Diagne, Souleymane Bachir. "Négritude." In *The Stanford Encyclopedia of Philosophy* (Summer 2018 edition), edited by Edward N. Zalta. https://plato.stanford.edu/archives/sum2018/entries/negritude/.

Dibeltulo, Martino. "The Revival of Tantrism: Tibetan Buddhism and Modern China." PhD diss., The University of Michigan, 2015.

Dickson, Alnis. "Organizing Religion: Situating the Three-Vow Texts of the Tibetan Buddhist Renaissance." Thesis, McGill University, 2009.

Diemberger, Hildegard. "The First Samding Dorje Pakmo, Chokyi Dronma." *Treasury of Lives* BCRC P2CZ7891 (2014). https://treasuryoflives.org/biographies/view/First-Samding-Dorje-Pakmo-Chokyi-Dronma/13205.

Diemberger, Hildegard. *When a Woman Becomes a Religious Dynasty: The* Samding Dorje Phagmo *of Tibet*. New York: Columbia University Press, 2007.

Dirks, Nicholas B. *Castes of Mind: Colonialism and the Making of Modern India*. Princeton, NJ: Princeton University Press, 2001.

Divall, Jennifer. "Empty Stone Caves and Celestial Palaces: Embedding the Transcendent in the Tibetan Landscape in Godrakpa's 'Songs of Realization.'" *The Tibet Journal* 39.2 (Autumn/Winter 2014): 37–56.

Dobbins, James. "The Biography of Shinran: Apotheosis of a Japanese Buddhist Visionary." *History of Religions* 30.2 (Nov. 1990): 179–196.

Dolce, Lucia. "Criticism and Appropriation: Nichiren's Attitude Toward Esoteric Buddhism." *Japanese Journal of Religious Studies* 26.3/4 (Fall 1999): 349–382.

Doney, Lewis. "Early Bodhisattva-Kingship in Tibet: The Case of Tri Songdétsen." *Cahiers d'Extrême-Asie* 24 (2015): 29–47.

Doniger, Wendy. *The Hindus: An Alternative History*. New York: Penguin Press, 2009.

Donnelly, Paul B. "Pilgrimage in Buddhist Tibet." *Oxford Research Encyclopedia of Religion*. Oxford: Oxford University Press, 2018. DOI: 10.1093/acrefore/9780199340378.013.625.

Dorje, Gyurme. "The Guhyagarbhatantra and Its XIVth Century Commentary *phyogs-bcu mun-sel*." PhD diss., School of Oriental and African Studies, University of London, 1987.

Dowman, Keith. *The Divine Madman: The Sublime Life and Songs of Drukpa Kunley*. Clear Lake, CA: Dawn Horse Press, 1980.

Dowman, Keith. *Masters of Mahamudra: Songs and Histories of the Eighty-Four Buddhist Siddhas*. Albany: State University of New York Press, 1985.

Drewes, David. "The Forest Hypothesis." In *Setting out on the Great Way: Essays on Early Mahāyāna Buddhism*, edited by Paul Harrison, 73–93. Sheffield, UK: Equinox, 2018.

Dreyfus, George. "The Shuk-den Affair: History and Nature of a Quarrel." *Journal of the International Association of Buddhist Studies* 21.2 (1998): 227–270.

Drummond, Donald. "Negotiating Influence: The Pilgrimage Diary of Monastic Imperial Prince Kakuhō—*Omurogosho Kōyasan gosanrō nikki*. PhD diss., Graduate Theological Union, Berkeley, 2007.

Dubuisson, Daniel. *The Western Construction of Religion: Myths, Knowledge, and Ideology*. Translated by William Sayers. Baltimore: Johns Hopkins University Press, 2003.

Dumoulin, Heinrich. *Zen Buddhism: A History. Volume 1: India and China*. Translated by James W. Heisig and Paul Knitter. New York: Macmillan, 1988.

Dykstra, Yoshiko K. "Miraculous Tales of the Lotus Sutra: The *Dainihonkoku Hokkegenki*." *Monumenta Nipponica* 32.2 (Summer 1977): 189–210.

E

Earhart, H. Byron. *A Religious Study of the Mount Haguro Sect of Shugendō: An Example of Japanese Mountain Religion*. Tokyo: Sophia University, 1970.

Eastman, Elizabeth. "Incense at a Funeral: The Rise and Fall of an American Shingon Temple." In *TransBuddhism: Transmission, Translation, Transformation*, edited by Nalini Bhushan, Jay L. Garfield, and Abraham Zablocki, 69–85. Amherst: University of Massachusetts Press, 2009.

Eckel, Malcolm David. "The Ghost at the Table: On the Study of Buddhism and the Study of Religion." *Journal of the American Academy of Religion* 62.4 (Winter 1994): 1085–1110.

Eddy, Glenys. "A Strand of Contemporary Tantra: Its Discourse and Practice in the FPMT." *Journal of Global Buddhism* 8 (2007): 81–106. http:// https://www.globalbuddhism.org/article/view/1135.

Edou, Jérôme. *Machig Labdrön and the Foundations of Chöd*. Ithaca, NY: Snow Lion, 1996.

Eliade, Mircea. *The Myth of the Eternal Return: Cosmos and History*. 1954. Reprint. Princeton, NJ: Princeton University Press, 2018.

Eliade, Mircea. *The Sacred and The Profane: The Nature of Religion*. Translated by Willard R. Trask. San Diego, CA: Harcourt, Brace, Jovanovich, 1987.

Eliade, Mircea. *Shamanism: Archaic Techniques of Ecstasy*. Princeton, NJ: Princeton University Press, 1964.

Ellis, Thomas B. "Disgusting Bodies, Disgusting Religion: The Biology of Tantra." *Journal of the American Academy of Religion* 79.4 (December 2011): 879–927.

Elverskog, Johan. *Buddhism and Islam on the Silk Road*. Philadelphia: University of Philadelphia Press, 2010.

Elverskog, Johan. "Buddhist and Muslim Interactions in Asian History." In *The Oxford Research Encyclopedias: Asian History*. New York: Oxford University Press, 2019. doi.org/10.1093/acrefore/9780190277727.013.418.

Englehardt, Isrun. "Nazis of Tibet: A Twentieth Century Myth." http://info-buddhism.com/Nazis-of-Tibet-A-Twentieth-Century-Myth_Engelhardt.html.

F

Farmer, Steve, Richard Sproat, and Michael Witzel. "The Collapse of the Indus-Script Thesis: The Myth of a Literate Harappan Civilization" *Electronic Journal of Vedic Studies* 11.2 (2004): 19–57.

Fitzgerald, Timothy. *Discourse on Civility and Barbarity: A Critical History of Religion and Related Categories*. Oxford: Oxford University Press, 2007.

Fitzgerald, Timothy. *The Ideology of Religious Studies*. Oxford: Oxford University Press, 2000.

Flint, Valerie I. J. *The Rise of Magic in Early Medieval Europe*. Princeton, NJ: Princeton University Press, 1991.

Flood, Gavin. *Beyond Phenomenology: Rethinking the Study of Religion*. London: Cassell, 1999.

Flood, Gavin, ed. *The Blackwell Companion to Hinduism*. Oxford: Blackwell, 2003.

Flood, Gavin. *An Introduction to Hinduism*. Cambridge: Cambridge University Press, 1996.

Flood, Gavin. *The Tantric Body: The Secret Tradition of Hindu Religion.* London: I.B. Taurus, 2006.

Fogelin, Lars. "History, Ethnography, and Essentialism: The Archeaology of Religion and Ritual in South Asia." In *The Archaeology of Ritual*, edited by Evangelos Kyriakidis, 23–42. Los Angeles: Cotsen Institute of Archaeology, University of California, Los Angeles, 2007.

Foltz, Richard C. *Religions of the Silk Road: Overland Trade and Cultural Exchange from Antiquity to the Fifteenth Century.* New York: St. Martin's Press, 1999.

Forte, Antonino. *The Hostage An Shigao and His Offspring.* Italian School of East Asian Studies Occasional Papers, no. 6. Kyoto: Istituto Italiano di Cultura Scuola di Studi sull'Asia Orientale, 1995.

Forte, Antonino. "Iranians in China: Buddhism, Zoroastrianism, and Bureaus of Commerce." *Cahiers d'Extrême-Asie* 11 (1999–2000): 277–290. http://www.persee.fr.

Forte, Antonino, ed. *Tang China and Beyond: Studies on East Asia frome the Seventh to the Tenth Century.* Italian School of East Asian Studies Essays, vol. 1. Kyoto: Istituto Italiano de Cultura, Scuola di Studi sull'Asia Orientale, 1988.

Forte, Antonino, and Federico Masini, eds. *A Life Journey to the East: Sinological Studies in Memory of Giuliano Bertuccioli (1923–2001).* Italian School of East Asian Studies Essays, vol. 2. Kyoto: Scuola Italiana di Studi sull'Asia Orientale, 2002.

Fortson, Benjamin W., IV. *Indo-European Language and Culture.* Chichester, UK: Wiley-Blackwell, 2010.

Foulk, Griffith. "The Chan *Zong* in Medieval China: School, Lineage, or What?" *The Pacific World: Journal of the Institute of Buddhist Studies*, n.s. 8 (1992): 18–31; reprinted in Richard K. Payne, ed., *Shin Buddhism: Historical, Textual, and Interpretive Studies*), 25–45. Berkeley, CA: Institute of Buddhist Studies, and the Numata Center for Buddhist Translation and Research, 2007.

Foulk, Griffith. "Ritual in Japanese Zen Buddhism." In *Zen Ritual: Studies of Zen Buddhist Theory in Practice*, edited by Steven Heine and Dale S. Wright, 21–82. Oxford: Oxford University Press, 2008.

Foulk, T. Griffith, and Robert H. Sharf. "On the Ritual Use of Chan Portraiture in Medieval China." In *Chan Buddhism in Ritual Context*, edited by Bernard Faure, 74–150. London: RoutledgeCurzon, 2003.

Foxeus, Niklas. "'I Am the Buddha, the Buddha Is Me': Concentration Meditation and Esoteric Modern Buddhism in Burma/Myanmar." *Numen* 63 (2016): 411–445.

Frankopan, Peter. *The Silk Roads: A New History of the World.* New York: Alfred A Knopf, 2016.

Fronsdal, Gil., trans. *The Dhammapada: A New Translation of the Buddhist Classic with Annotations.* Boston: Shambhala, 2006.

G

Gadamer, Hans Georg. *Truth and Method.* Translated by Joel Weinsheimer and Donald G. Marshall. Rev. 2nd ed. 2004. London: Bloomsbury, 2013.

Gamble, Ruth. *Reincarnation in Tibetan Buddhism: The Third Karmapa and the Invention of a Tradition.* Oxford: Oxford University Press, 2018.

Gardiner, David L. *Kūkai: Japan's First Vajrayana Visionary.* Berkeley, CA: Institute of Buddhist Studies, and BDK America, 2024.

Gardiner, David L. "Tantric Buddhism in Japan: Shingon, Tendai, and the Esotericization of Japanese Buddhisms." In *Oxford Research Encyclopedia of Religion/Buddhism*, edited by Richard K. Payne and Georgios Halkias, n.p. Oxford: Oxford University Press, 2018. DOI: 10.1093/acrefore/9780199340378.013.619.

Garrett, Francis. *Religion, Medicine and the Human Embryo in Tibet.* Oxon, UK: Routledge, 2015.

Garry, Ron. "Dudjom Lingpa." https://treasuryoflives.org/biographies/view/Dudjom-Lingpa/9688.

Gasparri, Luca, and Diego Marconi. "Word Meaning." In *The Stanford Encyclopedia of Philosophy* (Fall 2019 edition), edited by Edward N. Zalta. https://plato.stanford.edu/archives/fall2019/entries/word-meaning/.

Geeraerts, Dirk. "Lexical Semantics from Speculative Etymology to Structuralist Semantics." In *The Oxford Handbook of the History of Linguistics*, edited by Keith Allan. Oxford: Oxford University Press, 2013. DOI: 10.1093/oxfordhb/9780199585847.013.0025.

Gellner, David. "Himalayan Conundrum? A Puzzling Absence in Ronald M. Davidson's *Indian Esoteric Buddhism*" *Journal of the International Association of Buddhist Studies* 27.2 (2004): 411–417.

Gellner, David. *Monk, Householder, and Tantric Priest: Newar Buddhism and Its Hierarchy of Ritual*. Cambridge: Cambridge University Press, 1992.

Gentry, James Duncan. "Tibetan Buddhist Power Objects." In *The Oxford Encyclopedia of Buddhism*, edited by Richard K. Payne and Georgios T. Halkias. New York: Oxford University Press, online 2019: https://doi.org/10.1093/acrefore/9780199340378.013.657.

Gethin, Rupert. *The Foundations of Buddhism*. Oxford: Oxford University Press, 1998.

Giddings, William J. "The Sūtra on the Dhāraṇī of the Vast, Complete, and Unobstructed Great Compassion of the Bodhisattva Avalokiteśvara with a Thousand Hands and a Thousand Eyes." In *Buddhism and Medicine: An Anthology of Premodern Sources*, edited by C. Pierce Salguero, 252–285. New York: Columbia University Press, 2017.

Giebel, Rolf, trans. *The Vairocanābhisaṃbodhi Sutra*. Berkeley, CA: Numata Center for Buddhist Translation and Research, 2005. Note: there are different versions of this text, with different pagination. The printed version is referenced here.

Gifford, Julie A. *Buddhist Practice and Visual Culture: The Visual Rhetoric of Borobudur*. New York: Routledge, 2011.

Gilday, Edmund T. "Power Plays: An Introduction to Japanese Festivals." *Journal of Ritual Studies* 4.2 (Summer 1990): 263–295.

Gimello, Robert M. "The Mañjuśrī of a Thousand Arms and a Thousand Bowls: A Preliminary Report on an Apocryphal Image and Its Origin in an Apocryphal Tantra." Conference presentation, Society for Tantric Studies, Flagstaff, AZ, Oct. 3–4, 1977.

Gleig, Ann. "Enacting Social Change Through Buddhist Meditation." In *The Oxford Handbook of Meditation*, edited by Miguel Farias, David Brazier, and Mansur Lalljee. New York: Oxford University Press, online 2020: doi.org/10.1093/oxfordhb/9780198808640.013.38.

Glucklich, Ariel. *The End of Magic*. Oxford: Oxford University Press, 1997.

Glucklich, Ariel. *The Strides of Vishnu: Hindu Culture in Historical Perspective*. Oxford: Oxford University Press, 2008.

Goble, Geoffrey C. "Chinese Esoteric Buddhism: Amoghavajra and the Ruling Elite." PhD diss., Indiana University, May 2012.

Goble, Geoffrey C. *Chinese Esoteric Buddhism: Amoghavajra, the Ruling Elite, and the Emergence of a Tradition*. New York: Columbia University Press, 2019.

Goff, Philip, William Seager, and Sean Allen-Hermanson. "Panpsychism." In *The Stanford Encyclopedia of Philosophy* (Winter 2017 edition), edited by Edward N. Zalta. https://plato.stanford.edu/archives/win2017/entries/panpsychism/.

Goldstein, Melvyn C. *A History of Modern Tibet: Vol. 1: 1913–1951, The Demise of the Lamaist State*. Berkeley: University of California Press, 1989.

Goldstein, Melvyn C. *A History of Modern Tibet: Vol. 2, The Calm before the Storm: 1951–1955*. Berkeley: University of California Press, 2007.

Gombrich, Richard F. *How Buddhism Began: The Conditioned Genesis of the Early Teachings*. London: Athlone, 1996.

Gómez, Luis O. "Meditation." In *Encyclopedia of Buddhism*, edited by Robert Buswell, 525. New York: Macmillan, 2004.

Gómez, Luis O. "Oriental Wisdom and the Cure of Souls: Jung and the Indian East." In *Curators of the Buddha: The Study of Buddhism under Colonialism*, edited by Donald S. Lopez, Jr., 197–250. Chicago: University of Chicago Press, 1995.

Goodell, Eric. "Taixu." In *The Oxford Encyclopedia of Buddhism*, edited by Richard K. Payne and Georgios Halkias, 2277–2301. Oxford: Oxford University Press, online 2022: https://doi.org/10.1093/acrefore/9780199340378.013.1018.

Goodman, Amanda. "The *Ritual Instructions for Altar Methods (Tanfa yize)*: Prolegomenon to the Study of a Chinese Esoteric Buddhist Ritual Compendium from Late-Medieval Dunhuang." PhD diss., University of California, Berkeley, 2013.

Goodman, Amanda. *The Varjagarbha Bodhisattva Three-Syllable Visualization: A Chinese Buddhist Sādhana Text from Tenth Century Dunhuang*. BuddhistRoad Paper 2.5. Bochum, Germany: Center for Religious Studies, Ruhr-University Bochum, 2022.

Goodwin, Janet. "Alms for Kasagi Temple." *The Journal of Asian Studies* 46.4 (Nov. 1987): 827–841.

Goodwin, Janet. *Alms and Vagabonds: Buddhist Temples and Popular Patronage in Medieval Japan*. Honolulu: University of Hawaiʻi Press, 1994.

Gough, Ellen. "Jain *Mantraśāstra* and the *Ṛṣimaṇḍala Yantra*." Centre of Jain Studies Newsletter, March 2009, no. 4: 36–38.

Gough, Ellen. "Jain Tantric Diagrams of the Goddess Padmāvatī." In *The Oxford Handbook of Tantric Studies*, edited by Richard K. Payne and Glen A. Hayes, 679–702. Oxford: Oxford University Press, forthcoming.

Gough, Ellen. *Making a Mantra: Tantric Ritual and Renunciation on the Jain Path to Liberation*. Chicago: University of Chicago Press, 2021.

Graham, Jack L. "Nonreligious Buddhism: Understanding Secular Buddhism as the Result of a Dialogue Between Victorian Constructions of 'Buddhism' and the Discourse of Non-Religion." Postgraduate diss., University of Oxford, 2018.

Grapard, Allan G. "Flying Mountains and Walkers of Emptiness: Toward a Definition of Sacred Space in Japanese Religions." *History of Religions* 21.3 (1982): 195–221.

Grapard, Allan G. "Institution, Ritual, and Ideology: The Twenty-Two Shrine-Temple Multiplexes of Heian Japan." *History of Religions* 27.3 (Feb. 1988): 246–269.

Gray, David B. *The Buddhist Tantras*. New York: Oxford University Press, 2023.

Gray, David B. *The* Cakrasamvara Tantra *(The Discourse of Śrī Heruka)*. New York: The American Institute of Buddhist Studies at Columbia University, and Columbia University's Center for Buddhist Studies and Tibet House US, 2007.

Gray, David B. "Eating the Heart of the Brahmin: Representations of Alterity and the Formation of Identity in Tantric Buddhist Discourse." *History of Religions* 45.1 (August 2005): 45–69.

Gray, David B. "Imprints of the "Great Seal"—On the Expanding Semantic Range of the Term of Mudrā in Eighth Through Eleventh Century Indian Buddhist Literature." *Journal of the International Association of Buddhist Studies* 34.1–2 (2011; published in 2013): 421–481.

Gray, David B. "On the Very Idea of a Tantric Canon: Myth, Politics, and the Formation of the Bka' 'gyur." *Journal of the International Association of Tibetan Studies* 5 (Dec. 2009): 1–37.

Gray, David B. "Skull Imagery and Skull Magic in the *Yoginī* Tantras." *Pacific World: Journal of the Institute of Buddhist Studies* third series, no. 8 (Fall 2006): 21–39.

Gray, David B. "Tantra and Tantric Traditions of Hinduism and Buddhism." In *The Oxford Encyclopedia of Buddhism*, edited by Richard K. Payne and Georgios T. Halkias, 2301–2324. New York: Oxford University Press, 2024. DOI: 10.1093/acrefore/9780199340378.013.59.

Green, Jivan Tova. "Jivan Tova Green's Reflection." In *The Hidden Lamp: Stories from Twenty-Five Centuries of Awakened Women*, edited by Florence Caplow and Susan Moon, 339–341. Somerville, MA: Wisdom Publications, 2013.

Green, Phillip Scott Ellis. "A Century of Confusion: The Brick Reliefs of Cambodia's Phnom Trap Towers." *Journal of the International Association of Buddhist Studies* 40 (2017): 27–62. DOI: 10.2143/JIABS.40.0.3269004.

Green, Phillip Scott Ellis. "The Many Faces of Lokeśvara: Tantric Connections in Cambodia and Campā Between the Tenth and Thirteenth Centuries." *History of Religions* 54.1 (Aug. 2014): 69–93.

Green, Ron. "The Mysterious Mirror of Writing: Kūkai's Poetry and Literary Theory." http://ww2.coastal.edu/rgreen/kukaipoetry.htm.

Greene, Eric. "Death in a Cave: Meditation, Deathbed Ritual, and Skeletal Imagery at Tape Shotor." *Artibus Asiae* 83.2 (2013): 265–294.

Greene, Eric. "Healing Breaths and Rotting Bones: On the Relationship Between Buddhist and Chinese Meditation Practices During the Eastern Han and Three Kingdoms Period." *Journal of Chinese Religions* 42.2 (Nov. 2014): 145–184.

Grether, Holly. "The Ritual Interplay of Fire and Water in Hindu and Buddhist Tantras." In *Homa Variations: The Study of Ritual Change Across the* Longue Durée, edited by Richard K. Payne and Michael Witzel, 47–66. Oxford: Oxford University Press, 2016.

Grieve, Gregory Price, and Daniel Veidlinger. "Buddhism and Media Technologies." In *The Oxford Handbook of Contemporary Buddhism*, edited by Michael Jerryson, ed., 469–484. Oxford: Oxford University Press, 2017. DOI: 10.1093/oxfordhb/9780199362387.013.25.

Griffiths, Arlo. "The 'Greatly Ferocious Spell' (*Mahāraudra-Nāma-Hṛdaya*): A Dhāraṇī Inscribed on a Lead-Bronze Foil Unearthed Near Borobudur." In *Epigraphic Evidence in the Pre-Modern Buddhist World*, edited by Kurt Tropper, 1–36. Vienna: Arbeitskreis für Tibetische und Buddhistische Studien, 2014.

Griffiths, Caitlin. "Tracing the Itinerant Path: Jishū Nuns of Medieval Japan." PhD diss., University of Toronto, 2010.

Griffiths, Caitlin. *Tracing the Itinerant Path: Jishū Nuns of Medieval Japan*. Honolulu: University of Hawai'i Press, 2016.

Guan, Kwa Chong. "The Maritime Silk Road: History of an Idea." Nalanda–Sriwijaya Centre Working Paper Series, no. 23. Singapore: The Nalanda Sriwijaya Centre, 2016.

Guenther, Herbert. *Ecstatic Spontaneity: Saraha's* Three Cycles of Dohā. Nanzan Studies in Asian Religions, 4. Berkeley, CA: Asian Humanities Press, 1993.

Guenther, Herbert. *The Life and Teaching of Naropa*. London: Oxford University Press, 1963.

Guenther, Herbert. *The Royal Song of Saraha: A Study in the History of Buddhist Thought*. 1968. Reprint. Berkeley, CA: Shambala, 1973.

Guenther, Herbert. *The Tantric View of Life*. Berkeley, CA: Shambhala, 1972.

Guenther, Herbert. *Yuganaddha: The Tantric View of Life*. 2nd ed., rev. Varanasi: The Chowkhambha Sanskrit Series, 1969.

Guenther, Herbert V., and Chögyam Trungpa. *The Dawn of Tantra*. 1975. Reprint. Boston: Shambhala, 2001.

Gunaratna, V. F., trans. "The Peacock's Prayer for Protection." No. 8 in *The Book of Protection:* Paritta. Access to Insight. https://www.accesstoinsight.org/lib/authors/piyadassi/protection.html#s8.

Gupta, P. "Hymns of Garutman in Atharva Veda." *Proceedings of the Indian History Congress* 47.1 (1986): 130–137.

Gupta, Sanjukta. "Modes of Worship and Meditation." In *Hindu Tantrism*, edited by Sanjukta Gupta, Dirk Jan Hoens, and Teun Goudriaan, 120–185. Leiden: E.J. Brill, 1979.

Gyältsän, Ngawang Losang Tempa. *Medicine Buddha Sadhana*. Translated by Lama Thubten Zopa Rinpoche. Taos, NM: FPMT (Foundation for the Preservation of the Mahayana Tradition), 2004.

Gyatso, Janet. "The Logic of Legitimation in the Tibetan Treasure Tradition." *History of Religions* 33.2 (Nov. 1993): 97–134.

Gyatso, Khedrup Norsang. *Ornament of Stainless Light: An Exposition of the Kālacakra Tantra*. Translated by Gavin Kilty. The Library of Tibetan Classics, vol. 14. Boston: Wisdom Publications, 2004.

Gyatso, Tenzin (Bstan-'dzin-rgya-mtsho, H.H. The Dalai Lama). *Kalachakra Tantra: Rite of Initiation*. Translated and edited by Jeffrey Hopkins. 1985. Rev. ed. Boston: Wisdom Publications, 1989.

Gyōnen. *The Essentials of the Eight Traditions.* Translated by Leo M. Pruden. Berkeley, CA: Numata Center for Buddhist Translation and Research, 1994.

H

Hakeda, Yoshito S. *Kūkai: Major Works.* New York: Columbia University Press, 1972.

Halbfass, Wilhelm. *India and Europe: An Essay in Understanding.* Albany: State University of New York, 1988.

Halkias, Georgios T. "Buddhist Meditation in Tibet: Exosteric and Esoteric Orientations." In *The Oxford Handbook of Meditation*, edited by Miguel Farias, David Brazier, and Mansur Lalljee, 263–287. Oxford: Oxford University Press, 2021. DOI: 10.1093/oxfordhb/9780198808640.013.52.

Halkias, Georgios T., and Richard K. Payne. "Editor's Introduction." In *Pure Lands in Asian Texts and Contexts: An Anthology*, edited by Georgios T. Halkias and Richard K. Payne, 1–25. Honolulu: University of Hawai'i Press, 2019.

Hallisey, Charles. *Therigatha: Poems of the First Buddhist Women.* Cambridge, MA: Harvard University Press, 2015.

Hamar, Imre. "Deconstructing and Reconstructing Yogācāra: Ten Levels of Consciousness-only/One-mind in Huayan Buddhism." In *Avataṃsaka (Huayan, Kegon, Flower Ornament) Buddhism in East Asia: Origins and Adaptation of a Visual Culture*, edited by Robert Gimello, Frédéric Girard, and Imre Hamar, 53–71. Wiesbaden: Harrassowitz Verlag, 2012.

Hanegraaff, Wouter J. *New Age Religion and Western Culture: Esotericism in the Light of Secular Thought.* Albany: State University of New York Press, 1998.

Hansen, Valerie. *The Silk Road: A New History.* Oxford: Oxford University Press, 2012.

Hardacre, Helen. *Shinto: A History.* New York: Oxford University Press, 2017.

Harding, Sarah. "Translator's Introduction." In *Chöd: The Sacred Teachings on Severance*, edited by Jamgön Kongtrul and translated by Sarah Harding, xi–xxii. Boulder, CO: Snow Lion, 2016.

Harding, Sarah. "Translator's Introduction." In *Zhije: The Pacification of Suffering*, edited by Jamgön Kongtrul and translated by Sarah Harding, xi–xxiii. Boulder, CO: Snow Lion, 2019.

Harrington, Laura. "Exorcising the Mandala: Kālacakra and the Neo-Pentecostal Response." *Journal of Global Buddhism* 13 (2012): 147–171.

Harrington, Laura. "Mañjuśrī." In *The Oxford Encyclopedia of Buddhism*, edited by Richard K. Payne and Georgios T. Halkias, 1497–1512. New York: Oxford University Press, 2024.

Harris, Ian. *Cambodian Buddhism: History and Practice.* Honolulu: University of Hawai'i Press, 2005.

Harrison, Paul. "An Shigao." Edited by Robert E. Buswell, ed. 2 vols. I: 24. *Encyclopedia of Buddhism.* New York: Macmillan Reference.

Harrison, Paul. "Buddhanusmṛti in the Pratyutpanna-Buddha-Saṃmukhāvasthita-Samādhi-sūtra." *Journal of Indian Philosophy* 6 (1978): 35–57.

Harrison, Paul. "Buddhism: A Religion of Revelation After All?" Review of Peter Masefield, *Divine Revelation in Pali Buddhism*, in *Numen* XXXIV, fasc. 2 (1987): 256–264.

Harrison, Paul. "Early Mahāyāna: Laying out the Field." In *Setting Out on the Great Way: Essays on Early Mahayana Buddhism*, edited by Paul Harrison, 7–31. Sheffield, UK: Equinox, 2018.

Harrison, Paul. "Mañjuśrī and the Cult of Celestial Bodhisattvas." *Chung-Hwa Buddhist Journal* 13.2 (2000): 157–193.

Harrison, Paul. "Mediums and Messages: Reflections on the Production of Mahāyāna Sūtras." *The Eastern Buddhist* XXXV.1–2 (2003): 115–151.

Harrison, Paul. *The* Samādhi *of Direct Encounter with the Buddhas of the Present.* Tokyo: The International Institute for Buddhist Studies, 1990.

Hartmann, Jens-Uwe. "Poetry: South Asia." In *Brill's Encyclopedia of Buddhism, vol. I: Literature and Languages*, edited by Jonathan A. Silk, 532–540. Leiden: Brill, 2015.

Hartzell, James F. "The Buddhist Sanskrit Tantras: 'The *Samādhi* of the Plowed Row.'" *Pacific World: Journal of the Institute of Buddhist Studies* third series, no. 14 (Fall 2012): 63–178.
Hartzell, James F. "Tantric Yoga: A Study of the Vedic Precursors, Historical Evolution, Literatures, Cultures, Doctrines, and Practices of the 11th Century Kaśmīri Śaivite and Buddhist Unexcelled Tantric Yogas." PhD diss., Columbia University, 1997.
Harvey, Friedhelm. *The Religious Culture of India: Power, Love and Wisdom.* Cambridge: Cambridge University Press, 1994.
Hatcher, Brian A. *Bourgeois Hinduism, or the Faith of the Modern Vedantists: Rare Discourses from Early Colonial Bengal.* Oxford: Oxford University Press, 2008.
Hatley, Shaman. "Converting the Ḍākinī: Goddess Cults and the Tantras of the Yoginīs Between Buddhism and Śaivism." In *Tantric Traditions in Transmission and Translation,* edited by David Gray and Richard Ryan Overbey, 37–86. Oxford: Oxford University Press, 2016. DOI: 10.1093/acprof:oso/9780199763689.003.0003.
Hatley, Shaman. "From *Mātṛ* to *Yoginī*: Continuity and Transformation in the South Asian Cults of the Mother Goddesses." In *Transformations and Transfer of Tantra in Asia and Beyond,* edited by István Keul, 99–129. Berlin: Walter de Gruyter, 2012.
Hatley, Shaman. "The Lotus Garland (*padmamālā*) and Cord of Power (*śaktitantu*): The *Brahmayāmala*'s Integration of Inner and Outer Ritual." In *Śaivism and the Tantric Traditions: Essays in Honour of Alexis G.J.S. Sanderson,* edited by Dominic Goodall et al., 387–408. Leiden: Brill, 2020.
Hatley, Shaman. "Mapping the Esoteric Body in Bengali Islamic Yoga." *History of Religions* 46.4 (2007): 352–368.
Hatley, Shaman. "Tantric Śaivism in Early Medieval India: Recent Research and Future Directions." *Religion Compass* 4.10 (Oct. 2010): 615–628. DOI: 10.1111/j.1749-8171.2010.00240.x.
Hausner, Sondra L. *Wandering with Sadhus: Ascetics in the Hindu Himalayas.* Bloomington: Indiana University Press, 2007.
Hawley, John Stratton, and Mark Juergensmeyer. *Songs of the Saints of India.* New Delhi: Oxford University Press, 1988.
Hayes, Glen A. "Exploring Metaphors and Conceptual Blending in Vaiṣṇava Sahajiyā Texts." In *The Oxford Handbook of Tantric Studies,* edited by Richard K. Payne and Glen A. Hayes, 755–786. Oxford: Oxford University Press, 2024; online 2023: https://doi.org/10.1093/oxfordhb/9780197549889.013.28.
Heine, Steven. "Did Dōgen go to China? Problematizing Dōgen's Relation to Ju-Ching and Chinese Ch'an." *Japanese Journal of Religious Studies* 30.1–2 (2003): 27–59.
Helderman, Ira. *Prescribing the Dharma: Psychotherapists, Buddhist Traditions, and Defining Religion.* Chapel Hill: University of North Carolina Press, 2019.
Herling, Bradley L. *A Beginner's Guide to the Study of Religion.* 2nd ed. London: Bloomsbury, 2016.
Heruka, Tsangyön. *The Hundred Thousand Songs of Milarepa.* Translated by Garma C.C. Chang. 1962. Reprint. Boston: Shambhala, 1999.
Heruka, Tsangyön. *The Hundred Thousand Songs of Milarepa: A New Translation.* Translated by Christopher Stagg. Boulder, CO: Shambhala, 2016.
Heruka, Tsangyön. *The Life of Milarepa.* Translated by Andrew Quintman. New York: Penguin, 2010.
Hickey, Wakoh Shannon. *Mind Cure: How Meditation Became Medicine.* Oxford: Oxford University Press, 2019.
Hickey, Wakoh Shannon. "Two Buddhisms, Three Buddhisms, and Racism." *Journal of Global Buddhism* 11 (2010): 1–25. Revised version in Scott A. Mitchell and Natalie E. F. Quli, eds., *Buddhism Beyond Borders: New Perspectives on Buddhism in the United* States, 35–56. Albany: State University of New York, 2015.
Hidas, Gergely. *Mahāpratisarā-Mahāvidyārājñī: The Great Amulet, The Great Queen of Spells.* New Delhi: International Academy of Indian Culture and Aditya Prakashan, 2012.

Higgins, David. "An Introduction to the Tibetan Dzogchen (Great Perfection) Philosophy of Mind." *Religion Compass* 6.10 (2012): 441–450.

Higham, Charles F. W. "The Origins of the Civilization of Angkor." In *Proceedings of the British Academy*, vol. 121: 2002 Lectures, edited by P. J. Marshall, 41–89. British Academy Scholarship Online, 2012. DOI: 10.5871/bacad/9780197263037.001.0001.

Higham, Charles F. W. "Ritual and Religion in South-East Asia." In *The Oxford Handbook of the Archaeology of Ritual and Religion*, edited by Timothy Insoll, 470–481. New York: Oxford University Press, 2011. DOI: 10.1093/oxfordhb/9780199232444.013.0031.

Hitoshi, Miyake. *Shugendō: Essays on the Structure of Japanese Folk Religion.* Ann Arbor: Center for Japanese Studies, University of Michigan, 2001.

Ho, Chi Chen. "The Śūraṃgama Dhāraṇī in Sinitic Buddhist Context: from the Tang Dynasty through the Contemporary Period." PhD diss., UCLA, 2010.

Hodge, Stephen. "Considerations on the Dating and Geographical Origins of the *Mahāvairocanābhisaṃbodhi-sūtra.*" *The Buddhist Forum* 3 (1991–1993): 57–83. https://www.shin-ibs.edu/research/archived-publications-and-research-projects/the-buddhist-forum/the-buddhist-forum-volume-iii/.

Hodge, Stephen, trans. *The Mahā-Vairocana-Abhisaṃbodhi Tantra with Buddhaguhya's Commentary.* London: RoutledgeCurzon, 2003.

Hoffman, Helmut. *The Religions of Tibet.* Translated by Edward Fitzgerald. London: George Allen & Unwin, 1961.

Holt, John Clifford. *The Buddhist Visnu: Religious Transformation, Politics, and Culture.* New York: Columbia University Press, 2004.

Holt, John Clifford. *Theravada Traditions: Buddhist Ritual Cultures in Contemporary Southeast Asia and Sri Lanka.* Honolulu: University of Hawai'i Press, 2017.

Hooykaas, C. *Balinese Bauddha Brahmans.* Amsterdam: North-Holland, 1973.

Hopkins, Jeffrey. "Preface." In Tsongkhapa, *The Great Exposition of Secret Mantra, Volume One: Tantra in Tibet*, translated and edited by Jeffrey Hopkins, vii–xii. 1977. Rev. ed. Boulder, CO: Snow Lion, 2016.

Hopkins, Jeffrey. "Supplement." In *The Great Exposition of Secret Mantra, Vol. 1: Tantra in Tibet*, translated and edited by Jeffrey Hopkins, 163–171. 1977. Reprint. Boulder, CO: Snow Lion, 2016.

Hopkirk, Peter. *Trespassers on the Roof of the World: The Secret Exploration of Tibet.* 1982. Reprint. Tokyo: Kodansha, 1995.

Hori, Ichiro. "Mountains and Their Importance for the Idea of the Other World in Japanese Folk Religion." *History of Religions* 6.1 (Aug. 1966): 1–23.

Hori, Ichiro. "On the Concept of the Hijiri (Holy-Man)." *Numen* 5.2 (April 1958): 128–160.

Hori, Ichiro. "On the Concept of the Hijiri (Holy-Man) (continued)." *Numen* 5.3 (Sept. 1958): 199–232.

Hoshino Eiki. "Pilgrimage and Peregrination: Contextualizing the Saikoku *Junrei* and the Shikoku *Henro.*" *Japanese Journal of Religious Studies* 24.3–4 (1997): 271–299.

Howard, Angela F. "The *Dhāraṇī* Pillar of Kunming, Yunnan: A Legacy of Esoteric Buddhism and Burial Rites of the Bai People in the Kingdom of Dali (937–1253)." *Artibus Asiae* 57.1/2 (1997): 33–72.

Howard, Angela F. "On 'Art in the Dark' and Meditation in Central Asian Buddhist Caves." *The Eastern Buddhist* 46.2 (2017): 19–39.

Howard, Donald R. *Writers and Pilgrims: Medieval Pilgrimage Narratives and Their Posterity.* Berkeley: University of California Press, 1980.

Hsing, I-Tien, and William G. Crowell. "Heracles in the East: The Diffusion and Transformation of His Image in the Arts of Central Asia, India, and China." *Asia Major* 18.2 (2005): 103–154.

Huang, Shih-shan Susan. "Illustrating the Efficacy of the *Diamond Sutra* in Vernacular Buddhism." *National Palace Museum Quarterly* (2018): 35–120.

Huber, Toni. *The Holy Land Reborn: Pilgrimage and the Tibetan Reinvention of Buddhist India.* Chicago: The University of Chicago Press, 2008.

Hunter, Harriet. "The *Rishukyō* Mandara Said to Have Been Introduced by Shūei." *Cahiers d'Extrême-Asie* 8 (1995): 371–388.

Huntington, C. W., Jr. "History, Tradition and Truth." *History of Religions* 46.3 (Feb. 2007): 187–227.

Huntington, Eric. "Buddhist Cosmology." In *The Oxford Encyclopedia of Buddhism*, edited by Richard K. Payne and Georgios T. Halkias, 478–493. New York: Oxford University Press, 2024; online: https://doi.org/10.1093/acrefore/9780199340378.013.1050.

I

Isaacson, Harunaga. "Tantric Buddhism in India (from c. A.D. 800 to c. A.D. 1200)." In *Buddhismus in Geschichte und Gegenwart. Band II*, 23–49. Hamburg: Hamburg University, 1998.

Isaacson, Harunaga, and Francesco Sferra. "Tantric Literature: Overview South Asia." In *Brill's Encyclopedia of Buddhism*, vol. I: Literature and Languages, edited by Jonathan A. Silk, 307–319. Leiden: Brill, 2015.

J

Jackson, David. "The *bsTan rim* ("Stages of the Doctrine") and Similar Graded Expositions of the Bodhisattva's Path." In *Tibetan Literature: Studies in Genre*, edited by José Ignacio Cabezón and Roger R. Jackson, 229–243. Ithaca, NY: Snow Lion, 1996.

Jackson, David, trans. "Dhāraṇī of the Jewel Torch." 84000: Translating the Words of the Buddha. 2020. https://read.84000.co/translation/toh145.html.

Jackson, Roger. "Guenther's Saraha: A Detailed Review of *Ecstatic Spontaneity*." *Journal of the International Association of Buddhist Studies* 17.1 (Summer 1994): 111–143.

Jackson, Roger. *Is Enlightenment Possible? Dharmakīrti and Rgyal Tshab Rje on Knowledge, Rebirth, No-Self and Liberation.* Boston: Snow Lion, 1993.

Jackson, Roger. "Mahāmudrā in India and Tibet." In *The Oxford Encyclopedia of Buddhism*, edited by Richard K. Payne and Georgios T. Halkias, 1472–1496. New York: Oxford University Press, 2024; online, 2016; DOI: 10.1093/acrefore/9780199340378.013.184.

Jackson, Roger. "Mahāmudrā: Natural Mind in Indian and Tibetan Buddhism." *Religion Compass* 5/7 (2011): 286–299. DOI: 10.1111/j.1749-8171.2011.00283.x.

Jackson, Roger. *Mind Seeing Mind: Mahāmudrā and the Geluk Tradition of Tibetan Buddhism.* Boston: Wisdom Publishing, 2019.

Jackson, Roger. "'Poetry' in Tibet: *Glu, mGur, sNyan ngag* and 'Songs of Experience.'" In *Tibetan Literature: Studies in Genre*, edited by José Ignacio Cabezón and Roger R. Jackson, 368–392. Ithaca NY: Snow Lion, 1996.

Jackson, Roger. "Sa skya paṇḍita's Account of the bSam yas Debate: History as Polemic." *Journal of the International Association of Buddhist Studies* 5.1 (1982): 89–99.

Jackson, Roger. *Saraha: Poet of Blissful Awareness.* Boulder, CO: Shambhala, 2024.

Jaini, Padmanabh. *The Jaina Path of Purification.* Berkeley: University of California Press, 1979.

Jakobson, Roman. "On Linguistic Aspects of Translation." In *On Translation*, edited by R. A. Brower, 232–239. Cambridge, MA: Harvard University Press, 1959.

Jamison, Stephanie W. *The Ravenous Hyenas and the Wounded Sun: Myth and Ritual in Ancient India.* Ithaca, NY: Cornell University Press, 1991.

Jamison, Stephanie W., and Michael Witzel. "Vedic Hinduism." In *The Study of Hinduism*, edited by Arvind Sharma, 65–113. Columbia: University of South Carolina Press, 2003.

References here are to the "long version" dated 1992, available online at http://www.people.fas.harvard.edu/~witzel/vedica.pdf.

Jarrige, Jean-Franois, and Richard H. Meadow. "The Antecedents of Civilization in the Indus Valley." *Scientific American* 243.2 (August 1980): 122–133.

Jinpa, Thupten, ed. and trans. *Essence of the Heart Sutra: The Dalai Lama's Heart of Wisdom Teachings*. Boston: Wisdom Publications, 2005.

Jinpa, Thupten, and Jaś Elsner, ed. and trans. *Songs of Spiritual Experience: Tibetan Buddhist Poems of Insight and Awakening*. Boston: Shambhala, 2000.

Jones, Ryan. "Fresh Bread from an Old Recipe: Chögryam Trungpa's Transmission of Buddhism to North America, 1970–1977. *Canadian Journal of Buddhist Studies* 13 (2018): 30–74.

Jordaan, Roy E. "Tārā and Nyai Lara Kidul: Images of the Divine Feminine in Java." *Asian Folklore Studies* 56.2 (1997): 285–312.

Jordaan, Roy E. "The Tārā Temple of Kalasan in Central Java." *Bulletin de l'École française d'Extrême-Orient* 85 (1998): 163–183.

Jordaan, Roy E., and Robert Wessing. "Construction Sacrifice in India, 'Seen from the East.'" In *Violence Denied: Violence, Non-Violence, and the Rationalization of Violence in South Asian Cultural History*, edited by Jan E. M. Houben and Karel R. van Kooij, 211–247. Leiden: Brill, 1991.

Josephson, Jason Ānanda. *The Invention of Religion in Japan*. Chicago: University of Chicago Press, 2012.

Joshi, M. C. "Historical and Iconographic Aspects of Śakta Tantrism." In *The Roots of Tantra*, edited by Katherine Anne Harper and Robert L. Brown, 39–56. Albany: State University of New York Press, 2002.

Juergensmeyer, Mark. "Thinking Globally about Religion." In *The Oxford Handbook of Global Religions*, edited by Mark Juergensmeyer, 3–12. Oxford: Oxford University Press, 2006; online 2009: DOI: 10.1093/oxfordhb/9780195137989.003.0001.

K

Kakar, Sudhir. *Shamans, Mystics and Doctors: A Psychological Inquiry into India and Its Healing Traditions*. Chicago: University of Chicago Press, 1982.

Kandahjaya, Hudaya. "The Lord of All Virtues." *Pacific World: Journal of the Institute of Buddhist Studies*, third series, no. 11 (Fall 2009): 1–24.

Kandahjaya, Hudaya. "A Study on the Origin and Significance of Borobudur." PhD diss., Graduate Theological Union, Berkeley, 2004.

Kane, Lee. "Great Compassion Mantra: Purification, Healing and Protection, the Maha Karuna Dharani Sutra—Benefiting All Beings." https://buddhaweekly.com/great-compassion-mantra-purification-healing-protection-maha-karuna-dharani-sutra-benefiting-beings.

Kano, Kazuo. "Vairocanābhisaṃbodhi." In *Brill's Encyclopedia of Buddhism*, vol. I: Literature and Languages, edited by Jonathan A. Silk, 382–389. Leiden: Brill, 2015.

Kapstein, Matthew T. "Introduction: Mediation and Margins." In *Buddhism Between Tibet and China*, edited by Matthew Kapstein, 1–18. Boston: Wisdom Publications, 2009.

Kapstein, Matthew T. "Review of *Mahamudra: The Quintessence of Mind and Meditation* by Tashi Nambyal [translated by Lobsang Lhalungpa]." *Journal of the International Association of Buddhist Studies* 13.1 (1990): 101–114.

Kapstein, Matthew T. *The Tibetan Assimilation of Buddhism: Conversion, Contestation, and Memory*. Oxford: Oxford University Press, 2000.

Karetzky, Patricia Eichenbaum. "Esoteric Buddhism and the Famensi Finds." *Archives of Asian Art* 47 (1994): 78–85.

Kasai, Yukio. *The Bodhisattva Mañjuśrī, Mt. Wutai, and Uyghur Pilgrims*. BuddhistRoad Paper 5.4, Bochum, Germany: Center for Religious Studies, Ruhr–University Bochum, 2020.

Kemp, Casey Alexandra. "Merging Ignorance and Luminosity in Early Bka' brgyud *Bsre ba* Literature." *Zentralasiatische Studien* 44 (2015): 35–50.

Kemp, Casey Alexandra. "Tibetan Book of the Dead (*Bardo Thödol*)." In *The Oxford Encyclopedia of Buddhism*, edited by Richard K. Payne and Georgios T. Halkias, 2467–2487. New York: Oxford University Press, 2024; online, 2016; DOI: 10.1093/acrefore/9780199340378.013.200.

Keyworth, George A. "Did the Silk Road(s) Extend from Dunhuang, Mount Wutai, and Chang'an to Kyoto, Japan? A Reassessment Based on Material Culture from the Temple Gate Tendai Tradition of Miidera." In *Buddhism in Central Asia II—Practices and Rituals, Visual and Material Transfer*, edited by Yukiyo Kasai and Henrik H. Sørensen, 17–67. Leiden: Brill, 2022.

Keyworth, George A. "How the Mount Wutai Cult Stimulated the Development of Chinese Chan in Southern China at Qingliang Monasteries." In *What Happened after Mañjuśrī Migrated to China? The Sinification of the Mañjuśrī Faith and the Globalization of the Wutai Cult*, edited by Jinhua Chen, Guang Kuan, and Hu Fo, 89–112. London: Routledge, 2022.

Keyworth, George A. "Yixing." In *Esoteric Buddhism and the Tantras in East Asia*, edited by Charles Orzech, Henrik Sørensen, and Richard K. Payne, 342–344. Leiden: Brill, 2011.

Khyentse, Dzongsar Jamyang. *The Guru Drinks Bourbon?* Edited by Amira Ben-Yehuda. Boulder, CO: Shambhala, 2016.

Kilty, Gavin. "Translator's Introduction." In Tsongkhapa, *A Lamp to Illuminate the Five Stages: Teachings on* Guhyasamāja Tantra, translated by Gavin Kilty, 1–16. Boston: Wisdom Publications, 2013.

Kim, Sunkyung. "Seeing Buddhas in Cave Sanctuaries." *Asia Major* 24.1 (2011): 87–126.

King, Richard. "Meditation and the Modern Encounter Between Asia and the West." In *The Oxford Handbook of Meditation*, edited by Miguel Farias, David Brazier, and Mansur Lalljee, n.p. New York: Oxford University Press, 2019. DOI: 10.1093/oxfordhb/9780198808640.013.2.

King, Richard. *Orientalism and Religion: Postcolonial Theory, India, and "The Mystic East."* London: Routledge, 1999.

Kinnard, Jacob N. "Reevaluating the Eighth–Ninth Century Pāla Milieu: Icono-Conservatism and the Persistence of Śākyamuni." *Journal of the International Association of Buddhist Studies* 19.2 (Winter 1996): 281–300.

Kinsley, David. *Tantric Visions of the Divine Feminine: The Ten Mahāvidyās.* Berkeley: University of California Press, 1997.

Klimkeit, Hans-J. "Buddhism in Turkish Central Asia." *Numen* 37.1 (1990): 53–69.

Klimkeit, Hans-J. "Christentum und Buddhismus in der innerasiatischen Religionsbewegung." *Zeitschrift für Religions- und Geistesgeschichte* 333 (1981): 208–220.

Klimkeit, Hans-J. "Jesus' Entry into Parinirvāṇa: Manichaean Identity in Buddhist Central Asia." *Numen* 33.2 (1986): 225–240.

Knipe, David M. *Vedic Voices: Intimate Narratives of Living Andhra Traditions.* New York: Oxford University Press, 2015.

Kochinski, Lisa. "Negotiations Between the *Kami* and Buddha Realms: The Establishment of Shrine-Temples in the Eighth Century." *Journal of Asian Studies at Kyushu University* 1 (Spring 2016): 39–45.

Kokhan, Igor. "The 'Ten Rites' (*Daśakriyā*) in Kuladatta's *Kriyāsaṁgrhapañjikā*." PhD diss., University of the West, 2020.

Kollmar-Paulenz, Karénina. "Ma gcig lab sgron ma—The Life of a Tibetan Woman Mystic Between Adaptation and Rebellion." *The Tibet Journal* 23.2 (Summer 1998): 11–32.

Kongtrul, Jamgön. "Beloved Garden: Brief Notes on the Offering and Gift of the Body." In *Chöd: The Sacred Teachings on Severance*, edited by Jamgön Kongtrul and translated by Sarah Harding, 483–501. Boulder, CO: Snow Lion, 2016.

Kongtrul, Jamgön. "Essence of Auspicious Renown: A Ritual of Offering and Supplication to All the Gurus of the Holy Dharmas of Pacification and Object Severance Together." In

Chöd: The Sacred Teachings of Severance, edited by Jamgön Kongtrul and translated by Sarah Harding, 503–535. Boulder, CO: Snow Lion, 2016.

Kongtrul, Jamgön. *Systems of Buddhist Tantra: The Indestructible Way of Secret Mantra*. Translated by Elio Guarisco and Ingrid McLeod. Ithaca, NY: Snow Lion, 2005.

Kongtrul, Jamgon, ed. *Timeless Rapture: Inspired Verse of the Shangpa Masters*. Translated by Ngawang Zangpo. Ithaca, NY: Snow Lion, 2003.

Kopf, David. *British Orientalism and the Bengal Renaissance: The Dynamics of Indian Modernization, 1773–1835*. Berkeley: University of California Press, 1969.

Koyasan Beikoku Betsuin. "Koyasan Buddhist Temple of Los Angeles" (Los Angeles, 2016). https://www.koyasanbetsuin.org/.

Koyasan University. *Studies of Esoteric Buddhism and Tantrism: In Commemoration of the 1,150th Anniversary of the founding of Koyasan*. Koyasan, Japan: Koyasan University, 1965.

Kragh, Ulrich Timme. *Tibetan Yoga and Mysticism: A Textual Study of the Yogas of Nāropa and Mahāmudrā Meditation in the Medieval Tradition of Dags po*. Tokyo: The International Institute for Buddhist Studies, 2015.

Kuhn, Thomas S. *The Structure of Scientific Revolutions*, 4th ed. Chicago: University of Chicago Press, 2012.

Kūkai. *Tantric Poetry of Kukai*. Translated and edited by Morgan Gibson and Hiroshi Murakami. Fredonia, NY: White Pine Press, 1987.

Kulke, Hermann. "Śrīvijaya Revisited: Reflections on State Formation of a Southeast Asian Thalasoccracy." *Bulletin de l'École française d'Extrême-Orient* 102 (2016): 45–96.

Kunga, Lama, and Brian Cutillo, ed. and trans. *Drinking the Mountain Stream: Songs of Tibet's Beloved Saint, Milarepa*. Boston: Wisdom Publications, 1995.

Kuo, Liying. "Dhāraṇī Pillars in China: Functions and Symbols." In *China and Beyond in the Mediaeval Period: Cultural Crossings and Inter-Regional Connections*, edited by Dorothy C. Wang, and Gustav Heldt, 351–385. New Delhi: Manohar, 2014.

Kuroda Toshio. "The Development of the *Kenmitsu* System as Japan's Medieval Orthodoxy." Translated by James Dobbins. *Japanese Journal of Religious Studies* 23.3–4 (1996): 233–269.

Kvaerne, Per. *An Anthology of Buddhist Tantric Songs: A Study of the* Caryāgīti. Oslo: Universitetsforlaget, 1977.

Kvaerne, Per. "On the Concept of Sahaja in Indian Buddhist Tantric Literature." Temenos XI (1975): 88–135; reprint in *Buddhism: Critical Concepts in Religious Studies*, vol. VI: Tantric Buddhism (including China and Japan); Buddhism in Nepal and Tibet, edited by Paul Williams, 162–208. London: Routledge, 2005.

Kwon, Do-Kyun. "Sarva Tathāgata Tattva Saṃgraha, Compendium of All the Tathāgatas: A Study of Its Origin, Structure and Teachings." PhD diss., School of Oriental and African Studies, 2002.

L

LaFleur, William R. *The Karma of Words*. Berkeley: Universiy of California Press, 1983.

Lancaster, Lewis. "Buddhist Literature: Its Canons, Scribes, and Editors." In *The Critical Study of Texts*, edited by Wendy Doniger O'Flaherty, 215–229. Berkeley, CA: Graduate Theological Union, 1979.

Lancaster, Lewis. "The Editing of Buddhist Texts." In *Buddhist Thought and Asian Civilization: Essays in Honor of Herbert B. Guenther on His Sixtieth Birthday*, edited by Leslie S. Kawamura and Keith Scott, 145–151. Berkeley, CA: Dharma Publishing, 1977.

Lancaster, Lewis. "Fixed, Portable, Measurable Sanctity: Buddhism and the Mountains of China." Unpublished essay, n.d. https://www.academia.edu/44112072/Fixed_Portable_Measurable_Sanctity_Buddhism_and_the_Mountains_of_China.

Langenberg, Amy. "Buddhism andSexuality." In *The Oxford Handbook of Buddhist Ethics*, edited by Daniel Cozort and James Mark Shields, 567–591. Oxford: Oxford University Press, 2018. DOI: 10.1093/oxfordhb/9780198746140.013.22.

Langenberg, Amy. "Reading Against the Grain: Female Sexuality in Classical South Asian Buddhism." *Religion* 49.4 (2019): 728–734.
Lapdron, Machik. "The Essential Bundle." In *Chöd*, edited by Jamgön Kongtrul and translated by Sarah Harding, 143–156. Boulder, CO: Snow Lion, 2016.
Larson, Gerald James. "The Terms 'Tantra' and 'Yoga' as Portmanteau or Homographic Expressions." AAR paper 2008.
Learman, Linda. "Introduction." In *Buddhist Missionaries in the Era of Globalization*, edited by Linda Learman, 1–21. Honolulu: University of Hawai'i Press, 2005.
Lee, Sonya. "Buddhist Art and Architecture." In *Oxford Research Encyclopedias: Asian History*, n.p. Oxford: Oxford University Press, 2022. DOI: 10.1093/acrefore/9780190277727.013.398.
Lehnert, Martin. "Tantric Threads Between India and China." In *The Spread of Buddhism*, edited by Ann Heirman and Stephan Peter Bumbacher, 247–276. Leiden: Brill, 2007.
Lessing, Ferdinand. "The Thirteen Visions of a Yogācārya: A Preliminary Study." In *Ritual and Symbol: Collected Essays on Lamaism and Chinese Symbolism*, ed. Ferdinand Lessing, 65–87. Taipei: The Chinese Association for Folklore, 1976.
Lessing, Ferdinand D., and Alex Wayman, trans. *Mkhas grub rje's Fundamentals of the Buddhist Tantras*. The Hague: Mouton, 1968.
Lévi, Sylvain. "On a Tantrik Fragment from Kucha (Central Asia)." *The Indian Historical Quarterly* 12.2 (June 1936): 197–214.
LeVine, Sarah, and David N. Gellner. *Rebuilding Buddhism: The Theravada Movement in Twentieth-Century Nepal*. Cambridge, MA: Harvard University Press, 2005.
Levitt, Peggy. "Redefining the Boundaries of Belonging: The Institutional Character of Transnational Religious Life." *Sociology of Religion* 65(1): 1–18. DOI: 10.2307/3712504.
Lewin, Bruno. "Activity of the Aya and Hata in the Domain of the Sacred." Translated by Richard K. Payne, with Ellen Rozett. *Pacific World: Journal of the Institute of Buddhist Studies*, new series, no. 10 (1994): 219–230.
Lewis, Todd. "*Avadānas* and *Jātakas* in the Newar Traditions of the Kathmandu Valley: Ritual Performances of Mahāyāna Buddhist Narratives." *Religion Compass* 9.8 (2015): 233–253. DOI: 10.111/rec3.12159.
Lewis, Todd. *Popular Buddhist Texts from Nepal: Narratives and Rituals of Newar Buddhism*. Albany: State University of New York Press, 2000.
Lin, Li-Kouang. "Puṇyodaya (Na-T'i), Un Propagateur du Tantrisme en Chine et au Cambodge à l'époque de Hiuan-Tsang." *Journal Asiatique* 227 (1935): 83–100.
Lin, Wei-cheng. "Relocating and Relocalizing Mount Wutai: Vision and Visuality in Mogao Cave 62." *Artibus Asiae* 73.1 (2013): 77–136.
Lin, Yutang. "Forever in Our Hearts." http://www.yogichen.org/gurulin/efiles/mb/mbk02.html.
Lin, Yutang. "Homa Ritual Honoring Manjusri," http://yogichen.org/gurulin/efiles/e0/e0070.html.
Lindahl, Jared R. "The Ritual Veneration of Mongolia's Mountains." In *Tibetan Ritual*, edited by José Ignacio Cabezón, 225–248. Oxford: Oxford University Press, 2010.
Linrothe, Rob. "Beyond Sectarianism: Toward Reinterpreting the Iconography of Esoteric Buddhist Deities Trampling Hindu Gods." *Indian Journal of Buddhist Studies* 2.2 (1990): 16–25.
Linrothe, Rob, ed. *Holy Madness: Portraits of Tantric Siddhas*. New York: Ruben Museum of Art, 2006.
Linrothe, Rob. *Ruthless Compassion: Wrathful Deities in Early Indo-Tibetan Esoteric Buddhist Art*. London: Serindia, 1999.
Locke, Jessica. "Ethics and Buddhism." In *The Oxford Encyclopedia of Buddhism*, edited by Richard K. Payne and Georgios T. Halkias, 973–991. New York: Oxford University Press, 2024; online 2023: https://doi.org/10.1093/acrefore/9780199340378.013.714.
Londo, William Frank. "The Other Mountain: The Mt. Kōya Temple Complex in the Heian Era." PhD diss., University of Michigan, 2004.
Lopez, Carlos. "Food and Immortality in the Veda: A Gastronomic Theology?" *Electronic Journal of Vedic Studies* 3.3 (1997): 11–19.

Lopez, Donald S., Jr. "Authority and Orality in the Mahāyāna." *Numen* 42.1 (Jan. 1999): 21–47.

Lopez, Donald S., Jr. *Elaborations on Emptiness: Uses of the Heart Sutra*. Princeton, NJ: Princeton University Press, 1996.

Lopez, Donald S., Jr. "Foreigner at the Lama's Feet." In *Curators of the Buddha: Buddhism Under Colonialism*, edited by Donald Lopez, Jr., 251–295. Chicago: University of Chicago Press, 1995.

Lopez, Donald S., Jr. "A Prayer Flag for Tārā." In *Religions of Tibet in Practice*, edited by Donald S. Lopez, Jr., 548–552. Princeton, NJ: Princeton University Press, 1997.

Lopez, Donald S., Jr., ed. *Religions of Tibet in Practice*. Princeton, NJ: Princeton University Press, 1997.

Lopez, Donald S., Jr. *The Tibetan Book of the Dead: A Biography*. Princeton, NJ: Princeton University Press, 2011.

Lopez, Jr., Donald S., Jr., with Rebecca Bloom, Kevin Carr, Chun Wa Chan, Ha Nul Jun, Carla Sinopoli, and Keiko Yokota-Carter. *Hyecho's Journey: The World of Buddhism*. Chicago: University of Chicago Press, 2017.

Lorea, Carola Erika. "'I Am Afraid of Telling You This, Lest You'd Be Scared Shitless!': The Myth of Secrecy and the Study of the Esoteric Traditions of Bengal." *Religions* 9.6 (2018): 172; https://doi.org/10.3390/rel9060172.

Lorea, Carola Erika. "Singing Tantra: Aural Media and Sonic Soteriology in Bengali Esoteric Lineages." In *The Oxford Handbook of Tantric Studies*, edited by Richard K. Payne and Glen T. Hayes, 991–1021. New York: Oxford University Press, 2024.

Lorenzen, David N., ed. *Bhakti Religion in North India: Community Identity and Political Action*. Albany: State University of New York Press, 1995.

Lorenzen, David N. "New Data on the Kāpālikas." In *Criminal Gods and Demon Devotees: Essays on the Guardians of Popular Hinduism*, edited by Alf Hiltelbeitel, 231–238. Albany: State University of New York Press, 1989.

Lucia, Amanda. "Innovative Gurus: Tradition and Change in Contemporary Hinduism." *Journal of Hindu Studies* 18.2 (August 2014): 221–263.

Luczanits, Christian "The Eight Great Siddhas in Early Tibetan Painting." In *Holy Madness: Portraits of Tantric Siddhas*, edited by Rob Linrothe, 76–91. New York: Ruben Museum of Art, 2006.

Lutgendorf, Philip. "Five Heads and No Tale: Hanumān and the Popularization of Tantra." *International Journal of Hindu Studies* 5.3 (Dec. 2001): 269–296.

Lye, Hun Y. "Feeding Ghosts: A Study of the *Yuquie Yankou* Rite." PhD diss., University of Virginia, 2003.

Lye, Hun Y. "Song Tiantai Ghost-Feeding Rituals." In *Esoteric Buddhism and the Tantras in East Asia*, edited by Charles D. Orzech, Henrik H. Sørensen, and Richard K. Payne, 521–524. Leiden: Brill, 2011.

Lye, Hun Y. "*Yuquie Yankou* in the Ming-Qing." In *Esoteric Buddhism and the Tantras in East Asia*, edited by Charles D. Orzech, Henrik H. Sørensen, and Richard K. Payne, 562–567. Leiden: Brill, 2011.

M

MacArgel, Nicole. "Foundation for the Preservation of the Mahayana Tradition (FPMT): A Contemporary Organization for Transmitting the Dharma." MA thesis, Graduate Theological Union, Berkeley, 2017.

MacWilliams, Mark W. "Temple Myths and the Popularization of Kannon Pilgrimage in Japan: A Case Study of Ōya-ji on the Bandō Route." *Japanese Journal of Religious Studies* 24.3–4 (1997): 375–411.

Maffly-Kipp, Laurie F. "Eastward Ho! American Religion from the Perspective of the Pacific Rim." In *Retelling U.S. Religious History*, edited by Thomas A. Tweed, 127–148. Berkeley: University of California Press, 1997.

Mair, Victor H. "Introduction: Reconsidering and Reconfiguring the 'Silk Roads.'" In *The "Silk Roads" in Time and Space: Migrations, Motifs, and Materials*, edited by Victor H. Mair, 3–4. Sino-Platonic Papers, no. 228. Philadelphia: Department of East Asian Languages and Civilizations, University of Pennsylvania, 2012.

Mair, Victor H. *Painting and Performance: Chinese Picture Recitation and Its Indian Genesis.* Honolulu: Univesity of Hawai'i Press, 1988.

Malandra, Geri H. *Unfolding a Maṇḍala: The Buddhist Cave Temples at Ellora.* Albany: State University of New York Press, 1993.

Mallinson, James. "*Kālavañcana* in the Konkan: How a Vajrayāna *Haṭhayoga* Tradition Cheated Buddhism's Death in India." *Religions* 10 (2019): article no. 273. DOI: 10.3390/rel10040273.

Malpas, Jeff. "Hans-Georg Gadamer." In *The Stanford Encyclopedia of Philosophy* (Fall 2022 edition), edited by Edward N. Zalta. https://plato.stanford.edu/archives/fall2022/entries/gadamer/.

Mang, Stefan, trans. "One-Syllable Prajñāpāramitā." Lotsawa House, 2019. https://www.lotsawahouse.org/words-of-the-buddha/one-syllable-perfection-of-wisdom.

Mann, Richard D. "Material Culture and the Study of Hinduism and Buddhism." *Religion Compass* 8.8 (2014): 264–273. DOI: 10.1111/rec3.12116.

Martin, Dan. "Illusion Web—Locating the *Guhyagarbha Tantra* in Buddhist Intellectual History." In *Silver on Lapis: Tibetan Literary Culture and History*, edited by Christopher I. Beckwith, 175–220. Bloomington, IN: The Tibet Society, 1987.

Masson, J. L. "Sex and Yoga: Psychoanalysis and the Indian Religious Experience." *Journal of Indian Philosophy* 2 (1974): 307–320.

Masuzawa, Tomoko. *In Search of Dreamtime: The Quest for the Origin of Religion.* Chicago: University of Chicago Press, 1993.

Masuzawa, Tomoko. *The Invention of World Religions: Or, How European Universalism was Preserved in the Language of Pluralism.* Chicago: University of Chicago Press, 2005.

Mathes, Klaus-Dieter. "Blending the Sutras with the Tantras: The Influence of Maitripa and His Circle on the Formation of *Sūtra Mahāmudrā* in the Kagyu Schools." In *Tibetan Buddhist Literature and Praxis: Studies in Its Formative Period*, edited by R. M. Davidson and C. Wedemeyer, 201–227. Leiden: Brill, 2006.

Mathes, Klaus-Dieter. *A Fine Blend of* Mahāmudrā *and Madhyamaka: Maitripa's Collection of Texts on Non-Conceptual Realization* (Amanasīkara). Vienna: Austrian Academy of Sciences, 2015.

Mathes, Klaus-Dieter. "Mind and Its Co-emergent (*sahaja*) Nature in Advayavajra's Commentary on Saraha's *Dohākoṣa*." *Zentralasiatische Studien* 44 (2015): 17–34.

Matsunaga, Yukei. "A History of Tantric Buddhism in India, with Reference to Chinese Translations." In *Buddhist Thought and Asian Civilization: Essays in Honor of Herbert V. Guenther on His Sixtieth Birthday*, edited by Leslie S. Kawamura and Keith Scott, 167–181. Emeryville, CA: Dharma Publishing, 1977.

Maud, Jovan. "Buddhist Relics and Pilgrimage." In *The Oxford Handbook of Contemporary Buddhism*, edited by Michael Jerryson, 421–435. Oxford: Oxford University Press, 2017. DOI: 10.1093/oxfordhb/9780199362387.013.20.

Mayer, Robert. "The Figure of Maheśvara/Rudra in the rÑiṅ-ma-pa Tantric Tradition." *Journal of the International Association of Buddhist Studies* 21, no. 2 (1988): 271–310.

Mayer, Robert. "Rnyingma Tantras." In *Brill Encyclopedia of Buddhism: Literature and Languages*, edited by Jonathan Silk, Oskar von Hinuber, and Vincent Eltschinger, 390–397. Leiden: Brill, 2015.

Mayer, Robert. *A Scripture of the Ancient Tantra Collection: The* Phur-pa bcu-gnyis. Oxford: Kiscadale Publications, 1996.

McAra, S. A. "Indigenizing or Adapting? Importing Buddhism into a Settler-Colonial Society." *Journal of Global Buddhism* 8 (2007): 132–156.

McBride, Richard D., II. "*Dhāraṇī* and Mantra in Contemporary Korean Buddhism: An Ethnography of Spell Materials for Popular Consumption." *Journal of the International Association of Buddhist Studies* 42 (2019): 361–403.

McBride, Richard D., II. "Dhāraṇī and Spells in Medieval Sinitic Buddhism." *Journal of the International Association of Buddhist Studies* 28.1 (2005): 85–114.

McBride, Richard D., II. "Is There Really 'Esoteric" Buddhism?" *Journal of the International Association of Buddhist Studies* 27.2 (2004): 330–356.

McBride, Richard D., II. "Wish-Fulfilling Spells and Talismans, Efficacious Resonance, and Trilingual Spell Books: The *Mahāpratisarā-dhāraṇī* in Chosŏn Buddhism." *Pacific World: Journal of the Institute of Buddhist Studies*, n.s. 19 (2017): 55–93.

McClintock, Sarah. "Compassionate Trickster: The Buddha as a Literary Character in the Narrratives of Early Indian Buddhism." *Journal of the American Academy of Religion* 79.1 (March 2011): 90–112.

McCloud, Sean. "From Exotics to Brainwashers: Portraying New Religions in Mass Media." *Religion Compass* 1.1 (2007): 214–228. DOI: 10.1111/j.1749-8171.2006.00001.x.

McDaniel, June. *The Madness of the Saints: Ecstatic Religion in Bengal.* Chicago: University of Chicago Press, 1989.

McDaniel, June. *Offering Flowers, Feeding Skulls: Popular Goddess Worship in West Bengal.* Oxford: Oxford University Press, 2004.

McDaniel, Justin Thomas. *Architects of Buddhist Leisure: Socially Disengaged Buddhism in Asia's Museums, Monuments, and Amusement Parks.* Honolulu: University of Hawai'i Press, 2017.

McDonald, Robert C. "Slavoj Žižek and Communication Studies." In *The Oxford Research Encyclopedia of Communication*, n.p. New York: Oxford University Press, 2018. https://doi.org/10.1093/acrefore/9780190228613.013.593.

McGovern, Nathan. "Esoteric Buddhism in Southeast Asia." In *The Oxford Encyclopedia of Buddhism,* edited by Richard K. Payne and Georgios T. Halkias, 958–973. Oxford: Oxford University Press, 2024, online, 2017; DOI: 10.1093/acrefore/9780199340378.013.617.

McKay, Alex, ed. *Pilgrimage in Tibet.* Surrey, UK: Curzon Press, 1998.

McMahan, David L. *The Making of Buddhist Modernism.* Oxford: Oxford University Press, 2008.

McMahan, David L. "Modernity and the Early Discourse of Scientific Buddhism." *Journal of the American Academy of Religion* 72.4 (Dec. 2004): 897–933.

McMahan, David L. "Orality, Writing, and Authority in South Asian Buddhism: Visionary Literature and the Struggle for Legitimacy in the Mahāyāna." *History of Religions* 37.3 (Feb. 1998): 249–274.

McMahan, David L. "Transpositions of Metaphor and Imagery in the *Gaṇḍavyūha* and Tantric Buddhist Practice." *Pacific World: Journal of the Institute of Buddhist Studies* third series, no. 6 (Fall 2004): 181–194.

Mei, Ching Hsuan. "The Early Transmission of 'Pho ba Teachings." *The Tibet Journal* 29.4 (Winter 2004): 27–42.

Michaels, Axel. *Hinduism: Past and Present.* Princeton, NJ: Princeton University Press, 2004.

Michon, Daniel. "Pre–Angkor Khmer Religion and State." *Religion Compass* 5.1 (2011): 28–36. DOI: 10.1111/j.1749-8171.2010.00261.x.

Mikkonen, Kai. "The 'Narrative Is Travel' Metaphor: Between Spatial Sequence and Open Sequence." *Narrative* 15.3 (Oct. 2007): 286–305.

Miksic, John. "The Buddhist-Hindu Divide in Premodern Southeast Asia." Nalanda-Sriwijaya Centre Working Paper Series no. 1. Singapore: Institute of Southeast Asian Studies, 2010.

Miller, Seumas. "Social Institutions." In *The Stanford Encyclopedia of Philosophy* (Fall 2024 edition), edited by Edward N. Zalta and Uri Nodelman. https://plato.stanford.edu/archives/fall2024/entries/social-institutions/.

Miller, W. Blythe. "The Vagrant Poet and the Reluctant Scholar: A Study of the Balance of Iconoclasm and Civility in the Biographical Accounts of Two Founders of the 'Brug pa bka' brgyud Lineages." *Journal of the International Association of Buddhist Studies* 28.2 (2005): 369–410.

Mishra, Vijay. "The Religious Sublime." In *The Oxford Handbook of Religion and the Arts*, edited by Frank Burch Brown, 57–76. Oxford: Oxford University Press, 2014. DOI: 10.1093/oxfordhb/9780195176674.013.003.

Miyata, Taisen. *A Henro Pilgrimage Guide to the 88 Temples of Shikoku Island, Japan*. Sacramento: Northern California Koyasan Temple, 1984.

Moens, J. L. "Barabudur, Mendut, and Pawon, and Their Mutual Relationship." Translated by Mark Long. Privately published on www.borbudur.tv (website is defunct), 2007.

Mollier, Christine. *Buddhism and Taoism Face to Face: Scripture, Ritual, and Iconographic Exchange in Medieval China*. Honolulu: University of Hawai'i Press, 2009.

Moriyasu, Takao. "Chronology of West Uighur Buddhism: Re-examination of the Dating of the Wall-Paintings in Grünwedel's Cave No. 8 (New: No. 18), Bezelik." In *Aspects of Research into Central Asian Buddhism: In Memoriam Kōgi Kudara*, Silk Road Studies, no. XVI., edited by Peter Zieme, 191–227. Turnhout, Belgium: Brepols, 2008.

Muller, Wilhelm K. "Shingon-Mysticism: Śubhākarasiṁha and I-hsing's Commentary to the Mahāvairocana-sūtra, Chapter One, an Annotated Translation." PhD diss., University of California, Los Angeles, 1976.

Muller-Ortega, Paul. "Ciphering the Supreme: Mantric Encoding in Abhinavagupta's 'Tantrāloka.'" *International Journal of Hindu Studies* 7.1/3 (Feb. 2003): 1–30.

Mullin, Glenn, trans. and ed. *The Practice of the Six Yogas of Naropa*. Ithaca, NY: Snow Lion, 2006.

Mullin, Glenn. *The Six Yogas of Naropa*. Ithaca, NY: Snow Lion, 2005.

N

Nagasawa, Jake. "Buddhaguhya." *Treasury of Lives*, 2017. https://treasuryoflives.org/biographies/view/Buddhaguhya/10546.

Nakamura, Hajime. *Indian Buddhism: A Survey with Bibliographical Notes*. Reprint. Delhi: Motilal Banarsidass, 1987.

Nalanda Translation Committee. *The Rain of Wisdom*. Boston: Shambhala, 1999.

Namdak, Tenzin. "White Crystal Mirror." In *Chöd*, edited by Jamgön Kongtrul and translated by Sarah Harding, 257–296. Boulder, CO: Snow Lion, 2016.

Namgyal, Tsering. "Buton Rinchen Drub." In *The Treasury of Lives*, 2012. https://treasuryoflives.org/biographies/view/Buton-Rinchen-Drub/2845.

Nance, Richard F. "Indian Buddhist Preachers Inside and Outside the Sutras." *Religion Compass* 2.2 (March 2008): 134–159. doi.org/10.1111/j.1749-8171.2007.00057.x.

Nance, Richard F. *Speaking for Buddhas: Scriptural Commentary in Indian Buddhism*. New York: Columbia University Press, 2012.

Naquin, Susan, and Chün-fang Yü. "Pilgrimage in China." In *Pilgrims and Sacred Sites in China*, edited by Susan Naquin and Chün-fang Yü, 1–38. Berkeley: University of California Press, 1992.

Nash, Roderick Frazier. *Wilderness and the American Mind*. New Haven, CT: Yale Univesity Press, 1967; 5th ed. 2014.

Nattier, Jan. *A Few Good Men: The Bodhisattva Path according to* The Inquiry of Ugra (Ugraparipṛcchā). Honolulu: University of Hawai'i Press, 2003.

Nattier, Jan. "The Heart Sūtra: A Chinese Apocryphal Text?" *Journal of the International Journal of Buddhist Studies* 15.2 (1992): 153–223.

Nattier, Jan. *Once Upon a Future Time: Studies in the Buddhist Prophecy of Decline*. Berkeley, CA: Asian Humanities Press, 1991.

Naudou, Jean. *Les Bouddhists Kaśmīriens au Moyen Age*. Paris: Presses Univesitaires de France, 1968.

Needham, Rodney. "Polythetic Classification: Convergence and Consequences." *Man* 10.3 (1975): 349–369.

Neelis, Jason. *Early Buddhist Transmission and Trade Networks: Mobility and Exchange Within and Beyond the Northwestern Borderlands of South Asia.* Leiden: Brill, 2011.

Nelson, John. "Diasporic Buddhisms and Convert Communities." In *The Oxford Handbook of Contemporary Buddhism*, edited by Michael Jerryson, 381–397. Oxford: Oxford University Press, 2017. DOI: 10.1093/oxfordhb/9780199362387.013.21.

Nietupski, Paul. *Labrang Monastery: A Tibetan Buddhist Community on the Inner Asian Borderlands, 1709–1958.* Lanham, MD: Lexington Books, 2011.

Nihom, Max. "On Attracting Women and Tantric Initiation: Tilottamā and 'Hevajratantra,' II.v. 38–47 and I.vii. 8–9." *Bulletin of the School of Oriental and African Studies* 58.3 (1995): 521–531.

Nongbri, Brent. *Before Religion: A History of a Modern Concept.* New Haven, CT: Yale University Press, 2013.

Novetzke, Christian Lee. "Divining an Author: The Idea of Authorship in an Indian Religious Tradition." *History of Religions* 42.3 (Feb. 2003): 213–242.

O

Olivelle, Patrick. "Introduction." In *Life of the Buddha, by Aśvaghoṣa*, translated by Patrick Olivelle, xvii–lv. New York: New York University Press, 2008.

Openshaw, Jeanne. *Seeking Bāuls of Bengal.* Cambridge: Cambridge University Press, 2002.

Orlina, Roderick. "Epigraphical Evidence for the Cult of Mahāpratisarā in the Philippines." *Journal of the International Association of Buddhist Studies* 35.1–2 (2012 [2013]): 159–169.

Orzech, Charles. "Esoteric Buddhism in the Tang: From Atikūṭa to Amoghavajra (651–780)." In *Esoteric Buddhism and the Tantras in East Asia*, edited by Charles D. Orzech, Henrik H. Sørensen, and Richard K. Payne, 263–285. Leiden: Brill, 2011.

Orzech, Charles. "The 'Great Teaching of Yoga,' the Chinese Appropriation of the Tantras, and the Question of Esoteric Buddhism." *Journal of Chinese Religions* 34 (2006): 29–78.

Orzech, Charles. *Politics and Transcendent Wisdom: The Scripture of Humane Kings in the Creation of Chinese Buddhism.* University Park: Pennsylvania State University Press, 1998.

Orzech, Charles. "Seeing Chen-yen Buddhism: Traditional Scholarship and the Vajrayāna in China." *History of Religions* 29.2 (Nov. 1989): 87–114.

Orzech, Charles D., and Henrik H. Sørensen. "*Mudrā*, Mantra, Mandala." In *Esoteric Buddhism and the Tantras in East Asia*, edited by Charles D. Orzech, Henrik H. Sørensen, and Richard K. Payne, 76–89. Leiden: Brill, 2011.

Orzech, Charles D., Henrik H. Sørensen, and Richard K. Payne, eds. *Esoteric Buddhism and the Tantras in East Asia.* Leiden: Brill, 2011.

Osto, Douglas. "'Proto-Tantric' Elements in the *Gaṇḍavyūha-sūtra*" *Journal of Religious History* 33.2 (June 2009): 165–177.

Overbey, Ryan Richard. "Memory, Rhetoric, and Education in the Great Lamp of the Dharma Dhāraṇī Scripture." PhD diss., Harvard University, 2010.

Overbey, Ryan Richard. "Vicissitudes of Text and Rite in the *Great Peahen Queen of Spells.*" In *Tantric Traditions in Transmission and Translation*, ed. David B. Gray and Ryan Richard Overbey, 257–283. Oxford: Oxford University Press, 2016.

Overbey, Ryan Richard. "'Why Don't We Translate Spells in the Scriptures?': Medieval Chinese Exegesis on the Meaning and Function of *dhāraṇī* Language." *Journal of the International Association of Buddhist Studies* 42 (2019): 493–514.

Oxford Dictionary of Philosophy. New York: Oxford University Press, 2008; online 2016: https://www.oxfordreference.com/display/10.1093/acref/9780199541430.001.0001/acref-9780199541430-e-2285.

P

Padoux, André. "Contributions a l'étude du Mantraśāstra, I: La sélection des *mantra (mantroddhāra).*" *Bulletin de l'Ecole française d'Extrême-Orient* 65.1 (1978): 65–85.

Padoux, André. "Contributions a l'étude du Mantraśāstra, II: *nyāsa*: l'imposition rituelle des *mantra.*" *Bulletin de l'Ecole française d'Extrême-Orient* 67 (1980): 59–102.

Padoux, André. "Contributions a l'étude du Mantraśāstra, III: Le *japa.*" *Bulletin de l'Ecole française d'Extrême-Orient* 76 (1987): 117–164.

Padoux, André. *The Hindu Tantric World.* Chicago: University of Chicago Press, 2017.

Pankenier, David W. *Popular Astrology and Border Affairs in Early Imperial China: An Archaeological Confirmation.* Sino-Platonic Papers. 104. Philadelphia: Department of East Asian Languages and Civilizations, University of Pennsylvania (July 2000).

Pathak, Shubha. "Why Do Displaced Kings Become Poets in the Sanskrit Epics? Modeling *Dharma* in the Affirmative *Rāmāyaṇa* and the Interrogative *Mahābhārata.*" *Hindu Studies* 10 (2006): 127–149. DOI: 10.1007/s11407-006-9018-0.

Payne, Richard K. "Aparimitāyus: 'Tantra' *and* 'Pure Land' in Medieval Indian Buddhism?" *Pacific World: Journal of the Institute of Buddhist Studies*, third series, no. 9 (2007): 272–308.

Payne, Richard K. "Archetype and Emptiness: Comparisons, Critiques and Applications of Jung and Buddhism." With Greg Petropoulus. *The San Francisco Jung Institute Library Journal* 20.4 (2002): 33–73. (Name changed to *Jung Journal: Culture and Psyche* in 2007)

Payne, Richard K. "Authority of the Buddha: The Limits of Knowledge in Medieval Indian Buddhist Epistemology." *Acta Orientalia Vilnensia* 11, no. 1 (2010): 13–36.

Payne, Richard K. "Buddhism." In *The Cambridge Companion to Literature and Religion*, edited by Susan M. Felch, 169–185. New York: Cambridge University Press, 2016.

Payne, Richard K. "Buddhism and the Powers of the Mind." In *Buddhism in the Modern World*, edited by David L. McMahan, 233–255. London: Routledge, 2012.

Payne, Richard K. "Buddhist Studies Beyond the Nation-State." In *Oxford Handbook Topics in Religion*, edited by The Oxford Handbooks Editorial Board. 2016. DOI: 10.1093/oxfordhb/9780199935420.013.13.

Payne, Richard K. "Doctrine and Practice: Dialectic and Nondual." *The Berkeley Journal of Religion and Theology* 9.1 (2024): 122–152.

Payne, Richard K. "The Fourfold Training in Japanese Esoteric Buddhism." In *Esoteric Buddhism and the Tantras in East Asia*, edited by Charles D. Orzech, Henrik H. Sørensen, and Richard K. Payne, 1024–1028. Leiden: Brill, 2011.

Payne, Richard K. "From Vedic India to Buddhist Japan: Continuities and Discontinuities in Esoteric Ritual." In *Esoteric Buddhism and the Tantras in East Asia*, edited by Charles Orzech, Henrik Sørensen, and Richard K. Payne, 1040–1051. Leiden: Brill, 2011.

Payne, Richard K. "Global and Colonial Dynamics in the Religions of Japan." In *The Bloomsbury Handbook of Japanese Religions*, edited by Fabio Rambelli, Erica Baffelli, and Andrea Castiglioni, 99–106. New York: Bloomsbury, 2021.

Payne, Richard K. "Globalizing Tantric Buddhism." In *The Oxford Encyclopedia of Buddhism*, edited by Richard K. Payne and Georgios T. Halkias, 1131–1158. Oxford: Oxford University Press, 2024; online 2021: https://doi.org/10.1093/acrefore/9780199340378.013.1043.

Payne, Richard K. "Hiding in Plain Sight: The Invisibility of the Shingon Mission to the United States." In *Buddhist Missionaries in the Era of Globalization*, edited by Linda Learman, 101–122. Honolulu: University of Hawai'i Press, 2005.

Payne, Richard K. "How Not to Talk About Pure Land Buddhism: A Critique of Huston Smith's (Mis)Representations." In *Path of No-Path: Contemporary Studies in Pure Land Buddhism Honoring Roger Corless*, edited by Richard K. Payne, 147–172. Berkeley, CA: Institute of Buddhist Studies and Numata Center for Buddhist Translation and Research, 2009.

Payne, Richard K. "Integrating Christ and the Saints into Buddhist Ritual: The Christian *Homa* of Yogi Chen." *Buddhist–Christian Studies* 35 (2015): 37–48.

Payne, Richard K. "Introduction." In *Re-Visioning "Kamakura" Buddhism*, edited by Richard K. Payne, 1–23. Honolulu: University of Hawai'i Press, 1998.

Payne, Richard K. "'Japanese Buddhism': Constructions and Deconstructions." In *The Dao Companion to Japanese Buddhist Philosophy*, edited by Gereon Kopf, 3–51. Dordrecht: Springer Verlag, 2019.

Payne, Richard K. "Jesus Christ, Tantric Deity: Syntax and Semantics in Ritual Change." In *On Meaning and Mantra: Essays in Honor of Frits Staal*, edited by George Thompson and Richard K. Payne, 455–476. Berkeley, CA: Institute of Buddhist Studies and BDK America, 2016.

Payne, Richard K. *Language in the Buddhist Tantra of Japan: The Indic Roots*. London: Bloomsbury Press, 2018.

Payne, Richard K. "Lethal Fire: The Shingon Yamāntaka Abhicāra Homa." *Journal of Religion and Violence* 6.1 (2018): 11–31.

Payne, Richard K. "Mindfulness and the Moral Imperative for the Self to Improve the Self." In *Handbook of Mindfulness: Culture, Context, and Social Engagement*, edited by Ronald E. Purser, David Forbes, and Adam Burke, 121–134. Berlin: Springer, 2016.

Payne, Richard K. "On Not Understanding Extraordinary Language in the Buddhist Tantra of Japan." *Religions* 8.10:223 (2017). https://doi.org/10.3390/rel8100223.

Payne, Richard K. "On the Ritual Culture of Japan: Symbolism, Ritual, and the Arts." In *The Nanzan Guide to Japanese Religions*, edited by Paul L. Swanson and Clark Chilson, 235–256. Honolulu: University of Hawai'i Press, 2006.

Payne, Richard K. "Practicing the 'Three-Fold Mystery': Rethinking a Shingon Ritual from Dichtomy to Dialectic." *Journal of Contemplative Studies* 19.4 (2024): 1–29. https://doi.org/10.57010/XNID2516.

Payne, Richard K. "Ritual, Rituals, and Ritualizing in American Buddhism." In *The Oxford Handbook of American Buddhism*, edited by Scott Mitchell and Ann Gleig, 339–358. Oxford: Oxford University Press, 2024.

Payne, Richard K. "Ritual Studies in the *Longue Durée*: Comparing Shingon and Śaiva Siddhanta *Homas*." *Pacific World: Journal of the Institute of Buddhist Studies*, third series, no. 13 (Fall 2011): 223–262.

Payne, Richard K., ed. *Secularizing Buddhism: New Perspectives on a Dynamic Tradition*. Boulder, CO: Shambhala, 2021.

Payne, Richard K. "Self-Representation and Cultural Expectations: Yogi Chen and Religious Practices of Life-Writing." *Entangled Religions* 3 (2016): 33–82.

Payne, Richard K. "Sex and Gestation: The Union of Opposites in European and Chinese Alchemy." *Ambix* 36.2 (1989): 66–81. http://dx.doi.org/10.1179/000269889790418612.

Payne, Richard K. "Shingon Services for the Dead." In *Religions of Japan in Practice*, edited by George J. Tanabe, Jr., 159–163. Princeton, NJ: Princeton University Press, 1999.

Payne, Richard K. "The Shingon Subordinating Fire Offering for Amitābha: Amida Kei Ai Goma." *Pacific World: Journal of the Institute of Buddhist Studies*, third series, no. 8 (2006): 191–236.

Payne, Richard K. *The Tantric Ritual of Japan: Feeding the Gods, The Shingon Fire Ritual.* Delhi: International Academy of Indian Culture, and Aditya Prakashan, 1991.

Payne, Richard K. "Tongues of Flame: Homologies in the Tantric Homa." In *The Roots of Tantra*, edited by Katherine Anne Harper and Robert L. Brown, 193–210. Albany: State University of New York Press, 2002.

Payne, Richard K. "Traditionalist Representations of Buddhism." *Pacific World: Journal of the Institute of Buddhist Studies*, third series, no. 10 (2008): 177–223.

Payne, Richard K. "Why 'Buddhist Theology' Is Not a Good Idea." *The Pure Land: Journal of the International Association of Shin Buddhist Studies* n.s., no. 27 (2012–2013): 37–71.

Payne, Richard K. "Yogi Chen and the Transformation of Tantric Ritual." Presentation for the "Buddhism Without Borders" conference, Institute of Buddhist Studies, Berkeley, CA, March 2010.

Payne, Richard K., and Glen T. Hayes, eds. *The Oxford Handbook of Tantric Studies.* New York: Oxford University Press, 2024.

Payne, Richard K., and Glen A. Hayes. "Tantric Studies: Issues, Methods and Scholarly Collaborations." In *The Oxford Handbook of Tantric Studies*, edited by Richard K. Payne and Glen A. Hayes, 1–26. Oxford: Oxford University Press, 2024.

Payne, Richard K., and Casey Alexandra Kemp. "Secular Buddhism." In *The Oxford Encyclopedia of Buddhism*, edited by Richard K. Payne and Georgios T. Halkias, 2125–2152. New York: Oxford University Press, 2024.

Payne, Richard K., and Michael Witzel, eds. *Homa Variations: Ritual Change Across the* Longue Durée. Oxford: Oxford University Press, 2016.

Pidaev, Shakirjan, Tukhtash Annaev, and Gérard Fussman. *Monuments Bouddhiques de Termez/Termez Buddhist Monuments* I.1 and I.2. Publications of l'Institut de Civilizations Indienne, fasc. 79. 1 and 79.2. Paris: Collège de France, 2011.

Pinte, Klaus Leon Roger A. "The Samaya Code: Esotericization of Buddhist Precepts in Japan." PhD diss., Ghent University, 2013. https://biblio.ugent.be/publication/5332680.

Piyadassi, trans. "Atanatiya Sutta: Discourse on Atanatiya." http://www.accesstoinsight.org/tipitaka/dn/dn.32.0.piya.html.

Plofker, Kim. *Mathematics in India: 500 BCE to 1800 CE.* Princeton: Princeton University Press, 2009.

Poceski, Mario. "Contemporary Chinese Buddhist Traditions." In *The Oxford Handbook of Contemporary Buddhism*, edited by Michael Jerryson, 79–99. Oxford: Oxford University Press, 2017; online 2016: DOI: 10.1093/oxfordhb/9780199362387.013.15.

Pollock, Sheldon. *Language of the Gods in the World of Men: Sanskrit, Power, and Culture in Premodern India.* Berkeley: University of California Press, 2006.

Possehl, Gregory L. *The Indus Civilization: A Contemporary Perspective.* Lanham, MD: Alta Mira, 2002.

Powers, John. *The Buddha Party: How the People's Republic of China Works to Define and Control Tibetan Buddhism.* Oxford: Oxford University Press, 2017.

Prebish, Charles, and Martin Baumann. "Introduction: Paying Homage to the Buddha in the West." In *Westward Dharma: Buddhism beyond Asia*, edited by Charles Prebish and Martin Baumann, 1–13. Berkeley: University of California Press, 2002.

Proffitt, Aaron. "Shingon." In *The Oxford Encyclopedia of Buddhism*, edited by Richard K. Payne and Georgios T. Halkias, 2173–2196 Oxford: Oxford University Press, 2024; online 2022: https://doi.org/10.1093/acrefore/9780199340378.013.767.

Pruden, Leo. "Translator's Introduction." In *The Essentials of the Eight Traditions.* Translated by Leo Pruden, 1–6. Berkeley, CA: Numata Center for Buddhist Translation and Research, 1994.

Pye, Michael. *Japanese Buddhist Pilgrimage.* Sheffield, UK: Equinox Publishing, 2015.

Q

"Qianshou jing." In *The Princeton Dictionary of Buddhism*, edited by Robert E. Buswell, Jr., and Donald S. Lopez, Jr., 689. Princeton, NJ: Princeton University Press, 2014.

Quinter, David. "Creating Bodhisattvas: Eison, *Hinin*, and the "Living Mañjuśrī." *Monumenta Nipponica* 62.4 (Winter 2007): 437–479.

Quinter, David. *From Outcasts to Emperors: Shingon Ritsu and the Mañuśrī Cult in Medieval Japan.* Leiden: Brill, 2015.

Quinter, David. "Mañjuśrī in East Asia." In *Brill's Encyclopedia of Buddhism*, Vol. II: Lives, edited by Jonathan A. Silk, 591–599. Leiden: Brill, 2019.

Quinter, David. "Moving Monks and Mountains: Chōgen and the Cults of Gyōki, Mañjuśrī, and Wutai." In *What Happened After Mañjuśrī Migrated to China? The Sinification of the Mañjuśrī Faith and the Globalization of the Wutai Cult*, edited by Jinhua Chen, Guang Kuan, and Hu Fo, 133–156. London: Routledge, 2022.

Quinter, David. "Visualization/Contemplation Sutras (*Guan Jing*)." In *The Oxford Encyclopedia of Buddhism*, edited by Richard K. Payne and Georgios T. Halkias. New York: Oxford University Press, 2021. doi.org/10.1093/acrefore/9780199340378.013.770.

Quinter, David. "Visualizing the *Mañjuśrī Parinirvāṇa Sūtra* as a Contemplation Sutra." *Asia Major* 23.2 (2010): 97–128.

Quintman, Andrew. *The Yogin and the Madman: Reading the Biographical Corpus of Tibet's Great Saint Milarepa*. New York: Columbia University Press, 2014.

Quli, Natalie. "Western Self, Asian Other: Modernity, Authenticity, and Nostalgia for 'Tradition' in Buddhist Studies." *Journal of Buddhist Ethics* 16 (2009): 1–38.

R

Rambelli, Fabio. "Buddhism and Shinto." In *The Oxford Encyclopedia of Buddhism*, edited by Richard K. Payne and Georgios T. Halkias, 332–349. New York: Oxford University Press, 2024; online, 2018: https://doi.org/10.1093/acrefore/9780199340378.013.612.

Rambelli, Fabio. "The Empire and the Signs: Semiotics, Cultural Identity and Ideology in Japanese History." *Versus: Quaderni di studi semiotici* 83/84 (May & December) 1999. Special issue: "Reconfiguring Cultural Semiotics: The Construction of Japanese Identity."

Rambelli, Fabio. "*Honji suijaku* at Work: Religion, Economics, and Ideology in Pre-Modern Japan." In *Buddhas and Kami in Japan:* Honji Suijaku *as a Combinatory Paradigm*, edited by Mark Teeuwen and Fabio Rambelli, 255–286. London: Routledge, 2003.

Rambelli, Fabio. "'Just Behave as You Like; Prohibitions and Impurities Are Not a Problem': Radical Amida Cults and Popular Religiosity in Premodern Japan." In *Approaching the Land of Bliss: Religious Praxis in the Cult of Amitābha*, edited by Richard K. Payne and Kenneth K. Tanaka, 169–201. Honolulu: University of Hawai'i Press, 2004.

Rambelli, Fabio. "Re-inscribing *Maṇḍala*: Semiotic Operations on a Word and Its Object." In *Studies in Central and East Asian Religions* 4 (1991): 1–24.

Rambelli, Fabio. "Religion, Ideology of Domination, and Nationalism: Kuroda Toshio on the Discourse of *Shinkoku*." *Japanese Journal of Religious Studies* 23.3–4 (1996): 387–426.

Rambelli, Fabio. "The Ritual World of Buddhist 'Shinto': The *Reikiki* and Initiations on Kami-Related Matters (*jingi kanjō*) in Late Medieval and Early-Modern Japan." *Japanese Journal of Religious Studies* 29.3–4 (2002): 266–297.

Rambelli, Fabio. "Secrecy in Japanese Esoteric Buddhism." In *The Culture of Secrecy in Japanese Religion*, edited by Berhard Scheid and Mark Teeuwen, 107–129. London: Routledge, 2006.

Rambelli, Fabio. "Semiotics as Soteriology: A Different Look at Medieval Japanese Buddhism." In *Buddhism and Linguistics: Theory and Philosophy*, edited by Manel Herat, 55–80. Cham, Switzerland: Palgrave Macmillan, 2018.

Rambelli, Fabio. "True Words, Silence, and the Adamantine Dance: On Japanese Mikkyō and the Formation of Shingon Discourse." *Japanese Journal of Religious Studies* 21.4 (1994): 373–405.

Rappaport, Roy. *Ritual and Religion in the Making of Humanity*. Cambridge: Cambridge University Press, 1999.

Rasmussen, Susan J. "Cultural Anthropology." In *The Oxford Handbook of Culture and Psychology*, edited by Jean Valsiner, 96–115. New York: Oxford University Press, 2012.

Ray, Reginald. *Buddhist Saints in India: A Study in Buddhist Values and Orientations*. Oxford: Oxford University Press, 1994.

Ray, Reginald. "Reading the Vajrayāna in Context: A Reassessment of Bengal Blackie." *Buddhist-Christian Studies* 5 (1985): 173–189.

Ray, Reginald. *Secret of the Vajra World: The Tantric Buddhism of Tibet*. Boston: Shambhala, 2001.

Reader, Ian. "Dead to the World: Pilgrims in Shikoku." In *Pilgrimage in Popular Culture*, edited by Ian Reader and Tony Walter, 107–136. Houndmills: The Macmillan Press, 1993.

Reader, Ian. "From Asceticism to the Package Tour—The Pilgrim's Progress in Japan." *Religion* 17 (1987): 133–148.
Reader, Ian. "Legends, Miracles, and Faith in Kōbō Daishi, and the Shikoku Pilgrimage." In *Religions of Japan in Practice*, edited by George J. Tanabe, Jr., 360–369. Princeton, NJ: Princeton University Press, 1999.
Reader, Ian. *Making Pilgrimages: Meaning and Practice in Shikoku*. Honolulu: University of Hawai'i Press, 2005.
Reader, Ian. "Miniaturization and Proliferation: A Study of Small-Scale Pilgrimages in Japan." *Studies in Central and East Asian Religions* 1 (September 1988): 50–66.
Reader, Ian. "Pilgrimage as Cult: The Shikoku Pilgrimage as a Window on Japanese Religion." In *Religion in Japan: Arrows to Heaven and Earth*, edited by P. F. Kornicki and I. J. McMullen, 267–287. Cambridge: Cambridge University Press, 1996.
Reader, Ian. *Religion in Contemporary Japan*. Honolulu: University of Hawai'i Press, 1991.
Reader, Ian, and John Schultz. *Pilgrims Until We Die: Unending Pilgrimage in Shikoku*. New York: Oxford University Press, 2021. https://doi.org/10.1093/oso/9780197573587.001.0001.
Reader, Ian, and Paul L. Swanson. "Pilgrimage in the Japanese Religious Tradition." *Japanese Journal of Religious Studies* 24.3–4 (1997): 225–270.
Regamey, Constantin. "Motifs Vichnouites ed Śivaïtes dans le Kāraṇḍavyūha." In *Études tibétaines: dédieés à la mémoire de Marcelle Lalou*, edited by Ariane Spanien, 411–432. Paris: Librairie d'Amerique et d'Orient, 1971.
Reichle, Natasha. *Violence and Serenity: Late Buddhist Sculpture from Indonesia*. Honolulu: University of Hawai'i Press, 2007.
Reis-Habito, Maria Dorothea. *Die Dhāraṇī des Großen Erbarmens des Bodhisattva Avalokiteśvara mit tausend Händen und Augen: Übersetzung und Untersuchung ihrer textlichen Grundlage sowie Erforschung ihres Kultes in China*. Nettetal: Steyler Verlag, 1993.
Repo, Joona. "Tsongkhapa Lobzang Drakpa." Treasury of Lives, http://treasuryoflives.org/biographies/view/Tsongkhapa-Lobzang-Drakpa/8986.
Reynolds, Frank E. "The Several Bodies of Buddha: Reflections on a Neglected Aspect of Theravada Tradition." *History of Religions* 16.4 (May 1977): 374–389.
Rhie, Marylin Martin. *Early Buddhist Art of China and Central Asia, Vol. One: Later Han, Three Kingdoms and Western Chin in China and Bactria to Shan-shan in Central Asia*. Leiden: Brill, 1999.
Rhie, Marylin Martin. *Early Buddhist Art of China and Central Asia, Vol. Two: The Eastern Chin and Sixteen Kingdoms Period in China and Tumshuk, Kucha and Karashahr in Central Asia—Text*. Leiden: Brill, 2002.
Rhodes, Robert F. *Genshin's* Ōjōyōshū *and the Construction of Pure Land Discourse in Medieval Japan*. Honolulu: University of Hawai'i Press, 2017.
Rhoton, Jared Douglas. "Introduction." In Sakya Pandita Kunga Gyaltshen, *A Clear Differentiation of the Three Codes: Essential Distinctions among the Individual Liberation, Great Vehicle, and Tantric Systems*, translated by Jared Douglas Rhoton, 3–35. Albany: State University of New York Press, 2002.
Rhys Davids, C. A. F., and K. R. Norman. *Poems of Early Buddhist Nuns*. Oxford: Pali Text Society, 1989.
Roberts, Peter Alan, trans. *Mahāmudrā and Related Instructions: Core Teachings of the Kagyü Schools*. The Library of Tibetan Classics, vol. 5. Boston: Wisdom Publications, 2011.
Roberts, Peter Alan. "Translating Translation: An Encounter with the Ninth-Century Tibetan Version of the *Kāraṇḍavyūha-sūtra*." *Journal of Contemporary Buddhist Studies* 2 (2012): 224–242.
Robertson, Matthew I. *Puruṣa: Personhood in Ancient India*. New York: Oxford University Press, 2023.
Roccasalvo, Joseph F. "The Debate at bSam yas: A Study in Religious Contrast and Correspondence." *Philosophy East and West* 30.4 (Oct. 1980): 505–520.

Rocha, Cristina. "Buddhism in Latin America." In *The Oxford Handbook of Contemporary Buddhism*, edited by Michael Jerryson, 299–315. Oxford: Oxford University Press, 2017. DOI: 10.1093/oxfordhb/9780199362387.013.18.

Roesler, Ulrike. "The Kadampa: A Formative Movement in Tibetan Buddhism." In *The Oxford Encyclopedia of Buddhism*, edited by Richard K. Payne and Georgios T. Halkias, 1393–1415. New York: Oxford University Press, 2024.

Rothkrug, Lionel. "Religious Practices and Collective Perceptions: Hidden Homologies in the Renaissance and Reformation." *Historical Reflections/Réflexions Historiques* (1980) 7: 1–251.

Ruegg, D(avid) Seyfort. "Aspects of the Study of the (Earlier) Indian Mahāyāna." *Journal of the International Association of Buddhist Studies* 27.1 (2004): 3–62.

Ruegg, D(avid) Seyfort. *The Literature of the Madhyamaka School of Philosophy in India.* A History of Indian Literature, vol. VII, fasc. 1. Wiesbaden: Otto Harrassowitz, 1981.

Ruegg, D(avid) Seyfort. "A Note on the Relationship Between Buddhist and 'Hindu' Divinities in Buddhist Literature and Iconology: the Laukika/Lokottara Contrast and the Notion of an Indian 'Religious Substratum.'" *Serie Orientale Roma* 92 (2001): 735–742.

Ruegg, D(avid) Seyfort. "On the Authorship of Some Works Ascribed to Bhāvaviveka/Bhavya." In *Earliest Buddhism and Madhyamaka*, edited by David Seyfort Ruegg and Lambert Schmithausen, 59–71. Leiden: E.J. Brill, 1990.

Ruegg, D(avid) Seyfort. "Sur les rapports entre le Bouddhisme et le 'substrat religieux' indien et tibétain." *Journal Asiatique* 252 (1964): 7–95.

Ruegg, D(avid) Seyfort. *The Symbiosis of Buddhism with Brahmanism/Hinduism in South Asia and of Buddhism with "Local Cults" in Tibet and the Himalayan Region.* Vienna: Österreichische Akademie der Wissenschaften, 2007.

S

Sakuma, Ruriko. "Visualization of Avalokiteśvara as the Divinity of Lust." *Journal of Indian and Buddhist Studies* 43.2 (March 1995): 1013–1009. https://www.jstage.jst.go.jp/browse/ibk1952.

Salguero, C. Pierce. "Buddhist Medicine and Its Circulation." *Oxford Research Encyclopedias, Asian History*; online 2018. doi.org/10.1093/acrefore/9780190277727.013.215.

Salomon, Richard. "An Unwieldy Canon: Observations on Some Distinctive Features of Canon Formation in Buddhism." In *Kanonisierung und Kanonbildung in der asiatischen Religionsgeschichte*, edited by Max Deeg, Oliver Freiberger, and Christoph Kleine, 161–207. Vienna: Verlag der Österreichischen Akademie der Wissenschaften, 2011.

Samuel, Geoffrey. *Civilized Shamans: Buddhism in Tibetan Societies.* Washington, DC: Smithsonian Institution Press, 1993.

Samuel, Geoffrey. "The Subtle Body in India and Beyond." In *Religion and the Subtle Body in Asia and the West: Between Mind and Body*, edited by Geoffrey Samuel and Jay Johnston, 33–47. London: Routledge, 2013.

Samuel, Geoffrey. *Tantric Revisionings: New Understandings of Tibetan Buddhism and Indian Religion.* Aldershot, UK: Ashgate, 2005.

Samuels, Jonathan. "Debate in the Tibetan Tradition." In *The Oxford Encyclopedia of Buddhism*, edited by Richard K. Payne and Georgios T. Halkias, 729–747. New York: Oxford University Press, 2024; online: 2021, https://doi.org/10.1093/acrefore/9780199340378.013.752.

Sanders, Fabian, and Margherita Pansa. "On Some *rDzogs chen* Aspects in a *gCod* Text from the *Bla ma dgongs 'dus*, a *gTer ma* Collection Discovered by Sangs rgyas gling pa (1341–1396)." *Revue d'Études Tibétaines* 35 (2016): 169–202.

Sanderson, Alexis. "The Śaiva Age." In *Genesis and Development of Tantrism*, edited by Shingo Einoo, 41–349. Tokyo: Institute of Oriental Culture, University of Tokyo, 2009.

Sanderson, Alexis. "The Śaiva Religion Among the Khmers, Part I." *Bulletin de l'École française d'Extrême-Orient* 90–91 (2003–2004): 349–462.

Sanderson, Alexis. "Vajrayāna: Origin and Function." In *Buddhism into the Year 2000: International Conference Proceedings*, edited by the Dhammakāya Foundation, 89–102. Bangkok: Dhammakāya Foundation, 1994.

Sanford, James H. "The Abominable Tachikawa-ryū Skull Ritual." *Monumenta Nipponica* 46.1 (1981): 1–20.

Sanford, James H. "Breath of Life: The Esoteric Nembutsu." In *Esoteric Buddhism in Japan*, edited by Ian Astley. Copenhagen: Seminar for Buddhist Studies, 1994; reprinted in *Esoteric Buddhism in East Asia*, edited by Richard K. Payne, 161–189. Boston: Wisdom Publications, 2006.

Sanford, James H. "The Nine Faces of Death: 'Su Tung-po's' *Kuzō-shi*." *The Eastern Buddhist* n.s., XXI.2 (Autumn 1988): 54–77.

Sango, Asuka. "Debate Traditions in Premodern Japan." In *The Oxford Encyclopedia of Buddhism*, edited by Richard K. Payne and Georgios T. Halkias, 747–763. New York: Oxford University Press, 2024; online 2022: https://doi.org/10.1093/acrefore/9780199340378.013.954.

Sangren, P. Steven. *History and Magical Power in a Chinese Community*. Stanford, CA: Stanford University Press, 1987.

Sansom, G. B. *Japan: A Short Cultural History*. 1931. Rev. ed. Stanford, CA: Stanford University Press, 1978.

Śāntideva. *The Bodhicaryāvatāra*. Translated by Kate Crosby and Andrew Skilton. Oxford: Oxford University Press, 1995.

Saso, Michael. "*Kuden*: The Oral Hermeneutics of Tendai Tantric Buddhism." *Japanese Journal of Religious Studies* 14.2–3 (1987): 235–246.

Schaeffer, Kurtis R. *Dreaming the Great Brahmin: Tibetan Traditions of the Buddhist Poest-Saint Saraha*. Oxford: Oxford University Press, 2005.

Schaeffer, Kurtis R. "Dying Like Milarépa: Death Accounts in a Tibetan Hagiographic Tradition." In *The Buddhist Dead: Practices, Discourse, Representations*, edited by Bryan J. Cuevas and Jacqueline Stone, 208–233. Studies in East Asian Buddhism, no. 20. Honolulu: University of Hawai'i Press, 2007.

Schaffalitzky de Muckadell, Caroline. "On Essentialism and Real Definitions of Religion." *Journal of the American Academy of Religion* 82.2 (June 2014): 495–520. DOI: 10.1093/jaarel/lfu015.

Scheid, Bernhard, and Mark Teeuwen, eds. *The Culture of Secrecy in Japanese Religion*. London: Routledge, 2006.

Scheier-Dolberg, Joseph. "Treasure House of Tibetan Culture: Canonization, Printing, and Power in the Derge Printing Hourse." PhD diss., Harvard University, 2005.

Scherer, Burkhard. "Interpreting the Diamond Way: Contemporary Convert Buddhism in Transition." *Journal of Global Buddhism* 10 (2009): 17–48.

Schilbrack, Kevin. "The Concept of Religion." In *The Stanford Encyclopedia of Philosophy* (Summer 2022 edition), edited by Edward N. Zalta. https://plato.stanford.edu/archives/sum2022/entries/concept-religion/.

Schomer, Karine, and W. H. McLeod, eds. *The Sants: Studies in a Devotional Tradition of India*. Berkeley, CA: Berkeley Religious Studies Series, 1987.

Schopen, Gregory. "Archaeology and Protestant Presuppositions in the Study of Indian Buddhism." *History of Religions* 31.1 (Aug. 1991): 1–23.

Schopen, Gregory. "On the Buddha and His Bones: The Conception of a Relic in the Inscriptions of Nāgārjunikoṇḍa." *Journal of the American Oriental Society* 108.4 (Oct.–Dec. 1988): 527–537.

Schopen, Gregory. "The Phrase '*sa pṛthivīpradeśaś caityabhūto bhavet*' in the *Vajracchedikā*: Notes on the Cult of the Book in Mahāyāna." *Indo-Iranian Journal* 17.3/4 (Nov./Dec. 1975): 147–181.

Schopen, Gregory. "The Text on the 'Dhāraṇī Stones from Abhayagiriya': A Minor Contribution to the Study of Mahāyāna Literature in Ceylon." *Journal of the International Association of Buddhist Studies* 5.1 (1982): 100–108.

Scott, Victoria R. M. "Introduction: The Tradition, the Teachings, and the Teacher." In Deshung Rinpoche, *The Three Levels of Spiritual Perception*, translated by Jared Rhoton and edited by Victoria R. M. Scott, xxvii–lxxi. Boston: Wisdom Publications, 1995.

Seidel, Anna. "Corruptible Body, Incorruptible Body, Substitute Body: Modes of Immortality in China." Evans-Wentz Lecture, Stanford University, 1988.

Sekimori, Gaynor. "Shugendō and Its Relationship with the Japanese Esoteric Sects: A Study of the Ritual Calendar of an Edo-Period Shugendō Shrine-Temple Complex." In *Esoteric Buddhism and the Tantras in East Asia*, edited by Charles D. Orzech, Henrik H. Sørensen, and Richard K. Payne, 997–1008. Leiden: Brill, 2011.

Sen, Tansen. "Yijing and the Buddhist Cosmopolis of the Seventh Century." In *Texts and Transformations: Essays in Honor of the 75th Birthday of Victor H. Mair*, edited by Haun Saussy, 345–368. Amherst, MA: Cambria Press, 2018.

Sharf, Robert H. "Art in the Dark: The Funerary Context of Buddhist Caves in Western China." In *Art of Merit: Studies in Buddhist Art and Its Conservation*, edited by David Park, Kuenga Wangmo, and Sharon Cather, 38–65. London: Archetype Publications, Courtauld Institute of Art, 2013.

Sharf, Robert H. *Coming to Terms with Chinese Buddhism: A Reading of the* Treasure Store Treatise. Honolulu: University of Hawai'i Press, 2002.

Sharf, Robert H. "Thinking Through Shingon Ritual." *Journal of the International Association of Buddhist Studies* 26.1 (2003): 51–96.

Sharrock, Peter D. "The Buddhist Pantheon of the Bàyon of Angkor: An Historical and Art Historical Reconstruction of the Bàyon Temple and Its Religious and Political Roots." PhD diss., School of African and Oriental Studies, University of London, 2006.

Sharrock, Peter D. "Hevajra at Bantéay Chmàr." *The Journal of the Walters Art Museum*: Curator's Choice: Essays in Honor of Hiram W. Woodward, Jr. vol. 64/65 (2006/2007).

Sharrock, Peter D. "Garuḍa, Vajrapāṇī and Religious Change in Jayavarman VII's Angkor." *Journal of Southeast Asian Studies* 40.1 (February 2009): 111–151.

Sharrock, Peter D. "Mandalas and Landscape in Maritime Asia." In *The Oxford Handbook of Tantric Studies*, edited by Richard K. Payne and Glenn A. Hayes, 557–580. New York: Oxford University Press, 2024.

Shaw, Miranda. *Buddhist Goddesses of India*. Princeton, NJ: Princeton University Press, 2006.

Shaw, Sarah. "Buddhist Meditation and Contemplation." In *The Oxford Encyclopedia of Buddhism*, edited by Richard K. Payne and Georgios T. Halkias, 506–527. New York: Oxford University Press, 2024.

Shaw, Sarah. *Introduction to Buddhist Meditation*. Abingdon, UK: Routledge, 2009.

Sherpa, Trungram Gyaltrul Rinpoche. "Gampopa, the Monk and the Yogi: His Life and Teachings." PhD diss., Harvard University, 2004.

Shikoku Hachi-ju Ha ka Sho. 2 vols. 1982, II.268.

Shinohara, Koichi. *Spells, Images, and Mandalas: Tracing the Evolution of Esoteric Buddhist Rituals*. New York: Columbia University Press, 2014.

Shoji, Rafael. "'Buddhism in Syncretic Shape': Lessons of Shingon in Brazil." *Journal of Global Buddhism* 4 (2003): 70–107.

Siegel, Lee. "Bengal Blackie and the Sacred Slut: A Sahajayāna Buddhist Song." *Buddhist-Christian Studies* 1 (1981): 51–58.

Siegel, Lee. "Bengal Blackie Rides Again." *Buddhist-Christian Studies* 5 (1985): 191–192.

Sihlé, Nicolas. "Towards a Comparative Anthropology of the Buddhist Gift (and Other Transfers)." *Religion Compass* 9.11 (2015): 352–385.

Sihlé, Nicolas. "Written Texts at the Juncture of the Local and the Global: Some Anthropological Considerations on the Local Corpus of Tantric Ritual Manuals (Lower Mustang, Nepal)."

In *Tibetan Ritual*, edited by José Ignacio Cabezón, 35–52. New York: Oxford University Press, 2010.

Silburn, Lilian. *Kundalini: Energy of the Depths, A Comprehensive Study Based on Scriptures of Nondualistic Kaśmir Śaivism*. Translated by Jacques Gontier. Albany: State University of New York Press, 1988.

Silk, Jonathan. "The Most Important Buddhist Scripture?" Paper presented at the 12th Conference of the International Association of Buddhist Studies, Université of Lausanne, Lausanne, Switzerland, August 27, 1999.

Silk, Jonathan. "What, If Anything, Is Mahāyāna Buddhism? Problems of Definitions and Classifications." *Numen: International Review for the History of Religions* 49 (2002): 355–405.

Sinor, Denis. "Introduction: The Concept of Inner Asia." In *The Cambridge History of Early Inner Asia*, edited by Denis Sinor, 1–18. Cambridge: Cambridge University Press, 1990.

Skilling, Peter. "An Oṃ Maṇipadme Hūṃ Inscription from South East Asia." *Aséanie* 11 (2003): 13–20.

Skilling, Peter. "How the Unborn Was Born: The Riddle of Mahāyāna Origins." In *Setting Out on the Great Way: Essays on Early Mahāyāna Buddhism*, edited by Paul Harrison, 31–71. Sheffield, UK: Equinox, 2018.

Skilling, Peter. "The Rakṣā Literature of the Śrāvakayāna." *Journal of the Pali Text Society* XVI (1992): 109–182.

Skilton, Andrew. *A Concise History of Buddhism*. 2nd ed. Birmingham, UK: Windhorse Publications, 1997.

Skinner, G. William. "Cities and the Hierarchy of Local Systems" In *The City in Late Imperial China*, edited by G. William Skinner, 275–351. Stanford, CA: Stanford University Press, 1977.

Skinner, G. William. "Marketing and Social Structure in Rural China, Part I." *Journal of Asian Studies* 24.1 (1964): 3–43.

Smith, Frederick M. "The Āvasathya Fire in the Vedic Ritual." *Adyar Library Bulletin* 46 (1982): 73–92.

Smith, Frederick M. *The Self Possessed: Deity and Spirit Possession in South Asian Literature and Civilization*. New York: Columbia University Press, 2006.

Smith, Huston. *The World's Religions*. New York: HarperCollins, 1991 [1958].

Smith, Jonathan Z. *Imagining Religion: From Babylon to Jonestown*. Chicago: University of Chicago Press, 1982.

Snellgrove, David. *Indo-Tibetan Buddhism: Indian Buddhists and their Tibetan Successors*. Boston: Shambhala, 2002 [1987].

Snellgrove, David. "Introduction." In *Sarva-Tathāgata-tattva-saṅgraha: facsimile reproduction of a tenth century Sanskrit manuscript from Nepal*, edited by Lokesh Chandra and D. L. Snellgrove, 5–67. Delhi: Sharada Rani, 1981.

Snodgrass, Adrian. *The Matrix and Diamond World Mandalas in Shingon Buddhism*. 2 vols. New Delhi: Aditya Prakashan 1988.

Snodgrass, Adrian. *The Symbolism of the Stupa*. Ithaca, NY: Cornell Southeast Asia Program, 1985.

Sobisch, Jan-Ulrich. *Hevajra and* Lam 'bras *Literature of India and Tibet as Seen Through the Eyes of A-mes-Zhabs*. Contributions to Tibetan Studies, vol. 6. Wiesbaden: Dr. Ludwig Reichert Verlag, 2008.

Sobisch, Jan-Ulrich. *Three-Vow Theories in Tibetan Buddhism: A Comparative Study of Major Traditions from the Twelfth through Nineteenth Centuries*. Wiesbaden: Dr. Ludwig Reichert Verlag, 2002.

Sodargye, Khenpo, and Dan Smyer Yü. "Revisioning Buddhism as a Science of Mind in a Secularized China: A Tibetan perspective." *Journal of Global Buddhism* 18 (2017): 91–111.

Soekmono, Raden. *Chandi Borobudur: A Monument of Mankind*. Amsterdam: Van Gorcum, 1976.

Soma. "The Way of Mindfulness: The Satipatthana Sutta and Its Commentary." Access to Insight, 1998. https://www.accesstoinsight.org/lib/authors/soma/wayof.html#cemetery.

Sopa, Lhundub, Roger Jackson, and John Newman. *The Wheel of Time: The Kalachakra in Context.* Edited by Beth Simon. Madison, WI: Deer Park Books, 1985.

Sørensen, Henrik H. "Early Esoteric Buddhism in Korea: Three Kingdoms and Unified Silla (ca. 600–918)." In *Esoteric Buddhism and the Tantras in East Asia*, edited by Charles D. Orzech, Henrik Sørensen, and Richard K. Payne, 575–596. Leiden: Brill, 2011.

Sørensen, Henrik H. "Esoteric Buddhism Under the Chosŏn." In *Esoteric Buddhism and the Tantras in East Asia*, edited by Charles D. Orzech, Henrik Sørensen, and Richard K. Payne, 616–657. Leiden: Brill, 2011.

Sørensen, Henrik H. "Esoteric Buddhism Under the Koryŏ (918–1392)." In *Esoteric Buddhism and the Tantras in East Asia*, edited by Charles D. Orzech, Henrik Sørensen, and Richard K. Payne, 597–615. Leiden: Brill, 2011.

Sørensen, Henrik H. *Light on "Art in the Dark": On Buddhist Practice and Worship in the Mogao Caves.* BuddhistRoad Paper 5.6 Bochum, Germany: Center for Religious Studies, Ruhr-University Bochum, 2022.

Sørensen, Henrik H. "On Esoteric Buddhism in China: A Working Definition." In *Esoteric Buddhism and the Tantras in East Asia*, edited by Charles D. Orzech, Henrik H. Sørensen, and Richard K. Payne, 155–175. Leiden: Brill, 2011.

Sørensen, Henrik H. "The Spell of the Great, Golden Peacock Queen: The Origin, Practices, and Lore of an Early Esoteric Buddhist Tradition in China." *Pacific World: Journal of the Institute of Buddhist Studies*, third series, no. 8 (Fall 2006): 89–123.

Sørensen, Henrik H. "Spells and Magical Practices as Reflected in the Early Chinese Buddhist Sources (c. 300–600 CE) and Their Implications for the Rise and Development of Esoteric Buddhism." In *Chinese and Tibetan Esoteric Buddhism*, edited by Yael Bentor and Meir Shahar, 41–71. Leiden: Brill, 2017.

Sorensen, Michelle Janet. "Mahāmudrā Chöd? Rangjung Dorjé's Commentary on *The Great Speech Chapter* of Machik Labdrön." In *Wading Into the Stream of Wisdom: Essays in Honor of Leslie Kawamura*, edited by Sarah F. Haynes and Michelle J. Sorensen, 129–160. Berkeley, CA: Institute of Buddhist Studies and BDK America, 2013.

Sorensen, Michelle Janet. "Making the Old New Again and Again: Legitimation and Innovation in the Tibetan Buddhist Chöd Tradition." PhD diss., Columbia University, 2013.

Sorensen, Michelle Janet. "Padampa Sanngye." *Treasury of Lives* BDRC 1243 (2011). https://treasuryoflives.org/biographies/view/Padampa-Sanggye-/2510.

Sorensen, Per K. *Divinity Secularized: An Inquiry into the Nature and Form of the Songs Ascribed to the Sixth Dalai Lama.* Vienna: Arbeitskreis für Tibetische und Buddhistische Studien, Universität Wien, 1990.

Staal, Frits. *Agni: The Vedic Fire Ritual*, 2 vols. Berkeley, CA: Asian Humanities Press, 1983.

Staal, Frits. *Discovering the Vedas: Origins, Mantras, Rituals, Insights.* New Delhi: Penguin Books, 2008.

Staal, Frits. *Rules Without Meaning: Ritual, Mantras and the Human Sciences.* New York: Peter Lang Publishing, 1989.

Stache-Rosen, Valentina. "Gunavarman (367–431): A Comparatuve Analysis of the Biographies Found in the Chinese Tripitaka." *Bulletin of Tibetology* X.1: 5–54.

Stark, Rodney, and William Sims Bainbridge. "Of Churches, Sects, and Cults: Preliminary Concepts for a Theory of Religious Movements." *Journal for the Scientific Study of Religion* 18.2 (June 1979): 117–131.

Stark, Rodney, and William Sims Bainbridge. *A Theory of Religion.* 1987. Reprint. New Brunswick, NJ: Rutgers University Press, 1996.

Stearns, Cyrus. *King of the Empty Plain: The Tibetan Iron-Bridge Builder Tangtong Gyalpo.* Ithaca, NY: Snow Lion, 2007.

Stearns, Cyrus, ed. and trans. *Taking the Result as the Path: Core Teachings of the Sakya Lamdré Tradition.* Boston: Wisdom Publications, 2006.

Stein, Lisa, and Ngwang Zangpo, trans. *Butön's History of Buddhism in India and Its Spread to Tibet.* Boulder, CO: Snow Lion, 2013.

Stein, R. A. *Tibetan Civilization*. Translated by J. E. Stapleton Driver. Stanford, CA: Stanford University Press, 1972.

Sternberg, Ungern. "Komyo Shingon (Mantra of Light)." https://www.youtube.com/watch?v = jxTeTcWkL4Q.

Stevenson, Daniel B. "The Four Kinds of *Samādhi* in Early T'ien-t'ai Buddhism." In *Traditions of Meditation in Chinese Buddhism*, edited by Peter Gregory, 45–97. Honlulu: University of Hawai'i Press, 1986.

Stoddard, Heather. *Early Sino-Tibetan Art*. 2nd ed. Bangkok: Orchid Press, 2008.

Stone, Jacqueline. "Just Open Your Mouth and Say 'A': A-Syllable Practice for the Time of Death in Early Medieval Japan." *Pacific World: Journal of the Institute of Buddhist Studies*, third series, no. 8 (Fall 2006): 167–189.

Stone, Jacqueline. "Nichiren." In *The Oxford Encyclopedia of Buddhism*, edited by Richard K. Payne and Georgios T. Halkias, 1760–1779 New York: Oxford University Press, 2024, online 2020. https://doi.org/10.1093/acrefore/9780199340378.013.575.

Stone, Jacqueline. *Original Enlightenment and the Transformation of Medieval Japanese Buddhism*. Honolulu: University of Hawai'i Press, 1999.

Stone, Jacqueline. *Right Thoughts at the Last Moment: Buddhism and Deathbed Practices in Early Medieval Japan*. Honolulu: University of Hawai'i Press, 2016.

Strickmann, Michel. "Homa in East Asia." In *Agni: The Vedic Ritual of the Fire Altar*, ed. Frits Staal, 2 vols., II: 418–455. Berkeley, CA: Asian Humanities Press, 1983.

Strickmann, Michel. *Mantras et mandarins: Le bouddhisme tantrique en Chine*. Paris: Gallimard, 1996.

Stril-Rever, Sofia. *Kālachakra: Guide de l'Initiation et du Guru Yoga*. Paris: Desclée de Brouwer, 2002.

Stril-Rever, Sofia, trans. *Tantra de Kālachakra: Le Livre du Corps subtil*. Paris: Desclée de Brouwer, 2000.

Stril-Rever, Sofia. *Traité du maṇḍala: Tantra de Kālacakra*. Paris: Desclée de Brouwer, 2003.

Strube, Julian. *Global Tantra: Religion, Science and Nationalism in Global Modernity*. New York: Oxford University Press, 2022.

Studholme, Alexander. *The Origins of* Oṃ Maṇipadme Hūṃ*: A Study of the* Kāraṇḍavyūha Sūtra. Albany: State University of New York Press, 2002.

Styers, Randall. *Making Magic: Religion, Magic, and Science in the Modern World*. New York: Oxford University Press, 2004.

Sugiki, Tsunehiko. "On the Chronology of Buddhist Tantras." In *The Oxford Handbook of Tantric Studies*, edited by Richard K. Payne and Glen T. Hayes, 1057–1082. New York: Oxford University Press, 2024; online: doi.org/10.1093/oxfordhb/9780197549889.013.32.

Sujata, Victoria. *Tibetan Songs of Realization: Echoes from a Seventeenth-Century Scholar and Siddha in Amdo*. Leiden: Brill, 2005.

Sundberg, J(effrey). "The Abhayagirivihāra's *Pāṃśukūlika* Monks in Second Lambakaṇṇa Śrī Laṅka and Śailendra Java: The Flowering and Fall of a Cardinal Center of Influence in Early Esoteric Buddhism." *Pacific World: Journal of the Institute of Buddhist Studies*, third series, no. 16 (2014): 49–185.

Sundberg, J(effrey). "The Wilderness Monks of the Abhayagirivihara and the Origins of Sino-Javanese Esoteric Buddhism." *Bijdragen tot de Taal-, Land- en Volkendunde* 160.1 (2004): 95–123.

Sundberg, Jeffrey, in collaboration with Rolf Giebel. "The Life of the Tang-Court Monk Vajrabodhi as Chronicled by Lü Xiang (呂向): South-Indian and Śrī Laṅkān Antecedents to the Arrival of the Buddhist Vajrayāna in Eighth-Century Java and China." *Pacific World: Journal of the Institute of Buddhist Studies*, third series, no. 13 (2011): 129–222.

Swanson, Paul L. "Shugendō and the Yoshino-Kumano Pilgrimage: An Example of Mountain Pilgrimage." *Monumenta Nipponica* XXXVI.1 (Spring 1981): 55–84.

Swearer, Donald K. *The Buddhist World of Southeast Asia*. 2nd ed. Albany: State University of New York Press, 2010.

T

TAIRA Masayuki. "Kuroda Toshio and the *Kenmitsu Taisei* Theory." Translated by Thomas Kirchner. *Japanese Journal of Religious Studies* 23.3–4 (1996): 427–448.

Tajima, Ryūjun. *Étude sur le Mahāvairocana sūtra.* Paris, 1936; English translation in Alex Wayman, trans. and ed., *The Enlightenment of Vairocana.* Delhi: Motilal Banarsidass, 1992.

Tambiah, S(tanley) J. *World Conqueror and World Renouncer: A Study of Buddhism and Polity in Thailand against a Historical Background.* Cambridge: Cambridge University Press, 1976.

Tanabe, George, Jr. "The Founding of Mount Kōya and Kūkai's Eternal Meditation." In *Religions of Japan in Practice*, edited by George J. Tanabe, Jr., 354–359. Princeton, NJ: Princeton University Press, 1999.

Tanabe, George, Jr. *Myōe the Dreamkeeper: Fantasy and Knowledge in Early Kamakura Buddhism.* Cambridge, MA: Harvard University Asia Center, 1992.

Tanabe, Willa Jane. "Robes and Clothing." In *Encyclopedia of Buddhism*, edited by Robert E. Buswell, Jr., 731–735. New York: Macmillan, 2004.

Tatz, Mark. Asaṅga's Chapter on Ethics with the Commentary of Tsong-Kha-Pa. In *The Basic Path to Awakening, The Complete Bodhisattva.* Lewiston, NY: Edwin Mellen Press, 1986.

Tatz, Mark. "The Life of the Siddha-Philosopher Maitrīgupta." *Journal of the American Oriental Society* 107.4 (Oct.–Dec. 1987): 695–711.

Tayé, Jamgön Kongtrul Lodrö. *The Treasury of Knowledge: Book Six, Part Four; Systems of Buddhist Tantra.* Translated by Elio Guarisco and Ingrid McLeod. Ithaca, NY: Snow Lion, 2005.

Taylor, Mark C. "The Politics of Theo-ry." *Journal of the American Academy of Religion* 59.1 (Spring 1991): 1–37.

Teiser, Stephen. *The Ghost Festival in Medieval China.* Princeton, NJ: Princeton University Press, 1988.

ten Grotenhuis, Elizabeth. "Collapsing the Distinction Between Buddha and Believer: Human Hair in Japanese Esotericizing Embroideries." In *Esoteric Buddhism and the Tantras in East Asia*, edited by Charles D. Orzech, Henrik H. Sørensen, and Richard K. Payne, 876–892. Leiden: Brill, 2011.

Ṭhānissaro. *The Buddhist Monastic Code, II: The Khandhaka Rules.* Valley Center, CA: Metta Forest Monastery, 2001.

Ṭhānissaro. "The Establishing of Mindfulness Discourse Satipaṭṭhāna Sutta (MN 10)." https://www.dhammatalks.org/suttas/MN/MN10.html.

Ṭhānissaro. *Japanese Mandalas: Representations of Sacred Geography.* Honolulu: University of Hawai'i Press, 1999.

Ṭhānissaro. "Kayagata-sati sutta, Mindfulness Immersed in the Body." Access to Insight, 1997. https://www.accesstoinsight.org/tipitaka/mn/mn.119.than.html, updated version at https://www.dhammatalks.org/suttas/MN/MN119.html.

Ṭhānissaro. "Khp 7. Tirokuḍḍa Kaṇḍa—(Hungry Ghosts) Outside the Walls." https://www.dhammatalks.org/suttas/KN/Khp/khp7.html.

Ṭhānissaro. "Khuddaka Nikāya: The Short Collection." https://www.dhammatalks.org/suttas/KN/index_KN.html.

Thapar, Romila. *Early India: From the Origins to AD 1300.* Berkeley: University of California Press, 2002.

Thapar, Romila. *The Past Before Us: Historical Traditions of Early North India.* Cambridge, MA: Harvard University Press, 2013.

Thompson, Ashley. "Contemporary Cambodian Buddhist Traditions: Seen from the Past." In *The Oxford Handbook of Contemporary Buddhism*, edited by Michael Jerryson, 236–257. New York: Oxford University Press, 2017. DOI: 10.1093/oxfordhb/9780199362387.013.32.

Thrangu, Khenchen. *A Song for the King: Saraha on Mahāmudrā Meditation.* Edited by Michele Martin and translated by Peter O'Hearn. Boston: Wisdom Publications, 2006.

Thurman, Robert. "Buddhist Hermeneutics." *Journal of the American Academy of Religion* 46.1 (March 1978): 19–39.

Tibetan Classics Translators Guild of New York, trans. *The Noble Procedure for Mañjuśrī's Single-Syllable Mantra.* 84000: https://read.84000.co/translation/toh550.html.

Timalsina, Sthaneswar. "Attention, Memory, and the Imagination: A Cognitive Analysis of Tantric Visualization." In *The Oxford Handbook of Tantric Studies*, edited by Richard K. Payne and Glen A. Hayes, 731–751. Oxford: Oxford University Press, online 2023: https://doi.org/10.1093/oxfordhb/9780197549889.013.53.

Timalsina, Sthaneswar. "Metaphor, *Rasa*, and *Dhvani*: Suggested Meaning in Tantric Esotericism." *Method and Theory in the Study of Religion* 19 (2007): 134–162.

Timalsina, Sthaneswar. "Reconstructing the Tantric Body: Elements of the Symbolism of Body in the Monistic Kaula and Trika Tantric Traditions." *International Journal of Hindu Studies* 16.1 (April 2012): 57–91. DOI: 10.1007/s11407-012-9111-5.

Timalsina, Sthaneswar. "Songs of Transformation: Vernacular Josmanī Literature and the Yoga of Cosmic Awareness." *International Journal of Hindu Studies* 14.2–3 (2010): 201–228.

Timalsina, Sthaneswar. "Terrifying Beauty: Interplay of the Sanskritic and Vernacular Rituals of Siddhilakṣmī." *International Journal of Hindu Studies* 10.1 (April 2006): 59–73.

Todaro, Dale Allen. "A Study of the Earliest *Garbha Vidhi* of the Shingon Sect." *Journal of the International Association of Buddhist Studies* 9.2 (1986): 109–146.

Toshio Kuroda. "The Development of the *Kenmitsu* System as Japan's Medieval Orthodoxy." *Japanese Journal of Religious Studies* 23.3–4 (1996): 233–270.

Toulmin, Stephen. *Cosmopolis: The Hidden Agenda of Modernity.* Chicago: University of Chicago Press, 1992.

Trainor, Kevin. *Relics, Ritual, and Representation in Buddhism: Rematerializing the Sri Lankan Tradition.* Cambridge: Cambridge University Press, 1997.

Trainor, Kevin, and Paula Arai. "Introduction: Embodiment and Sense Experience." In *The Oxford Handbook of Buddhist Practice*, edited by Kevin Trainor and Paula Arai, 1–18. New York: Oxford University Press, 2022. https://doi.org/10.1093/oxfordhb/9780190632922.013.40.

Tribe, Anthony. "Mañjuśrī: Origins, Role and Significance (Parts 1 & 2)." *The Western Buddhist Review* 2 (1997): 1–47.

Tsongkhapa, *A Lamp to Illuminate the Five Stages: Teachings on* Guhyasamāja Tantra. Translated by Gavin Kilty. Boston: Wisdom Publications, 2013.

Tsong Khapa Losang Drakpa. *Brilliant Illumination of the Lamp of the Five Stages* (rin lnga rab tu gsal ba'i sgron me): Practical Instruction in the King of Tantras The Glorious Esoteric Community. Translated by Robert A. F. Thurman. New York: Columbia University, 2010.

Tsuda Shin'ichi. "A Critical Tantrism." *Memoirs of the Research Department of the Toyo Bunko* 36 (1978): 167–231.

Tsuda Shin'ichi. "The Original Formation and Performance of the 'Secret Assembly' (*guhyasamāja*), an Integration of the *Guhyasamāja-tantra* into the History of Tantric Buddhism in India." *Journal of the International College for Advanced Buddhist Studies* 2 (1999): 103–146 (or 310–267).

Tuladhar-Douglas, Will. *Remaking Buddhism for Medieval Nepal: The Fifteenth-Century Reformation of Newar Buddhism.* London: Routledge, 2006.

Tuttle, Gray. "Challenging Central Tibet's Dominance of History: The *Oceanic Book*, a 19th Century Politico-Religious Geographic History." In *Mapping the Modern in Tibet*, edited by Gray Tuttle, 135–182. Andiast, Switzerland: International Institute for Tibetan and Buddhist Studies, 2011.

Tuttle, Gray. "Uniting Religion and Politics in a Bid for Autonomy: Lamas in Exile in China and America." In *Buddhist Missionaries in the Era of Globalization*, edited by Linda Learman, 210–232. Honolulu: University of Hawai'i Press, 2005.

Tweed, Thomas A. "American Occultism and Japanese Buddhism: Albert J. Edmunds, D.T. Suzuki, and Translocative History." *Japanese Journal of Religious Studies* 32.2 (2005): 249–281.

Tweed, Thomas A. "Introduction: Narrating U.S. Religious History." In *Retelling U.S. Religious History*, edited by Thomas A. Tweed, 1–23. Berkeley: University of California Press, 1997.

Tweed, Thomas A. "Toward a Translocative History of Occult Buddhism: Flows and Confluences, 1881–1912. *History of Religions* 54.4 (May 2015): 423–433.

U

Ullrey, Aaron Michael. "Grim Grimoires: Pragmatic Ritual in the Magic Tantras." PhD diss., Univesity of California, Santa Barbara, 2016.

Unno, Mark. *Shingon Refractions: Myōe and the Mantra of Light*. Boston: Wisdom Publications, 2004.

Urban, Hugh B. *The Economics of Ecstasy: Tantra, Secrecy, and Power in Colonial Bengal*. New York: Oxford University Press, 2001.

Urban, Hugh B. "The Extreme Orient: The Construction of 'Tantrism' as a Category in the Orientalist Imagination." *Religion* 29 (1999): 123–146.

Urban, Hugh B. *Magia Sexualis: Sex, Magic, and Liberation in Modern Western Esotericism*. Berkeley: University of California Press, 2006.

Urban, Hugh B. *The Power of Tantra: Religion, Sexuality and the Politics of South Asian Studies*. London: I.B. Tauris, 2009.

Urban, Hugh B. *Songs of Ecstasy: Tantric and Devotional Songs from Colonial Bengal*. New York: Oxford University Press, 2001.

Urban, Hugh B. *Tantra: Sex, Secrecy, Politics, and Power in the Study of Religion*. Berkeley: University of California Press, 2003.

Urban, Hugh B. "The Yoga of Sex: Tantra, Orientalism, and Sex Magic in the Ordo Templi Orientis." In *Hidden Intercourse: Eros and Sexuality in the History of Western Esotericism*, edited by Wouter J. Hanegraaff and Jeffrey J. Kripal, 401–443. New York: Fordham University Press, 2011.

V

van der Kujip, Leonard W. J. "The Lives of Bu ston Rin chen grub and the Date and Sources of His *Chos 'byung*, a Chronicle of Buddhism in India and Tibet." *Revue d'Etudes Tibétains* 35 (2016): 203–308.

van der Kujip, Leonard W. J. "Some Remarks on the Textual Transmission and Text of Bu ston Rin chen grub's *Chos 'byung*, a Chronicle of Buddhism in India and Tibet." *Revue d'Etudes Tibétains* 25 (2013): 115–193.

van der Veere, Hendrik. "Pilgrimage in Japanese Buddhism." In *The Wiley Blackwell Companion to East and Inner Asian Buddhism*, edited by Mario Poceski, 259–277. Chichester, UK: John Wiley & Sons, 2014.

van Schaik, Sam. *Approaching the Great Perfection: Simultaneous and Gradual Methods of Dzogchen Practice in the Longchen Nyingtig*. Boston: Wisdom Publications, 2004.

van Schaik, Sam. "A Definition of Mahāyoga: Soures from the Dunhuang Manuscripts." *Tantric Studies* 1 (2008): 45–88.

van Schaik, Sam. "The Early Days of the Great Perfection." *Journal of the International Association of Buddhist Studies* 27.1 (2004): 165–206.

van Schaik, Sam. "The Internalisation of the Vajrāsana." In *Precious Treasures from the Diamond Throne: Finds from the Site of the Buddha's Enlightenment*, edited by Sam van

Schaik, Daniela DeSimone, Gergely Hidas, and Michael Willis, 65–70. London: The British Museum, 2021.

van Schaik, Sam. "The Limits of Transgression: The *Samaya* Vows of Mahāyoga." In *Esoteric Buddhism at Dunhuang: Rites and Teachings for This Life and Beyond*, edited by Matthew Kapstein and Sam van Schaik, 61–84. Leiden: Brill, 2010.

van Schaik, Sam. "The Sweet Sage and *The Four Yogas*: A Lost Mahāyoga Treatise from Dunhuang." *Journal of the International Association of Tibetan Studies* 4 (Dec. 2008): 1–67.

van Schaik, Sam. *The Taming of the Demons: Violence and Liberation in Tibetan Buddhism.* New Haven, CT: Yale University Press, 2011.

van Schaik, Sam. *Tibetan Zen: Discovering a Lost Tradition.* Boston: Snow Lion, 2015.

Vásquez, Manuel A., and David Garbin. "Globalization." In *The Oxford Handbook of the Study of Religion*, edited by Michael Strausberg and Steven Engler, 682–701. Oxford: Oxford University Press, 2016; online, 2017: DOI: 10.1093/oxfordhb/9780198729570.013.46.

Veidlinger, Daniel M. *Spreading the Dhamma: Writing, Orality, and Textual Transmission in Buddhist Northern Thailand.* Honolulu: University of Hawai'i Press, 2006.

Veidlinger, Daniel M. "Transmission of Buddhist Media and Texts." In *The Oxford Encyclopedia of Buddhism*, edited by Richard K. Payne and Georgios T. Halkias, 2553–2574. New York: Oxford University Press, 2024; online, 2018. DOI: 10.1093/acrefore/9780199340378.013.515.

Viswanathan, Gauri. "Colonialism and the Construction of Hinduism." In *The Blackwell Companion to Hinduism*, edited by Gavin Flood, 23–44. Oxford: Blackwell Publishing, 2003.

von Brück, Michael. *Einführung in den Buddhismus.* Frankfurt: Verlag der Weltreligionen, 2007.

von Glasenapp. Helmuth. *Buddhistische Mysterien: Die Geheimen Lehren und Riten des Diamant-Fahrzeugs.* Stuttgart: W. Spemann Verlag, 1940.

W

Waddell, L.(aurence) Austine. *Tibetan Buddhism: With Its Mystic Cults, Symbolism, and Mythology.* New York: Dover, 1972.

Wallace, B. Alan, trans, *Heart of the Great Perfection: Düdjom Lingpa's Visions of the Great Perfection.* Vol. I. Somerville, MA: Wisdom Publications, 2015.

Wallace, Vesna. *The Inner Kālacakratantra: A Buddhist Tantric View of the Individual.* Oxford: Oxford University Press, 2001.

Wallace, Vesna. "Introduction." In *Buddhism in Mongolian History, Culture, and Society*, edited by Vesna Wallace, xv–xxii. Oxford: Oxford University Press, 2015.

Wallace, Vesna. "Kālacakra-Maṇḍala: Symbolism and Construction." In *The Oxford Encyclopedia of Buddhism*, edited by Richard K. Payne and Georgios T. Halkias, 1416–1433. New York: Oxford University Press, 2024.

Wallis, Glenn. *Mediating the Power of the Buddhas: Ritual in the* Mañjuśrīmūlakalpa. Albany: State University of New York Press, 2002.

Walshe, Maurice. *The Long Discourses of the Buddha.* 1987. Reprint. Boston: Wisdom Publications, 1995.

Walter, Mariko Namba. *Sogdians and Buddhism.* Sino-Platonic Papers, no. 174. Philadelphia: Department of East Asian Languages and Civilizations, University of Pennsylvania, 2006. www.sino-platonic.org.

Walter, Mariko Namba. *Tokharian Buddhism in Kucha: Buddhism of Indo-European Centum Speakers in Chinese Turkestan before the 10th Century C.E.* Sino-Platonic Papers, no. 85. Philadelphia: Department of East Asian Languages and Civilizations, University of Pennsylvania, 1998. www.sino-platonic.org.

Walter, Michael. "Jābir, The Buddhist Yogi: Part One" *Journal of Indian Philosophy* 20 (1992): 425–438.

Walter, Michael. "Jābir, The Buddhist Yogi: Part Two, 'Winds' and Immortality." *Journal of Indian Philosophy* 24 (1996): 145–164.

Walton, Matthew J. "Buddhism, Nationalism, and Governance." In *The Oxford Handbook of Contemporary Buddhism*, edited by Michael Jerryson, 532–535. Oxford: Oxford University Press, 2017. DOI: 10.1093/oxfordhb/9780199362387.013.41

Wang, Michelle C. "Dunhuang Art." in *The Oxford Encyclopedia of Buddhism*, edited by Richard K. Payne and Georgios T. Halkias, 781–806. New York: Oxford University Press, 2024; online: 2018, https://doi.org/10.1093/acrefore/9780199340378.013.173.

Wang, Michelle C. "The Thousand-Armed Mañjuśrī at Dunhuang and Paired Images in Buddhist Visual Culture." *Archives of Asian Art* 66.1 (2016): 81–105.

Wangchug, Shakya Gelong Kelsan Thubten. *A Manual for the Self-Generation of the Mandala of the Seven Gone to Thus*. Translated by Fabrizio Palloti. Portland, OR: FPMT (Foundation for the Preservation of the Mahayana Tradition), 2011.

Wangchuk, Dorji. "An Eleventh-Century Defence of the Authenticity of the *Guhyagarbha Tantra*." In *The Many Canons of Tibetan Buddhism*, edited by Helmut Eimer and David Germano, 265–291. Leiden: Brill, 2002.

Wangyal, Tenzin. *The Tibetan Yogas of Dream and Sleep*. Ithaca, NY: Snow Lion, 1998.

Watkins, Calvert. *How to Kill a Dragon: Aspects of Indo-European Poetics*. Oxford: Oxford University Press, 1995.

Wayman, Alex. *The Buddhist Tantras: Light on Indo-Tibetan Esotericism*. 1973. Reprint. London: Routledge, 2008.

Wayman, Alex. "Contributions on the Symbolism of the Mandala-Palace." In *Études Tibétaines: Dédiées À La Mémoire De Marcelle Lalou*, edited by André Bareau, 557–566. Paris: Libraire d'Amérique et d'Orient, 1971.

Wayman, Alex. *The Enlightenment of Vairocana*. Delhi: Motilal Banarsidass, 1992.

Wedemeyer, Christian K. "Locating Tantric Antinomianism: An Essay Toward an Intellectual History of the 'Practices/Practice Observance' (*caryā/caryāvrata*)." *Journal of the International Association of Buddhist Studies* 34.1–2 (2011 [2012]): 349–419.

Wedemeyer, Christian K. *Making Sense of Tantric Buddhism: History, Semiology, and Transgression in the Indian Traditions*. New York: Columbia University Press, 2013.

Wedemeyer, Christian K. "Tropes, Typologies, and Turnarounds: A Brief Genealogy of the Historiography of Tantric Buddhism." *History of Religions* 40.3 (2001): 223–259.

Weinberger, Steven. "The Significance of Yoga Tantra and the *Compendium of Principles (Tattvasaṃgraha Tantra)* within Tantric Buddhism in India and Tibet." PhD diss., University of Virginia, 2003.

Weinberger, Steven. "The Yoga Tantras and the Social Context of Their Transmission to Tibet." *Chung-Hwa Buddhist Journal* 23 (2010): 131–166.

Welch, Holmes. *The Practice of Chinese Buddhism, 1900–1950*. Cambridge, MA: Harvard University Press, 1967.

West, M. L. *Indo-European Poetry and Myth*. Oxford: Oxford University Press, 2007

Westerhoff, Jan. *The Dispeller of Disputes: Nāgārjuna's* Vigrahavyāvartanī. Oxford: Oxford University Press, 2010.

Westerhoff, Jan. *Nāgārjuna's Madhyamaka: A Philosophical Introduction*. Oxford: Oxford University Press, 2009.

White, David Gordon. *The Alchemical Body: Siddha Traditions in Medieval India* Chicago: University of Chicago Press, 1996.

White, David Gordon. *Kiss of the Yoginī: "Tantric Sex" in Its South Asian Contexts*. Chicago: University of Chicago Press, 2003.

White, David Gordon. "Tantra in Practice: Mapping a Tradition." In *Tantra in Practice*, edited by David Gordon White, 3–38. Princeton, NJ: Princeton University Press, 2000.

White, Erick. "Contemporary Buddhism and Magic." In *The Oxford Handbook of Contemporary Buddhism*, edited by Michael Jerryson, 591–605. Oxford: Oxford University Press, 2017.

White, Hayden. *Metahistory: The Historical Imagination in Nineteenth-Century Europe.* Baltimore: Johns Hopkins University Press, 1973.

Whitfield, Susan. "Introduction: A Part of All Our Histories." In *The Silk Road: Trade, Travel, War and Faith*, edited by Susan Whitfield, 13–18. Chicago: Serindia Publications, 2004.

Willemen, Charles. "Tripitaka Shan-wu-wei's Name: A Chinese Translation from Prākrit." *T'oung Pao* 67 (1981): 362–365.

Williams, Ben. "Cosmogenesis and Phonematic Emanation." In *The Oxford Handbook of Tantric Studies*, edited by Richard K. Payne and Glen A. Hayes, 795–818. New York: Oxford University Press, 2024.

Williams, Paul. "Some Mahāyāna Buddhist Perspectives on the Body." In *Religion and the Body*, edited by Sarah Coakley, 205–230. Cambridge: Cambridge University Press, 1997.

Williams, Paul, with Anthony Tribe. *Buddhist Thought: A Complete Introduction to the Indian Tradition.* London: Routledge, 2000.

Wilson, Jeff. *Dixie Dharma: Inside a Buddhist Temple in the American South.* Chapel Hill: The University of North Carolina Press, 2014.

Winfield, Pamela. *Icons and Iconoclasm in Japanese Buddhism: Kūkai and Dōgen on the Art of Enlightenment.* Oxford: Oxford University Press, 2013.

Winfield, Pamela. "Kyoto Pilgrimage Past and Present." *Crosscurrents* Sept. 2009: 349–357.

Witzel, (E. J.) Michael. *The Origins of the World's Mythologies.* New York: Oxford University Press, 2013.

Witzel, (E. J.) Michael. "Reminiscences of Frits Staal and the *Agnicayana*." In *On Meaning and Mantra: Essays in Honor of Frits Staal*, edited by George Thompson and Richard K. Payne, 601–622. Berkeley, CA: Institute of Buddhist Studies, 2016.

Witzel, (E. J.) Michael. "Vedas and Upaniṣads." In *The Blackwell Companion to Hinduism*, edited by Gavin Flood, 68–98. Oxford: Blackwell, 2003.

Wolpert, Stanley. *India.* 3rd ed. Berkeley: University of California Press, 2005.

Wong, Dorothy C. "The Art of *Avataṃsaka* Buddhism in the Courts of Empress Wu and Emperor Shōmu/Empress Kōmyō." In *Avataṃsaka (Huayan, Kegon, Flower Ornament) Buddhism in East Asia: Origins and Adaptation of a Visual Culture*, edited by Robert Gimello, Frédéric Girard, and Imre Hamar, 223–260. Wiesbaden: Harrassowitz Verlag, 2012.

Woodward, Hiram. "Bianhong: Mastermind of Borobudur?" *Pacific World: Journal of the Institute of Buddhist Studies*, third series, no. 11 (2009): 25–60.

Woodward, Hiram. "Esoteric Buddhism in Southeast Asia in the Light of Recent Scholarship." *Journal of Southeast Asian Studies* 35.2 (June 2004): 329–354. DOI: 10.1017/S0022463404000177.

Woodward, Hiram. "Tantric Buddhism at Angkor Thom." *Ars Orientalis* 12 (1981): 57–67.

Wright, Dale S. "Introduction: Rethinking Ritual Practice in Zen Buddhism." In *Zen Ritual: Studies of Zen Theory in Practice*, edited by Steven Heine and Dale Wright, 3–20. Oxford: Oxford University Press, 2007.

Wright, Dale S. *What Is Buddhist Enlightenment?* Oxford: Oxford University Press, 2016.

Wright, Rita P. *The Ancient Indus: Urbanism, Economy, and Society.* Cambridge: Cambridge University Press, 2010.

Wright, Robert. *Why Buddhism Is True: The Science and Philosophy of Meditation and Enlightenment.* New York: Simon and Schuster, 2017.

Wu, Emily Shao-Fan. "Fengshui Plus Buddhism Equals What? An Initial Analysis of Black Sect Tantric Buddhism in the United States." MA thesis, Boston University, 2003.

Wu, Wei. *Esoteric Buddhism in China: Engaging Japanese and Tibetan Traditions, 1912–1949.* New York: Columbia University Press, 2024.

Wujastyk, Dominik. "The Science of Medicine." In *The Blackwell Companion to Hinduism*, edited by Gavin Flood, 393–409. Oxford: Blackwell, 2003.

X

Xinjiang, Rong. *Land Route or Sea Route? Commentary on the Study of the Paths of Transmission and Areas in Which Buddhism Was Disseminated During the Han Period.* Translated by Xiuqun Zhou, Sino-Platonic Papers, no. 144. Philadelphia: Department of East Asian Languages and Civilizations, University of Pennsylvania, 2004.

Y

Yamaguchi, Shinobu. "A Sanskrti Text of the Nepalese Buddhist Homa." *Journal of Indian and Buddhist Studies* 50.1 (Dec. 2001): 489–484 (rtlp: right to left pagination). https://www.jstage.jst.go.jp/browse/ibk1952.

Yamaguchi, Shinobu. "The Three Meditations of the Cakrasaṃvaramaṇḍala" *Journal of Indian and Buddhist Studies* 51.1 (Dec. 2002): 503–449 (rtlp: right to left pagination). https://www.jstage.jst.go.jp/browse/ibk1952.

Yamamoto, Carl S. "The Historical Roots of Tibetan Scholasticism." *Religion Compass* 3/5 (2009): 823–835. DOI: 10.1111/j.1749-8171.2009.00170.x.

Yamashita, Tsutomu. "Sanskrit Medical Literature." In *The Oxford Handbook of Science and Medicine in the Classical World*, edited by Paul T. Keyser and John Scarborough, 95–104. Oxford: Oxford University Press, 2018; doi.org/10.1093/oxfordhb/9780199734146.013.66.

Yang, Bin. *Cowrie Shells and Cowrie Money: A Global History.* London: Routledge, 2019.

Yang, Bin. "Horses, Silver, and Cowries: Yunnan in Global Perspective." *Journal of World History* 15.3 (2004): 281–322.

Yelle, Robert A. *Explaining Mantras: Ritual, Rhetoric, and the Dream of a Natural Language in Hindu Tantra.* New York: Routledge, 2003.

Yi-liang, Chou. "Tantrism in China." *Harvard Journal of Asiatic Studies* 8.3/4 (March 1945): 241–332. Reprinted in *Tantric Buddhism in East Asia*, edited by Richard K. Payne, 33–60. Boston: Wisdom Publications, 2005.

Young, Serinity. *Courtesans and Tantric Consorts: Sexualities in Buddhist Narrative, Iconography, and Ritual.* London: Routledge, 2004.

Yu, Anthony C. "Two Literary Examples of Religious Pilgrimage: The Commedia and The Journey to the West." *History of Religions* 22.3 (Feb. 1983): 202–230.

Yu, Jimmy. "Revisiting the Notion of *Zong*: Contextualizing the Dharma Drum Lineage of Modern Chan Buddhism." *Chung-Hwa Buddhist Journal* 26 (2013): 113–151.

Z

Zaehner, R. C. *Mysticism, Sacred and Profane: An Inquiry into Some Varieties of Praeternatural Experience.* 1957. Reprint. Oxford: Oxford University Press, 1980.

Zakharov, Anton O. "The Śailendras Reconsidered." Singapore: The Nalanda–Sriwijaya Centre, Institute of Southeast Asian Studies, 2012.

Zuidervaart, Lambert. "Theodor W. Adorno." In *The Stanford Encyclopedia of Philosophy* (Winter 2015 edition), edited by Edward N. Zalta. https://plato.stanford.edu/archives/win2015/entries/adorno/.

Zürcher, Eric. *The Buddhist Conquest of China.* 2 vols. Leiden: Brill, 1959.

Zysk, Kenneth G. "The Science of Respiration and the Doctrine of Bodily Winds in Ancient India." *Journal of the American Oriental Society* 113.2 (April–June 1993): 198–213.

Index

For the benefit of digital users, indexed terms that span two pages (e.g., 52–53) may, on occasion, appear on only one of those pages.

Abé, Ryūichi, 88–89
Abhayagiri Vihāra and Abhayagiri lineage, 124–25
abhidharma, 40–41, 143, 219
abhiṣeka, 51–57, 204–5, 219
abridged version of a tantra, 48, 219
Acalanātha Vidyārāja, 3, 219. *See also* Fudō Myōō; Immovable Wisdom King
ācārya, 28–29, 52–53, 219
Acri, Andrea, 112, 121–22, 166–67
adamantine songs, 63–65, 219. See also *caryagīti*; *dōha*; *vajragīti*
ādibuddha, 219
ādyanutpāda, 54, 219
agency, 78–79
Agni, 3, 35, 219
agnicayana, 34–35, 219
All-Gathering Maṇḍala Ceremony, 45–46
already awakened buddha mind, 219
Amida, 101–2
Amitābha, 82, 99, 107
Amoghavajra, 28–29, 83, 84–85, 86–87, 118–19, 126–27, 157, 167, 173, 204–5, 206, 219
Analayo, Bhikkhu, 140–41
Andrews, Susan, 183–84
Angkor, 114, 118, 120, 174
  mandala, 117–19
anitya, 138–39, 219
Anurādhapura, 124
anuttarayoga tantras, 47, 59–60, 219
Apabraṃśa, 63–64
Aparimitāyus, 78–79. *See also* Amitābha
apramāṇa, 153, 219
apratiṣṭhā-nirvāṇa, 51, 219
Arai, Paula, 157–58
argha, 53–54, 219
Aryans, 195
asanas, 17, 219
Asaṅga, 82, 83
Assavavirulhakarn, Prapod, 113, 114, 115
aṣṭamahāśmaśāna, 120–21n.52
aśubhabhāvanā, 140, 219
Atharvaveda, 80–81
Atikūṭa, 44–45
Atiśa, 122–23, 167, 168–69
attachments, severing, 153–56
austerities, 93–94, 101, 203–4, 219
Avalokiteśvara, 79, 81–82, 106–7, 108–9, 168, 203, 215–16, 219
āvaraṇa, 58, 219
Avataṃsaka sūtra, 96, 128, 131–32, 219
avidyā, 212–13, 219
awakened being, 51
awakened ones, 49–50, 51, 170–71, 219
awakening, 61–62, 93–94, 211–13, 219
āyurveda, 60–61

Babhala, 69–70
Balaputra, 168
banners, 86–87, 220
bardo, 61–62, 220
Barrett, T. H., 183
Bat Cum, 118–19
"becoming awakened in this body," 220
"Beloved Garden" (Kongtrul), 153
Bentor, Yael, 58
Berkwitz, Stephen, 201, 203, 205
Bhaiṣajya guru, 52, 220
bhikṣus, 203–4
Bible, 26–27, 193–94
Blackburn, Anne, 25–26, 172, 181
Bodhgayā, 129–30
bodhi, 93–94
Bodhicaryāvatāra, 142–43
bodhicitta, 50, 56, 69–70, 116, 153, 158, 213–14, 220
bodhi-mind, 50, 220
Bodhisattvabhūmi, 82
bodhisattvas, 49–50, 51–52, 54–55, 74, 78, 79, 108, 177–80, 215–16
bodily postures, 17, 220
body donation practice, 149, 153–54, 153n.71, 160, 220
Bolle, Kees, 13–14

Bond, George, 139–40
Borobudur, 94, 105, 109, 127–33, 168, 169
brāhmaṇa, 194–95, 220
Brahmanical rules, 136
Brahmanic ritual, 57
Braitstein, Lara, 65–66, 72
breath, or "winds," 60–61, 220
Brilliant Illumination of the Lamp of the Five Stages, 67
Brooks, Douglas Renfrew, 19
Buddhaghosa, 138, 141–43, 142n.23, 159
Buddhaguhya, 49–50, 59–60n.116
Buddhahood, 48
buddhavacana, 170–71, 220
Buddhist canons, 25–26, 181, 209
Buddhist cosmopolis (ADD), 4–5, 134, 160, 161–62, 163, 167, 171–72, 175, 176, 186, 187, 217–18
Bukong, 204, 220
Burnouf, Eugène, 196–97

cakras, 60–61, 69–70
Cakrasaṃvara tantra, 47
cakravāla, 128, 220
cakravartin, 47
caṇḍālī, 70
caryagīti, 220. See also *dohā*; *mgur*; *vajragīti*
Casparis, J. G. de, 191–92
caste, 136, 194–95, 203–4, 220
caturmahārāja, 6, 220
celestial musicians, 51, 220
central deity, 1, 3, 15–16, 45, 71, 112–13, 220. *See also* chief deity; *honzon*
cessation, 93–94, 220
Chandi Mendut, 94
Chandra, Lokesh, 80–82
Chang'an, 84–85, 87–88, 220
channels, 60–61, 220
charnel ground practices, 120–21n.52, 136–38, 142–44, 145, 146, 148–49
Chemburkar, Swati, 116, 129–30, 132–33, 169
Chen, Jinhua, 30–31
Chen, Yogi, 161–62, 174–76, 185, 186, 187
chief deity, 92–93, 220. *See also* central deity; *honzon*
Chih Ch'ien, 84–85
Chinese Buddhism, 31–32, 118–19, 175–76, 204–5
  Zhenyan, 84–85, 189
chingo kokka, 98, 220
chöd, 32–33, 136, 138, 148–58, 159–60, 216–17, 220
Chokyi Dronma, 151–52
Chola, 124, 167–68
Christianity, 12, 26–27, 189–95, 199–200, 201
chuang, 86–87
Chu Lü- yen, 84–85
"circulatory pilgrimage," 220. *See also* pilgrimages
citta, 50
Clausen, Christopher, 199
Clear Light Mantra, 104–5, 158
clear light practices, 61–62
Col, Cynthia, 171–72
cold water austerities, 220
Colebrooke, H. T., 195, 196–97
collections of *dhāraṇī* practices (*dhāraṇīsaṃgraha*), 44–45, 220
compassion, 51, 156, 179, 213–14
Compassionate Honored One, 220
comprehensive resource for practice (*kalpa*), 180, 221
concentration, 53–54, 141, 221
conditioned coproduction, 138–39, 221
conditioning habits, 50, 221
Confucianism, 175–76, 205
consciousness, 16, 61–62
contemplation of the foulness and impurity of human bodies, 138–49, 221
"Contemplation of the Nine Appearances," 146–48, 221
corpse meditation, 144–46
Cruijsen, Thomas, 28
Cūḷavaṃsa, 125
cult of the book, 170–71

Da Guan-ding jing, 221
Daigo, 90
Daihō in, 99
Dainichi ji, 98
Dainichi Nyorai, 90, 221
Daizong, 162n.2, 221
ḍākinī, 66, 221
Dalai Lama, 1–3, 52, 108–9, 202
Dalton, Jacob, 26–27, 47, 58–60, 59–60n.116, 121
dana-parāmitā, 51, 221
Daoism, 101
Davidson, Ronald M., 15–16, 24–25, 28, 38–39, 40–41, 44–45, 46, 47, 52, 63–64, 76, 115, 181
death and decay, 135–36, 138–49, 159–60, 216–17
decadence, 195–98
  rhetoric of, 12, 189, 195, 196, 198–202
deity yoga, 21, 221

delusion, 141–42, 221
severing, 153–56
Derge, 169–73, 176, 221
dhāraṇī, 6–7, 10, 22, 32–33, 73, 74, 221
agency and, 78–79
collections, 44–45, 220
dharmadhāraṇī, 76–77, 221
Great Compassion Dhāraṇī, 79, 104–5
as ground for Zhenyan, 84–85
"Hungry Ghost Dhāraṇī Scripture," 157
"Incantation of the Glorious Buddha's Crown," 86–87
from Indic Buddhism, 80–84
Karaṇḍamudrā Dhāraṇī, 17–18, 17n.54
kṣāntilābābhāya dhāraṇī, 76–77, 224
for Mahāpratisarā, 126–27, 127n.85
mantra and, 44, 75–76, 79–80n.24, 82–83, 84
mantradhāraṇī, 76–77, 225
"Noble Dhāraṇī of the Tathāgata Jñānolka That Purifies All Rebirths, The," 77–78
Noble King of the Sound of the Drum dhāraṇī, 76–77
praxes, 77, 79, 86–87, 104–5
Silk Road in transmission of, 165
during Tang dynasty, 84–85, 86–87
as tantric institution, 74, 75–91, 105
in tantric praxes, 44–45, 76–77, 78, 86, 104–5, 126–27
"Dhāraṇī 'Essence of Immeasurable Longevity and Wisdom,' The," 77, 78–79
dhārānī pillars, 86–87, 221
dhāraṇīsaṃgraha, 44–45, 221
dharma, 54, 61n.125, 86, 107–8
dharmabhāṇaka, 38, 107–8, 221
dharmadhāraṇī, 76–77, 221
dharmadhātu, 158
Dharmakīrtiśri, 122–23, 168
Dharmapāla, 117, 167
dharma phrases, 54
dhyana, 142–43, 221
dialectic, 12–13, 13n.34, 189, 209–14
diamond body, 116, 221
diamond realm, 87–88
Diamond Sutra, 84
dīkṣā, 17, 221
Dīpaṃkara Śrijñana, 167
disappearing tradition narrative, 200–6
"Discourse of the Dhāraṇī of the Buddha's Essence, The," 77–78
discriminative consciousness, 50, 221
Dispeller of all Hindrances, 106–8
displacement, 96–97
Divyadevī, 118–19
doctrine, 209, 210–11, 213
Dōgen Zenji, 6–7, 7n.16
dohā, 221. See also *caryagīti*; *mgur*; *vajragīti*
ḍombī, 70
dualism, 57, 59–60, 209–10
dual-mandala system, 126
dual-occupancy sites, 96–99, 221
dukkha, 139–40, 221
Dunhuang, 184–85
Durbodhāloka, 168
dveṣa, 141–42, 221
Dzogchen, 151

Edo period, 7–8
Eison, 216, 221
Eliade, Mircea, 153n.71
Ellora, 129
Elverskog, Johan, 42
Emmei ji, 102
emptiness, 51, 53–54, 68, 138–39, 222
Enchin, 102
Enlightenment, 50, 55, 211
Ennin, 222
En no Ozunu, 101
"entering me, me entering," 222
esoteric Buddhism, 28–29, 47, 112, 117, 124, 167–68, 205, 222 See also *mikkyō*
esoteric physiology, 129, 131
esoteric treasury, 222
"Essence of Auspicious Renown," 155, 158
"Essential Bundle, The," 157
expansive visionary text, 180, 222
expedient means, 213–14, 222
explanatory tantras, 25–26

festivals, 157–58, 202–3, 222
feudal system of vassal relations, 41, 222
five-element stupa, 131, 222
fletcheress, 66, 67, 70
Flood, Gavin, 137
Foltz, Richard C., 206n.62
four great kings, 6, 222
four immeasurables, 153, 222
Freud, Sigmund, 192–93, 192n.11
Fudō Myōō, 8, 222 *See also* Acalanātha Vidyārāja; Immovable Wisdom King
Fushimi Inari, 7–9, 35

gandharva, 51, 222
Gandhavyuha Sutra, 179–80, 184–85
Gaozong, 173, 174
garbhadhātu, 87–88, 222
*garbhadhātu maṇḍala, 222

gatha, 56–57, 222
Gathering of Intentions, 26–27
Gellner, David, 201
generosity, perfection of, 51, 222
Gethin, Rupert, 210–11
Ghaznavid dynasty, 42
ghost festivals, 157–58
Ghuri, Muhammad, 42
Giddings, William J., 82
Gien, 99
Gifford, Julie, 112–13, 128, 129–30, 131
Gilday, Edmund, 190–92
Goble, Andrew, 28–29, 206
gods, 96–97, 97n.99, 98–99, 165, 222
goma, 2, 222. *See also* homa; *saitō goma*
gongen, 99, 222
gorintō, 131, 222
Gōshōji, 102
Gough, Ellen, 37–38
Grapard, Allan, 98
Gray, David, 45–46, 47
Great Compassion Dhāraṇī, 79, 104–5
"Great Exegesis of Abhidharma," 143–44
Great Mandalas, 117–21
"great monasteries," 40–41, 222
Great Peahen Queen of Spells, 80, 101
"great seal," 64, 72, 222
Great Speech Chapter, The, 150
"Great Teaching of Yoga," 204–5, 207, 207n.64, 222
great vow, 137, 223
great yoga tantras, 47, 59–60, 223
greed, 141–42, 223
Greene, Eric, 145, 145n.32
grhya, 35, 223
Griffiths, Arlo, 28
gtum mo, 61–62, 223
guardian deity, 6, 223
Guenther, Herbert, 65–66
Guhyagarbha tantra, 26–27, 67
Guhyasamāja tantra, 26–27, 47
Gumonji practice, 100
Gupta, 40
Gyōgi, 100–1, 223
Gyōnen, 102

Hachiman shrine, 99
Halkias, Georgios T., 120–21n.52
Hanta ji, 102
Harding, Sarah, 149, 152
Hardy, Friedhelm, 24
Harrington, Laura, 180
Harrison, Paul, 177–78
Hatley, Shaman, 57–58n.110
hatred, 141–42, 223
Hayes, Glen A., 11n.29
Heart of Wisdom teachings, 1
Heart Sutra, 2, 75, 84, 151, 158
Heaven of the Thirty-three, 157–58, 223
Hegel, G. W. F., 12n.32
Heian period, 88–89, 92–93, 103–4, 124
Herling, Bradley L., 19–20
Hevajra Tantra, 118, 122–23
Hiei-zan, 95
Himalayan tradition, 42
Hinduism, 17, 24–25, 36, 37–38, 111, 115, 193–95, 201, 203–4
Hindu Śakta tantra, 19
hinin, 216, 223
historiography, 195–208
Ho, Chi Chen, 104–5
Hodge, Stephen, 46
holy men of Kōyasan, 90–91, 223
homa, 3–4, 7–8, 54–55, 58, 85n.47, 181, 185–86, 204–5, 223. See also *goma*; *saitō goma*
Hōnen, 102
honzon, 3, 223. *See also* central deity; chief deity
Hopkins, Jeffrey, 21
hosshin, 93–94, 223
Hotsu-Misaki ji, 100
how things actually are, 212–13, 223
Huiguo, 223
human person, 15, 223
"Hungry Ghost Dhāraṇī Scripture," 157
hungry ghosts, 155–58, 160, 223
Hutuktu, Lola, 175–76

Ichi no Miya shrine, 98
Ido ji, 100
ignorance, 212–13, 223
"Illuminating the Unfathomable," 168
illusory body, 61–62
image worship, 45
Immovable Wisdom King, 3, 223. See also Fudō Myōō, and Acalanātha Vidyārāja
imperial maṇḍala rites, 15–16
imperial temples, 96
impermanence, 135–36, 138–39, 146, 223
impurity, 140, 145, 223
"Incantation of the Glorious Buddha's Crown," 86–87
India-China maritime trade routes, 126, 134
Indian Buddhism, tantra in, 24–25, 38–48, 117
  changing social and political context of, 40–42
  collapse of Gupta and Vākāṭaka, 40
  dhāraṇī and *dhāraṇī* collections in, 44–45, 80–84

Himalayan tradition and, 42
literary history of, 42–48
Mahāyāna and, 40–41, 202–3
mid-eighth to mid-ninth century developments in, 46–47
Muslim conquest and, 41–42
networks in transmission of, 167–69
during Pāla dynasty, 41, 72–73
second wave of transmission from, 118–19
systematic texts in, 45–46
Vairocanābhisaṃbodhi tantra, 46, 48–57, 72–73
initiation, 2–3, 51–57, 107, 216–17, 223
initiation rituals, 47
inner heat, 61–62, 223
insightful awareness, 186, 223
insight meditation, 140
institutional designations, 206–8
institutionalization, of tantra, 32–33, 74, 84–85, 88, 89–90, 103, 198–99
intention toward awakening, 158, 213–14, 223
interiorization of ritual, 57–62
internal yogas, 58–59
"Introduction to the Practices of Awakening," 142–43
Ippen shōnin, 102, 223
Iwaya ji, 95–96

Jackson, Roger, 65–66
Jainism, 24–25, 37–38
Jamison, Stephanie, 36
Japanese Buddhism
Mahāyāna, 7n.18
nine faces of death in, 146–49
Shingon in, 6–8, 22, 87–91, 89n.69, 126, 131–32, 138, 158, 185–86, 204, 205
Java, classical central, 124–27
Jayavarman II, 118
Jayavarman VI, 118
Jayavarman VII, 118, 119, 121
Jayavarma VIII, 119
Jesus Christ, 200
jingūji, 97, 224
Ji sect, 92–93, 102
Ji-shū, 102, 224
jiva, 15, 224
jñāna, 186, 224
jñeyāvaraṇa, 138–39, 185
Jōdo ji, 101–2

Kagyü, 71
Kaiyuanzong, 84–85, 224
Kakurin ji, 95
Kālacakra tantra, 48, 180, 181
Kalingga, 224
kalpa, 23–24, 180, 181, 224
kāmaloka, 128, 157, 224
kami, 96–97, 97n.99, 98–99, 165
Kandahjaya, Hudaya, 127, 129
Kanjur, 170, 224
Kannon, 101–2
Kāpālika, 137–38
Karaṇḍamudrā Dhāraṇī, 17–18, 17n.54
Kāraṇḍavyūha sūtra, 106–9, 168
karuṇā, 213–14
Karuṇāmaya, 203
kāṣāya, 139–40, 224
Kayagata-sati sutta, 140
Kayumwungan, 127–28
Kesariya, 133
Keyworth, George, 165
khaṭvāṅga, 137, 224
Khmer Buddhism, 118–19
Khmer Empire, 117–18, 174–75
Khuddaka Nikāya, 156
Khuddakapāṭha, 156
king of kings, 15–16, 224
kleśa, 149
kleśāvaraṇa, 138–39
Klokke, Marijke J., 28
knowledge, 212–13, 224
Kōbō Daishi, 90, 95–96, 99–100, 103
Kokubun ji, 96, 224
kokushi, 102
Kokuzo, 100
kōmyō shingon, 104–5, 224
Kongō fuku ji, 96
Kongō-ji, 145
Kongtrul, Jamgön, 149, 153–54, 155, 158
Kōnomine ji, 99
Kopf, David, 195
Kōshō, 99
Kōya hijiri, 90–91, 91n.74, 224
Kōyama ji, 99–100
Kōya Myōjin, 224
Kōyasan, 90–91, 92, 95, 103–4, 131–32
kṣāntilābābhāya dhāraṇī, 76–77, 224
kṣatriya, 194–95, 224
Kūkai, 73, 87–91, 92–93, 97, 126, 138, 224
"Contemplation of the Nine Appearances" by, 146–48, 221
life story of, dynamics of temple origins and, 99–104
mantra, 74, 75
pilgrimages and, 74, 75, 103–4, 105
Shingon, tantric praxes and, 88, 90–91
on *Vairocanābhisaṃbodhi tantra*, 87–88
kūṭāgāra, 129, 224

Kuya shōnin, 101–2
Kvaerne, Per, 69–70

laghu-tantra, 48, 224
Larson, Gerald, 24
lay practitioners, 79, 224
Lee, Sonya, 62
Lehnert, Martin, 109n.8
Lewis, Todd, 202–3
Licchavi dynasty, 203
Lin, Yutang, 176
lineage, 212, 224
Lingpa, Dudjom, 150
liu, 224
"Lives of Eminent Monks Composed in the Song," 85–86n.52, 224
lobha, 141–42, 225
Lokakṣema, 178, 179
lokapāla, 6–7, 225
Lokeśvara, 203
Lopez, Donald, 23–24
Lorenzen, David N., 137
Lotus Sutra, 79, 84, 87, 179–80, 215–16
lucid awareness, 61–62
lus byin, 149, 225

Mabbett, I. W., 191–92
Macchendra, 203
Machik Labdron, 150–52, 153–54, 155, 157, 159
Madhyamaka, 40–41, 51, 72, 123, 225
Maegami ji, 99
Mahābhairava, 120–21
Mahābodhi temple, 128, 129–30, 130n.107, 176–77
Mahākalparāja, 225
Mahāmayūrī-rājñi-saṃyuktāṛddhidhāraṇī sūtra, 225
Mahāmayūrīvidyārajñī, 80, 101
mahāmudrā, 64, 71, 72, 225
Mahāpratisarā, 126–27, 127n.85
Mahāpratisarāmahāvidyārājñī, 126–27
mahasattvas, 116
mahāsiddhas, 47, 62, 63–72, 225
  Saraha, 63–73
  tantric character of, 71–72, 225
Mahātantrarāja,
Mahāvairocana, 52, 55, 87–88, 90
mahāvihara, 40–41, 125, 225
mahāvrata, 137, 225
Mahāyāna, 56–57, 116, 118, 125
  bodhisattva, Śākyamuni as, 37
  dhāraṇī in, 76
  "Great Teaching of Yoga" and, 204–5
  Indian Buddhism and, 40–41, 202–3
  in Japanese Buddhism, 7n.18
  Mañjuśrī and, 177–78, 179–80, 184–85, 186
  mantrayāna in, 28
  in Southeast Asia, 111
  sutra and mantra vehicles of, 21
  sutras, 106, 215–16
  systematic texts in, 45–46
  Vairocanābhisaṃbodhi tantra in, 49, 51
mahāyānavaipulyasūtra, 180, 225
mahāyoga tantras, 47, 59–60, 64, 225
Maheśvara, 120–21
Mahidharapura, 118
Maitreya, 23–24, 90–91, 225
Malandra, Geri H., 129
Malla dynasty, 203–4
Mandala of Angkor, 117–19
mandalas, 37–38, 45, 47, 100, 109, 155–56
  Borobudur and, 129–30, 132
  circa first to ninth century, 115–17
  in Derge, 171–73
  dual-mandala system, 126
  Great Mandaḷas, circa ninth to thirteenth century, 117–21
  initiation to, 51–57, 107
  mantra and, 56
  nation-states and, 109, 110–11, 113
  Parkhang, 171–72
  of Śailendra, 122, 124–27
  as social, political, and religious category, 112–15
  of Srivijaya, 122–24
  stūpa and, 131–32
  at Tabo, 132, 169
  Zanning on, 204–5
Mandara ji, 100
Mañjuśri, 46–47, 161–62, 177–81, 182–86, 187, 216–17
Mañjuśrīmūlakalpa, 180–81
Mañjuśrī parinirvāṇa sūtra, 178–79, 183, 216
mantra, 8, 13–14, 17, 29, 225
  Clear Light Mantra, 104–5, 158
  dhāraṇī and, 44, 75–76, 79–80n.24, 82–83, 84
  dharma phrases, 54
  emptiness of, 51
  Heart Sutra and, 151
  in *Kāraṇḍavyūha sūtra*, 107, 108–9
  Kūkai, 74, 75
  mandala and, 56
  mantraśāstra and, 37–38
  vidyāmantra, 107
  yantra and, 116
mantradhāraṇī, 76–77, 225
mantranaya, 27–28, 29, 204, 225
mantra path, 116

mantraśāstra, 37–38, 225
mantra school, 84–85
mantra teachings, 54
mantrayāna, 27–28, 29–30, 116, 118, 225
mantrin, 52–53, 225
maraṇānusmṛti, 135–36, 225
Marpa, 61
Mātangīsūtra, 84–85, 85n.47
material aspects of existents, 50, 225
Maud, Jovan, 103
McMahan, David, 215–16
Medicine Buddha, 1–4, 225
meditation, 1–2, 29, 54, 225
  corpse meditation on Silk Road, 144–46
  on foulness of decaying human body, 138–49
  ritual and, 57, 213–14
meditative concentration, 53–54, 56, 90, 141, 225
Meiji era, 98, 99
Mendut, 132
merchants and farmers, 194–95, 225
"methods of recalling and reciting," 225
mgur, 63–64, 225. See also *caryagīti*; *dohā*; *vajragīti*.
Michaels, Axel, 17
mikkyō, 29–30, 226. *See also* esoteric Buddhism
Miksic, John, 116–17, 122–23, 124, 166, 167
Milarepa, 61
mind-body dualism, 57, 59–60, 209–10
mindfulness of death, 135–36, 140, 141–42, 226
mind of awakening, 50, 56, 69–70, 116, 153, 158, 213–14, 226
Minobusan, 226
misplaced affections, 138–39, 185, 226
mistaken conceptions, 138–39, 185, 226
"mixed" esoteric Buddhism, 226
mizong, 29–30, 84–85, 226
Moens, J. L., 132
moha, 141–42, 226
monothetic approach to defining tantra, 14–16, 21
Mo teng ch'ieh ching, 84–85
mudra, 8, 17, 56, 226
mūlakleśa, 141–42, 226
Mulian, 157–58
multifactorial monothetic approaches to defining tantra, 16, 17–18

nāḍī, 60–61, 226
Nagārjuna, 72
Nalānda, 41, 117, 168
Nāmasaṃgīti, 46–47, 180–81
Nance, Richard, 5
Nandā, Abhirūpā, 135
Nara period, 88–89
Nāropa, 62, 66n.149
Naropa chos drug, 61
Nāsadīya, 193–94
national master, 102, 226
nation-states, 109, 110–11, 113
Neelis, Jason, 165
nehan, 93–94
Nepalese Buddhism, 202–4
networks, 161–69, 173, 182–84, 187
Newar tradition, 202–3
nine faces of death, 146–49
Ningai, 226
nirupadhiśeṣa-nirvāṇa, 51, 226
nirvana, 51, 93–94, 226
nirvana without remainder, 51, 226
Niutsuhime, 226
"Noble Dhāraṇī of the Tathāgata Jñānolka That Purifies All Rebirths, The," 77–78
Noble King of the Sound of the Drum dhāraṇī, 76–77
Nongbri, Brent, 190
Northern California Koyasan Temple, 2, 3–5, 7–8, 35
Northern Wei dynasty, 183–84
Nyingma texts and tradition, 25–27, 202–3

obscurations, 58, 149, 226
Oda Nobunaga, 6
Okunoin, 90, 226
oral transmission, 131–32, 226
ordinary monastics, 203–4, 226
ordination, 17, 226
originally unborn, 54, 226
Orlina, Roderick, 126–27
Orzech, Charles, 55, 115, 204–8
outcasts, 216, 226
Overbey, Ryan Richard, 77n.13
overdetermination, 192n.11, 192–95

pacification, 54–55, 150, 155, 227
Pacification of Suffering, 151
Padampa Sanggye, 150–52, 155
Padoux, André, 13–14
Pāla dynasty, 41, 72–73, 124, 129–30
Palembang, 115, 116–17
Pāli Buddhism, 7n.18, 76, 111
Pāli texts, 80–81, 112, 139–40, 156
Pandyan dynasty, 125
paññā, 139–40, 141
paradise of a saving buddha, 227
Paramādibuddha, 48
parāmitā, 51, 65, 65n.144, 227
pāramitāyāna, 28, 116, 227

paritta, 80–81, 227
Parkhang, 170–72
Path of Purification, The (Buddhaghosa), 141–42, 142n.23, 159
Pawon, 94, 132
perception, 50, 227
Perfection of Wisdom, 75, 149, 151, 168, 179–80
perfection path, 116, 227
Perfection Path Buddhism, 116
perfections, 51, 227
Perfection Vehicle, 151
perfumed water, 53–54, 227
Philippines, 126–27
phowa, 61–62, 227
pilgrimages, 32–33, 73
  to dual-occupancy sites, 96–97, 98
  Kūkai and, 74, 75, 103–4, 105
  localization of, 103
  Shikoku, 74, 91–94, 98, 103–4, 105, 130n.107, 182n.72
  Wutai shan in, 182–83
Plato, 194–95
poems in the Japanese style, 147–48, 227
"Poems of the Nine Stages," 147–48
pollution, 136, 139–40, 227
polythetic approaches to defining tantra, 18–22
power/potency, 137, 227
practical canon, for Buddhist tantra, 25–26, 181
practice, 93–94, 95–96, 180, 227
prajñā, 141, 227
Prajñāpāramitā, 118–19
prana, 60–61, 227
pranidāna, 116, 227
prāsāda, 131–32, 227
pratisara, 45
pratityasamutpada, 138–39, 227
praxis, 208, 209–16. *See also* tantric praxes
priests, 2, 194–95, 227
primary afflictions, 141–42, 227
primitive *shugenja*, 227
"Procedure for Mañjuśrī's Single-Syllable Mantra, The," 75–76
protector deity, 10, 22
Protestant Christianity, 12, 189–95, 199–200, 209, 211n.74, 217
Protestant Reformation, 199, 200, 211
proto-tantric, 39, 44n.47, 45
pūjā, 17, 36, 227
Puṇyodaya, 161–62, 173–75, 176, 187
"pure" esoteric Buddhism, 227
Pure Land Buddhism, 92–93, 102
Pure Land sutras, 82
purity, 136, 139–40
Pye, Michael, 96–97

Quinter, David, 178, 216

radical nonduality, 71–72
radish girl, 66, 67, 70
rājādhirāja, 47, 227
Rambelli, Fabio, 97n.99
ratnatraya, 53, 227
Reader, Ian, 92
"realization" or "attainment," 2–3
realm of desire, 128, 227
Reichle, Natasha, 116
religion
  defining, 11–12, 18–20, 190
  dualistic value system of Western religious culture, 209
  fear of death and, 159
  institutional designations in study of, 206–8
  narrative of disappearing tradition in study of, 200–6
  praxis in study of, 208, 209–16
  religious studies and, 189–95, 214–15
  rhetoric of decadence as narrative structure of history of, 198–202
  state and, 110–11
religious practices in the mountains, 228
remaining in the world as an awakened being, 228, 51, 219
renunciates, 37, 138–39, 228
Ṛg Veda, 36
rhetoric of decadence, 12, 189, 195, 196, 198–202
Richthofen, Ferdinand von, 165
right view, 212–13, 228
Rinpoche, Gelu, 175–76
Rinzai, 92–93
ritual
  Borobudur and, 129–30, 131, 132
  Brahmanic, 57
  for feeding hungry ghosts, 157, 158
  homa, 3–4, 7–8, 54–55, 58, 85n.47, 181, 185–86, 204–5, 223
  initiation, 47
  interiorizing, 57–62
  Mātangīsūtra on, 84–85
  meditation and, 57, 213–14
  Vedic, 14–15, 29, 34–39, 57, 76, 185, 192, 216–17
ritual identification, 14–16, 185, 213
ritual specialists, 203–4, 228
robes that a monk wears, 139–40, 228
Root Manual of the Rites of Mañjuśrī, 23–24
Rudra, 120–21, 120–21n.52
rules of the order, 139–40, 228. See also *vinaya*
rūpa, 50, 228
Ryōkō ji, 99

sacred diagrams, 17, 228. *See also* mandala
sacrifice of Puruṣa, 193–95

sādhana, 1–4, 17, 52, 181, 228
Saga, 96
Saichō, 6, 87–88, 228
Śailendra, 114, 122, 124–28
saitō goma, 7–8, 228. *See also* goma; homa
Śaiva Siddhānta, 15, 228
Śaiva tantra, 43
Śaiva tradition, 117–18, 119–20, 121, 174
śāktization, 43, 228
śākyabhikṣus, 203–4, 228
Śākyamuni Buddha, 61n.125, 99, 139, 170–71, 182n.72, 192
 in Buddhist cosmopolis, 4–5
 in Buddhist modernism, 192
 charnel ground practices and, 137–39
 in disappearing tradition narrative, 201–2
 early tantras taught by, 46
 Parkhang and, 171–72
 in praxis, 176–77, 178
 in rhetoric of decadence narrative, 200
 samaya vows and, 56
 stupa as memorial mounds for, 131
 Theravāda and, 111
 Vajrapāṇi in state formation and, 118–19
 Vedic rituals and, 34–35, 37
Salguero, C. Pierce, 60–61, 174
samādhi, 53–54, 56, 90, 141, 228
samanta, 41, 228
Samantabhadra, 49–50, 184–85
samaya, 54–56, 158, 228
Samding Dorje Phagmo, 151–52
samjñā, 50, 228
saṃsāra, 58, 139–40
saṃskāra, 50, 228
Saṃvarodaya tantra, 129
samyak dṛṣṭi, 212–13, 228
Samye, 169
Sanderson, Alexis, 43, 117–18
Sanford, James, 147–48
sangha, 2, 2n.4, 3, 4–5, 228
Sangharakshita, 175
Sang Hyang Kamahāyānikan, 127–28
Sanskrit, 42, 54, 63–64, 76–77, 111, 112
Śāntideva, 142–43
śāntika, 54–55, 228
Sanzen-in, 6
Saraha, 63–73
Sarvanīvaraṇaviṣkambhin, 106–8
Sarvatathāgatatattvasaṃgraha tantra, 26–27, 46, 55, 118–19, 133, 204–5
Satipaṭṭhana sutta, 138, 140
Schaeffer, Kurtis R., 65–66
Schaffalitzky de Muckadell, Caroline, 18–19
Schaik, Sam van, 129–30
school, 228
Schopen, Gregory, 17–18, 17n.54
"Scripture on the Twelve Gates," 145
Second Lambakaṇṇa dynasty, 124–25
Secret of the Golden Flower, 69n.162
"secret" or "esoteric" teachings, 29–30, 228
Seidenstrasse, 165. *See also* Silk Road/ Silk Route
self, 16
self-ordained, 228
sensation, 50, 228
separation of kami and buddhas, 98, 228
Sera Monastery, 92
serfs and servants, 194–95, 228
severance/Severance, 32–33, 136, 138, 148–58, 159–60, 216–17, 228
sex and sexuality, 67–71
sexual desire, 141, 145–46
sexual practices, 47, 59–60, 188
Sharrock, Peter, 118–19, 121–22, 174–75
Shikoku, 73, 96, 229
 pilgrimages, 74, 91–94, 98, 103–4, 105, 130n.107, 182n.72
shinbutsu bunri, 98, 229. *See also* separation of kami and buddhas
Shingon, 6–8, 22, 87–91, 89n.69, 126, 131–32, 138, 158, 185–86, 204, 205. See also *tōmitsu*
Shingon Ritsu school, 216
Shinohara, Koichi, 45–46
Shinran, 102
Shintō, 8, 96–97, 99, 100
Shiramine ji, 102
Shōmu, 96, 100–1
Shōsan-ji, 95
Shugendō, 7–8, 101, 229
shugyō, 93–94, 229
Shusshaka ji, 99–100
Siddhartha, 55
siddhas, 47, 62, 62n.132, 63–64, 229
siddhi, 137, 229
sīla, 141, 229
Silk, Jonathan, 179
Silk Road/Silk Route, 126, 134, 144–46, 164–66, 169. See also *Seidenstrasse*
single charismatic figure pilgrimage, 229
single deity pilgrimage, 229
Śiva, 15, 120–21, 203, 229
Śiva-Kapālin, 137
"Six Dharmas of Naropa," 61, 61n.125
skull-topped staff, 137, 229
Smith, Jonathan Z., 19
Society for Tantric Studies, 19
soma, 34–35, 36–37, 36n.14, 229
Sönam Pelden, 151–52
Song dynasty, 85–86n.52, 204–5, 207n.64
"songs of awakening" or "songs of realization," 63–64, 229

Sørensen, Henrik, 19, 55
Soshitchikara kyō, 229
Sōtoku, 99
Sōtō Zen, 6–7, 7n.16, 92–93
Southern Silk Route, 164, 166–67
Spice Route, 164
śramana, 37, 138–39, 229
śrauta, 35–36, 229
Śri Lanka, 124–25
Srivijaya, 114, 115, 116–17, 122–24, 167–69
Staal, Frits, 111
state formation, 105, 109, 118–19, 162n.2, 229
  subjugation and, 120–21
  tantra in, 110–11, 115, 134, 162, 216–17
state protection, 98, 229
sthaṇḍila, 38, 229
Strickmann, Michel, 14–15, 21, 44n.47
Strube, Julian, 23n.69
stūpa, 129, 131–32, 148, 215–16, 229
Śubhākarasimha, 28–29, 84–85, 118–19, 173, 229
subjugation, 120–21
sublation, 12, 12n.32, 189, 190–92
subtle body, 60–61, 64–65, 68, 69–70, 72–73
śūdra, 194–95, 229
suffering, 51, 151, 154, 229
Sugiki, Tsunehiko, 42–43
Sukhāvatī, 82
sūkṣmakāya, 60–61
Sumatra, 122–24
Sumeru, 129, 163
Sundberg, Jeffrey, 124–26
sunyatā, 68, 138–39, 229
supreme yoga tantras, 59–60, 229
Susiddhikara tantra, 26–27
Sūtra of the Basket's Display, 106–8
sutras, 48–49
  Diamond Sutra, 84
  Gandhavyuha Sutra, 179–80, 184–85
  Heart Sutra, 2, 75, 84, 151, 158
  Lotus Sutra, 79, 84, 87, 179–80, 215–16
  Mahāyāna, 106, 215–16
  Mañjuśrī, 178–80
  Pure Land, 82
  tantra and, 30, 106
  Vimalakīrti nirdesa, 179–80, 184–85
Suzong, 162n.2
syncretism, 98

Tabo monastery, 132–33, 169
taimitsu, 229. *See also* Tendai
Tairyō ji, 95, 100
Taixu, 175–76, 229
Taizong, 85–86n.52, 229
Taizu, 229
Talang Tuwo, 116
Tamura Shrine, 99
Tanabe, George, 90–91
Tang dynasty, 28–29, 31n.99, 84–85, 86–87, 118–19, 124, 129–30, 167, 204, 205
tantra. *See also* Indian Buddhism, tantra in
  abridged version of, 48, 219
  as bibliographic category, 23–27
  category terms pointing to movement, 27–30
  as coherent and continuous movement, 11
  context, use, and designation in delineating, 22–23
  continuous tradition of, 202
  death and decay in, 135–36
  as decadent, 195–98
  definitional strategies for, 13–22
  delineating, strategies for, 12–30
  in Derge, 171–72
  disappearing tradition narrative on, 206
  explanatory, 25–26
  facets of, 32–33
  at Fushimi Inari, 7–9, 35
  hungry ghosts in East Asian, 157–58
  institutional categories and, 206–7, 208
  institutionalization of, 32–33, 74, 84–85, 88, 89–90, 103, 198–99
  interiorization of ritual in, 57–62
  invisibility of, 10
  Madhyamaka and, 72
  mahāsiddhas and, 71–72
  methodological issues in study of, 11–12, 133–34
  monothetic approaches to defining, 14–16, 21
  as movement and praxis, 208, 209–10, 217–18
  multifactorial monothetic approaches to defining, 16, 17–18
  Nepalese Buddhism and, 203–4
  networks in transmission of, 167–69, 187
  at Northern California Koyasan Temple in Sacramento, 2, 3–5, 7–8, 35
  in Ohara, 6–7, 8–9, 10, 22, 89
  overdetermined representations of, 192–93
  as pervasive, 9–10
  polythetic approaches to defining, 18–22
  practical canon for, 25–26, 181
  in the present, 1–9
  ritual identification in practice, 14–16
  during Śailendra dynasty, 124–27
  at Shoreline Amphitheater, 1–3, 4–5, 52
  in Southeast Asia, 109–15, 117–27, 134
  during Srivijaya dynasty, 122–24

in state formation, 110–11, 115, 134, 162, 216–17
subjugation narratives and, 121
sutra and, 30, 106
texts, 42–48
Vedic ritual and, 35–39
Zen and, 6–7, 7n.16
tantric consorts, 66–69, 70
tantric institutions, 74, 216–17
dhāraṇī, 74, 75–91, 105
Shikoku pilgrimage, 74, 91–94, 103–4, 105
tantric praxes, 5, 7–8, 11, 12, 208, 217–18
agency in, 78
All-Gathering Maṇḍala Ceremony in, 45–46
Davidson on sources of, 38–39
dhāraṇī in, 44–45, 76–77, 78, 86, 104–5, 126–27
impermanence in, 135–36
Indo-Iranian influences on, 37
as instantiations of tantric Buddhism, 176–77
interiorization in, 58–59
of Mañjuśrī, 177–79, 180, 182–85, 187, 216–17
organizing schema of ground, path, and goal in, 211–12
ritual identification in, 15–16
Severance, 149, 159
Shingon, Kūkai and, 88, 90–91
in Southeast Asia, 111
terms to identify, 27
Vairocanābhisaṃbodhi tantra and, 49, 56
value judgments of, 209–10
tantric yogas, 57, 61–62, 71
yogic sexual practices, 47
Tārā, 150, 153–54, 168
tathāgatas, 49–50, 56, 69n.162, 158, 229
tathatā, 212–13, 229
"teaching of yoga," 230
temple origins, dynamics of, 94–104
dual occupancy, 96–99
imperial temples, 96
life story of Kūkai in, 99–104
practice, 95–96
trade routes, 94–95
Tendai, 6–8, 87, 92–93, 102, 230 See also *taimitsu*
Tenjur, 170, 230
Tennō ji, 99
Tenpa Tsering, 170
Theragātha, 63–64, 141 See also "Verses of the Elder Monks"
Theravāda Buddhism, 111–12, 114, 125, 133–34, 139–40, 192, 201–2
Therīgātha, 63–64
Thompson, Ashley, 111–12
"three countries" model of Buddhist history, 85n.50, 230
three evil paths, 230
Three Jewels, 53, 230
three poisons, 141–42, 230
Thurman, Robert, 31n.99, 67
Tiantai, 87, 102
Tibetan Buddhism, 42, 148–49, 150, 151–52, 168, 169–70, 175, 202–3
Tibetan canon, 75–76
Tibetan Mahāmudrā, 71
Tibetan Renaissance, 123
Tilopa, 61, 62
Tirokuḍḍa Kaṇḍa, 156–57
Tokugawa era, 89–90, 92–93
tōmitsu, 230. *See also* Shingon
torii, 99
trade routes, 94–95
Trailokyavijaya, 118–19, 120–21, 120n.50
transfer of consciousness, 61–62, 230
transgression, 136–37
travel and travelers, 161–62, 173–76, 187
Trāyastrimśa Heaven, 157–58, 230
Tribe, Anthony, 179–80, 186
triple refuge, 53, 230
triśaraṇa, 53, 230
triviṣa, 141–42, 230
"true word," 29–30, 230
Tsongkhapa, 21–22, 67, 92
Tuladhar-Douglas, Will, 42

Umādevā, 120–21
unexcelled yoga tantras, 47
upāya, 51, 65, 65n.144, 213–14, 230
Upen ji, 95
Uttaratantra, 23–24

Vairocana, 37, 46, 49–50, 51–52, 53, 54, 56–57, 120–21
Vairocanābhisaṃbodhi tantra, 26–27, 88–89, 107, 213–14, 216–17, 230
Buddhaguhya on, 59–60n.116
Indian Buddhism and, 46, 48–57, 72–73
Kūkai on, 87–88
on mandala and *abhiṣeka*, 51–57
on Trailokyavijaya, 120n.50
Vaiśnava tradition, 117–18
vaiśya, 194–95, 230
vajra, 28, 30, 120–21, 204–5, 230
Vajrabodhi, 28–29, 84–85, 118–19, 167, 173, 230
vajrācāryas, 203–4, 230
Vajradhara, 37

vajradharas, 49–50, 230
vajradhātu, 55, 87–88, 120–21, 230
Vajradhātu maṇḍala, 132–33, 169, 230
vajragīti, 63–65, 230
vajra holders, 49–50, 230
Vajrapāṇi, 37, 37n.20, 50, 51–52, 56–57, 118–19, 120–21
Vajrapāṇyabhiṣeka, 46
Vajrāsana Buddha, 129–30
vajraśarīra, 116, 231
Vajrasattva, 55, 175–76
Vajraśekhara tantra, 46–47, 88–89, 231
Vajravārāhī Buddha, 153–54
"vajra vehicle of yoga, the," 204–5, 205n.57, 230
Vajrayāna, 27–28, 29, 30, 71–72, 117–18, 125, 203, 204–5, 230
Vajrayoginī, 153–54
Vajroṣṇīṣa, 52
Vākāṭaka, 40
vaṃsas, 125
varna, 194–95, 231
vedanā, 50, 231
Vedas, 17, 36, 37, 193–95, 196. *See also* Atharvaveda
Vedic India, 195–96
Vedic ritual, 14–15, 29, 34–39, 57, 76, 185, 192, 216–17
Veidlinger, Daniel, 170
verses, 56–57, 231
"Verses of the Elder Monks," 63–64, 141
vidhis, 181
vidyā, 212–13, 231
vidyāmantra, 107
vidyārājas, 231
vihāra, 124, 129, 231
vijñāna, 50, 231
Vimalakīrti nirdesa sutra, 179–80, 184–85
vinaya, 139–40, 231
virtue, 141, 231
Visuddhimagga, 138, 141–42, 142n.23
vows, 54–56, 231

waka, 147–48, 231
Wang, Michelle C., 184–85
Wangchuk, Dorji, 26–27
Warring States period, 6
warriors, 194–95, 231
Wayman, Alex, 198
Wedemeyer, Christian, 198
Weinberger, Steven, 26–27
Western direction pure land, 231
"we two traveling, or practicing together," 231
"Wheel of Instruction and Command," 204–5, 207, 207n.64, 231
White, David Gordon, 62n.132
white bone contemplation, 145
Whitfield, Susan, 165–66
wisdom, 139–40, 141, 231
Witzel, Michael, 36
womb, 231
womb realm, 87–88
women, in Tibetan Buddhism, 151–52
Woodward, Hiram, 116, 118, 167–68
word of the Buddha, 170–71, 231
Wright, Dale, 211n.74
Wujastyk, Dominik, 60–61
Wutai shan, 182–84
Wuxing, 46
Wuzong, 231

Xiaowendi, 183
Xuanzang, 173, 174
Xufa, Boting, 83

Yang, Bin, 166
yantra, 17, 37–38, 116, 231
Yijing, 173–74
Yixing, 231
yoga, 48, 57, 58–59, 63–64, 69–70, 73, 204–5
Yogācāra, 23–24, 40–41, 173, 231
Yogaratnamala, 122–23
yoga tantras, 47–48, 59–60, 59–60n.116, 231
yogic anatomy, 129
yogic sexual practices, 47
yogic technology, 61
Yoginī tantras, 47, 64, 118, 129, 168
Yokomine ji, 95
Yoshino River, 94–95
Young, Serinity, 67, 68, 70
yulanben, 157–58, 232

Zakharov, Anton, 124
Zanning, 85–86n.52, 115, 204–5, 207n.64
Zaō-gongen, 99
Zen, 6–7, 7n.16, 8–9, 10, 22
Zentsū ji, 99–100, 102
Zhenla, 114, 174
Zhenyan, 29–30, 84–85, 189, 204
Zhi byed, 150
Zhiyi, 232
zong, 232

www.ingramcontent.com/pod-product-compliance
Ingram Content Group UK Ltd.
Pitfield, Milton Keynes, MK11 3LW, UK
UKHW041534050226
467683UK00011B/32

9 780195 368475